M000116340

Fraud and Fraud Detection

The Wiley Corporate F&A series provides information, tools, and insights to corporate professionals responsible for issues affecting the profitability of their company, from accounting and finance to internal controls and performance management.

Founded in 1807, John Wiley & Sons is the oldest independent publishing company in the United States. With offices in North America, Europe, Asia, and Australia, Wiley is globally committed to developing and marketing print and electronic products and services for our customers' professional and personal knowledge and understanding.

Fraud and Fraud Detection

A Data Analytics Approach

SUNDER GEE

For general information on our other products and services or for technical support, please contact our Customer Care Department within the United States at (800) 762-2974, outside the United States at (317) 572-3993 or fax (317) 572-4002.

Wiley publishes in a variety of print and electronic formats and by print-on-demand. Some material included with standard print versions of this book may not be included in e-books or in print-on-demand. If this book refers to media such as a CD or DVD that is not included in the version you purchased, you may download this material at http://booksupport.wiley.com. For more information about Wiley products, visit www.wiley.com.

Library of Congress Cataloging-in-Publication Data:
Gee, Sunder.
 Fraud and fraud detection : a data analytics approach/Sunder Gee.
    pages cm. — (Wiley corporate F&A series)
 Includes index.
   ISBN 978-1-118-77965-1 (hardback) — ISBN 978-1-118-77967-5 (ePDF) — ISBN 978-1-118-77966-8 (ePub) — ISBN 978-1-118-93676-4 (oBook)
  1. Fraud.   2. Managerial accounting.   3. Data mining.   I. Title.
  HV6691.G44 2014
  658.4'73—dc23
                                                           2014021352

Printed in the United States of America

10 9 8 7 6 5 4 3 2 1

Contents

Foreword

I MET SUNDER MANY YEARS ago when he was researching advanced methods to improve his work through Benford's Law analysis. He immediately displayed a passion and excitement for thinking outside of the box that inspired a professional relationship based on our common enthusiasm for IDEA. Being a long-time IDEA user with experience in various types of audits, I have always been keen on learning new and innovative ways to use the tool and push it to its limits, especially now working on the development side of the product.

Today's fast-paced society has enabled most actions, transactions, and activities to be captured and saved on various databases in a matter of minutes. Because of this, fraud has grown in sophistication and become increasingly difficult to identify. However, this influx of technology and data capturing has also provided fraud examiners with the ability to use fraud detection methods that rival perpetrators of fraud in both complexity and innovation. The increased amount of data collected by innumerable systems in turn increases the possibilities available to fraud examiners. It is through the use of data analytics that fraud examiners can combat fraud and detect anomalies in a timely and efficient manner.

This book will lead you through the possibilities I have mentioned and will explain in full detail the different mathematic models and advanced analytics available for use in the identification of suspicious transactions. It is with great enthusiasm that I recommend this book to enhance your fraud detection process. I am certain that this book will inspire all who read it to approach fraud creatively regardless of experience level. While the subject matter within this book may appear to be complex, Sunder eloquently outlines his ideas and experience along with research into various theoretical concepts that result in an easily digested guide by even the most novice of auditors while still providing valuable insight to seasoned auditors as well.

Sunder's experience in electronic commerce audit is highly recognizable in this book as it reveals countless real-life examples of applying innovative fraud detection methods. Sunder's longstanding expertise as an IDEA user since the days of DOS prevails in the pages of this book. His knowledge of computer-assisted audit technology and techniques combined with an ability to think creatively will lead readers on a journey that opens their eyes to the various possibilities available when a thirst for knowledge and an analytic mind-set are combined.

Alain Soublière, CPA, CGA, CIDA
Director, Product Strategy, CaseWare IDEA Inc.

Preface

FRAUD AND FRAUD DETECTION takes a data analytics approach to detecting anomalies in data that are indicators of fraud. The book starts by introducing the reader to the basics of fraud and fraud detection followed by practical steps for obtaining and organizing data in usable formats for analysis. Written by an auditor for auditors, accountants, and investigators, *Fraud and Fraud Detection* enables the reader to understand and apply statistics and statistical-sampling techniques. The major types of occupational fraud are reviewed and specific data analytical detection tests for each type are discussed along with step-by-step examples. A case study shows how zapper or electronic suppression of sales fraud in point-of-sales systems can be detected and quantified.

Any data analytic software may be used with the concepts of this book. However, this book uses CaseWare IDEA software to detail its step-by-step analytical procedures. The companion website provides access to a fully functional demonstration version of the latest IDEA software. The site also includes useful IDEAScripts that automate many of the data analytic tests.

Fraud and Fraud Detection provides insights that enhance the reader's data analytic skills. Readers will learn to:

- Understand the different areas of fraud and their specific detection methods.
- Evaluate point-of-sales system data files for zapper fraud.
- Understand data requirements, file format types, and apply data verification procedures.
- Understand and apply statistical sampling techniques.
- Apply correlation and trend analysis to data and evaluate the results.
- Identify anomalies and risk areas using computerized techniques.
- Distinguish between anomalies and fraud.
- Develop a step-by-step plan for detecting fraud through data analytics.
- Utilize IDEA software to automate detection and identification procedures.

The delineation of detection techniques for each type of fraud makes this book a must-have for students and new fraud-prevention professionals, and the step-by-step guidance to automation and complex analytics will prove useful for experienced examiners. With data sets growing exponentially, increasing both the speed and sensitivity of detection helps fraud professionals stay ahead of the game. *Fraud and Fraud Detection* is a guide to more efficient, more effective fraud identification.

HOW THIS BOOK IS ORGANIZED

This book is about identifying fraud with the aid of data analytic techniques. It includes some data analytical tests that you probably have not considered. It may also expose you to some useful features of IDEA and how to apply procedures to make you a more effective IDEA user. This is a list of the chapters in *Fraud and Fraud Detection*:

- **Chapter 1, "Introduction."** This chapter provides a simple definition of fraud to distinguish it from abuse. Different types of frauds are outlined. The chapter includes a discussion of why a certain amount of fraud risk is acceptable to organizations and how risk assessments enable us to evaluate and focus on areas with a higher potential risk of fraud.
- **Chapter 2, "Fraud Detection."** Occupational fraud is hard to detect as employees know their systems inside out. There are both fraudulent inclusions and fraudulent exclusions to be evaluated. This chapter discusses recognizing the red flags of fraud and different types of anomalies. Accounting and analytic anomalies are distinguished, as well as whether procedures are considered to be data mining or data analytics.
- **Chapter 3, "The Data Analysis Cycle."** The data analysis cycle steps include evaluation, technology, and auditing the results from the analysis. Before you can do any analysis, you must have good data. This chapter defines the steps in obtaining the data, such as necessary files, fields, file formats, the download, and techniques to verify data integrity. The next steps of preparing for data analysis include examples of data-familiarization techniques along with arranging and organizing the data.
- **Chapter 4, "Statistics and Sampling."** Knowledge of statistics can help to better understand and evaluate anomalies, of which some are deviations from the normal. Results of sampling methods can also be more effectively analyzed and interpreted. This chapter explains basic statistics that can easily be understood by auditors, accountants, and investigators. The chapter includes both descriptive and inferential statistics, the measure of center points, and variability from the center. Standard deviation and its usefulness in comparing data is discussed. Both statistical and nonstatistical sampling methods that include attribute, monetary unit, classical variable, discovery, and random sampling are demonstrated along with explanations of why sampling is not enough.
- **Chapter 5, "Data Analytical Tests."** Data analytical tests allow for the detection of anomalies over entire data sets. The tests can evaluate 100 percent of the transactions or records to reduce potentially millions of records to a reasonable amount of high-risk transactions for review. General data analytical tests can be applied in most situations and are ideal as a starting point for an audit when there is no specific fraud or target identified. Benford's Law for detecting abnormal duplications in data is explained for the primary, advanced, and associated tests. Examples of these are demonstrated using IDEA's Benford's Law built-in tests to provide understanding, application, and evaluations of the results. Z-score, relative size factor, number duplication, same-same-same, same-same-different, and even amounts tests are shown with step-by-step instructions of how they can be manually applied using IDEA.
- **Chapter 6, "Advanced Data Analytical Tests."** Correlation, trend analysis, and time-series analysis are explained in this chapter and demonstrated using IDEA's

built-in features. Relationship tests known as GEL-1 and GEL-2 are shown with step-by-step instructions of how they can be manually applied using IDEA. The reader will be able to analyze and evaluate the results from these advanced tests.

- **Chapter 7, "Skimming and Cash Larceny."** In this chapter, we will look at the differences and similarities of skimming and cash larceny. This type of fraud has fewer data analytical tests that can be performed as the fraud is not recorded in the business system's databases or is well concealed. Less attention is paid to this area, as the losses are generally not as significant as in other types of fraud. Methods of skimming and larceny are discussed to provide an understanding of these types of frauds. A short case study using two years of sample sales data highlights possible data analytical tests that use charts and pivot tables to provide views for different analytical perspectives.

- **Chapter 8, "Billing Schemes."** Billing schemes occur through accounts payable and are centered on trade and expenses payable. The objective for reviewing accounts payable does not stop at looking for fraud by corrupt employees, but it is also useful for detecting errors and inefficiencies in the system. Most of the case study involves real-life payment data of over 2 million records. Data analytical tests from Chapter 5 are applied in practice and demonstrated using the IDEA software. Other specific tests include isolating payments without purchase orders, comparing invoice dates to payment dates, searching the database for post office box numbers, matching employees' addresses to the suppliers' addresses, duplicate addresses in the supplier master file, payments made to suppliers not in the master file, and the usage of gap detection on check numbers.

- **Chapter 9, "Check Tampering Schemes."** This chapter includes discussions of electronic payment-systems fraud along with traditional check-tampering schemes to better understand both new and old schemes. Methods of obtaining checks and authorized signatures, along with concealment methods, are outlined. Data analytical tests and a short case study that uses sample data are used as examples.

- **Chapter 10, "Payroll Fraud."** Some form of payroll fraud happens in almost every organization; whether they are the simple claiming of excess overtime and hours worked or taking complex steps to set up nonexistent employees on the payroll. This chapter outlines data analytical tests to identify anomalies that can be evaluated to determine payroll fraud. The case study uses real payroll payment data to illustrate step-by-step payroll analytical tests. Tests for the payroll register, payroll master, and commission files are discussed.

- **Chapter 11, "Expense Reimbursement Schemes."** Travel and entertainment expenses are open to abuse by employees, as improperly reimbursed amounts puts extra money in their pockets. This chapter uses actual travel expense data to highlight analytical tests to identify anomalies that require additional analysis and review. The case study includes methodologies to make the inconsistent data usable in a field that contains the travel destinations. Tests for purchase cards are also discussed.

- **Chapter 12, "Register Disbursement Schemes."** This chapter distinguishes between register disbursement schemes, skimming, and cash larceny. It provides an understanding of false returns, adjustments, and voids used to perpetrate this type of fraud. Concealment methods are discussed. The case study uses data analytics to detect anomalies in voids and coupon redemptions. Tests, such as identifying transactions where the same person both registers the sale and authorizes the void, and matching all sales with all voids are illustrated.

■ **Chapter 13, "Noncash Misappropriations."** Noncash misappropriations frequently involve assets such as inventory, materials, and supplies. This type of fraud is easy to commit, difficult to conceal, and requires conversion of the assets to cash. Noncash schemes, such as misuse, unconcealed misappropriations, and transfer of assets are discussed. Concealment strategies by falsifying inventory records, sales, and purchases records are noted. The types of data file and data analytical tests to detect potential are suggested.

■ **Chapter 14, "Corruption."** Corruption is insidious as it involves an employee of the organization. Corruption schemes are difficult to detect as the gain to the employee is paid by an outside party and not recorded in the organization's records. Corruption schemes include bribery, tender or bid rigging, kickbacks, illegal gratuities, extortion, and conflict of interest. Data analytics can expose transactions that may be associated with corruptions schemes. One of the most powerful tests that can be applied to data sets is a relationship-linking test, as demonstrated in this chapter.

■ **Chapter 15, "Money Laundering."** This chapter introduces the reader to money-laundering schemes and how to detect them. Anti-money-laundering organizations are listed to provide resource information on this subject matter. Techniques used to convert illicit funds to what appear to be legitimate funds in the placement, layering, and integration stages are discussed. Nontraditional banking systems and new payment methods are included in this introduction. Data analytical tests to detect money laundering are outlined.

■ **Chapter 16, "Zapper Fraud."** Zappers, or electronic suppression-of-sale devices, are being used to delete sales transactions from point-of-sales systems. This is a worldwide problem that is of great concern to taxation authorities and commercial landlords that base rental revenue on a percentage of sales. This chapter provides some background information on POS systems and zappers. Step-by-step instructions are shown on how to prepare POS files for analysis and on using various analytic techniques to analyze, detect, evaluate, and quantify deleted sales in IDEA.

■ **Chapter 17, "Automation and IDEAScript."** This chapter introduces the automation tools of IDEAScript, Visual Script, and custom functions. Automating procedures, especially complex ones, can save much time. Considerations for automation are discussed. The benefits of IDEAScript are compared with those of Visual Script. Creating Visual Script and IDEAScript from the recording of procedures manually done in IDEA are shown. In addition, a look into how IDEAScript can create a script from the history log file is included in this chapter. IDEAScript resources are outlined, including useful completed scripts that are available from the companion website.

■ **Chapter 18, "Conclusion."** This chapter explains why using data analytics to initially detect financial-statement fraud is not appropriate. Features, equations, and functions demonstrated throughout the book are summarized here. The project overview feature within IDEA is briefly discussed, showing how it brings together all the databases used in the project and how they relate to one another. There are some final words regarding data analytic challenges and future needs.

Acknowledgments

I WOULD LIKE TO THANK Athena Mailloux, who developed my interest in occupational fraud and fraud detection. Without her insistence that I join her in teaching a financial-fraud program that she developed for a local college, I would not have found the enthusiasm for fraud detection.

Alain Soublière and all the wonderful people at CaseWare IDEA Inc. deserve much credit for their assistance, support, and professionalism. CaseWare IDEA allowed me to combine fraud detection with data analytics.

A special thanks to Brian Element, an IDEAScript master. Without Brian, the automated IDEAScripts offered in the companion website would not exist. I met Brian, a chartered professional accountant, at an advanced IDEA course that he presented in 2011. We started chatting and it came out the Brian wanted to learn IDEAScripting. Brian said that he would have to come up with a scenario for his self-learning IDEAScript project. At the time, I had given much thought to the detection of anomalies through the use of data analytics, so I said to him, "Have I got a deal for you!" Since that time we have been working together on ideas for scripts for fraud detection that Brian programs. From self-learning, Brian has become the world's leading expert in IDEAScripts and he has been conferred the certified IDEAScript expert (CISE) designation by CaseWare IDEA. At the time of writing, Brian is the sole holder of this designation.

Most important, I would like to thank my family, friends, and associates for all their support and encouragement to be able to complete this book.

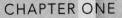

## CHAPTER ONE

Introduction

ORGANIZATIONS GENERATE AND RETAIN more information stored in electronic format than ever before, yet even though there is more analysis performed with the available data, fraud persists. With such vast amounts of data, abusive scheme transactions are hidden and are difficult to detect by traditional means. Data analytics can assist in uncovering signs of potential fraud with the aid of software to sort through large amounts of data to highlight anomalies.

This book will help you understand fraud and the different types of occupational fraud schemes. Specific data analytical tests are demonstrated along with suggested tests on how to uncover these frauds through the use of data analytics.

DEFINING FRAUD

A short definition of fraud is outlined in *Black's Law Dictionary*:

> An act of intentional deception or dishonesty perpetrated by one or more individuals, generally for financial gain.[1]

This simple definition mandates a number of elements that must be addressed in order to prove fraud:

- The statement must be false and material.
- The individual must know that the statement is untrue.
- The intent to deceive the victim.
- The victim relied on the statement.
- The victim is injured financially or otherwise.

The false statement must substantially impact the victim's decision to proceed with the transaction and that perpetrator must know the statement is false. A simple error or mistake is not fraudulent when it is not made to mislead the victim. The victim reasonably relied on the statement that caused injury to the victim or placed him or her at a disadvantage.

It is intentional deception that induces the victim to take a course of action that results in a loss that distinguishes the theft act.

In addition to the employer suffering a financial or other loss, occupational fraud involves an employee violating the trust associated with the job and hiding the fraud. The employee takes action to conceal the fraud and hopes it will not be discovered at all or until it is too late.

The word *abuse* is employed when the elements for defining fraud do not explicitly exist. In terms of occupational abuse, common examples include actions of employees:

- Accessing Internet sites such as Facebook and eBay for personal reasons.
- Taking a sick day when not sick.
- Making personal phone calls.
- Deliberately underperforming.
- Taking office supplies for personal use.
- Not earning the day's pay while working offsite or telecommuting.

There is an endless list that can fall under the term *abuse*, but no reasonable employer would use this word to describe any employee unless the actions were excessive. Organizations may have policies in place for some of these items, such as an Acceptable Internet Use Policy, but most would be considered on a case-by-case basis, as the issue is a matter of degree that can be highly subjective. There would unlikely be any legal actions taken against an employee who participated in a mild form of abuse.

ANOMALIES VERSUS FRAUD

In the data analysis process, "Detecting a fraud is like finding the proverbial needle in the haystack."[2] Typically, fraudulent transactions in electronic records are few in relation to the large amount of records in data sets. Fraudulent transactions are not the norm. Other anomalies, such as accounting records anomalies, are due to inadequate procedures or other internal control weaknesses. These weaknesses would be repetitive and will occur frequently in the data set. Sometimes, they would regularly and consistently happen at specific intervals, such as at month- or year-end. Understanding the business and its practices and procedures helps to explain most anomalies.

TYPES OF FRAUD

The Association of Certified Fraud Examiners (ACFE) in the 2012 Report to the Nations[3] outlines the three categories of occupational fraud and their subcategories in Figure 1.1.

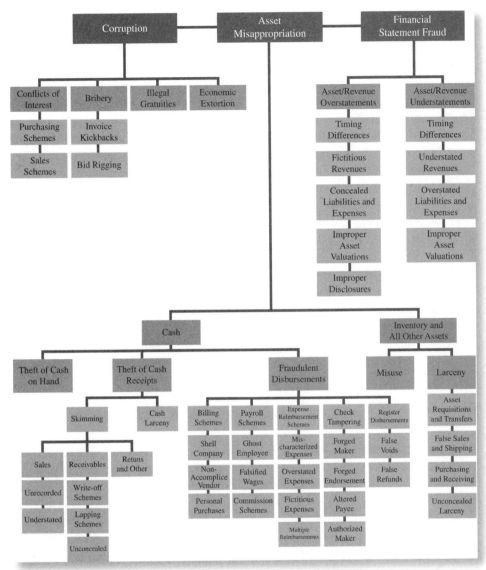

FIGURE 1.1 Occupational Fraud and Abuse Classification System

Source: Association of Certified Fraud Examiners

It was found that:

> As in our previous studies, asset misappropriation schemes were by far the most common type of occupational fraud, comprising 87% of the cases reported to us; they were also the least costly form of fraud, with a median loss of $120,000. Financial statement fraud schemes made up just 8% of the cases in our study, but caused the greatest median loss at $1 million. Corruption schemes fell in the middle, occurring in just over one-third of reported cases and causing a median loss of $250,000.[4]

Among the three major categories—corruption, asset misappropriation, and financial statement fraud—there are far more types of occupational fraud in the asset-misappropriation category. There are many known schemes and areas where fraud may occur. Thefts of cash on hand have been occurring ever since there was cash. With globalization and the availability of the Internet, newer and more innovative types of fraud are coming to light.

An example is the case study published in Verizon's security blog titled "Pro-Active Log Review Might Be a Good Idea."[5] A U.S.-based corporation had requested Verizon to assist them in reviewing virtual private network logs that showed an employee logging in from China while he was sitting at his desk in the United States. Investigation revealed that the employee had outsourced his job to a Chinese consulting firm at a fraction of his earnings. The employee spent most of his day on personal matters on the Internet. The blog notes that the employee's performance reviews showed that "he received excellent remarks. His code was clean, well written, and submitted in a timely fashion. Quarter after quarter, his performance review noted him as the best developer in the building."

Clearly there was no dispute with the quality of work submitted and he had met all deadlines. While the employee did misrepresent that the work was his, the company did not suffer any direct financial loss. Other than violating security policy of permitting unauthorized access to the network, at most, the employee abused company resources by browsing the Internet for most of his workday.

Would any of this have been an issue if the employee were a contractor who subcontracted his work out (assuming that there were no objections with the login procedures)?

ASSESS THE RISK OF FRAUD

It is not possible to eliminate fraud risk in any given area other than to avoid it all together. A company may choose not to deal with a particular vendor or purchaser. They may choose not to acquire assets that need a high level of protection or to expand or do business in an unstable country. Alternatively, they may select an exit strategy if the risk is found to be too great. Avoidance would have been the result of either a formal or informal risk assessment. A risk analysis would have been considered and found that the cost outweighs the benefits.

Some risks will be assumed without additional control features being implemented, since the cost of implementation would be higher than the expected loss. For example, banks issuing credit cards may be able to reduce fraudulent charges if they implement new high-tech security measures, but the cost in terms of dollars or customer inconvenience would be higher than the cost of fraudulent transactions. Fraud is a cost of doing business and it needs a cost-to-benefit or return-on-investment analysis. The risk assessment aids in the determination of the level of controls to implement while balancing acceptable risk tolerance against costs of reducing the risk.

$$\text{Risk} = \text{Impact} \times \text{Probability (threats and vulnerabilities)}$$

In most cases, the company will seek to mitigate the risks by implementing controls. These could be preventative, monitoring, or detection controls. Risk can also be mitigated by purchasing insurance or, in the case of certain employees, requiring them to be bonded.

It may be determined that costs exceed the benefits of preventing fraud in a particular area. However, investments in measures to detect rather than prevent the fraud may be an acceptable risk given the lower costs and likelihood of high losses. Detective measures must also be factored into any risk assessment.

The decision on how far to go will depend on the risk assessment and the reason for performing the risk assessment. It is a management decision as to what level to take the response to the risk of fraud. The decision will be primarily based on why the fraud risk assessment was undertaken in the first place. Was it due to audit or regulatory requirements? Was it management's desire to evaluate the internal control system? Was it to reduce the cost for fraud?

A risk assessment will identify potential areas of fraud, whether internal or external, directly or indirectly, and how vulnerable or how likely the threat is to occur. Factors that determine the probability component include:

- The industry or nature of the business
- The values and ethics of senior management and employees
- Internal controls—preventive and detective
- Business environment—local versus multinational, small versus large, brick-and-mortar versus Internet, geographic location, economic conditions
- Likelihood
- Industry trends
- History
- Resources
- Internal control
- Complexity
- Volume
- Standards
- Whistleblower
- Complaints
- Moral
- Impact
- Value
- Maximum exposure

Other issues that must be considered when performing a risk assessment include the possibility of adverse publicity resulting in a loss of consumer confidence, potential lawsuits, violating laws, and the overall impairment to carrying on normal business.

Appendix D of *Managing the Business Risk of Fraud*[6] is an excellent example of the fraud-risk assessment framework for revenue recognition risk that can be used as a template for any organization. It can also be modified to encompass any type of risk.

The template lists various fraud risks and schemes and then associates the following with each of the schemes:

- Likelihood of occurrence
- Significance to the organization

- People and/or department subject to the risk
- Existing antifraud internal controls
- Assessment of internal control effectiveness
- Residual risks
- Fraud-risk response

 ## CONCLUSION

Understanding what fraud is and the types of frauds allows us to focus on occupational fraud in this book. Being able to assess fraud risk provides us with priorities as to where to invest time and resources to have the largest impact in detecting and reducing incidents of fraud.

 ## NOTES

1. *Black's Law Dictionary*, "What Is FRAUD?," accessed June 17, 2013, http://thelawdictionary .org/fraud-2.
2. Steve W. Albrecht et al., *Fraud Examination*, 4th ed. (Mason, OH: Cengage Learning, 2012).
3. "Association of Certified Fraud Examiners—2012 Report to the Nations," accessed June 17, 2013, www.acfe.com/rttn.aspx.
4. Ibid.
5. Andrew Valentine, "Case Study: Pro-Active Log Review Might Be a Good Idea," Verizon Enterprise Solutions, accessed April 24, 2014, www.verizonenterprise.com/security/ blog/index.xml?postid=1626.
6. Institute of Internal Auditors, the American Institute of Certified Public Accountants, and Association of Certified Fraud Examiners, *Managing the Business Risk of Fraud: A Practical Guide*, https://na.theiia.org/standards-guidance/Public%20Documents/ fraud%20paper.pdf.

CHAPTER TWO

Fraud Detection

O CCUPATIONAL FRAUD IS DIFFICULT to detect. While companies have policies and procedures in place, an employee committing fraud tries to circumvent those policies and procedures. The employee is a trusted employee who has legitimate access to various systems and, in the course of their duties, would learn how the systems work. They are well versed in the workings of the business in the normal course of their duties and would have encountered weaknesses in the system. In fact, the employee is likely to have worked around the normal procedures to resolve an issue on behalf of the employer. These sanctioned attempts in circumventing normal procedure would expose a weakness in the system.

While policies and procedures are good at stating the employer's position and also designed to bring common errors and mistakes to light, an employee committing fraud is not making a mistake but deliberately circumventing the systems. Added to this, the employee attempts to use various methods to conceal their actions. Lies are told. Documents are falsified. Transaction recordings are misrepresented. Internal controls are abused.

It is impossible for any business to operate efficiently if too many restrictions or controls are put in place to thwart fraud. Employees must be trusted to perform their duties diligently and honestly. They are trusted with assets, tools, and information to do this.

Even with honest employees, flaws in the systems or unintentional errors on the part of employees also produce errors.

One must balance the risk of potential fraud and the continued operations of an ongoing business concern.

 ## RECOGNIZING FRAUD

We can only observe indicators, symptoms, or red flags of fraud. Once detected, they should be investigated to determine whether there is actual fraud. There will be large numbers of false positives in this area. Because of the volume, many of these are not given the attention that they deserve. For instance, after clearing a recognized symptom in a particular area, other red flags in the same area may be dismissed.

Red flags may be internal control irregularities, accounting anomalies, analytical anomalies, tips, and behavioral changes.

Business systems are in place to operate a business efficiently. Recording transactions is part of this process. Throughout the processes, there are controls to ensure that the business runs smoothly, safeguards assets, and has accurate recording and reporting. Fraud prevention, deterrence, and detection are objectives of internal controls. Internal control overrides or weaknesses contribute to the most common types of frauds and compromise the purpose of fraud prevention and deterrence. In some cases, there is a legitimate reason to circumvent an internal control. For instance, where there is a new situation not originally contemplated in the design of the control, employees deliberately look for ways to effectively do their job and carry on with the business process. These actions may or may not be formally sanctioned.

Good internal control includes:

- Separation of duties where collusion with someone else is needed to go around the controls.
- Physical safeguards of assets, including information in computer systems.
- Independent checks through monitoring and audits.
- Proper records and supporting documents to validate the transactions and to leave an adequate audit trail.
- Proper authorization for transactions, records, and other activities to ensure approvals and control independent authorization limits.

Detection techniques should be focused on any weaknesses in internal controls. Irregularities should be examined and the appropriate actions taken documented. The documentation will assist in implementing corrective measures to the internal controls if necessary.

Accounting anomalies are those unusual items associated with the accounting system. The anomalies would be with entries and with backup documents. By their nature, journal entries are to adjust unusual items that are outside of the normal day-to-day accounting system flow. Journal entries are a high-risk area as they allow for concealment of fraud activities. Manual journal entries should be reviewed with care and automated journal entries should be tested. Many accounting anomalies also fall under analytical anomalies.

Analytical anomalies are anything that is out of the norm. Things falling outside of normal patterns or new patterns formed can be analytical anomalies. They are anything that is unusual. Examples include:

- Outliers
- Inliers where they are not expected
- Too many or too few transactions
- Unexplained items
- Unusual relationships between items

- Unexpected timing of transactions or events
- Unusual accounts or account balances
- Inconsistencies
- Gaps or duplicates of item numbers
- Unexpected payment methods
- Unreasonable items

Analytical anomalies may easily occur in business systems where they are not integrated. Unlike enterprise resource planning (ERP) systems where data entered in one module populates all the related modules, many organizations have business systems that do not communicate directly with each other. Extra care has to be taken where data from one system is manually transferred to the consolidation or other systems.

Expect a high number of analytical anomalies. One must distinguish high-risk anomalies and low-risk anomalies. Eliminate from review those that normally would occur. Therefore, one must understand the business systems, understand the business, and also understand the industry. Knowledge of these will allow you to separate the normal and expected anomalies from those that have fraud potential.

For internal auditors, it is expected that they would have a thorough knowledge of the workings of the business. For external auditors, forensic accountants, consultants, and investigators, they must make themselves familiar with the business entity and its industry. Standard audit steps such as the following must be employed.

- Tour the business premises to obtain an overview of the business operations.
- Analyze financial statements, reports, and other relevant documents.
- Review the flow of accounting data and other information within the organization.
- Interview relevant employees from different areas and levels. Interviews with auditors, IT staff, and corporate security employees should also be included.
- Obtain the assistance of an experienced employee to assist and to answer questions. While an internal audit employee may be a logical choice to obtain aid, care should be taken that internal audit staff does not provide direct assistance to external auditors where prohibited. The Financial Reporting Council in the United Kingdom introduced this prohibition, effective for audits of financial statement periods ending on or after June 15, 2014.[1]

For detailed flow of business systems, Section 404 of the Sarbanes-Oxley Act enacted by the United States in 2002[2] (or its counterpart in other countries) is invaluable. In order to annually assess the effectiveness of its internal controls, management must document and evaluate controls that form part of the financial-reporting process. This report outlines in much detail the business systems. Flowcharts typically accompany the report, which would facilitate understanding the business flow. Not only should one have knowledge of the organization, but one should also be familiar with industry practices and with some of the organization's competitors to establish a baseline or normal business practices.

Another red flag area is tips and complaints about alleged frauds or of witnessing unusual events. Tips are investigated more vigorously than most other irregularities or anomalies. It is recognized that people are reluctant to provide tips of fraud or suspicion of fraud. They do not know for sure that the fraud is taking place. Most people shy away from squealing on people whom they associate with and know. They believe that informing on people is just plain wrong or that they are siding with management. There is also the fear of being found out that they informed and will be ostracized by other employees. There may be potential reprisals not only from the alleged perpetrator but also from the supervisor, who may not find the tip credible or may be involved in the fraud. Also many organizations do not have a whistleblowing or integrity hotline procedures in place to make it easy and anonymous for people to provide the tips. The 2012 ACFE Report to the Nations[3] shows tips as the most common way fraud was initially detected in occupational fraud at 43.3 percent. This is an increase over the 2010 report of 40.2 percent. With whistleblowing legislation in place and organizations implementing tools to facilitate this process for people, the volume of tips will hopefully increase.

Employees are in the best place to witness and detect fraud. They are the best source for information. However, it should be recognized that some tips are provided with malicious intent. The allegations may be false and the tips provided to make trouble for the alleged perpetrator. A tip should be recognized as merely a red flag or fraud symptom and require investigation like any other symptom. An open mind and professional skepticism are needed.

Behavioral and lifestyle changes are another area where employees are best positioned to observe these anomalies. Auditors would likely have no base to compare changes to as they do not know the employee, whereas coworkers see and interact with other employees on a day-to-day basis. Lifestyle changes would be obvious to coworkers. While observed assets can be easily explained away by way of lottery winnings, inheritance, or disposition of investments, the explanation can be just as easily verified.

Similarly, behavioral changes—whether detrimental or good—are best noticed by other staff members. Perpetrating fraud is a stressful action that involves a fear of being caught. The stress triggers unusual behaviour that should be looked into by the organization. This may be out of concern for the employee's physical and mental health, as well as to determine whether it impairs the organization in its day-to-day operation. The employee may be dealing with personal issues that are causing changes in behavior. This proactive approach is beneficial to the employee and may reduce one of the pressures contributing to committing fraud.

 ## DATA MINING VERSUS DATA ANALYSIS AND ANALYTICS

BusinessDictionary.com defines *data mining* as:

> sifting through very large amounts of data for useful information. Data mining uses artificial intelligence techniques, neural networks, and advanced statistical tools (such as cluster analysis) to reveal trends, patterns, and relationships, which might otherwise have remained undetected.[4]

Data mining is the searching of large amounts of computerized data to find trends, patterns, or relationships without testing a hypothesis. No specific results or outcomes are anticipated.

BusinessDictionary.com defines *data analysis* as:

> the process of evaluating data using analytical and logical reasoning to examine each component of the data provided. This form of analysis is just one of the many steps that must be completed when conducting a research experiment. Data from various sources is gathered, reviewed, and then analyzed to form some sort of finding or conclusion. There are a variety of specific data analysis method, some of which include data mining, text analytics, business intelligence, and data visualizations.[5]

Data mining is a subset of data analysis or analytics. Data analytics starts with a hypothesis that is to be confirmed or proven to be false. A conclusion is made based on inference from the findings.

The definition and types of data analytics can be further refined as to exploratory data analysis (EDA), confirmatory data analysis (CDA), and qualitative data analysis (QDA).

EDA is the initial stage where the data is explored when little is known about the data's relationships. It is here those hypotheses are formed and new patterns of features of the data are discovered. Most EDA techniques are visual and graphical. They consist of plotting the data in various types of statistical graphs to obtain an insight to the data.

CDA is where testing takes place and the hypotheses are proven correct or false. Results from samples are applied to the entire database. Causal or cause-and-effect relationships are verified. A cause-and-effect relationship is where one variable is independent and the other dependent. That is, the cause is the independent variable that impacts the dependent effect. An example would be citing the amount of rainfall as causing the growth of grass; care must be taken, as many events appear to be associated but may not actually have a cause-and-effect relationship.

Online analytical processing (OLAP) tools are frequently used with the CDA process. They allow the user to extract data selectively and view the data from different perspectives or dimensions.

QDA is used to draw conclusions from nonquantitative or non-numerical data such as images or text. While typically employed in the social sciences, it can be used in organizational audits of controls, procedures, and processes.

Data analytics provide insight into the dataset, discover underlying data relationships and structures, test assumptions and hypothesis, identify variables of causal relationships, and detect anomalies.

DATA ANALYTICAL SOFTWARE

There are a number of software programs that analyze data. Software such as Microsoft Access[6] or Microsoft Excel[7] is familiar to many people and used by many businesses and individuals. Indeed, Excel is favored and frequently use by accountants and auditors. Access and Excel is suitable when the dataset is not large and the analysis not complex.

While it is possible to do more complex procedures, many steps are necessary. The user may need to perform operations and formulas that are not commonly used.

These products are not recommended as professional analytic tools; their complex functions are time consuming to learn and lack data integrity. It is easy to inadvertently change the content of cells by accidentally touching the wrong key. Processing speed is also slow and can be cumbersome when applied to large amounts of data.

Professional or dedicated data analysis software, such as ACL,[8] Arbutus,[9] and IDEA[10] are specifically designed for use with large and very large data sets. Features of this type of software include:

- The data source is protected
- Can provide quick analysis
- Retains audit trails
- Built-in data analytical functions
- User friendly
- Can import from various data sources and file formats
- Able to analyze 100 percent of transactions
- Field statistics
- Various types of sampling techniques
- Benford's Law analysis
- Correlation and trend analysis
- Drill-down features
- Aging
- Stratification
- Fuzzy matching
- Sophisticated duplicate testing
- Auto-run or automated procedures

ActiveData[11] is an Excel add-in that has data analytical capabilities. It is a cross between Excel/Access and the more powerful data analytical software. It is feature-rich with an attractive low price.

 ## ANOMALIES VERSUS FRAUD WITHIN DATA

Data anomalies are a fact of life. There will always be inconsistencies, abnormal, or incorrect data residing in databases. This is quite normal. Database anomalies could be the result of missing or unmatched information caused by human error and flaws and limitations in the database. Bugs in the database can occur whenever a record is entered, modified, or deleted.

Insertion anomalies occur when data is being entered into the database. One form of this anomaly is where the information cannot be entered until additional information from another source is entered. A new employee's shift scheduling cannot be entered until the employee has a payroll number. The payroll number may not be assigned immediately as the new employee's first pay will not occur until two weeks from starting employment.

Data must be entered in a format that is consistent. The most common insertion errors are missing or incorrectly formatted entries. Well-designed software should have error-checking capabilities that provide an error message and prevent recording of the record if there is a blank entry where data is expected. Error checking or validation should also prevent an entry that does not fall within an acceptable range. For instance, the program would not accept a number outside of 01 to 12 where the field is a numeric month field. It may not accept a single digit for a month if the validation was designed to require a leading zero where the month normally would be a single digit. This helps to reduce errors where the operator meant to enter 12 but entered a 1 instead.

Deletion anomalies occur when the last record for a particular group of information is deleted. Removing that record may remove relevant information associated with the record. The deletion of information or facts about one entity automatically deletes other facts regarding that entity.

Let's say an employee has left to work for another employer. The former employee shift schedule information is deleted but the associated address information might also be contained in that last record for the employee. Where would the employer send the employee's last paycheck or accumulated vacation pay?

Modification or update anomalies are where incorrect information needs to be changed that may require many other record changes. This leads to the possibility that some items may be updated incorrectly.

When we analyze data for anomalies for fraud items, we are not interested in insertion, deletion, or modification anomalies caused by the business systems (other than to note poor system designs that lead to internal control problems). What we are interested in are unexpected or strange items, such as outliers or too many inliers. We target suspicious transactions or transactions that are too typical to be natural. We look at the unusual in relationship to the usual.

Anomalies in datasets will be common. Most will be errors and very few, if any, may pertain to fraud. It is unlikely that any fraud can be proven solely based on analyzing data. Analyzing data to identify anomalies or patterns gives the auditor or investigator a starting point of where to do further analyses. One must follow the audit trail to review source documents and supporting factors that lead to the records to review.

It is important to employ professional skepticism at this point by:

- Critically assessing the anomalies without making a conclusion.
- Having no biases caused by being overly suspicious or cynical.
- Not accepting evidence or information gathered at face value.
- Ensuring that all evidence or information is complete.
- Pursuing the facts through the critical review of documents associated with the data anomaly.
- Assessing whether information provided by staff lacks objectivity or there is lack of knowledge.

What is the anomaly for the numbers 1987 and 2013? It took 26 years to pass before the year contained all four different digits again. This anomaly is neither an error nor fraud, but rather just an observation.

FRAUDULENT DATA INCLUSIONS AND DELETIONS

Many staff members have access to business systems as part of their duties to update, create, delete, and modify transaction records. Some employees, such as managers, owners, and shareholders, may have additional or higher access rights. Without the proper controls these accesses are vulnerable to errors and potential fraud.

The modification or substitution recording of the proper transaction can be classified as a fraudulent inclusion. Falling under a fraudulent deletion can be failing to record the transaction when it should be entered.

Concealing theft of inventory can be done by altering inventory records to match the physical count. Alternatively, if the fraudster is involved in the physical count, changing the count numbers to match the perpetual inventory records would also conceal the shrinkage. Reclassifying the missing inventory as obsolete would accomplish the same results. More sophisticated fraudsters may create a sale of the inventory to an old existing account that may be due for write-off.

Recharacterizing expenses as capital expenditures increases net income that may constitute financial statement fraud. One of the simplest ways to show higher income is to just omit the recording of liabilities and expenses until another period. While it is easy for management to do, it is hard for the auditors to detect as it leaves no audit trail. Improper recording can be examined but it is far more difficult to look for something that should exist but does not.

True deletion of electronic records is akin to the shredding of paper documents. Most business systems do not allow deletion without it being logged in the audit-trail file. Some systems record a deletion as a reversal of a previous transaction, therefore maintaining the integrity of the system. An excellent example of transaction deletions are "zappers and phantom-ware facilitate the systematic skimming of cash receipts by deleting records of cash sales, re-numbering receipts to disguise the deletion, and the production of conforming financial reports. In some cases, these programs can be so thorough that they reach out beyond the ECR and the sale system itself to bring inventory and employee time records into line with the deletions."[12]

 CONCLUSION

Fraud occurs in any organization as it is not possible to invoke the level of control needed to eliminate fraud. If there are too many restrictions or controls in place, those restrictions prevent employees from doing their jobs properly.

As auditors or investigators, we can only test for red flags of fraud. Data analytical software can assist us in sifting through all the transactions to flag anomalies. Being able to recognize fraud may allow us to further refine our tests to reduce the number of anomalies to investigate.

Before we can perform data analytics, we must understand the data analysis cycle and know how to obtain the electronic data files for our audit or analysis. We must ensure that the data is usable, complete, and accurate.

NOTES

1. Financial Reporting Council, "FRC Prohibits the Use of Internal Audit Staff on the External Audit Team," accessed July 2, 2013, www.frc.org.uk/News-and-Events/FRC-Press/Press/2013/June/FRC-prohibits-the-use-of-internal-audit-staff-on-t.aspx?goback=%2Egde_107948_member_251979920.
2. U.S. Securities and Exchange Commission, "Final Rule: Management's Report on Internal Control Over Financial Reporting and Certification of Disclosure in Exchange Act Periodic Reports; Rel. No. 33-8238," accessed June 30, 2013, www.sec.gov/rules/final/33-8238.htm.
3. "Association of Certified Fraud Examiners—2012 Report to the Nations," accessed June 17, 2013, www.acfe.com/rttn.aspx.
4. BusinessDictionary.com, "Data Mining," accessed July 1, 2013, www.businessdictionary.com/definition/data-mining.html.
5. BusinessDictionary.com, "Data Analysis?," accessed July 1, 2013, www.businessdictionary.com/definition/data-analysis.html.
6. Microsoft Office, "Access Database Software and Applications," accessed July 13, 2013, http://office.microsoft.com/en-ca/access.
7. Microsoft Office, "Spreadsheet Software, Microsoft Excel," accessed July 13, 2013, http://office.microsoft.com/en-ca/excel.
8. "ACL Compliance, Audit, Governance & Risk Software—Data Analytics and Cloud-Based GRC Management," accessed July 13, 2013, www.acl.com.
9. "Arbutus Audit and Compliance Analytics, and Continuous Monitoring Solutions," accessed July 13, 2013, www.arbutussoftware.com.
10. "IDEA–CaseWare International," accessed July 13, 2013, www.caseware.com/products/idea.
11. "InformationActive.com—Data Analytics for Excel and SQL Databases," accessed July 13, 2013, www.informationactive.com.
12. Richard Ainsworth, "Zappers & Phantom-Ware: A Global Demand for Tax Fraud Technology," accessed November 20, 2013, http://taxblog.com/rainsworth/zappers-phantom-ware-a-global-demand-for-tax-fraud-technology.

CHAPTER THREE

The Data Analysis Cycle

T HE DATA ANALYSIS CYCLE is a three-stage cycle that is constantly changing, and which must be adjusted to in order to be effective. The stages are evaluation and analysis, software and technology, and the audit and investigation stage.

 ## EVALUATION AND ANALYSIS

To start the cycle one must understand the whole business well and, specifically, the subsidiary, division, or business unit being reviewed. A good understanding of the industry in general, along with the business environment, will give you a baseline for comparison purposes.

This cycle includes evaluating areas of potential fraud and identifying symptoms or red flags for frauds. This knowledge allows you to tailor your evaluation strategies to the organization. You cannot apply all the same steps and procedures universally to every business, as business practices in different industries, as well as within the same industries, differ greatly.

With this knowledge, the next step is to identify weaknesses or areas where potential fraud may exist within the business systems. It would be impossible to perform this task on the business organization as a whole. You need to break down the organization to at least the business-unit level to be able to focus on a more detailed level. Each area has different elements and risks. For instance, one area may be dealing with cash or payments and another with access controls and authorities. The risk assessments discussed earlier need to be tailored specifically to the function under review.

The audit team should employ the requirements of the Statement on Auditing Standards No. 99 (SAS 99) from the American Institute of Certified Public Accountants. As all transactions contribute toward the financial statements, team members should participate in "an exchange of ideas or 'brainstorming' among the audit team members, including the auditor with final responsibility for the audit, about how and where they believe the entity's financial statements might be susceptible to material misstatement due to fraud" as outlined in the AU 316.14 section of the professional standards.[1] The brainstorming exercise combines the experiences and thoughts of team members to identify risk areas.

The collaboration will also assist with the third step of listing red flags and symptoms of possible fraud in the functional or business unit being audited. Once completed as discussed in "Recognizing Fraud" in Chapter 2, you can move on to the Software and Technology segment of the data analysis cycle.

Software and Technology

Utilizing the identified red flags or symptoms, various software and hardware tools can be deployed to source information and data. Analysis can then be done against the data and information obtained. If issues are identified, automated technology can be used to minimize or prevent future occurrences.

With a list of symptoms in hand, one can decide what data is needed to perform meaningful analysis to conform to the audit objectives. With data in hand, analytical software such as IDEA can do tests to target the selected areas. It should be noted that some general tests, such as Benford's Law, highlight anomalies and can be used to compliment the specific testing.

The audit plan needs to be expanded to review and investigate suspicious items or anomalies. Most of the anomalies will be false positives that can be explained after additional investigation. Actual fraudulent transactions are normally few and far apart. If actual issues are determined, automated procedures and processes, such as continuous monitoring, can be implemented to immediately flag the issue to mitigate the risk of reoccurrence. Continuous monitoring can be both proactive and detective. This may come after the audit and investigative stage.

Audit and Investigative

No amount of technology can confirm a fraud. Technology can merely provide a starting point or identify potential transactions that may or may not indicate fraud. Technology reduces the amount of daily routine transactions to those that are high risk and require further review. Risk analysis is used to dictate whether further resources should be allocated to expand the audit or to investigate specific transactions. The audit trail must be followed and source documents should be reviewed. It may also be necessary to interview staff to obtain additional information, clarification, or reasoning behind the transaction. This may cycle back to the need for better understanding the business in more detail in the evaluation and analysis stage.

Once a fraudulent transaction is identified, technology may be able to assist in quantifying or for rooting out additional fraudulent transactions of the same type. The result of the audit or investigation determines additional procedures necessary to be implemented or included in the automated monitoring procedures.

The three stages of the cycle are ever evolving and continuous. They need to be proactive as new methods of fraud are constantly arising, especially with the rapid changes in technology. While technology may assist the auditor or investigator with new detection methods, technology also provides new tools for the fraudster to attack systems and perpetrate fraud. Where one area may be secured by various controls today, it may be compromised tomorrow. An auditor must include routine checks, like a night watchman on patrol who checks that doors are locked properly several times during the routine patrol. Have a plan but constantly adjust the plan accordingly!

 OBTAINING DATA FILES

In order to proceed with any data analytical tests, you have to be able to obtain data in a usable format that includes the record fields that you might need for your analysis. In addition to getting the data, the data must be scrubbed or cleansed to correct it from inherent errors to be useful. At times, even perfectly good data must be reorganized in order to perform certain calculations for tests.

Sometimes obtaining useful data requires high-tech knowledge and significant preplanning. For example, SAP,[2] enterprise resource-planning software from SAP AG, has more than 70,000 tables—and each table has many fields. The Accounting Document Header table (BKPF) has more than 100 fields.

The information under the subhead Audit Objectives to the end of the subhead Documenting the Results has been extracted and slightly modified (to remove references to appendices not reproduced) from *A Practical Guide to Obtaining Data for Auditors*,[3] published by CaseWare IDEA Inc. IDEA data analytical software is produced by CaseWare IDEA Inc. The author wrote the guide for CaseWare IDEA and the publisher granted permission to include these segments. The reproduced information is generic and can generally be applied in conjunction with other data analytical software.

IDEA licensees can access the full guide at http://ideasupport.caseware.com/media/viewpost.aspx?postid=1418.

Audit Objectives*

Data exists in various formats, maybe in a single file, possibly within a database, or perhaps even spread over a number of business systems that are not linked to one another. The audit objectives should be the determining factor of the data requirements.

For example, a routine financial audit using IDEA—whether it be to verify mechanical accuracy, valuation, existence, validity, completeness, cut-off, and analysis for other audit steps—may only require data from the accounting system. Files may include the general ledger, detail transactions, accounts payable, inventory, and sales.

For a fraud audit, in conjunction with the accounting system files, data both from access logs and from human resources may be needed. Computer or physical entry log date and times may be compared with accounting postings or authorizations. Personnel records of addresses may be matched to vendor records.

Additional electronic data may be required for forensic and other specific-purpose audits and reviews.

---

*This section is adapted, with permission, from CaseWare IDEA Inc.

Determine Whether IDEA Is Appropriate

IDEA is most useful when there is a problem to solve on an audit or used for substantive testing. IDEA should always be used subject to consideration of data volume and the cost of obtaining the required electronic data.

Data analysis techniques are necessary where there is a large volume of transactions. The greater the number of records, the more valuable IDEA is. When the number of records is low, using IDEA may not provide much benefit over a manual audit.

Consideration must also be given to the costs incurred in obtaining the data. Costs may be direct monetary cost in using outside services or cost in time for both the auditors and IT specialists. There may be major costs involved in determining the files and fields needed, writing queries, processing, and transferring the resulting data from the host computer to the auditor's computer or IDEA server. Time needs to be budgeted to examine the resulting files to ensure completeness and accuracy. Additional time may be required to investigate and correct data issues.

Data Requirements

Once the audit objectives have been well defined and it is determined that IDEA is the appropriate tool, the next step is to determine the data requirements. In order to do so, you must first identify the business or computer system, the business software used, and the files and fields needed to meet the audit objectives.

Hardware and Operating System

Identifying the computer system hardware and operating system will allow the auditor to determine whether IT support is needed. Computer hardware may be of entry level, business class, workstations and servers, mainframe, or supercomputers.

Operating systems include Windows, Mac OS, iOS, UNIX, Linux, and IBM OS.

Software

Software can include off-the-shelf, add-ons, ERP, and custom-designed packages.

Files

Though it may be simpler with off-the-shelf packages, you must still decide whether to obtain the raw data files and use your own copy of the package to convert the data to be readable by IDEA or to accept an export. The simplest types of export that most packages can handle are Microsoft Excel and print/pdf reports. Though there are disadvantages to both, no specialized skills are required.

For ERP and customized packages from large systems, IT support is required. At times, the expertise lies outside of the organization and third parties or consultants may be required.

Data Dictionary

For small packages, getting everything is simpler.

For large data packages, you need to determine which fields are relevant to the audit objectives. Files may be too large if everything is obtained. Also, many fields may not be relevant to the audit, such as budget, statistical, and nonfinancial fields. Consideration should also be given to the time and cost related to queries and processing.

Data Requirements

- **Volume:** While it is easier to ask an IT specialist for the entire file, as they would not need to create a query or do processing, it may not be practical due to the volume of data and additional work by the auditor to define every field in the record layout for IDEA.
- **Ease of download:** IT specialists are generally unconcerned with performing processing on their server because server memory is usually plentiful. However, the network is the bottleneck in the download process. Transferring data over the network may tie up resources. Transferring large amounts of data over a network may prevent or slow work for other users in the company. There may also be some security concerns.
- **Master files:** When obtaining any detailed files, you should also obtain the related master files. For example, vendor files may only contain vendor numbers, and you will need to obtain the vendor master file to join other relevant information, such as vendor name and address, to the detailed file.
- **Flags, codes, and references:** All fields containing flags, codes, and references should be reviewed and the translation chart obtained either in hardcopy or as a file. These flags and codes are usually meaningful and it is important that you understand their meaning.

Required Files and Fields Special attention should be given to date fields. For example, the posting date may be just as relevant as the transaction date for your audit objectives. When in doubt, include the field and then document its usefulness for the next time. Ensure fields with references can be traced to the source documents.

File Formats Determine the most suitable file-output format under the circumstances.

Transfer Method Determine what the most appropriate data transfer method is for the circumstances. Data transfer methods, include:

- Direct connect to the network server
- Internet
- FTP server: Care should be taken when transferring EBCDIC data as it converts to ASCII unless transfer options are set as binary. You may lose valuable data in the conversion process.
- Removable media (DVD, external USB drives, flash drives)

Other Questions to Consider
- Where is the data located?
- Is it live or archived?
- Is the requested data period available?
- Can it be accessed?

- Is it readable?
- How long are data being retained?
- How large are the estimated file sizes?

Once the data requirements have been established, a data request should be made in writing and include:

- Data parameters including files, fields, and the review period.
- File format.
- Transfer method.
- Date when the data should be available.
- Contact information for the auditor.
- For reconciliation purposes, you may also want to request the number of records and totals for each file, as well as printouts of the first 50 records for each file. Verification items can also be requested from other sources. For example, you could request the trial balance files in order to verify sales or accounts receivable files.

 ## PERFORMING THE AUDIT

Obtain Test Files

Where there might be a large volume of data that would be time consuming for the client to provide, you may wish to agree to obtain test files first with a limited number of records.

Obtaining sample files ensures that the fields and layout are as desired. This also ensures that the output format is readable and the data transfer method is tested. Any errors or integrity issues can be dealt with on the smaller scale.

If successful, the client should use the same query but expand the date range to cover all the records for the period for which data is requested.

IDEA Import

Once obtained, the data can be imported into IDEA.

After Import

Data quality can be assessed by its accuracy, integrity, completeness, validity, consistency, and uniformity.

Completeness and uniformity are the result of a well-designed and implemented data request, since this is based on the original computer data. Completeness checks for unwarranted inclusions or required data that is omitted.

Data irregularities such as incomplete data can cause nonuniformity. Nonuniform data may cause issues such as skewed columns or make it difficult to distinguish the data. Nonuniformity between files may create issues for procedures that require a common key between the files.

To evaluate data quality received, steps that can be taken include:

- **Reconciliation:** Reconciling the data to an independent source is a good indicator that the data is complete. The data may include unintentional nonfinancial, budgetary, or statistical information, which will be detected by reconciliation. However, this process cannot tell you whether some of the records are at a summary level rather than the desired detailed level.
- **Count:** A total count of the number of records imported into IDEA matching the total number of records from the output can contribute to the assurance of complete data.
- **Control total:** Similar to the count, summing the amounts in a numeric field and matching it to the expected total is assuring. Debit, credit, and other fields may be summed. For some files, such as a trial balance, the control total in a net amount field is expected to be zero.
- **Field statistics:** IDEA's Field Statistics easily displays information such as net value, number of zero items, minimum value, maximum and number of data errors, which can assist in the determination of the data integrity. Reviewing the Earliest Date and Latest Date statistic tests the boundary of the data for the beginning and ending period range.
- **Browse data:** A quick browse while scrolling through the data may reveal data integrity issues, such as the actual data layout is not the same as in the file layout provided to the auditor. Browsing allows for obvious omissions or inclusion errors possibly due to query issues.
- **Data dump printout:** Matching the IDEA sample records contents to the same sample records printed from the system can confirm data content and confirm whether fields are populated with proper data.

Cleaning Up the Data

Data received may not always be as anticipated. At times, some adjustments may be required. For example, both the first and last names of people are in a single field rather than appearing in separate fields. In that case, functions such as @split and @simplesplit may be applied.

For files from different systems that need to be joined, the common character field may have different lengths; for instance, one file may have a leading zero and the other does not.

Typically the common field in two files will be of different field types. This can be resolved by simply changing the field type in one file to match.

Sometimes it is more efficient to make IT aware of the problem and have them rerun the job rather than try to fix all the issues yourself. This also establishes the correct routine for future data requests.

Documenting the Results

Results of the download should be documented so that the process can be simplified for the next time the files are needed. Procedures for cleaning up the data for efficient usage should also be noted. If the download was successful the first time with no data adjustments required, this should also be documented. Obtaining a copy of the query for your own file is a good practice.

FILE FORMAT TYPES

Data analytical software can import many types of file formats into the software. Most business software packages can produce or export files into a number of formats. The selected format should be the one most appropriate under the circumstances. Reliability, ease of import, and ease of export are all considerations as to which format type should be selected when there are choices.

Typical file formats that can be accepted in data analytical software include dBASE, Microsoft Access, Microsoft Excel, ODBC, print reports, Adobe PDF, delimited text, and XML. Manual definitions can also be defined to import various other types of files.

Microsoft Access and dBASE files are common formats on personal computers and are simple to import. Field names are included in the files, eliminating the need to define the file name headers.

Microsoft Excel is a popular export format and can be simple to import into data analytical software if each row is a separate record. Sometimes, the first row contains the field names that the software would recognize and would be included in the import. Where the spreadsheet includes headers, subtotals, totals, and other extraneous details, you can save the Microsoft Excel file as a report or Adobe PDF file for further processing.

The Open Database Connectivity (ODBC) option can bring data into the data analytical software where you have the appropriate ODBC driver to connect to the data source. See Figure 3.1 as an example.

An excellent, detailed discussion of how to use ODBC, with examples, can be found at Indiana University at http://rt.uits.iu.edu/visualization/analytics/odbc.pdf.

Print report files and Adobe PDF files are everywhere and are readily available. While there are no doubts that direct access data is better, PDF reports are available from most software packages. You have no control over the query, so you will not get all of the relevant fields available in the source data that are not printed out in the reports. While extra steps are involved to import the information into the data analytical software, you will not need to define the record layout or have to select desired fields from data dictionaries. Some reports will have totals to assist in the reconciliation of the imported data with the reports.

Report and PDF files can be imported by applying the internal data analytical software's feature, such as Arbutus Print Image (Figure 3.2) or IDEA's Report Reader (Figure 3.3). The producers of ActiveData recommend the use of third-party software such as Monarch (www.datawatch.com), ABBYY PDF Transformer (http://pdftransformer.abbyy.com), or Able2Extract PDF Converter (www.able2extract .com) to convert files into Microsoft Excel format.

PREPARATION FOR DATA ANALYSIS

Most of the techniques and examples in the rest of this book will be demonstrated using the IDEA Version 9.1 software. The concepts can be applied to other data analytic software.

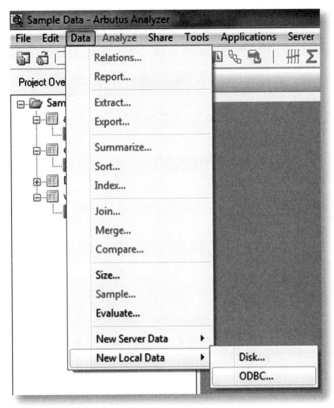

FIGURE 3.1   Arbutus Analyzer ODBC Data Import

Source: Arbutus Software Inc.

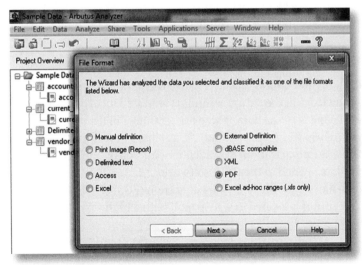

FIGURE 3.2   Arbutus Analyzer Data Import by Arbutus Software Inc.

Source: Arbutus Software Inc.

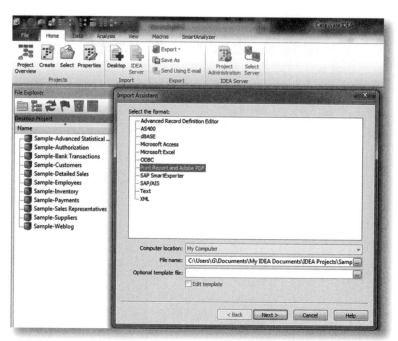

FIGURE 3.3　IDEA Data Import Assistant by CaseWare IDEA Inc.

Once you have good data in your data analytic software, you are almost ready to start your analysis. Foremost, you have to be familiar with your data. You need to know what the data contains in order to decide what tests can be applied or formulated. It is important to know whether critical fields are populated and to what extent. At times, the data is not laid out well for you to perform desired analysis techniques and needs further work. You can rearrange and reorganize the data within the data analytical software.

Data Familiarization

Know your data! You cannot effectively use the data if you are not aware of what it contains. Knowledge of the data at summary and statistical overview levels will give a good sense of what is in the data. There are a number of features and options that can be employed to help you profile the data. Available features in IDEA are Control Total, Field Statistics, Summarization, Stratification, and Pivot Table. Figure 3.4 shows payment tender data opened in the IDEA software.

This data file is from the point-of-sale system (POS) of a fast-food, take-out restaurant. The restaurant is located in a strip mall with a high school nearby. It is open:

Monday to Thursdays	11:00 A.M. to 10:00 P.M.
Friday	11:00 A.M. to 11:00 P.M.
Saturday	12:00 noon to 11:00 P.M.
Sunday	12:00 noon to 10:00 P.M.

Payment Tender Net.IMD

	TXNID	NO_OF_RECS	PAYAMOUNT_SUM	TENDERTYPEID	TENDERDESC1	SPLIT	PAYTIME_DATE	PAYTIME_TIME	YEAR
84676	178394	1	6.50	1	Cash	0	01/11/2011	12:02:05	2011
84677	178395	1	6.50	3	Visa	0	01/11/2011	12:02:34	2011
84678	178396	1	13.00	4	Debit	0	01/11/2011	12:10:09	2011
84679	178397	1	13.00	4	Debit	0	01/11/2011	12:11:24	2011
84680	178398	1	3.10	1	Cash	0	01/11/2011	12:12:09	2011
84681	178399	1	9.32	1	Cash	0	01/11/2011	12:12:35	2011
84682	178400	1	6.50	1	Cash	0	01/11/2011	12:13:53	2011
84683	178401	1	6.50	1	Cash	0	01/11/2011	12:17:39	2011
84684	178402	1	6.50	1	Cash	0	01/11/2011	12:21:57	2011
84685	178403	1	18.93	4	Debit	0	01/11/2011	12:27:03	2011
84686	178405	1	16.16	4	Debit	0	01/11/2011	12:37:16	2011
84687	178406	1	6.50	1	Cash	0	01/11/2011	12:43:38	2011
84688	178407	1	6.50	1	Cash	0	01/11/2011	12:53:22	2011
84689	178408	1	6.50	4	Debit	0	01/11/2011	12:57:12	2011
84690	178409	1	40.63	4	Debit	0	01/11/2011	13:38:40	2011
84691	178410	1	8.76	4	Debit	0	01/11/2011	13:27:02	2011
84692	178411	1	7.06	1	Cash	0	01/11/2011	13:43:19	2011
84693	178413	1	27.40	4	Debit	0	01/11/2011	14:06:50	2011
84694	178414	1	7.63	4	Debit	0	01/11/2011	14:41:52	2011
84695	178417	1	26.04	4	Debit	0	01/11/2011	15:25:43	2011
84696	178426	1	25.20	3	Visa	0	01/11/2011	16:13:25	2011
84697	178427	1	32.66	4	Debit	0	01/11/2011	16:16:04	2011
84698	178429	1	18.08	4	Debit	0	01/11/2011	16:21:47	2011
84699	178431	1	27.92	2	MasterCard	0	01/11/2011	17:14:37	2011
84700	178433	1	12.32	4	Debit	0	01/11/2011	17:02:31	2011

FIGURE 3.4 Payment Tender Type File Example in IDEA

Numeric, date, and time fields are displayed in field statistics in Figure 3.5. The only numeric field that is of use is the pay amount field, which we will look at closer in Figure 3.6.

Payment Tender Net.IMD

Numeric Statistics	TXNID	NO_OF_RECS	PAYAMOUNT_...	TENDERTYPEID	SPLIT	YEAR
Net Value	7,838,755,876	97,446	1,650,363.85	263,318	27	170,214,28
Absolute Value	7,838,755,876	97,446	1,650,368.69	263,318	27	170,214,28
# of Records	84,718	84,718	84,718	84,718	84,718	84,71
# of Zero Items	0	0	7	0	84,706	
Positive Value	7,838,755,876	97,446	1,650,366.27	263,318	27	170,214,28
Negative Value	0	0	-2.42	0	0	
# of Positive Records	84,718	84,718	84,709	84,718	12	84,71
# of Negative Records	0	0	2	0	0	
# of Data Errors	0	0	0	0	0	
# of Valid Values	84,718	84,718	84,718	84,718	84,718	84,71
Average Value	92,527.63	1.15	19.48	3.11	0.00	2,009.1
Minimum Value	1	1	-1.26	1	0	2,00
Maximum Value	178,466	6	380.13	6	4	2,01
Record # of Min	1	2	63,463	1	1	
Record # of Max	84,718	45,901	65,663	10,266	68,968	65,72
Sample Std Dev	54,319.83	0.37	15.17	1.28	0.03	1.3
Sample Variance	2,950,644,018.32	0.14	230.08	1.64	0.00	1.7
Pop Std Dev	54,319.51	0.37	15.17	1.28	0.03	1.3
Pop Variance	2,950,609,189.31	0.14	230.07	1.64	0.00	1.7
Pop Skewness	-0.050981	2.296986	3.007330	-0.838264	94.960362	-0.08424
Pop Kurtosis	-1.295230	5.233666	23.976610	-1.050269	9,960.911662	0.71347

FIGURE 3.5 Field Statistics of the Payment Tender File

The net value is the total of the field or column, which equals the control total. By putting your cursor over items it turns into a hand icon, and those items can be clicked on to drill down to detail levels and display the records pertaining to those items. There are seven records with zero value. Note that the average payment for the sales is $19.48. Both the minimum value and maximum value amount should be examined in detail. A discussion of the sample and population standard deviation values follows in Chapter 4.

The statistics for the date field shows the date of the earliest and latest record so you know the date range for the data you will be analyzing. The most frequent or common day of the week is Friday and the most common month is September. Therefore, the

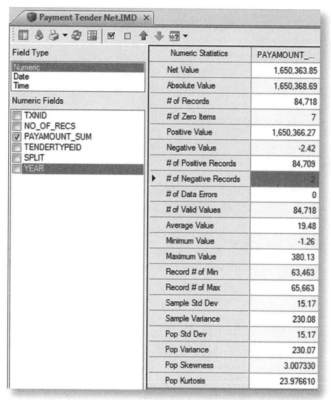

FIGURE 3.6   Isolating the Field Statistics of the Payment Amount

most frequent payments and sales occur on Fridays and September was the best month for the client. The monthly and daily number of transactions are also displayed in field statistics, as shown in Figure 3.7.

The payment time also provides valuable information in Figure 3.8. The most payments are processed after the noon hour, with 80,609 or 95 percent of transactions taking place. This makes perfect sense, since the business opens either at 11:00 A.M. or at noon, depending on the day of the week. If you were to apply sampling techniques, you would want to pull more samples from after the noon hour.

The tender or payment type can be summarized to identify the number of transactions for each category and total the amounts as shown in Figure 3.9.

We can see in Figure 3.10, that debit cards are used most frequently, followed by cash payments. Visa, MasterCard, and American Express (AME) are accepted but are not as popular with their customers.

Now that you are aware that the average payment is $19.48, you can stratify the amounts to give you a range of how many transactions occurred in each range as displayed in Figure 3.11. The ranges can be at a fixed increment or, better yet, you can set the explicit ranges to produce results that are more meaningful to the context of the data. You can group the output if you wish. In this case, we selected the tender payment field to group so that cash, debit, MasterCard, Visa, and so on amounts will be displayed

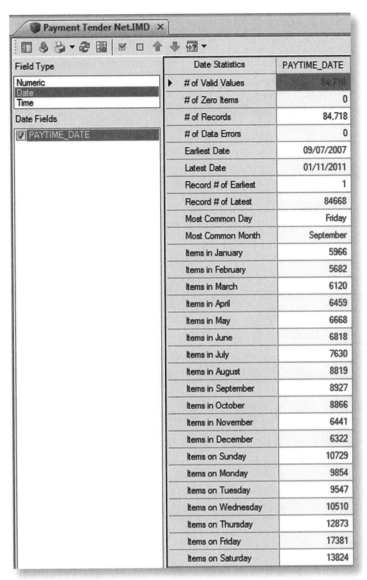

Field Type		Date Statistics	PAYTIME_DATE
Numeric	▶	# of Valid Values	84,718
Date		# of Zero Items	0
Time		# of Records	84,718
Date Fields		# of Data Errors	0
☑ PAYTIME_DATE		Earliest Date	09/07/2007
		Latest Date	01/11/2011
		Record # of Earliest	1
		Record # of Latest	84668
		Most Common Day	Friday
		Most Common Month	September
		Items in January	5966
		Items in February	5682
		Items in March	6120
		Items in April	6459
		Items in May	6668
		Items in June	6818
		Items in July	7630
		Items in August	8819
		Items in September	8927
		Items in October	8866
		Items in November	6441
		Items in December	6322
		Items on Sunday	10729
		Items on Monday	9854
		Items on Tuesday	9547
		Items on Wednesday	10510
		Items on Thursday	12873
		Items on Friday	17381
		Items on Saturday	13824

FIGURE 3.7 Date Field Statistics

in ranges. We determined that there were only these six tender or payment types when we summarized the data.

Stratifying the debit card payments shows that 97 percent of the transactions and 90 percent of the total dollar values are $50 dollars and below. There are no negative amounts for debit card transactions as seen in Figure 3.12. Similarly, there are no negatives for Visa, MasterCard, and AME (not shown).

The stratification of cash payments shows one negative amount in Figure 3.13. It is also interesting to note that neither the percentage of number of records nor the percentage of the payment amounts follows the same pattern as the debit card payments.

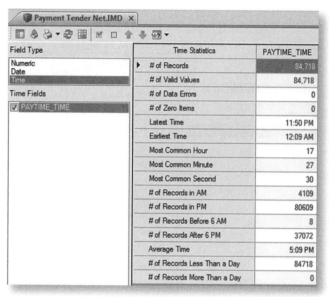

FIGURE 3.8 Time Field Statistics

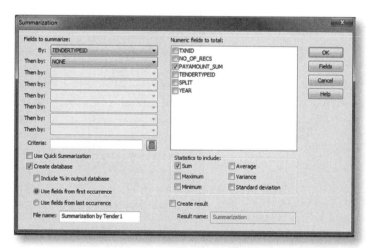

FIGURE 3.9 Summarization of Payment Tender Types

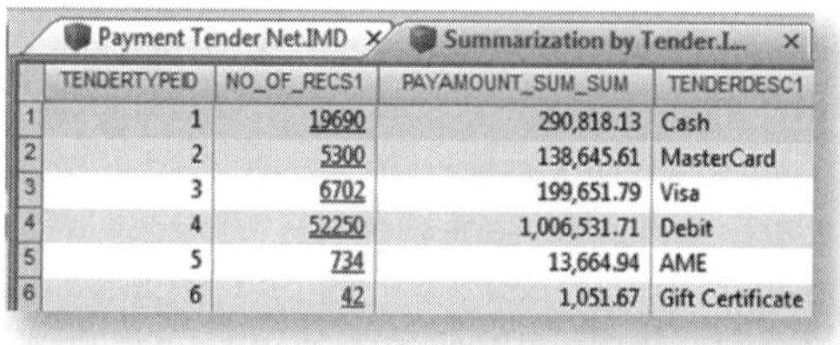

	TENDERTYPEID	NO_OF_RECS1	PAYAMOUNT_SUM_SUM	TENDERDESC1
1	1	19690	290,818.13	Cash
2	2	5300	138,645.61	MasterCard
3	3	6702	199,651.79	Visa
4	4	52250	1,006,531.71	Debit
5	5	734	13,664.94	AME
6	6	42	1,051.67	Gift Certificate

FIGURE 3.10 Summarization of Tender Type Results

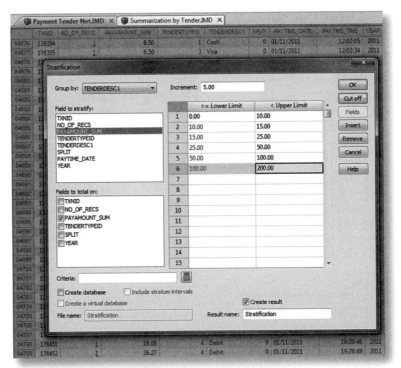

FIGURE 3.11   Stratification of Payment Amounts by Tender Types

Stratum #	>= L Limit	< U Limit	# Records	(%) # Records	PAYAMOUNT_SUM	(%) PAYAMOUNT_SUM
1	0.00	10.00	15,312	29.31	121,362.00	12.06
2	10.00	15.00	7,928	15.17	92,900.47	9.23
3	15.00	25.00	15,824	30.29	305,987.71	30.40
4	25.00	50.00	11,633	22.26	386,676.15	38.42
5	50.00	100.00	1,491	2.85	91,511.45	9.09
6	100.00	200.00	58	0.11	7,085.67	0.70
		Lower limit exceptions:	0	0.00	0.00	0.00
		Upper limit exceptions:	4	0.01	1,008.26	0.10
		Totals:	52,250	100.00	1,006,531.71	100.00

Totalled on: PAYAMOUNT_SUM   TENDERDESC1= Debit

FIGURE 3.12   Results of the Stratification for Debit Card Payments

The year field was previously added, so now we can perform additional data profiling using the year field.

Pivot Table allows data to be displayed, organized, and summarized in different views (Figure 3.14). It allows for a better overall picture to analyze data. In this example, we display by row the tender payment type and by column the year. The amounts are

Stratum #	>= L Limit	< U Limit	# Records	(%) # Records	PAYAMOUNT_SUM	(%) PAYAMOUNT_SUM
1	0.00	10.00	10,373	52.68	71,138.21	24.46
2	10.00	15.00	3,063	15.56	35,440.42	12.19
3	15.00	25.00	3,033	15.40	57,629.77	19.82
4	25.00	50.00	2,729	13.86	93,630.16	32.20
5	50.00	100.00	450	2.29	27,418.95	9.43
6	100.00	200.00	38	0.19	4,765.51	1.64
		Lower limit exceptions:	1	0.01	-1.16	0.00
		Upper limit exceptions:	3	0.02	796.27	0.27
		Totals:	19,690	100.00	290,818.13	100.00

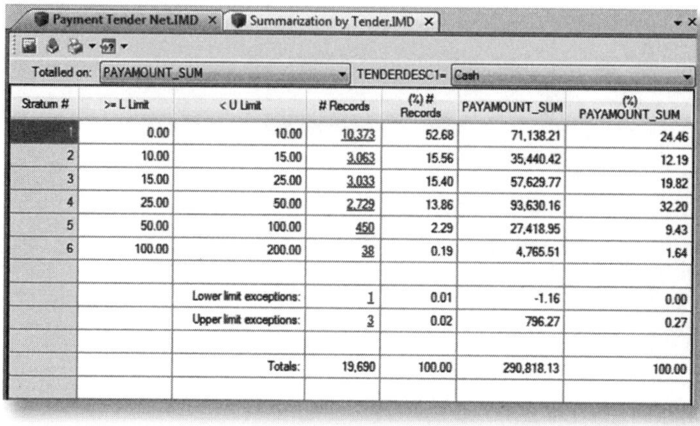

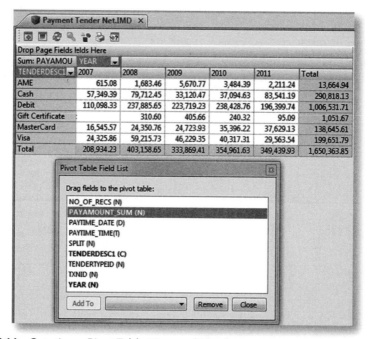

FIGURE 3.13 Results of the Stratification for Cash Payments

TENDERDESC1	2007	2008	2009	2010	2011	Total
AME	615.08	1,683.46	5,670.77	3,484.39	2,211.24	13,664.94
Cash	57,349.39	79,712.45	33,120.47	37,094.63	83,541.19	290,818.13
Debit	110,098.33	237,885.65	223,719.23	238,428.76	196,399.74	1,006,531.71
Gift Certificate		310.60	405.66	240.32	95.09	1,051.67
MasterCard	16,545.57	24,350.76	24,723.93	35,396.22	37,629.13	138,645.61
Visa	24,325.86	59,215.73	46,229.35	40,317.31	29,563.54	199,651.79
Total	208,934.23	403,158.65	333,869.41	354,961.63	349,439.93	1,650,363.85

FIGURE 3.14 Creating a Pivot Table View and Results

cross-tabulated both by rows and columns. This provides an understanding of how payments fluctuate from year to year. For instance, cash payments dropped significantly in 2009 and 2010 before increasing again in 2011. This is in contrast to debit card payments that remained consistent. Recall from the field statistics that the 2007 year had approximately 6 months' worth of transactions, while 2011 had only the first 10 months of transactions.

ARRANGING AND ORGANIZING DATA

The "Payment Tender Net" file previously displayed shows all the tender amounts listed in a single field or column. In order to do additional analysis steps, we need to have each of the different tender payment amounts in their own separate columns. All tender types are extracted into separate files and then joined back using the TXNID field to achieve this. Analytical software can easily rearrange and organize data into more useful layouts as shown in Figure 3.15 by using Direct Extraction to extract the

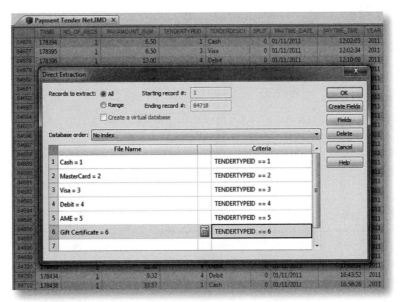

FIGURE 3.15   Direct File Extraction of Each Payment Tender Type

relevant fields and then using Visual Connector in Figure 3.16 to join them back to the desired layout as in Figure 3.17. This type of data layout is not uncommon and is highlighted in the example.

Data can further be enriched and transformed optimally for analysis, if you join information from other data files. This is especially so when data from separate systems is combined. A simple example is combining a dentist's electronic appointment scheduling software with the accounting software. Once this is done, it would be easy to determine if there are any errors in the recording of fees by filtering for appointments where there were no amounts paid or included in accounts receivable.

Compare the results displayed in Figure 3.17, which has individual tender columns, to the original layout in Figure 3.4, which has all the tender amounts in a single column.

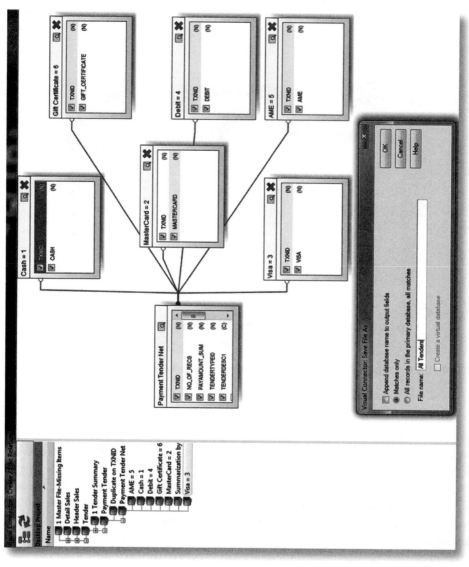

FIGURE 3.16 Using IDEA's Visual Connector to Join the Payment Tender Type Files

	TXNID	PAYAMOUNT_SUM	TENDERDESC1	CASH	DEBIT	MASTERCARD	VISA	AME	GIFT_CERTIFICATE	PAYTIME_DATE	PAYTIME_TIME
265	569	18.12	AME	0.00	0.00	0.00	0.00	18.12	0.00	22/07/2007	17:25:33
266	570	26.17	Debit	0.00	26.17	0.00	0.00	0.00	0.00	22/07/2007	17:30:14
267	571	8.55	Debit	0.00	8.55	0.00	0.00	0.00	0.00	22/07/2007	17:32:51
268	574	68.35	Cash	68.35	0.00	0.00	0.00	0.00	0.00	22/07/2007	18:19:04
269	579	50.04	MasterCard	0.00	0.00	50.04	0.00	0.00	0.00	22/07/2007	18:05:06
270	580	15.56	Debit	0.00	15.56	0.00	0.00	0.00	0.00	22/07/2007	18:03:44
271	582	50.04	Debit	0.00	50.04	0.00	0.00	0.00	0.00	22/07/2007	18:06:47
272	583	8.55	Debit	0.00	8.55	0.00	0.00	0.00	0.00	22/07/2007	18:06:42
273	585	17.33	Visa	0.00	0.00	0.00	17.33	0.00	0.00	22/07/2007	18:10:54
274	587	26.74	Debit	0.00	26.74	0.00	0.00	0.00	0.00	22/07/2007	18:18:48
275	588	23.89	Cash	23.89	0.00	0.00	0.00	0.00	0.00	22/07/2007	18:23:49
276	592	17.39	Cash	17.39	0.00	0.00	0.00	0.00	0.00	22/07/2007	18:28:20
277	598	19.38	Cash	19.38	0.00	0.00	0.00	0.00	0.00	22/07/2007	19:03:48
278	599	19.90	Cash	19.90	0.00	0.00	0.00	0.00	0.00	22/07/2007	18:48:33
279	600	19.90	Cash	19.90	0.00	0.00	0.00	0.00	0.00	22/07/2007	18:50:43
280	601	25.94	Visa	0.00	0.00	0.00	25.94	0.00	0.00	22/07/2007	18:57:18
281	602	23.82	Debit	0.00	23.82	0.00	0.00	0.00	0.00	22/07/2007	19:21:38
282	604	36.93	Cash	36.93	0.00	0.00	0.00	0.00	0.00	22/07/2007	19:03:14
283	610	20.64	Cash	20.64	0.00	0.00	0.00	0.00	0.00	22/07/2007	19:42:50
284	612	17.39	MasterCard	0.00	0.00	17.39	0.00	0.00	0.00	22/07/2007	19:49:59
285	614	12.26	Debit	0.00	12.26	0.00	0.00	0.00	0.00	22/07/2007	19:34:37
286	616	37.39	Debit	0.00	37.39	0.00	0.00	0.00	0.00	22/07/2007	22:08:04
287	618	7.93	Cash	7.93	0.00	0.00	0.00	0.00	0.00	22/07/2007	20:02:58
288	624	17.05	Visa	0.00	0.00	0.00	17.05	0.00	0.00	22/07/2007	20:46:59
289	626	46.74	Debit	0.00	46.74	0.00	0.00	0.00	0.00	22/07/2007	20:55:46
290	627	7.93	Debit	0.00	7.93	0.00	0.00	0.00	0.00	22/07/2007	21:32:40

FIGURE 3.17 Resulting Tender Master File with Each Tender Type in Individual Columns

CONCLUSION

After you have successfully completed the steps of obtaining the data in a format that you can use, ensured the data integrity, normalized the data, and prepared the data for analysis, you can apply various analytical tests. The general analytical tests are outlined in Chapter 5 and advanced tests in Chapter 6. Applicable tests to specific audit areas follow those two chapters. However, before we proceed to tests for anomalies, it is better to have a basic understanding and a review of statistics, which we discuss in Chapter 4.

NOTES

1. American Institute of Certified Public Accountants, "Consideration of Fraud in a Financial Statement Audit," www.aicpa.org/Research/Standards/AuditAttest/Downloadable Documents/AU-00316.pdf.
2. SAP, "SAP Business Solutions: Software, Applications & Data Management," accessed November 24, 2013, http://global.sap.com/campaign/na/usa/CRM-XH12-PPC-PPC-BRAND/index.html?SOURCEID=DE&campaigncode=CRM-XH13-PPC-CROBRND2DE& mid=s4G9sJJ8t%7cdc_2722p1v19626_27672116097_sap%2520ag_e&kwid=4G9sJJ8t.
3. CaseWare IDEA Inc., "A Practical Guide to Obtaining Data for Auditors," August 2013.

## CHAPTER FOUR

Statistics and Sampling

S TATISTICS INVOLVES THE STUDY of research designs, the collection of the data, describing the data, analyzing the data, and then forming a conclusion. We are interested mainly in the analysis of data that has already been collected for us by various business systems. We hope to be able to arrive at various conclusions after analyzing the data.

Understanding some basic statistics allows you to understand the makeup or distribution of your data files. This is especially useful when your data file is large and contains millions of records.

There are various types of statistical analysis, but the two major categories are descriptive statistics and inferential statistics.

DESCRIPTIVE STATISTICS

Descriptive statistics is where you describe information from the data set. It is used to summarize the data. Where the data have categories, they can be summarized in each group as to frequency or as a percentage that is a relative frequency. With numerical data, we determine the middle of the data or spread of how close or far the numbers are from that middle. We can determine ranges and possibly determine relationships between two variables. Data can also be summarized to ranges.

There are two main types of data: categorical (qualitative data) or numerical (quantitative data). Categorical data in a record describes qualities or characteristics of the record. For example, in a payroll record, the division or area field that the employee works in is categorical even if the division is coded as a number. Whether the employee is salaried or paid hourly is another categorical data field. Using pivot tables is a great way to see two categorical variables at once in a summarized fashion.

Numerical data includes items such as counts, amounts, or quantities in the record fields. Only actual numerical or quantitative data represent real numbers where calculations are done that make sense. It would not make sense to perform any mathematical operations on items represented by numbers in categorical fields.

Ordinal data is a third type that is a hybrid. The data is in categories, but the categories have a meaningful order. These can be analyzed as categorical data or, if the categories are represented by meaningful numeric values, basic calculations may be performed also. An example would be ranking or ratings such as 1 for poor, 2 for average, and 3 for superior.

INFERENTIAL STATISTICS

Inferential statistics is the use of sample statistics to make inferences about the population parameters. A parameter is a characteristic of the population.

Suppose you sampled 100 records out of the entire data set or population. Assuming that the 100 samples are representative of the total population, you can take the results of those 100 samples and infer the results over the entire population or data set.

Let us say that the 100 records were from the sales data set of a retail store, and you wish to pull and examine the sales invoices to attempt to determine whether the customer was female or male. This information would help the store better target their advertising. If the results were that there were 35 sales to males and 65 sales to females, you would conclude that females made 65 percent of all purchases, as you cannot review every sales invoice. In this case, the statistic is 65 percent and the parameter is females.

With data analytic software, you can perform calculations on the entire data set or population. Therefore, we will focus on descriptive statistics whether the data fields are categorical or numerical. Inferential statistics are discussed more in the sampling segment of this chapter.

MEASURES OF CENTER

In a data set, you want to know where the middle of the data is and what the typical or frequent value is. The most common way to summarize numerical data is to determine its center by describing the mean or average and the median.

The *mean* is merely a term for the average of all the numbers. In terms of the dataset, it would be the total of all the numbers in a particular field divided by the number of records. The mean amount may not even appear in a transaction in the data set as it is a calculated amount. For a PAID_AMOUNT field of 1,000 records, where the total of those records is $250,000, the mean (or average) is $250. IDEA's field statistics show averages for each numeric field. When you summarize a file in IDEA, you may also select for it to output the average for each key or group in the newly summarized file.

You need to take care when considering the mean. It is very sensitive to extremes or outliers. A few very large or a very few small amounts may make the mean not representative of the data. If there was a single transaction of $200,000 in the previous example and you exclude this outlier, the mean would be $50 rather than $250.

The median measurement is not sensitive to outliers. The median is the midpoint in the distribution of the data. It is the point that divides the distribution into two, with one half being equal to or less than the median and the other half being equal to or greater than the median. Again, there may not be an actual record amount that corresponds to the median amount. It is merely a positional value.

Data must be arranged as indexed or sorted, in either descending or ascending order, before you can successfully apply the formula. Once the data is ordered, determine if there are an odd or even number of records.

If the data contains an odd number of records, then the median is the one exactly in the middle of the ordered records.

In the example of numbers 1, 2, 4, 5, and 5, the middle or median position number is the third number, which has a value of 4.

If the data contains an even number of records, the median is the average of the two numbers appearing in the middle.

In the example of numbers 1, 2, 4, 7, 8, and 8, the two middle numbers are 4 and 7. The median position is between 4 and 7, which is the 3.5 spot. By adding those two middle numbers and dividing by 2, the result of 5.5 is the median value.

To calculate the position of the median, you may use this formula:

$$\text{Median} = (N+1)/2$$

The letter N (in uppercase) represents the number of records in the field or population. A lowercase letter n represents the number of cases in a sample. This is used when the median position is needed in a sample.

In applying the formula for the odd number of the five records above, the median position calculation is $(5 + 1)/2 = 3$ with a value of 4 in that position.

For the even number example of six records, the median position calculation is $(6 + 1)/2 = 3.5$, with a value of 5.5 in that position.

When the mean and median values are far from each other, it is good to be aware of both values. You now know that there are outliers in the data that need to be addressed.

Along with the mean and median, the *mode* is frequently mentioned as a measure of center. The mode refers to the most frequently occurring value in a distribution or data set. It is determined by counting the frequency of each result. In the discussion of Benford's Law in Chapter 5, it can be seen that the leading digit 1 for the first-digit test is the mode or the number that most frequently appears in data sets. While we will not be using the mode for any calculations, you should be aware of what it represents.

 ## MEASURE OF DISPERSION

In order to understand the data, you need to be aware of the dispersion or variability of the data. To do so, you need more information than just the mean. Different distributions may have the same mean, so the mean alone is not that informative.

The range measures variability and is merely the lowest item and the highest item. IDEA's field statistics displays a minimum value and a maximum value, which is the range of the data in that particular field. The range gives some indication of the distribution of the data. Certainly, it advises you of the extremes. For example, data in a particular accounts payable file may have a range from $9.00 to $1,004,462.00. While this may not be meaningful alone, additional information will give you a better sense of the data. More useful types of ranges might include transaction numbers, check numbers, or transaction date starting and ending information.

MEASURE OF VARIABILITY

Measuring variability is the determination of how far the data is spread out. It is the extent to which data points in a data set diverge from the mean or average value. Knowledge of the variability of the data provides the auditor or investigator with a sense of whether transactions are outside of the normal area or pattern.

Deviations from the Mean

Deviation from the mean is how far a number is away from the mean of the distribution. This is calculated by subtracting the mean from the individual numbers. Some numbers will be below the mean, resulting in negative differences, and some will be above the mean, resulting in positive differences. The total or sum of these differences will always net to zero.

The Mean Deviation

This is also known as the average deviation that describes (on the average) how far each number is from the mean. This is calculated by subtracting the mean from the individual numbers, but the differences are in absolute values—that is, the negative signs are ignored. The sums of these differences are calculated and then divided by the number of records in the distribution.

The Variance

The variance is a measure of dispersion that eliminates the issue of differences totaling to zero and also the issue of negative numbers. You calculate it by squaring each of the differences, taking the total of the squared differences, and then dividing that total by the number of records.

IDEA's field statistics provides the population variance information of the dataset.

The Standard Deviation

The most common measure of variability is the standard deviation. It is the distance of the number from the center or average. The standard deviation is the square root of the variance.

You calculate it by squaring each of the differences, taking the total of the squared difference, dividing that total by the number of records, and then applying the square root to the resulting number. The standard deviation tells us the variability in the distribution of the data. It tells us how far each number is away from the mean. The further the number deviates from the mean, the larger the standard deviation amount. It can be used as a measure of relativity between the numbers. This can be also used as a comparison to different data sets. Since standard deviation is relative, it eliminates issues of comparing difference scales or bases as a ratio is calculated. If you were comparing test scores, whether they are calculated out of 100 or 125, the standard deviation can be compared without any additional calculations.

Standard Deviation of a Population versus Standard Deviation of a Sample

The standard deviation calculation discussed earlier is for a population standard deviation. The total of the squared differences is divided by the number of records or n.

When calculating the standard deviation of a sample, the total of the squared differences is divided by the number of records minus 1 or $n-1$. Subtracting 1 is a correction factor. The reduction in the denominator results in a larger standard deviation in a sample and should be more representative of the true standard deviation of the population.

The accuracy of the standard deviation of a sample increases with the increase of the sample size. As you increase the sample size, you get closer to having a standard deviation that is the standard deviation of the population. As you increase the sample size, or n, the correction factor has less impact. Applying division with a denominator of, say 4 ($5-1$, where the sample size is 5) would have a greater impact than dividing by 499 ($500-1$, where the sample size is 500).

IDEA's field statistics provides both the population and sample deviation information of the dataset.

Z-scores or standard scores tell us how far a number is away from the mean. It is a good example of how it applies the standard deviation in the formula. Z-scores are discussed further along in the book.

 ## SAMPLING

Merriam-Webster defines *sampling* as:

> the act, process, or technique of selecting a representative part of a population for the purpose of determining parameters or characteristics of the whole population.[1]

Simply put, sampling is a process of selecting a subset of the population or a number of records from the data set for the purpose of making inferences or conclusions to the entire population or data set.

Audit sampling is the audit procedure of examining of a portion of items within a class of transactions in order to evaluate one or more characteristics of that entire class. Either statistical or nonstatistical sampling methods may be used against a part of the entire data set to make a conclusion regarding the entire data set.

Sampling is effective when the audit procedure or step does not require a 100 percent review of the population of the class, but a decision or conclusion is required and it is not cost effective to audit 100 percent of the transactions.

Statistical Sampling

Statistical sampling uses statistical mathematical calculations for selecting and then evaluating a sample from the data set. Statistical sampling outlines in numeric terms the parameters and precision levels associated with the sample conclusion.

One such use of statistical sampling that we are most familiar with are polls used to determine candidates' current standings in upcoming elections or in popularity surveys.

In a November 2013 poll, Toronto's mayor Rob Ford maintained his 42 percent approval rating after he "admitted he has smoked crack, bought illegal drugs, and might have driven drunk,"[2] among other issues. The poll of 1,049 Toronto residents determined the 42 percent rating with accuracy results of plus or minus 3 percent, 19 times out of 20.

The 19 times out of 20 translates to a confidence level of 95 percent, so the 1,049 sample results can be applied to the general population of Toronto with a confidence level of 95 percent that the approval rating is between 39 percent and 45 percent.

An auditor may be verifying an account balance through statistical sampling and conclude that it is $100,000 plus or minus 5 percent or $5,000 each way ($95,000 to $105,000), 19 times out of 20. The conclusion would be that given the precision of the sample at 5 percent (plus or minus $5,000), there is assurance that the balance is correct with a confidence level of 95 percent. In addition, if the materiality was predetermined to be at 7 percent, then it can be concluded that there would no material error based on the precision level.

Confidence level is the remaining factor when the acceptable sampling risk is eliminated. In the example of selecting a 95 percent confidence level, you allow only a 5 percent chance of getting the wrong sample that does not adequately represent the entire population.

Using statistical samples to obtain familiarity with the data set might be useful but if it is not used to reach a conclusion, it cannot be considered as part of the audit procedure. In addition to formulating a conclusion, statistical sampling must use statistical calculations, and the sample must be random.

Proper use of statistical sampling is beneficial because it:

- Requires a scientifically accepted and defined approach.
- Allows the auditor to maintain professional judgment in regard to audit risks and materiality.
- Displays the sample results and conclusion in relation to the selected data set population along with defined judgment selections.

Nonstatistical Sampling

Nonstatistical sampling does not involve the use of statistical calculations. It relies on the subjective sampling selections by the auditor and has less of a standardized approach.

Nonstatistical sampling is beneficial where:

- The auditor needs to employ professional subjective judgment.
- There is a unique issue where there is a need for a less rigid standardized approach.
- The auditor should not be restricted to explicit numbers as to materiality or risk.

In order to effectively perform nonstatistical sampling, the auditor must have a good knowledge of the data set. Knowing the contents of the data or population allows for a supportable sample selection choice and also supports the conclusion of the results. Sample selection may be based on random sampling or other nonmathematical techniques such as judgmental, haphazard, or block selection.

Judgmental selection is frequently used when the auditor is very experienced and selects samples based on sound judgment. Typically, the auditor will make the selections based on a combination of representativeness of the population, value of the items, and relative risk of the items.

Haphazard selection is where the auditor picks items without basis of any mathematical formula. The auditor believes that the items selected are representative of the population and no intentional bias was applied to any of the included or excluded items.

Block selection is where a contiguous sequence of items is selected as samples. These blocks may be invoice numbers from 1000 to 1100 or a specific type of transactions for the month of March. Block selection effectiveness can be much improved by sampling several blocks.

Sampling Risk

The sample selected either through statistical sampling or nonstatistical sampling methods might not truly reflect the population even if done with the utmost care. This is the cause for sampling risk, where the auditor's conclusion based on the selected sample may differ from the reality of the conditions of the entire population of the data set. Sampling risk occurs due to limited time and resources that prevent an audit of the entire population.

Alpha or Type I risk is the risk of incorrect rejection. That is, the auditor incorrectly concludes from the sample that the population errors are worse than they actually are.

Beta or Type II risk is the risk of incorrect acceptance. That is, the auditor incorrectly concludes from the sample that the errors in the population are better than they really are.

Auditors are usually more interested in beta (Type II) risks, as they are concerned about the failure to detect material misstatements.

Nonsampling Risk

Auditors may draw incorrect conclusions from using sampling techniques where the wrong inferences are not because of the selected samples themselves, but for other reasons not directly connected with the sample contents.

Nonsampling risk is where the auditor may have selected an appropriate sample but arrived at a wrong conclusion. Examples include employing inappropriate audit procedures, failure to recognize errors present, or misinterpreting the results or evidence.

Nonstatistical Sampling Methods

The nonstatistical sampling features built into IDEA are shown in Figure 4.1.

IDEA has easy-to-use random, systematic, and stratified random sampling built in.

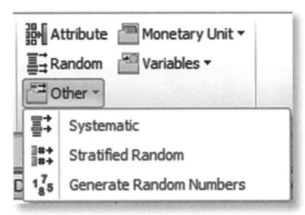

FIGURE 4.1 Nonstatistical Sampling Feature in IDEA

To use the random sampling method, select Random and enter the number of records you wish to select for sampling. IDEA inputs the start and ending record number based on the records in the data set. IDEA suggests a random seed number (it changes every time you use the random record sampling feature) that you may change if desired to perform the random record sampling extraction. The History file in IDEA records the seed number used. In the example in Figure 4.2, it was decided that approximately 1 percent or 90 records would be examined.

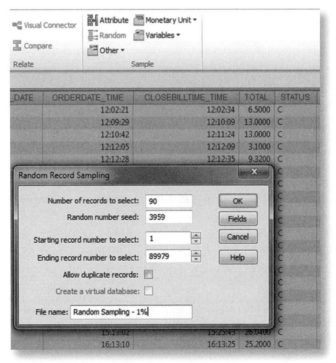

FIGURE 4.2 Applying Random Record Sampling in IDEA

IDEA outputs 90 records and creates a SAM_RECNO field that tells you which record number from the original file of 89,979 records it was randomly selected from as displayed in Figure 4.3.

	BUSDATE_DATE	BUSDATE_TIME	TXNID	ORDERDATE_DATE	ORDERDATE_TIME	CLOSEBILLTIME_TIME	TOTAL	STATUS	SAM_RECNO
77	29/03/2010	00:00:00	115563	29/03/2010	17:01:37	17:01:57	7.3500	C	55406
78	30/01/2011	00:00:00	150201	30/01/2011	18:20:33	18:21:02	18.4200	C	71874
79	07/10/2008	00:00:00	54040	07/10/2008	17:48:12	17:48:59	34.6300	C	27610
80	05/01/2009	00:00:00	65170	05/01/2009	14:42:36	14:43:06	5.2500	C	32423
81	05/07/2009	00:00:00	85430	05/07/2009	12:03:48	12:04:50	9.3200	C	41687
82	06/02/2009	00:00:00	68600	06/02/2009	18:35:15	18:49:54	17.5200	C	33935
83	24/04/2010	00:00:00	118520	24/04/2010	20:36:30	20:37:36	20.5700	C	56813
84	01/04/2011	00:00:00	156609	01/04/2011	20:42:19	20:42:36	16.9000	C	75109
85	07/01/2008	00:00:00	21058	07/01/2008	11:47:35	11:47:43	8.1900	C	11313
86	15/02/2011	00:00:00	151818	15/02/2011	16:34:25	16:34:46	26.2700	C	72692
87	27/07/2008	00:00:00	45344	27/07/2008	18:16:43	18:17:29	18.3100	C	23337
88	30/12/2010	00:00:00	146759	30/12/2010	20:31:51	20:32:05	9.3200	C	70191
89	17/03/2009	00:00:00	72866	17/03/2009	12:45:47	12:47:12	21.4200	C	35890
90	15/10/2007	00:00:00	11017	15/10/2007	18:46:56	18:47:44	8.5500	C	5990

FIGURE 4.3 Output of Random Sampling

Systematic record sampling extracts a number of records from a database at equal intervals to a separate database. You may input the number of records and IDEA will compute the interval size. In the example in Figure 4.4, we enter 90 records and IDEA calculates the selection interval of 1,010. Conversely, you may enter the selection interval and IDEA will calculate the required number of records.

Systematic Sample

Number of Records | Selection Interval

Selection interval: 1010
Number of records to select: 90
Starting record number to select: 1
Ending record number to select: 89979
File name: Systematic Sampling

Fields
Compute
Help

Create a virtual database | OK | Cancel

FIGURE 4.4 Applying Systematic Record Sampling

Stratified random sampling is used to extract a random sample with a specified number of records from each of a series of bands. This method requires the database to first be stratified into a series of numeric, character, or date bands. Based on your knowledge of the data set, select the bands' lower and upper limits as displayed in Figure 4.5.

You are then presented with a table displaying the number of records within each band, in which you must decide and enter the number of sample records to be extracted

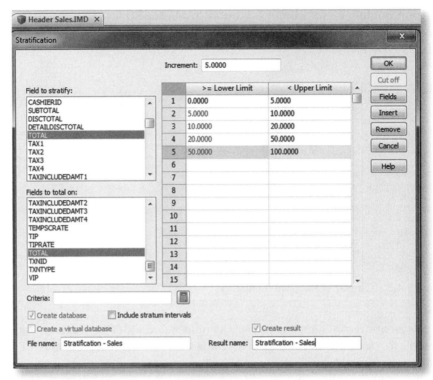

FIGURE 4.5 Selecting the Ranges for Stratified Random Sampling

at random from each band. In this example, you decide to select more records from higher sales dollar amounts, including 50 records to sample from the 330 records that exceed the maximum upper limit of $100.00 shown in Figure 4.6.

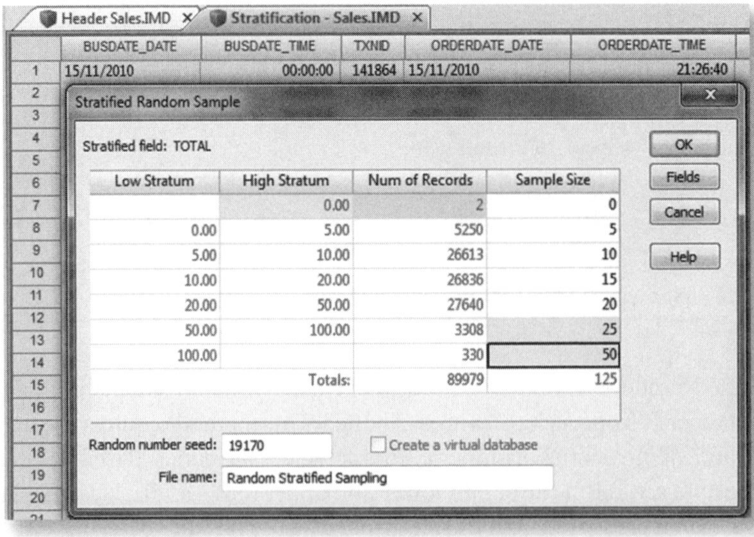

FIGURE 4.6 Selecting the Number of Records to Sample in Stratified Random Sampling

Using stratified random sampling eliminates independence of the sample as the auditor makes the judgment to select the sample size from each band or stratum. Care should be taken if employing the results in any statistical application.

Statistical Sampling Methods

There are three basic types of sampling methods that auditors may use. The choice of methods depends on the main purpose of the sample and substantive test.

Probability Proportional-to-Size Sampling (PPS)

This method is used to estimate the total monetary amount of potential misstatement in a population. PPS uses monetary unit sampling (MUS) or dollar unit sampling (DUS). While other methods are based on occurrences or number of records, this method is based on dollar values where the higher monetary value transactions have a higher likelihood of being chosen in a sample. MUS is similar to systematic sampling, but where systematic sampling may sample every thousandth record, MUS will sample every thousandth dollar. It is typically used to determine the accuracy of financial accounts, where size is the most important factor, and where errors are expected to be few and far between. MUS provides a substantive assessment of error or misstatement in dollar figures and is specifically designed to predict overall error.

MUS should be used when:

- The process audited is well established and known to be reliable.
- The likelihood of errors (misstatements) is low.
- Obtaining a small sample size is important.
- You want to target larger dollar transactions, and expect to see some spikes in the data.

Performing MUS sampling involves the following steps.

Planning
- Determine the objectives of the exercise.
- Define the population.
- Define what a misstatement means.
- Determine sample size, using the following:
  - **Confidence level.** A percentage value comfort level that the sample will be representative and that you have the capabilities to interpret the results correctly.
  - **Tolerable error.** The point of no return past which you would no longer have faith in the process audited, nor the validity of the sample.
  - **Expected error.** The amount of errors or misstatements that are reasonably expected in a population.

Performing MUS Sampling Procedures
- Select the samples.
- Perform the audit procedures.
- Record and analyze any errors observed.

Evaluation

- Create a projected misstatement by summarizing errors and extrapolating these across population.
- Compare ranges of the projected misstatement against the tolerable error limit.
- Draw final conclusions.

As seen in Figure 4.7, IDEA will simplify all these steps for you.

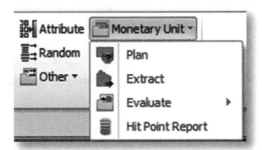

FIGURE 4.7 Monetary Unit Sampling Feature

In the example of testing sales, seen in Figure 4.8, we select absolute values as there are a few credit or refund values that are negative amounts in the Total field. We select a confidence level of 95 percent. Confidence levels below 90 percent are not generally recommended for MUS sampling. It should be recognized that the higher the confidence level, the larger the sample size needed.

The tolerable error amount or percentage must be entered. This is the absolute error limit that can be tolerated. The higher the tolerable error, the more errors you can accept and the lower the sample size needs to be. In this example, with sales in excess of $1.7 million, 1 percent or $17,000 was decided as the maximum tolerable error. A 1 percent loss would be material enough to take actions such as to initiate an investigation or redesign the sales system. Since MUS is only to be used for processes where there is a high degree of confidence based on actual experience, significant errors may indicate fraud, embezzlement, or untrained or incompetent staff.

The expected error is the anticipated misstatement that is a realistic estimate of likely errors expected to found in the process. It is historical experience that dictates the estimate amount. Both the expected error and tolerable error can be entered either as an amount or percentage. In this example, management estimates that approximately 10 percent or $1,700 is the expected error.

When the Estimate button is selected, IDEA's MUS calculation determines that in order to be 95 percent confident, it is necessary to set the sample size at 363 records and that there should be no more than 36.25 percent tainting or total percentage of errors found.

Once the Accept button is selected, the Monetary Unit Sampling—Extract screen appears as displayed in Figure 4.9.

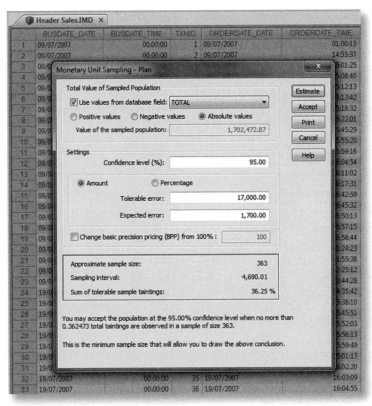

FIGURE 4.8   Monetary Unit Sampling Planning

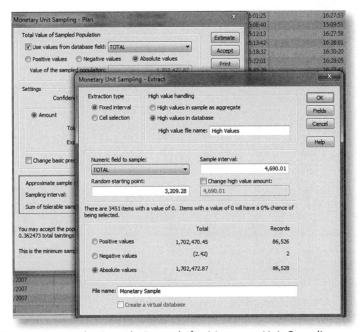

FIGURE 4.9   Extracting the Sample Records for Monetary Unit Sampling

Three hundred sixty-three records are then extracted and an AUDIT_AMT field is created as in Figure 4.10. The value of this field is equal to the field being audited but can be changed to reflect the proper amount determined during the execution of the audit procedures.

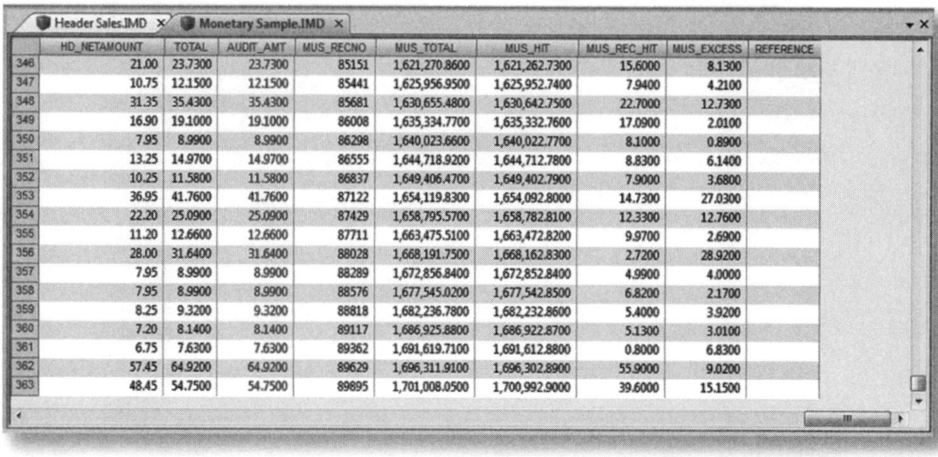

	HD_NETAMOUNT	TOTAL	AUDIT_AMT	MUS_RECNO	MUS_TOTAL	MUS_HIT	MUS_REC_HIT	MUS_EXCESS	REFERENCE
346	21.00	23.7300	23.7300	85151	1,621,270.8600	1,621,262.7300	15.6000	8.1300	
347	10.75	12.1500	12.1500	85441	1,625,956.9500	1,625,952.7400	7.9400	4.2100	
348	31.35	35.4300	35.4300	85681	1,630,655.4800	1,630,642.7500	22.7000	12.7300	
349	16.90	19.1000	19.1000	86008	1,635,334.7700	1,635,332.7600	17.0900	2.0100	
350	7.95	8.9900	8.9900	86298	1,640,023.6600	1,640,022.7700	8.1000	0.8900	
351	13.25	14.9700	14.9700	86555	1,644,718.9200	1,644,712.7800	8.8300	6.1400	
352	10.25	11.5800	11.5800	86837	1,649,406.4700	1,649,402.7900	7.9000	3.6800	
353	36.95	41.7600	41.7600	87122	1,654,119.8300	1,654,092.8000	14.7300	27.0300	
354	22.20	25.0900	25.0900	87429	1,658,795.5700	1,658,782.8100	12.3300	12.7600	
355	11.20	12.6600	12.6600	87711	1,663,475.5100	1,663,472.8200	9.9700	2.6900	
356	28.00	31.6400	31.6400	88028	1,668,191.7500	1,668,162.8300	2.7200	28.9200	
357	7.95	8.9900	8.9900	88289	1,672,856.8400	1,672,852.8400	4.9900	4.0000	
358	7.95	8.9900	8.9900	88576	1,677,545.0200	1,677,542.8500	6.8200	2.1700	
359	8.25	9.3200	9.3200	88818	1,682,236.7800	1,682,232.8600	5.4000	3.9200	
360	7.20	8.1400	8.1400	89117	1,686,925.8800	1,686,922.8700	5.1300	3.0100	
361	6.75	7.6300	7.6300	89362	1,691,619.7100	1,691,612.8800	0.8000	6.8300	
362	57.45	64.9200	64.9200	89629	1,696,311.9100	1,696,302.8900	55.9000	9.0200	
363	48.45	54.7500	54.7500	89895	1,701,008.0500	1,700,992.9000	39.6000	15.1500	

FIGURE 4.10 Random Record Selection Results for Monetary Unit Sampling

Suppose three discrepancies were found, including the one in record number 250 where the actual amount was $60.00 instead of the $55.32 recorded in the sales system as shown in Figure 4.11. To evaluate the MUS sample, select the Single Sample option.

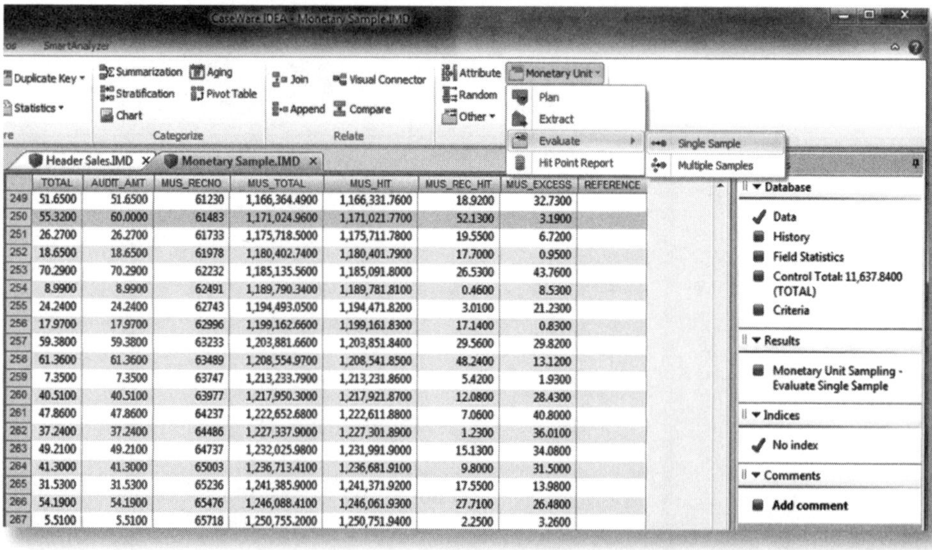

	TOTAL	AUDIT_AMT	MUS_RECNO	MUS_TOTAL	MUS_HIT	MUS_REC_HIT	MUS_EXCESS	REFERENCE
249	51.6500	51.6500	61230	1,166,364.4900	1,166,331.7600	18.9200	32.7300	
250	55.3200	60.0000	61483	1,171,024.9600	1,171,021.7700	52.1300	3.1900	
251	26.2700	26.2700	61733	1,175,718.5000	1,175,711.7800	19.5500	6.7200	
252	18.6500	18.6500	61978	1,180,402.7400	1,180,401.7900	17.7000	0.9500	
253	70.2900	70.2900	62232	1,185,135.5600	1,185,091.8000	26.5300	43.7600	
254	8.9900	8.9900	62491	1,189,790.3400	1,189,781.8100	0.4600	8.5300	
255	24.2400	24.2400	62743	1,194,493.0500	1,194,471.8200	3.0100	21.2300	
256	17.9700	17.9700	62996	1,199,162.6600	1,199,161.8300	17.1400	0.8300	
257	59.3800	59.3800	63233	1,203,881.6600	1,203,851.8400	29.5600	29.8200	
258	61.3600	61.3600	63489	1,208,554.9700	1,208,541.8500	48.2400	13.1200	
259	7.3500	7.3500	63747	1,213,233.7900	1,213,231.8600	5.4200	1.9300	
260	40.5100	40.5100	63977	1,217,950.3000	1,217,921.8700	12.0800	28.4300	
261	47.8600	47.8600	64237	1,222,652.6800	1,222,611.8800	7.0600	40.8000	
262	37.2400	37.2400	64486	1,227,337.9000	1,227,301.8900	1.2300	36.0100	
263	49.2100	49.2100	64737	1,232,025.9800	1,231,991.9000	15.1300	34.0800	
264	41.3000	41.3000	65003	1,236,713.4100	1,236,681.9100	9.8000	31.5000	
265	31.5300	31.5300	65236	1,241,385.9000	1,241,371.9200	17.5500	13.9800	
266	54.1900	54.1900	65476	1,246,088.4100	1,246,061.9300	27.7100	26.4800	
267	5.5100	5.5100	65718	1,250,755.2000	1,250,751.9400	2.2500	3.2600	

FIGURE 4.11 Audit Results of the Sampled Records

The screen in Figure 4.12 appears.

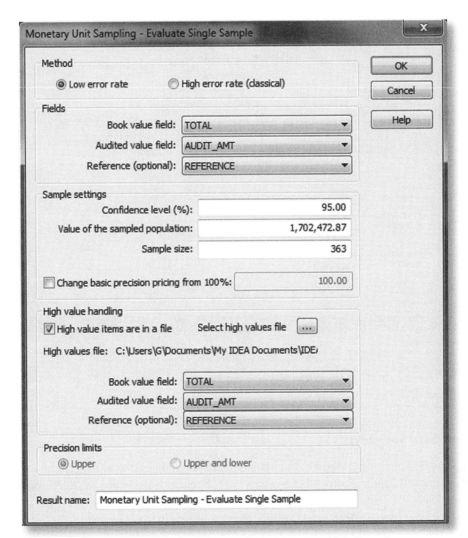

FIGURE 4.12   Evaluating Single Sample Results in Monetary Unit Sampling

Once OK is selected, the summary shown in Figure 4.13 appears displaying:

- Zero overstatements were discovered.
- Three understatements were discovered.
- The net most likely error is $1,512.47.
- Both the gross and net upper error limits are less than materiality (tolerable error) of $17,000.

The conclusion is that with 95 percent certainty the projected total errors based on errors found in the sample is within the accepted range and will not exceed the tolerable error of $17,000. That is, you are 95 percent assured that the sample is representative of the population and that no actions to investigate or redesign the sales system are needed.

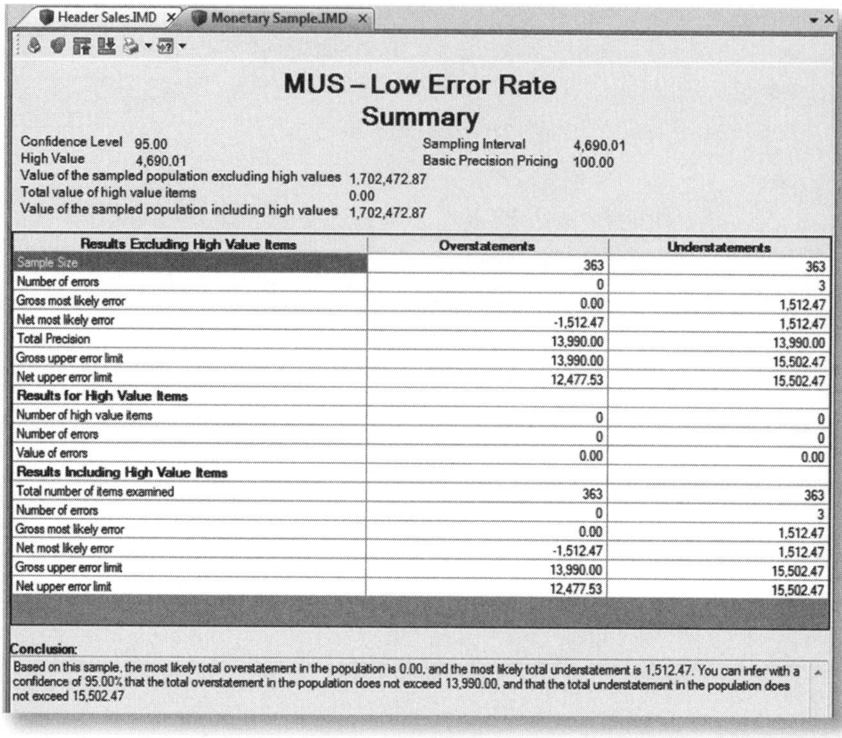

Header Sales.IMD × Monetary Sample.IMD ×

MUS – Low Error Rate
Summary

Confidence Level 95.00
High Value 4,690.01
Sampling Interval 4,690.01
Basic Precision Pricing 100.00
Value of the sampled population excluding high values 1,702,472.87
Total value of high value items 0.00
Value of the sampled population including high values 1,702,472.87

Results Excluding High Value Items	Overstatements	Understatements
Sample Size	363	363
Number of errors	0	3
Gross most likely error	0.00	1,512.47
Net most likely error	-1,512.47	1,512.47
Total Precision	13,990.00	13,990.00
Gross upper error limit	13,990.00	15,502.47
Net upper error limit	12,477.53	15,502.47
Results for High Value Items		
Number of high value items	0	0
Number of errors	0	0
Value of errors	0.00	0.00
Results Including High Value Items		
Total number of items examined	363	363
Number of errors	0	3
Gross most likely error	0.00	1,512.47
Net most likely error	-1,512.47	1,512.47
Gross upper error limit	13,990.00	15,502.47
Net upper error limit	12,477.53	15,502.47

Conclusion:
Based on this sample, the most likely total overstatement in the population is 0.00, and the most likely total understatement is 1,512.47. You can infer with a confidence of 95.00% that the total overstatement in the population does not exceed 13,990.00, and that the total understatement in the population does not exceed 15,502.47

FIGURE 4.13 Summary and Conclusion of Audit Results of MUS

Attribute Sampling

Attribute sampling is a statistical sampling technique often used to test internal controls; it evaluates the individual attributes of a record to be either true or false. Examples include:

- Having two required signatures for check authorizations over certain amounts.
- Whether account receivables are overdue.
- If travel expense claims are valid or not.

Attribute sampling should be used when:

- There is a need for a statistical sampling solution and judgmental sampling will not suffice.
- The objective of the review is to test compliance to internal controls.
- The compliance testing should evaluate to a true or false result.
- A random selection process will meet the objectives of your review.

Performing attribute sampling involves the following steps.

Planning

- Determine the objectives of the exercise.
- Define the population.

- Define what a misstatement means.
- Determine sample size, using the following:
  - **Confidence level.** A percentage-value comfort level that the sample will be representative and that you have the capabilities to interpret the results correctly.
  - **Tolerable error.** The point of no return past which you would no longer have faith in the process audited, nor the validity of the sample.
  - **Expected error.** The amount of errors or misstatements that are reasonably expected in a population.

Performing Attribute Sampling Procedures

- Select the sample.
- Perform the audit procedures.
- Record and analyze any errors observed.

Evaluation

- Create a projected misstatement by summarizing errors and extrapolating these across the population.
- Compare ranges of the projected misstatements against the tolerable error limit.
- Draw final conclusions.

Similar to MUS sampling, attribute sampling requires a user to set certain boundaries and tolerances for the calculations to be performed.

- **Tolerable deviation rate as a percentage.** Also known as tolerable error rate, this is the absolute maximum percentage of transactions in error (i.e., not in compliance) that is acceptable as a cost of doing business. If you have more errors than the tolerable error rate, this internal control is not working and must be redesigned. The higher the tolerable error, the more errors you can tolerate, and the lower the sample size needs to be.
- **Expected deviation rate as a percentage.** Also known as expected error rate, this is the percentage of errors (i.e., noncompliance) you would reasonably expect to see, based on experience. As a rule, the lower the expected error, the lower the sample size.
- **Confidence level as a percentage.** This is the likelihood that the sample records chosen are indeed representative of the population at large, and that you will correctly interpret the results. The more confident you need to be, the more samples you require.

In the example in Figure 4.14, management decided that the maximum percentage tolerable deviation rate is 10 percent. Anything above 10 percent would suggest that the control is not working and may need to be redesigned. Based on previous history, management expects a deviation rate of 3 percent. Management is happy to accept a confidence level of 90 percent that the sample is representative of the population or data set.

The population size or number of records is 89,979.

The population size, percentage tolerable deviation rate, percentage expected deviation rate, and the confidence level must be entered into the Planning tab of the Attribute Sampling box.

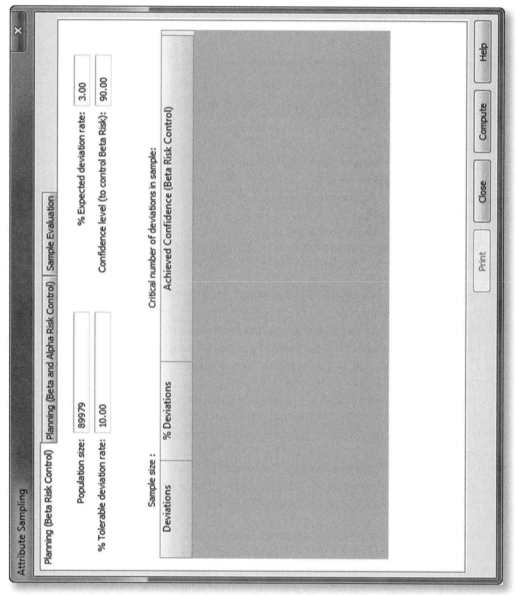

FIGURE 4.14 Planning for Attribute Sampling

Once the Compute button is clicked, based on the information entered, IDEA informs you that you would need a sample size of 52 and that there must not be more than two deviations or errors in the sample to achieve a 90 percent confidence level that deviation level of the population is not more than 10 percent. Refer to Figure 4.15.

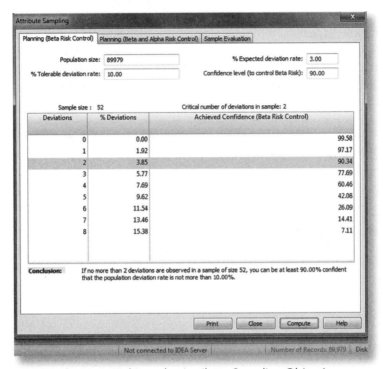

FIGURE 4.15 Conclusion to Achieve the Attribute Sampling Objective

The random record sampling feature in Figure 4.16 can be used to randomly select the 52 required records. A detailed audit of the 52 selected records determines whether the control was met. The number of deviations is noted.

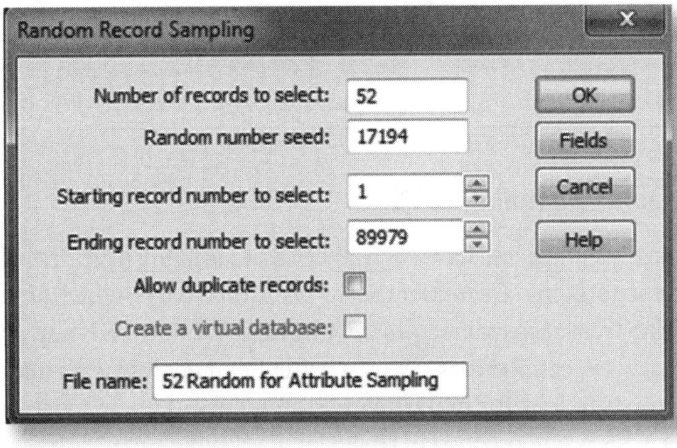

FIGURE 4.16 Obtaining the Samples for Attribute Sampling

In the Sample Evaluation tab of the Attribute Sampling box, entries for the population size, sample size, and percentage of desired confidence level are made again. The number of deviations (five) discovered during the audit of the 52 samples must also be included, as noted in Figure 4.17.

Since five deviations are more than the critical number of deviations (two) in the sample calculated in the planning stage, the conclusion is that there is 90 percent certainty that the number of deviations could be significantly higher in the overall population than the 10 percent tolerable percentage. It is 90 percent certain that there could be as many as 17.11 percent of errors if the entire population was audited. As such, this sample cannot be considered as representative and it is likely the control must be redesigned.

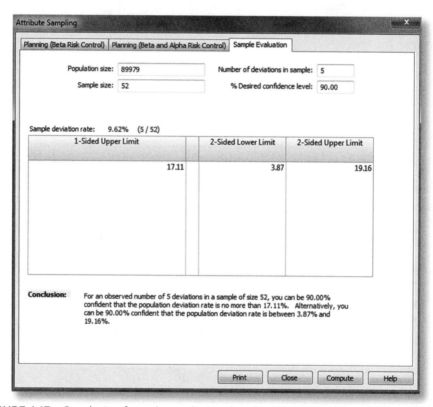

FIGURE 4.17 Conclusion from the Audit Results of Attribute Sampling

Classical Variables Sampling (CVS)

Classical variables sampling considers each record as a sampling unit. Therefore each record has an equal chance of being selected for the sample, unlike MUS, which favors higher dollar value records. MUS treat each dollar as a sampling unit. While MUS is best used in situations where there are few expected errors, CVS is a better fit for dealing with many exceptions.

If the purpose is to look for material misstatements in an account balance or class of transactions, CVS is a good choice. However, CVS typically requires a larger sample size than other sampling methods. It is mainly used to perform substantive audit tests.

Three common types of CVS are mean-per-unit estimation, ratio estimation, and difference estimation.

- Mean per unit uses the statistical concept of mean or average discussed earlier in the Measures of Center section. Using the average value (mean) of items in your sample, you can estimate the population value.

  If you had a data set of 1,000 records and determined that your sample size should be 20 out of the population of 1,000, you would total the 20 individual values and divide by the sample size to obtain the mean. Assume that the total amount for the 20 records is $5,000, so the mean is $250 ($5,000/20). With 1,000 records in your population, then the mean estimate is $250,000 ($250 × 1,000). Mean estimates can be used in conjunction with confidence level, sample risk, and error rate to project to the entire population.

- Ratio estimation uses the method of applying the sample ratio to the entire population. Assuming that the 20 audited samples result in total errors of $500 out of the total sample amount of $5,000, your misstatement ratio is 10 percent ($500/$5,000). If the total for the data set is $225,000, then the projected misstatement would be $22,500 ($225,000 × 10%).

- Similar to the ratio estimation, difference estimation uses a ratio but also incorporates the records in the population or data set. Suppose your data set has 1,000 records and your sample is 20 of those records. Your audit procedures determine $500 worth of errors. The estimated misstatement would be $25,000 (($500/20) × 1,000)).

IDEA calculates results for these three methods and more. To perform CVS, you need to determine a confidence level and the desired precision. Desired precision is the difference between the tolerable error and expected error. Small precision amounts allow for less margin of error that requires larger samples, while large precision amounts offer more leeway and require smaller samples. Determining the precision requires knowledge of the business, historical data, and past experience. Precision needs to be determined by management along with the auditor.

For statistical sampling to be considered valid, the sample size must be determined by statistical calculations and the samples taken randomly. The results of the review of the samples must then be evaluated statistically.

In this example, we believe that there may be issues with how sales are voided. From our sales database of 89,979 records, we extract 1,828 records of void sales. The total value of voided transactions is $52,104.18. We will perform CVS on the voided records.

Management believes that there are weaknesses in the POS system and that it may contain errors anywhere from 1 in 5 (20 percent) to as many as 1 in 3 cases (33 percent). Desired precision can be calculated as follows:

Tolerable Error	= $52,104.18×.33	= $17,194.38
Expected Error	= $52,104.18×.20	= $10,420.84
Desired Precision		= $ 6,773.54

By selecting the Preparation option in the Variables sample area of IDEA (Figure 4.18), the Classical Variables: Prepare–Stratify window appears as displayed

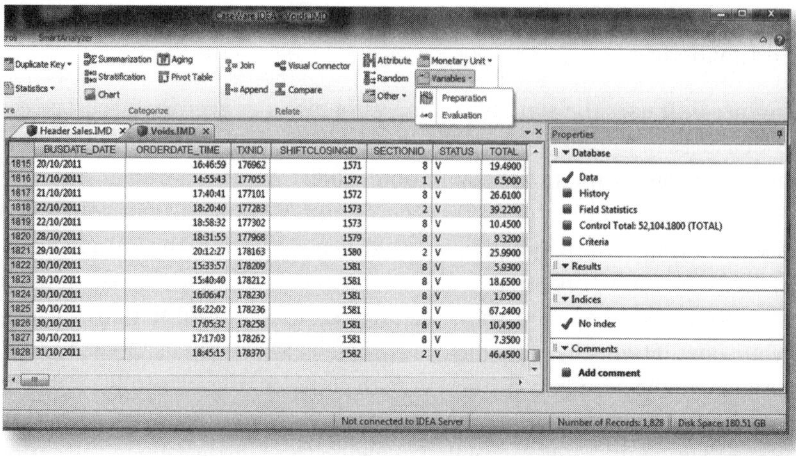

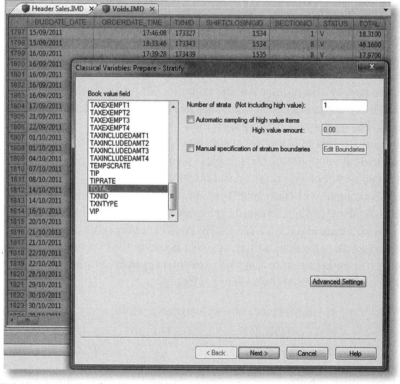

FIGURE 4.18 Classical Variables Sampling Feature of IDEA

in Figure 4.19. Normally, there is a considerable variance between the highest and the lowest values in data sets. Stratifying the data in bands or ranges produces better samples. However, this data set is from a fast-food restaurant where each record or transaction is of low value, so there would not be a need to stratify in this case. The number of strata is entered as 1 and the automatic sampling of high-value items box is unchecked.

FIGURE 4.19 Preparing for Classical Variables Sampling

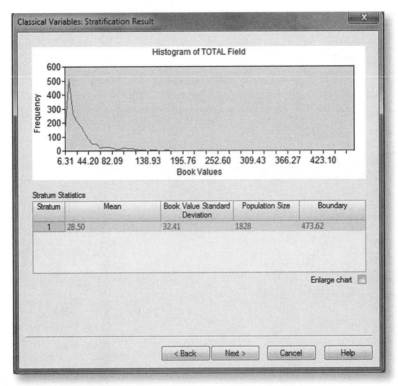

FIGURE 4.20 Classical Variables Sampling Stratification Results

By selecting the Next button, the Classical Variables: Stratification Result screen displays, as in Figure 4.20. The mean or average is 28.50 and the standard deviation is 32.41. The histogram is right-skewed, indicating that there are outliers in the higher value ranges.

A confidence level of 95 percent, desired precision of $6,773.54, and an expected proportion of errors in the population of 20 percent are entered to compute the sample size needed.

Due to the high confidence level of 95 percent, IDEA calculates a required sample size of 256, as shown in Figure 4.21.

The next step is to randomly extract 256 records to test. IDEA completes this process for you, including generating a random number seed as in Figure 4.22.

IDEA creates the AUDIT_AMT field where the auditor can input the correct amount if the audited amount from the sample is found to be incorrect. In this case, the audit determined that 21 of 256 samples were found to be incorrectly entered into the POS system.

In the Classical Variables: Evaluate box, shown in Figure 4.23, are displays for entry of the audit results from the samples extracted as outlined in Figure 4.22.

The graph in Figure 4.24 displays six types of statistical evaluations.

1. Mean per unit
2. Difference

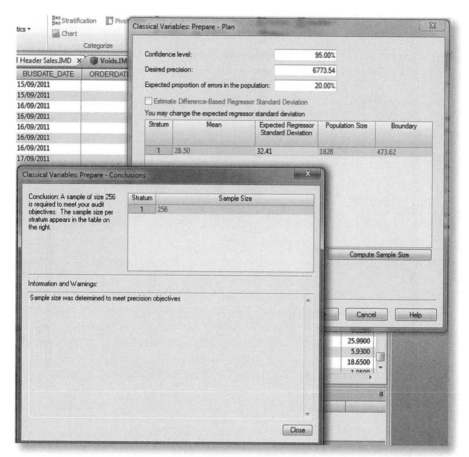

FIGURE 4.21 Obtaining the Required Sample Size to Meet the Classical Variables Sampling Objectives

3. Combined ratio
4. Separate ratio
5. Combined regression
6. Separate regression

By clicking on each of the types, the graph will display a report of each statistical evaluation. Since the mean-per-unit estimation method has the largest error, we will click on the word *mean* to open the mean-estimation report displayed in Figure 4.25.

Based on this report, it has been determined that it is 95 percent confident that the errors in voided transactions are in the range between –$15,144.76 and –$5,189.96. The most likely total error of $10,167.36 is the difference between the sample total of $52,104.18 and the projected audited amount (based on the 21 errors) of $41,936.82. Therefore the void amounts recorded are likely to be overstated by $10,167.36 either by error or as a result of fraud.

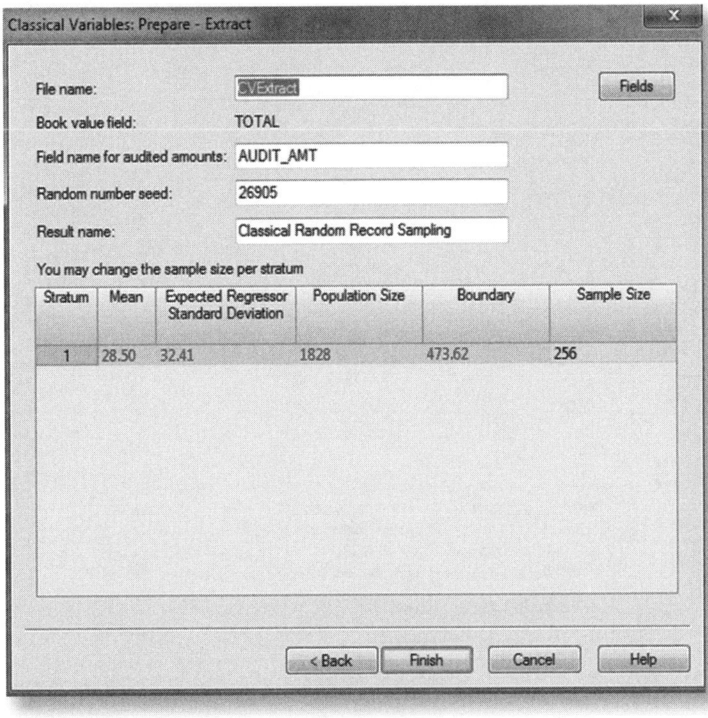

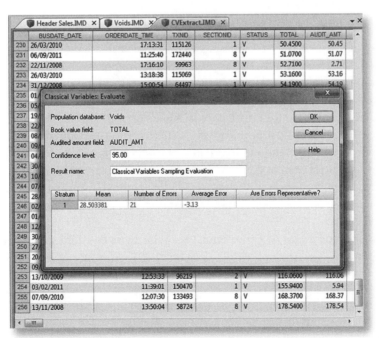

FIGURE 4.22 Extracting the Required Sample Size

FIGURE 4.23 Entering the Results of the Audit of the Classical Variables Samples to Be Evaluated

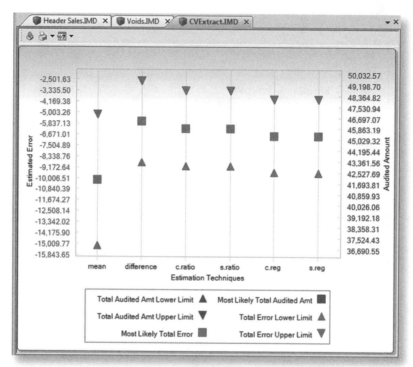

FIGURE 4.24 Statistical Evaluations of Classical Variables Sampling

Discovery Sampling

Discovery sampling is worth discussing, as it is frequently used to detect a fraudulent transaction.

A sample size is selected for discovery sampling. If the sample is error free, then the entire data set or population is accepted as error free. However, even if only a single error is discovered, then the entire population is rejected. The auditor is not as much interested in determining how many errors there are in the population as in the fact that there was an error. The auditor's concern would be that there is a possibility that the internal control system could be compromised. The one error may be sufficient to require an examination of the entire population or to formulate a new plan for further action. If one instance of fraud is found, the auditor is 100 percent confident that fraud exists.

On the practical side, deviations must be divided into categories as to whether the deviations are:

- Clearly errors
- Clearly fraudulent
- Highly suspicious for fraud

While the goal of discovery sampling is for not even a single critical deviation, an expected deviation rate of 1 percent is typically accepted.

Classical Variables Sampling Evaluation

Prepared by:		Report name:	
Input file name:	CVExtract	Period:	

Population Database:	Voids	Estimation Technique:	mean
Book Value Field:	TOTAL	Sample Size:	256
Audited Amount Field:	AUDIT_AMT	Planned Precision:	6,773.54
Confidence Level:	95.00	High Value Items Automatically Selected:	No

Quantity	Sample
Most Likely Total Audited Amt	41,936.82
Most Likely Total Error	-10,167.36
Achieved Precision	4,977.40
Total Audited Amt Upper Limit	46,914.22
Total Audited Amt Lower Limit	36,959.42
Total Error Upper Limit	-5,189.96
Total Error Lower Limit	-15,144.76

Stratified Sample Summary

Stratum	Size	Number of Errors	Mean Error Value	Estimated Regressor Standard Deviation
1	256	21	-3.13	23.86

CONCLUSION:

At the 95.00% confidence level the total population error is between -15,144.76 and -5,189.96, and the total value of AUDIT_AMT is between 36,959.42 and 46,914.22.

WARNINGS:

FIGURE 4.25 Mean Estimation Report Example of One of the Six Types Available

Discovery sampling's stringent requirement regarding errors makes it a good choice for fraud-detection audits.

Choice of Sampling Methods

An auditor first must decide whether to utilize statistical or nonstatistical sampling and then which method within the two choices.

There is much disagreement as to whether statistical or nonstatistical samples are more defensible, especially in court. Auditors tend to favor statistical sampling as sampling is independently and objectively determined. Measurements are mathematically calculated providing results that are quantitative. Auditors and accountants are comfortable with defined procedures and standards that produce specific numbers.

However, lawyers call upon expert witnesses to provide professional judgment and opinions. As such, it may be that nonstatistical sampling may produce better results as it is based on the judgment and experience of the auditor. The expert witness would explain to the court how, in their professional opinion, the sample is representative of the population. This may be more effective than having a statistician explain that for a 90 percent confidence level, the auditor's conclusion has a 10 percent risk of being wrong.

If statistical sampling is selected, then the type of statistical sample must be decided upon. The nature of the audit test should dictate the choice. If the primary purpose of the sample is to test a control, then attribute sampling is generally the best choice. CVS, while normally requiring larger sample sizes, is good for verifying account balances or a specific class of transactions. For auditing items where errors tend to be low, such as inventory or accounts receivable, PPS or MUS are better choices, as they require smaller sample sizes. The auditor must be aware that PPS has a higher probability of showing false positives due to its sensitivity of errors in projecting misstatements. For fraud detection, clearly the larger concern over any errors is the best selection.

Sampling Is Not Enough

While sampling is mandated for certain audit procedures and is very suitable to provide assurances of accuracy formally or for the auditor's own comfort, the inherent limitation is that sampling only examines a small segment of the population or dataset and not all transactions are tested. Sampling may be a practical approach due to the number of transactions; but detecting fraud is looking for needles in haystacks. In sampling, there are so many transactions that are never touched by the auditor. There is a high probability that certain transactions of interest would not be selected as part of the sample and therefore not reviewed in detail.

If MUS is selected as the sampling type and larger amounts are more likely to be randomly selected, smaller anomalies may escape attention. Some frauds consist of a number of lower-dollar transactions that may total to a significant amount. Regardless of the dollar amount, any fraud is serious and may indicate a weakness in the control system. Fraudulent transactions do not typically appear in data sets randomly. There is usually a pattern. The fraudster exploits that same control weakness over and over or may be limited to certain dollar amounts. The limit may be due to the control system or by design of the fraudster to escape attention. Very often, fraudsters are aware of auditors' concepts of materiality and scope.

Sampling works well when transactions are relatively consistent throughout the data set. If sampling is not effective to detect fraud, what are the measures or tests that can be applied? There are numerous analytical techniques and tests that are available, and ad hoc, repetitive, and continuous monitoring procedures can be used.

Ad hoc allows you to explore and seek out fraud or opportunity for potential fraud. You develop a theory of an area of fraud or that may lead to fraud. For example, you believe that there may be opportunity for vendor-payment fraud in the accounts payable department. One test might be in reviewing inactive vendors that suddenly start having payments made to them again. Did the company actually start using that vendor again or is it possible that payments are being made to a phantom company with a similar name? An employee who can issue payments but has no authority to create accounts may be using the inactive vendor account.

Suppose that you found payments posted to the formerly inactive account of ABC Co. but the checks were made out to ABC Inc. and mailed to a post office box. Obviously further investigation would be necessary. Regardless whether the discovered anomaly was indeed fraud, it is an area for *potential* fraud.

 ## CONCLUSION

Repetitive or continuous monitoring procedures are a good business practice.

Automating tests in various areas will allow you to identify issues or anomalies shortly after they occur when using repetitive testing. Repetitive testing can be employed for each audit cycle but, better yet, can be scheduled at more frequent intervals. Once the tests are in place, very little manual efforts are needed and only require someone to review any anomalies. Continuous monitoring identifies anomalies as they occur or at specified intervals. Continuous monitoring need not be in real time. The automated analytics can be executed daily, weekly, monthly, or for any logical business cycle timelines. Notifications can be set so that reports or e-mails are issued as soon as the anomalies are detected. Once the automated procedures are in place, timely exception notifications allow for the early detection of fraud. Automated procedures would allow you more time to investigate and develop new detection procedures in other areas. Over time, more and more automated analysis can be developed and implemented to mitigate the risks of fraud.

Automated analytical techniques may be looking for outliers and anomalies of transactions that are not the norm. Statistical calculations may be employed to highlight items too far from the standard deviation or expected averages. Some of the highest values and lowest values should be included in your review of abnormal items. Grouping transactions by specific classes, such as location or dates, may reveal unusual patterns that are not typical of other locations or dates. Automated techniques need to be adjusted along with the dynamic business environment. Modern-day businesses are ever changing, whether due to mergers, acquisitions, or implementing new products or business lines. Performing the same tests without consideration of the changing business structures and systems may make those tests and procedures obsolete.

These techniques and tests do not detect fraud but rather allow you the opportunity to detect fraud.

 ## NOTES

1. *Merriam-Webster*, "Sampling," accessed December 27, 2013, www.merriam-webster .com/dictionary/sampling.
2. Don Peat, "Mayor Rob Ford's Popularity Holding Steady, New Poll Shows," *Toronto Sun*, November 22, 2013, www.torontosun.com/2013/11/22/mayor-rob-fords-popularity-impressive-new-poll-shows.

## CHAPTER FIVE

Data Analytical Tests

DATA ANALYSIS USES TECHNOLOGY to detect anomalies, patterns, and risk indicators within the data set. It can be used to establish a hypothesis or to quantify detected issues if the hypothesis was found to correctly identify fraud.

The true power of data analytics is that the entire data set of the transactions can be tested. Unlike sampling where only a part of the population is tested, data analytics can test 100 percent of the transactions. Resulting anomalies can then all be reviewed or, if in large quantities, sampled.

While the analysis can provide a list of anomalies, it is not a list of fraudulent transactions. Unlike statistical sampling, there is no mathematical formula that provides the auditor with a listing of frauds.

The auditor needs to apply professional judgment, employ analytical skills, and use intuition. Typically, the auditor reviews the list of anomalies, audits some of the transactions, revises the hypothesis, adjusts the test, and performs additional analytical procedures to refine the list to reduce false-positive transactions. There will be numerous false positives of true data anomalies that are not fraud. This is a product of data analytics.

The circular process may continue several times. When completed, the test identifies transactions with a high risk of fraud. This manageable number of transactions can then be examined using fraud-audit procedures. Once a single fraudulent transaction is detected, the audit plan should be revised to expand the review and investigation.

Once the auditor is familiar with the data, the business systems, and the business environment, a number of general analytical tests can be applied against the entire data set or to a specific category or class of transactions.

General data analytical tests are those that can and should be applied against the entire data set to provide the auditor or investigator with a starting point for further audit or review. The general tests output transactions that are outliers, anomalies, or suspicious items. The tests can go through 100 percent of the transactions looking for the defined anomalies. It reduces potentially millions of transactions to a reasonable number to review. The tests may also reveal patterns of interest about what should not be there or should be there. General tests show the power of data analytics. It allows the auditor to perform much more than sampling and allows them to test hypothesis and potential fraud scenarios. Being able to examine transactions at the source level assures the auditor of the integrity of the information. It allows the auditor to obtain insights to potential indicators of fraud and to the effectiveness of internal controls. Often, small anomalies are missed but it is these small anomalies that indicate weaknesses in internal controls that can be exploited. Data analytics of transactional data is a proactive approach in detecting fraud.

 ## BENFORD'S LAW

"The Benford's Law–based tests signal abnormal duplications. The mathematics of Benford's Law gives us the expected or the normal duplications, and duplications above the norm are abnormal or excessive."[1]

Benford's Law forms part of many audit plans and is frequently used by auditors. However, it is not always well understood. The results of applying Benford's Law provide a starting point for the auditor.

Benford's Law analyzes the digits in numerical data, helps identifies anomalies, and detects systematic manipulation of data (that is, the making up of false numbers) based on the digital distribution in a natural population. Natural population could be almost anything, such as all the transactions in a general ledger, the transactions in accounts payable, or even the cubic meters of water in all the lakes in Africa.

Frank Benford published "The Law of Anomalous Numbers" in 1938; it postulated that the lower the leading digit of a number, the more often it would appear. Frank Benford used data from rivers, populations, newspapers, cost data, addresses, and many other categories to confirm his theory. Since then, many have furthered his research, particularly Mark J. Nigrini, PhD. He has written many articles and books on the subject, such as *Benford's Law: Applications for Forensic Accounting, Auditing, and Fraud Detection*.

In 1938, the research and calculations were performed manually, which was painstaking. Today, with computing power and the ease of accessing big data sets, one can see that Benford's Law of expected numbers is valid. One website (http://TestingBenfordsLaw.com) applies a number of data sets against Benford's Law. It tests data such as Twitter users by followers' count, most common iPhone passcodes, population of Spanish cities, U.K. government spending, and even includes the first 652,066 Fibonacci numbers.

The expected values for any data set of the first leading digit and also for the first two leading digits are outlined in Table 5.1.

For the first digit test, the first leading digit output is depicted in the graph in Figure 5.1. For example, the leading digit 1 appears 30 percent of the time, whereas the leading digit 9 appears 4.6 percent of the time. The bars are the actual data counts and the lines are the lower and upper boundaries along with the expected count. This data set conforms to Benford's Law.

TABLE 5.1 Benford's Law First Digit Frequency and First Two Digits Frequency

	First Digit Frequency	Second Digit Frequency
0	—	0.11968
1	0.30103	0.11389
2	0.17609	0.10882
3	0.12494	0.10433
4	0.09691	0.10031
5	0.07918	0.09668
6	0.06695	0.09337
7	0.05799	0.09035
8	0.05115	0.08757
9	0.04576	0.08500

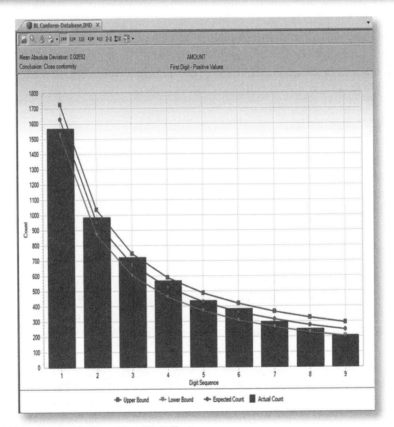

FIGURE 5.1 Benford's Law First Digit Test

For Benford's Law to be applicable, certain conditions must be met.

■ The numbers in the data set should describe the same object.
■ There should be no built-in maximum or minimum to the numbers.

- The numbers should not be assigned, such as telephone numbers, bank account numbers, social insurance, or social security numbers.
- Does not apply to uniform distributions such as lottery balls where the uniform balls are selected and not the actual numbers.

Primary Benford's Law tests are the first digit, first two digits, first three digits, and second digit tests. Advanced Benford's Law tests are summation and second order. Associated tests are last two digits, number duplication, and distortion factor model. All but the last two tests can be automatically executed from within the IDEA software.

The number duplication test identifies specific numbers causing spikes or anomalies in primary and summation tests. Spikes in the primary tests are caused by some specific numbers occurring abnormally too often. Abnormally large numbers in value cause spikes in the summation test.

The distortion factor model shows whether the data has an excess of lower digits or higher digits. It assumes that the true number is changed to a false number in the same range or percentage as the true number.

Most presentations and articles discuss using Benford's Law to detect numbers near their authorization limits. For example, if someone's authorization limit is $10,000, then many first two digits in the 99, 98, and 97 area will be detected using Benford's Law if they are trying to maximize authorizing expenditures. Some other practical applications include:

- Accounts payable (expenses) data
- Estimations (accruals) in the general ledger
- Sales
- Purchases
- Non-arm's-length transactions
- Customer refunds
- Bad debts
- Anti–money laundering

There is a potential to detect money laundering because money laundering flows money into the revenue stream that is not generated by the regular business. Since paying income tax on the false revenue is not desirable, corresponding expenses are made up to offset the false revenue. If there are enough of these made-up expenses or numbers, Benford's Law may detect the anomalies.

Not only is Benford's Law relevant to detecting anomalies in financial related data, it is applicable in other fields, too. A study was published in the *New Zealand Journal of Marine and Freshwater Research* entitled "Statistical Fraud Detection in a Commercial Lobster Fishery."[2] The study tested the reliability of fisheries' data in Canada. The study was prompted by the fact that lobster sales formed a large part of the underground economy. The Royal Canadian Mounted Police proceeds-of-crime unit first thought that large money transfers into a bank branch was from drug money, but later found them to be from cash sales of lobster. From highly regulated lobster fishery areas, the data was found to conform with the distribution as expected by Benford's Law. Lobster and snow-crab data from different, less regulated areas did not conform.

Another research paper titled "Not the First Digit! Using Benford's Law to Detect Fraudulent Scientific Data,"[3] found that there could be nonconformity with Benford's Law for the second or higher order tests for scientific data produced by researchers. Fabricated data may conform to the first digit test.

The paper "When Does the Second-Digit Benford's Law-Test Signal an Election Fraud? Facts or Misleading Test Results"[4] focused on Benford's Law and the conformity or nonconformity of election results.

The first digit test is a high-level test and is suitable for use with less than 300 transactions. The first three digits test is too detailed and will result in the need to investigate too many anomalies. The first two digits test is the most practical to use. Examples of applying the first two digits test are shown in Figures 5.2, 5.3, 5.4, and 5.5.

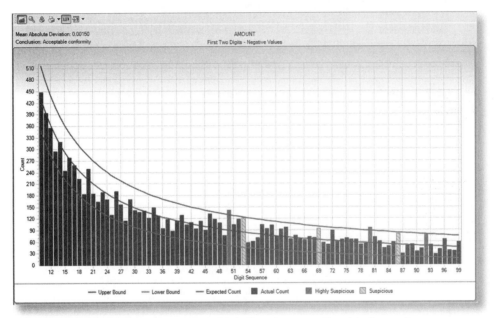

FIGURE 5.2 Benford's Law First Two Digit Test Accounts Payable from a Large Corporation Example Showing Conformity to Benford's Law

There are significant spikes for the first two digits of 19, 20, 21, . . . 31 and 32 in Figure 5.3. As this is an auto manufacturer, they sell cars to dealerships where sales of $19,000 to $32,000 are normal. Knowledge of the business allows you to eliminate this area for additional review.

Figure 5.4 clearly shows that Benford's Law identified the contents of this file as fabricated to be used to demonstrate payment data with the IDEA software.

The author generated the data in Figure 5.5 using the BenfordWiz software download from www.members.tripod.com/benfordwiz. This is to demonstrate and make auditors aware that where there are tools to detect fraud, there are always tools developed to prevent or circumvent detection.

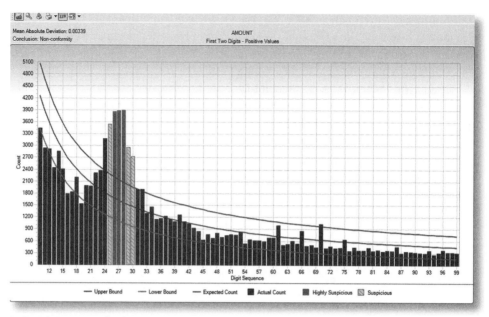

FIGURE 5.3 Benford's Law First Two Digits Test Accounts Receivable File of an Automotive Manufacturer Showing Nonconformity Spikes

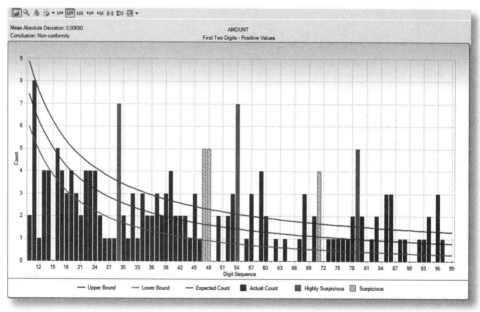

FIGURE 5.4 Sample Payment File Included with the IDEA Software Showing Nonconformity to the First Two Digits of Benford's Law

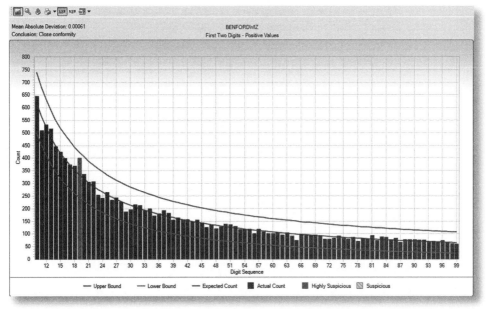

FIGURE 5.5 Benford's Law First Two Digits Test on Data Generated with Benfordwiz Software Showing General Conformity

Using Benford's Law in IDEA

The Benford's Law feature in IDEA can provide a valuable reasonableness test for large data sets.

- IDEA only tests positive numbers 10 and over in the data file.
- For negative numbers, values greater than minus 10 are excluded (exclude –9, –8, . . . –1).
- These steps eliminate immaterial items from the analysis.
- Positive and negative numbers are analyzed separately.

The positive and negative numbers are evaluated on their own due to the fact that positive numbers behave very differently from negative numbers. For example, where positive earnings are manipulated for management bonuses, there is motivation to increase the earnings, moving away from zero toward larger numbers. Where there are losses and management wishes to improve stock prices, there is incentive to move the larger negative number to a smaller one toward zero.

IDEA can apply most of the Benford's Law tests and can also display suspicious results in graphical format. Tests provided in IDEA are the first digit, first two digit, first three digits, second digit, last two digits, second order, and summation tests as shown in Figure 5.6.

Results that show a poor fit with Benford's Law should be examined, as they are an indicator of excessive duplications and anomalies.

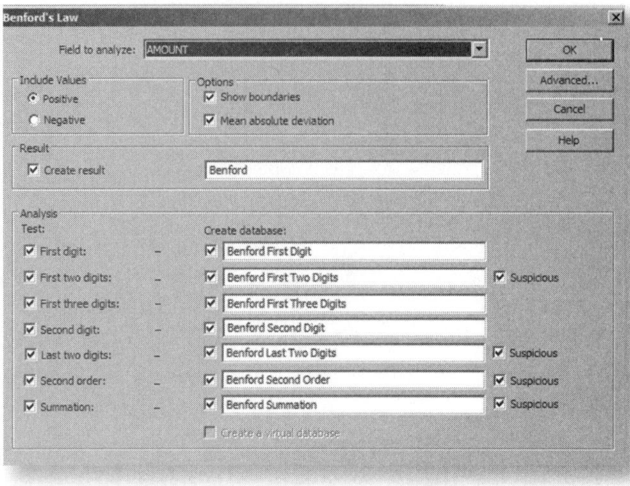

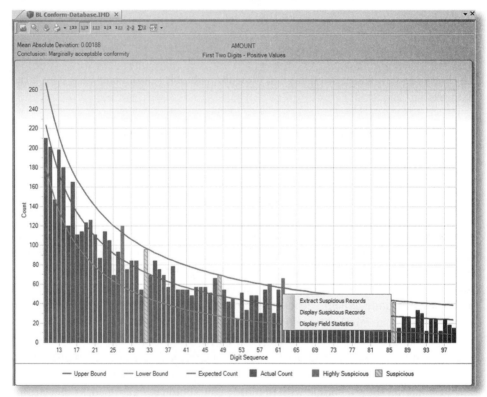

FIGURE 5.6   Applying the Benford's Law Feature in IDEA

This first two digits primary test output from IDEA indicates that it marginally conforms in Figure 5.7. The graph highlights the three most highly suspicious numbers and the three most suspicious items. By placing the cursor over any bar, such as the

FIGURE 5.7   First Two Digits Test Benford's Law Output with Suspicious Numbers Highlighted

highly suspicious 62 bar, options for extracting or displaying the records are offered. Field statistics may also be displayed.

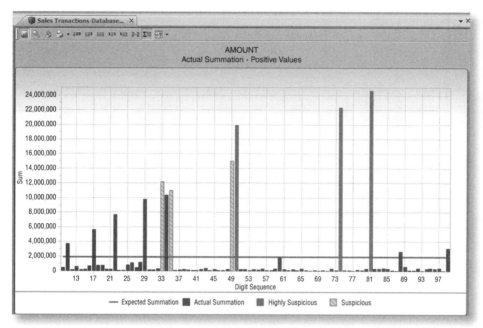

FIGURE 5.8 Benford's Law Summation Test Example

The summation test (Figure 5.8) analyzes the first two digits in the data by grouping the records of the first two digits together and then computing the sum of each group. Amounts with the same first two digits, such as 1200, 125, 12, 1234, and so on, are added together. Using the computed and summed values, the process determines whether a uniform distribution is followed. The summation test identifies excessively large numbers as compared to the rest of the data. The test is based on sums rather than on counts, as in the other Benford's Law tests. In theory, the sums of numbers with the same first two digits should be equal in distribution. However, in normal data sets, there are regular abnormal duplications of large numbers that may be caused by a few very large numbers or a high volume of moderately large numbers. Additional analysis will be needed.

The second order test is also based on the first two digits in the data. The data is sorted from the smallest to the largest and the differences between each pair of consecutive records are checked to determine whether they conform to the expectations of the first two digit distribution. Numbers of even tens—10, 20, 30, 40, 50, 60, 70, 80, and 90—on their own are expected to conform to the Benford's Law distribution and the rest of the numbers on their own are also expected to conform, as displayed in Figure 5.9.

The last two digits test groups the last two digits and computes the frequency. The grouped frequency is matched against the expected uniform distribution. In the accounts payable file shown in Figure 5.10, numbers ending in .00 significantly exceed the expected distribution but were found to be normal based on their actual payments.

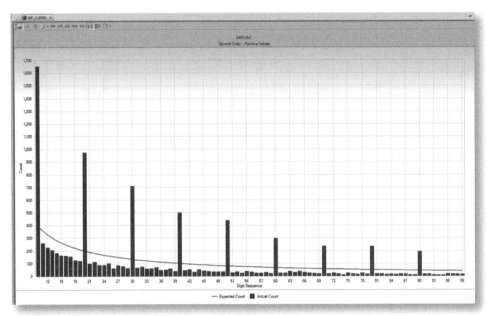

FIGURE 5.9 Benford's Law Second Order Test Example

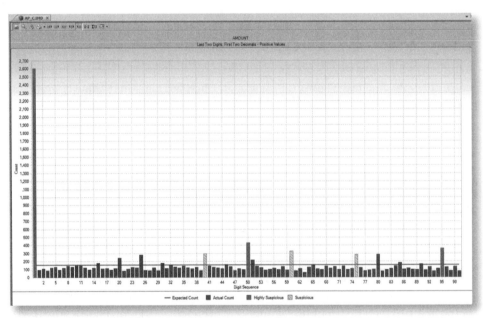

FIGURE 5.10 Benford's Law Last Two Digits Test Example

Usage Considerations of Benford's Law

- Users must consider whether a particular data set should be expected to fall into a Benford's Law distribution.
- What test should be run and how should the results of those tests be interpreted?
- When is Benford's Law ineffective?

For effective usage, amounts of less than $10.00 should be removed from the data. IDEA automatically does this task before performing the Benford's Law calculations. The auditor must bear in mind that there are costs associated with false positives (identifying a fraud condition when none is present) as well as with false negatives (failing to identify a fraud condition when one exists). The auditor must consider the level of significance to select for further investigation. A balance must be found so one does not investigate too many or too few transactions.

Are there categories of fraud that cannot be detected? As Benford's Law detects excessive duplications or made-up numbers, it is not appropriate for detecting deletions. If transactions were randomly deleted from sales, say from a point-of-sales system, the randomness would ensure that there would be no variation from the expected distribution of the original data set prior to any deletions.

Conclusion

- Benford's analysis, when used correctly, is a powerful tool for identifying suspect accounts or amounts for further analysis.
- Benford's analysis is a tool to complement additional tests/tools.
- Users have to gain expertise in interpreting results.

Benford's Law is a wonderful tool for initial risk assessment of the contents of a data set. It provides the auditor or investigator with a good starting point. The user must understand the business and the industry to effectively use this tool. Knowledge of the business can quickly eliminate false positives, such as in the example of the automotive manufacturer where sales of cars to dealerships caused spikes for the first two digits in the 18-to-32-digits range, as displayed in Figure 5.3.

 NUMBER DUPLICATION TEST

The number duplication test (NDT) is not specifically a Benford's Law test; rather it is an associated test that can be used to provide more information resulting from Benford's Law tests. The NDT can output specific numbers that caused the spikes in the first order tests (the first two digits test is one example) and the summation test, which is an advanced Benford's Law test.

Spikes from any first order test are caused by numbers occurring more frequently than expected while spikes in the summation test are usually due to high volumes of the same numbers repeating more often than normal. Mark Nigrini wrote, "The number duplication test was developed as a part of my PhD dissertation when I was looking for taxpayer amounts that were duplicated abnormally often. I believed that these abnormal duplications were there because taxpayers were inventing numbers and that, since we think alike, people would gravitate toward making up the same numbers. There were some interesting results for deduction fields such as charitable contributions."[5]

The NDT should be applied to different criteria in the data set.

- Greater than or equal to 10
- From 0.01 to 9.99

- From −0.01 to −9.99
- Less than or equal to −10

The output should show the amount that was duplicated and the count for each amount.

The ranking of the counts presents those with the highest number of duplicate amounts near the top of the results.

IDEA does not have an automated process for the NDT. However, it is not complex to perform this manually in IDEA.

We decided to use a travel expense data file to perform the NDT on. The travel expense file has fields for the various types of travel expenses, such as transportation, airfare, accommodation, meals, and so on. We will test the accommodation amounts, and for amounts greater than or equal to $10.00.

1. Summarize by our selected test field of ACCOMMODATION with the criteria of ACCOMMODATION > = 10 as shown in Figure 5.11.

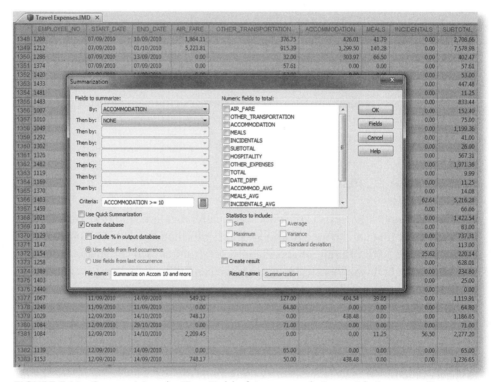

FIGURE 5.11 Summarizing the Test Field of Accommodations with Amounts Greater Than or Equal to $10.00

2. Create a new file using the Sort feature on the NO_OF_RECORDS field in descending order shown in Figure 5.12. This is our count field, which we will easily rank later as we had selected the sort to be in descending order. A sort creates a new database with the selected sort order physically set.

Number Duplication Test ■ **79**

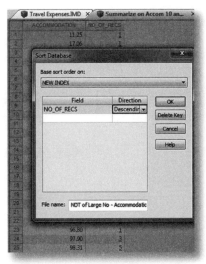

FIGURE 5.12   New Sorted File on Number of Records

3. We will create two new fields by using the Append field feature. Name the first new field as RANK set as a virtual numeric field with no decimals. Employ the function of @Precno( ), which returns the physical record number in the file that would remain the same even if the file was subsequently indexed differently. This would equate to the ranking that we would like to see.

In addition, we can pull out the first two digits from the accommodation amount for each record. Append a new field called FIRST_TWO set as a virtual numeric field with no decimal places. For the new field use the equation

@Val(@Left(@Str(ACCOMMODATION, 2, 2), 2))

This equation converts the ACCOMMODATION field to a character field using the @Str function to output a minimum of two characters. The second 2 is the number of decimal places. We could enter 0 or any number of decimal places, but the decimal places will be dropped because we specified that the new field would contain no decimal places. Two decimal places were used here as normally you would desire two decimal places, and also to provide an opportunity to make this point. The numeric ACCOMMODATION field must be changed to a character field in order to perform any position operations. We use the @Left function to extract the first two characters starting from the left position. Then we use the @Val function to convert everything back to numeric, as shown in Figure 5.13.

We now have all the accommodation expenses from the NO_OF_RECS field, so we know how many times those exact amounts appeared in the database in Figure 5.14. The top ranking of $174.02 appeared 52 times. We can click on the content of the NO_OF_RECS field to display the details.

The FIRST_TWO field displays numbers we would expect. That is, low first two digits ranked near the top as in our results to conform to Benford's Law, and not high first two digits such as 99, 98, 97, and so on.

Summarizing the data file by the FIRST_TWO field and indexing the resulting file on NO_OF_REC1 in descending order will give us the frequency of each two

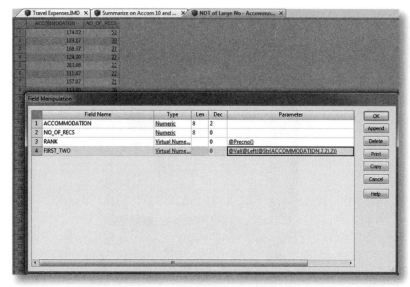

FIGURE 5.13   Appending the Two New Fields

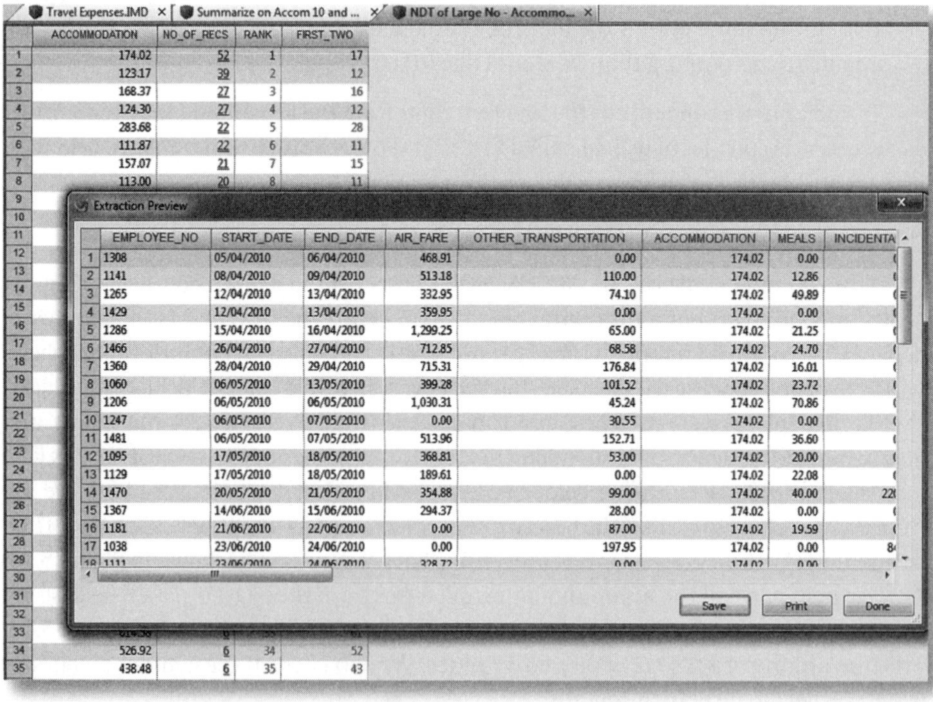

FIGURE 5.14   Results of the Number Duplication Test

digit number that further confirms conformity to Benford's Law as displayed in Figure 5.15.

	Summarize on First_Two.IMD ✕	
	FIRST_TWO	NO_OF_RECS1 ▼
1	11	37
2	12	35
3	10	32
4	16	29
5	15	27
6	17	26
7	13	24
8	14	23
9	18	22
10	23	21
11	26	20
12	22	18
13	19	17
14	20	15
15	40	14
16	36	14
17	28	14
18	29	13
19	24	13
20	34	12
21	25	12
22	33	11
23	27	11
24	38	10
25	32	10

FIGURE 5.15 Number Records for the First Two Digits

The NDT is a good provider of detailed information to identify spikes from the summation test and the first two digits test. This helps determine whether further investigation is necessary.

 Z-SCORE

The term Z-*score*, Z-*values*, Z-*ratio*, or Z is a statistical measurement of a number in relationship to the mean of the group of numbers. It refers to points along the base of the standardized normal curve. The center point of the curve has a Z-value of 0. Z-values to the right of 0 are positive and Z-values to the left are negative values. A Z-score is above the mean if to the right of 0 and is below the mean if left of the 0 center point. The distance from the mean is measured by standard deviations. If the Z-score is 0, it is 0 standard deviations from the mean and is equal to the mean.

Z-score is calculated by taking the difference between the number and the mean (average) and then dividing the difference obtained by the standard deviation.

$$Z = (X - \mu)/\sigma$$

X represents the raw number. The population mean is represented by μ and the standard deviation is the symbol σ.

A Z-score is standardized. It is irrelevant whether you are comparing Canadian dollars, U.S. dollars, euros, or British pounds. In fact, the unit may be measuring height, weight, education levels, or test scores. The Z-score is always relative to the mean that is the center or designated as zero. The Z-score tells you much about the distribution of the numbers in your data set and can highlight extremes.

With the Z-score, the area under the normal curve can be determined by computer calculation or by looking at tables. You can search the Internet for these tables. An example is located at www.sagepub.com/fitzgerald/study/materials/appendices/app_d .pdf.

A selected portion of a Z-score table is created in Table 5.2.

TABLE 5.2　Partial Z-Score Table

Z	Area between Mean and Z
0.30	.1179
0.50	.1915
0.80	.2881
1.00	.3413
1.50	.4332
1.80	.4649
1.96	.4750
2.58	.4951
3.90	.4999

A Z-score of 1.50 indicates that 43.32 percent of the area under the normal curve is located between the mean and the Z-score of 1.50. How much area under the curve would Z-scores between −1.96 and +1.96 be? Since we are looking at both the negative and positive sides of the mean, we multiply the area between the mean and Z by 2 (.4750 * 2), resulting in 95 percent. The higher the absolute value of the Z-score, the further the number is away from the mean or the norm. The auditor may wish to examine transactions that are extreme outliers.

Statistical theory states that 99.7 percent of the time, the Z-score will be between −3.00 and +3.00. It will be between −2.00 and +2.00 for 95 percent of the time, and 68 percent of the time, it will be between −1.00 and +1.00

IDEA does not automatically calculate the Z-score for you. However, it does have built-in calculations that make the calculation of the Z-score for each transaction easy.

Going back to our payment tender net database, let us take a look at the field statistics for the PAYAMOUNT_SUM field.

We note that the average value or the mean is \$19.48 and that the Pop Std Dev or population standard deviation is \$15.17 in Figure 5.16. These are calculated for you by IDEA.

Numeric Statistics	PAYAMOUNT_SUM
Net Value	1,650,363.85
Absolute Value	1,650,368.69
# of Records	84,718
# of Zero Items	7
Positive Value	1,650,366.27
Negative Value	-2.42
# of Positive Records	84,709
# of Negative Records	2
# of Data Errors	0
# of Valid Values	84,718
▶ Average Value	19.48
Minimum Value	-1.26
Maximum Value	380.13
Record # of Min	63,463
Record # of Max	65,663
Sample Std Dev	15.17
Sample Variance	230.08
Pop Std Dev	15.17
Pop Variance	230.07
Pop Skewness	3.007330
Pop Kurtosis	23.976610

FIGURE 5.16 Field Statistics for Payment Amounts

IDEA assigns numbers to be used with the @FieldStatistics function. The assigned number for the average or mean is 11 and 18 for the population standard deviation as shown in Figure 5.17.

The syntax for use of the function is @FieldStatistics("FieldName", Statistic).

We create or append a field called Z_SCORE by applying the formula for Z-score in the equation editor.

The formula obtains the average value and the population standard deviation amounts from the field statistics area to use in the equation shown in Figure 5.18.

When we index the Z_SCORE field by descending order, we can see that all of the 84,718 records, with the exception of 519 transactions, had Z-scores of 3.99 or below in Figure 5.19. In this particular data set, the Z-score goes as high as 23.78. The auditor needs to use judgment as to how many outliers should be examined in detail or to select the Z-score point for the examination cut-off.

When the Z_SCORE field is indexed by descending order, the PAYAMOUNT_SUM field would also have the largest amounts shown from the highest to lowest. While both fields indicate amount order, the Z-score provides you with a sense of how far each amount is from the mean so you can gauge the magnitude of the anomaly.

Assigned Numbers

- Numeric field statistics

# of Records	1
# of Zero Items	2
# of Valid Values	3
# of Data Errors	4
Net Value	5
Absolute Value	6
Positive Value	7
Negative Value	8
# of Positive Records	9
# of Negative Records	10
Average Value	11
Minimum Value	12
Maximum Value	13
Record # of Min	14
Record # of Max	15
Sample Std Dev	16
Sample Variance	17
Pop Std Dev	18
Pop Variance	19
Pop Skewness	20
Pop Kurtosis	21

FIGURE 5.17 Assigned Field Statistic Numbers to Be Used with the @Fieldstatistics Function

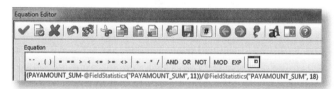

FIGURE 5.18 Equation for Calculating Z-Score Example

RELATIVE SIZE FACTOR TEST

The purpose of the relative size factor (RSF) test is to identify anomalies where the largest amount for subsets in a given key is outside the norm for those subsets. This test compares the top two amounts for each subset and calculates the RSF for each. The RSF test is based on Chapter 11 of Mark J. Nigrini's book, *Forensic Analytics: Methods and Techniques for Forensic Accounting Investigations.*[6]

In order to identify potential fraudulent activities in invoice payment data, one utilizes the largest and the second-largest amounts to calculate a ratio based on purchases that are grouped by vendors; this is often suggested in fraud-examination literature, such as *Principles of Fraud Examination* written by Joseph T. Wells.[7]

	TXNID	NO_OF_RECS	PAYAMOUNT_SUM	Z_SCORE ▾	TENDERTYPEID	TENDERDESC1	SPLIT	PAYTIME_DATE	PAYTIME ▲
503	22204	1	81.31	4.08	3	Visa	0	17/01/2008	21
504	136749	1	81.25	4.07	3	Visa	0	04/10/2010	16
505	25143	1	81.25	4.07	2	MasterCard	0	14/02/2008	18
506	64116	1	81.08	4.06	3	Visa	0	27/12/2008	16
507	50904	1	81.13	4.06	4	Debit	0	13/09/2008	16
508	171652	1	80.85	4.05	2	MasterCard	0	29/08/2011	15
509	140011	1	80.85	4.05	4	Debit	0	01/11/2010	10
510	136219	1	80.80	4.04	2	MasterCard	0	30/09/2010	21
511	19181	1	80.54	4.03	3	Visa	0	20/12/2007	21
512	178364	1	80.46	4.02	3	Visa	0	31/10/2011	19
513	139373	1	80.40	4.02	3	Visa	0	27/10/2010	18
514	111423	1	80.40	4.02	4	Debit	0	20/02/2010	16
515	21542	1	80.40	4.02	3	Visa	0	11/01/2008	22
516	105867	1	80.35	4.01	4	Debit	0	31/12/2009	18
517	173884	1	80.18	4.00	2	MasterCard	0	20/09/2011	18
518	149451	1	80.12	4.00	3	Visa	0	23/01/2011	17
519	72642	1	80.12	4.00	2	MasterCard	0	14/03/2009	18
520	178261	1	80.00	3.99	4	Debit	0	30/10/2011	17
521	136432	1	80.00	3.99	2	MasterCard	0	01/10/2010	22
522	132788	1	80.00	3.99	4	Debit	0	01/09/2010	17
523	10936	1	79.97	3.99	4	Debit	0	15/10/2007	17
524	174209	1	79.78	3.98	2	MasterCard	0	23/09/2011	19
525	112726	1	79.83	3.98	4	Debit	0	04/03/2010	17
526	94469	1	79.90	3.98	4	Debit	0	28/09/2009	17
527	69016	1	79.67	3.97	1	Cash	0	10/02/2009	21
528	19101	1	79.68	3.97	4	Debit	0	20/12/2007	14
529	92749	1	79.55	3.96	4	Debit	0	13/09/2009	17
530	173955	1	79.44	3.95	4	Debit	0	21/09/2011	17
531	145213	1	79.44	3.95	5	AME	0	16/12/2010	17
532	126634	1	79.38	3.95	4	Debit	0	02/07/2010	18
533	86105	1	79.44	3.95	4	Debit	0	11/07/2009	22
534	84036	1	79.44	3.95	4	Debit	0	21/06/2009	17
535	24881	1	79.33	3.95	3	Visa	0	12/02/2008	16

Properties

▾ Database
✓ Data
■ History
■ Field Statistics
■ Control Total: 1,650,363.85 (PAYAMOUNT_SUM)
■ Criteria

▾ Results
■ Stratification
■ Pivot Table

▾ Indices
■ No index
■ TENDERTYPEID/A
■ TENDERDESC1/A
✓ Z_SCORE/A
✓ Z_SCORE/D

▾ Comments
■ Add comment

Running Tasks

aged Project: POS Quick Service   Not connected to IDEA Server   Number of Records: 84,718   Disk Space: 160.56 GB

FIGURE 5.19   Results Displaying Z-Score Sequenced from Largest to Smallest

In Chapter 11 of Dr. Mark Nigirini's *Forensic Analytics* book, he introduces the RSF test, which expands on this concept and states, "In this chapter we compare large amounts to a benchmark to see how large they are relative to some norm, hence the name the RSF test. The RSF test is a powerful test for detecting errors. The test identifies subsets where the largest amount is out of line with the other amounts for that subset. This difference could be because the largest record either (a) actually belongs to another subset, or (b) belongs to the subset in question, but the numeric amount is incorrectly recorded. The RSF test is an important error-detecting test."

$$RSF = \frac{\text{Largest Record in a Subset}}{\text{Second-Largest Record in a Subset}}$$

Subsets in a data file are identified as *keys* in IDEA. An example would be vendors in an accounts payable file. The test identifies records that are outliers to the rest of the amounts within the subset groups. Outliers may not be the largest amounts in the entire data set, but are large in respects to particular members of the subset. Large differences might be attributed to errors such as the record belongs to another subset or that the amount was posted incorrectly (e.g., a shifted decimal point). Large differences may also be an indication of fraudulent activity, such as occupational accounts payable fraud, falsified invoices for HST or VAT input tax credits, offset money-laundering revenue, or product sales to related companies (offshore transfer pricing). In his book, Dr. Mark Nigrini discusses the forensic results regarding investigations of sales numbers, insurance claim payments, inventory numbers, and healthcare claims using the RSF test.

To enhance the information provided by the RSF test, the step-by-step instructions on how to perform the calculations will include a field that shows average amounts if we were to disregard the largest outlier. This will give the auditor a better feel of the data content relationships.

The Average_X_Largest field is the average of all positive or negative amounts (as determined by the user as the first step to the RSF calculations) excluding the largest amount. This field provides an indication of the typical amount within the subset members.

The step-by-step example uses a sample payment data set. The subset or key is the supplier number field (SUPPNO) performing the RSF calculations on the AMOUNT field.

Step 1. In reviewing the field statistics (Figure 5.20) for the AMOUNT field of the "Payment" file, we note that there are three negative values and one zero item. To run the RSF test on positive values, an AMOUNT of greater than 0 should be extracted. Name the new file "Extract RSF-1," as displayed in Figure 5.21.

Numeric Statistics	AMOUNT
Net Value	3,750,015.36
Absolute Value	3,757,791.70
# of Records	185
# of Zero Items	1
Positive Value	3,753,903.53
Negative Value	-3,888.17
# of Positive Records	181
# of Negative Records	3
# of Data Errors	0
# of Valid Values	185
Average Value	20,270.35
Minimum Value	-1,994.67
Maximum Value	97,376.40
Record # of Min	115
Record # of Max	97
Sample Std Dev	26,076.86
Sample Variance	680,002,723.38
Pop Std Dev	26,006.29
Pop Variance	676,327,032.98
Pop Skewness	1.324243
Pop Kurtosis	0.632613

FIGURE 5.20 Field Statistics of Payment Amounts

Step 2. After the extracting for all positive numbers, we need to create or append a field called RECNO using the @Precno( ) function as shown in Figure 5.22. This will track the physical record number in the data set. The record number will be needed for a future join of files.

Step 3. Using the "Extract RSF-1" file, sort the database by the SUPPNO field in ascending order and the AMOUNT field in descending order, as in Figure 5.23. This

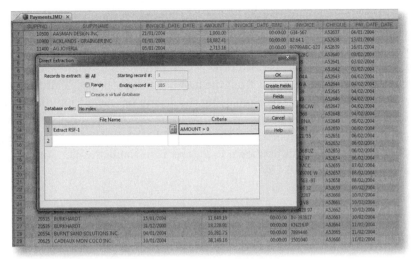

FIGURE 5.21 Preparing the File Extraction for Positive Amounts

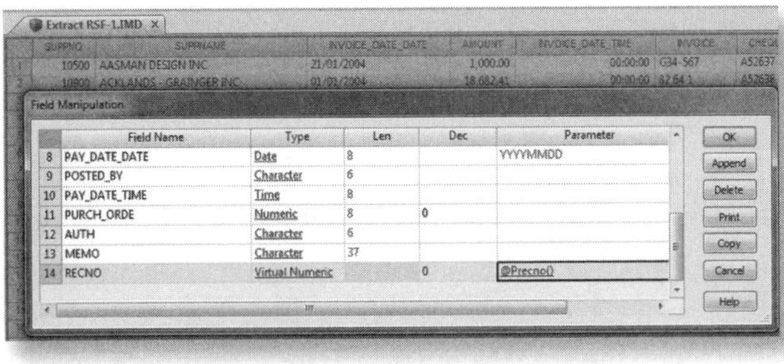

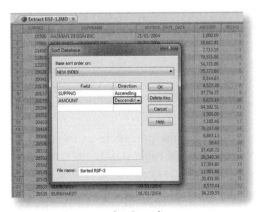

FIGURE 5.22 Adding a Field for Physical Record Numbers

FIGURE 5.23 Sorting Largest Amounts by Supplier

will place the largest amount as the first record by supplier number. Name the new file "Sorted RSF-3."

Step 4. Summarize the "Sorted RSF-3" file to give the total number of transactions along with the top amounts per SUPPNO. When performing a summarization, IDEA provides the options to use fields from the first occurrence or use fields from the last occurrence for additional fields. Employing the default use fields from the first occurrence selection, the highest or top amount from step 3 for each supplier number will result in the new file. Summarize by the field SUPPNO plus select Fields to include the AMOUNT and RECNO fields as shown in Figure 5.24. Name the file "Summarization RSF-4."

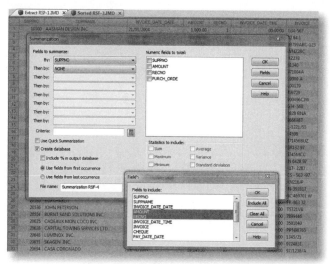

FIGURE 5.24 Obtaining the Total Number of Transactions by Supplier and the Largest Amounts

Step 5. Perform a join using the "Sorted RSF-3" file as the primary database and the "Summarization RSF-4" file as the secondary database. Use Match Key Felds with RECNO as the common key in both files. Select the records with no secondary match join option. The secondary file of "Summarization RSF-4" contains the largest amounts for each supplier. By creating a new file by using join databases with no secondary match, the new file will not contain the largest or top-most numbers as displayed in Figure 5.25. This will allow us to extract the next highest amounts that are in fact the second largest amounts. Name the new file "Join RSF-5."

Step 6. This is the exact same procedure as in step 3 to obtain the top-most amounts, but now with the actual highest amount removed from the data set. Sort the "Join RSF-5" file by the SUPPNO field in ascending order and the AMOUNT field in descending order as shown in Figure 5.26. We need to do the sort again as the join changes the orders of the records. This will allow us to later obtain the second largest amounts. Name the file "Sorted RSF-6."

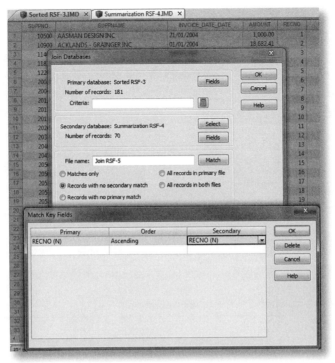

FIGURE 5.25 Preparing to Obtain the Second Largest Amounts

FIGURE 5.26 Sorting the Largest Amount by Supplier with the Top-Most Amount Excluded to Obtain the Second Largest Number

Step 7. Summarize the "RSF-6" file to obtain the average for the AMOUNT field. Summarize by the field SUPPNO with the AMOUNT field as the numeric field to total. Select average as the statistic to include. IDEA does not seem to allow you to perform a statistic on a field and add it as an additional field. We have to perform this step twice: once for the average and the second time for the top amount in the file in the next step. Name this file "Summarization RSF-7," as in Figure 5.27.

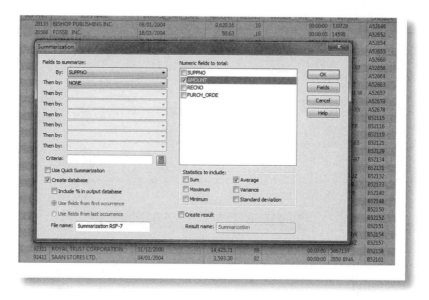

FIGURE 5.27 Calculating the Averages by Supplier

Step 8. Summarize the "RSF-6" file on the SUPPNO field and select the field to include of AMOUNT as displayed in Figure 5.28. Note the selection of the default "Use fields from first occurrence." This is identical to step 4 with the exception that RECNO does not have to be selected as a field to include. This will give us the largest numbers in the data set by supplier that are actually the second highest numbers. Name the file "Summarization RSF-8."

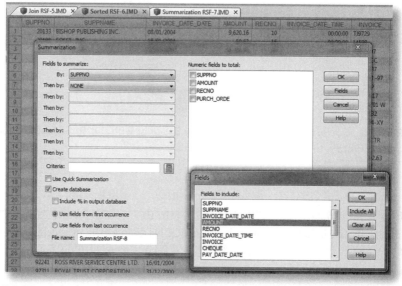

FIGURE 5.28 Calculating the Second Largest Number by Supplier

Step 9. Join as the primary file "Summarization RSF-8" to "Summarization RSF-7" as the secondary file. Use the SUPPNO for the Match Key Fields as in Figure 5.29. This will put together the second largest amount and the averages into one file. Include the SUPPNO and AMOUNT fields in the primary file. Include only the AMOUNT_AVERAGE field in the secondary file. Use the "Matches only" option for the join. Call the new file "Join RSF-9."

FIGURE 5.29 Putting Together the Second Largest Amount with the Average Amount

Step 10. Rename the AMOUNT and AMOUNT_AVERAGE fields to SECOND_LARGEST_AMT and AVERAGE_X_LARGEST respectively, as shown in Figure 5.30.

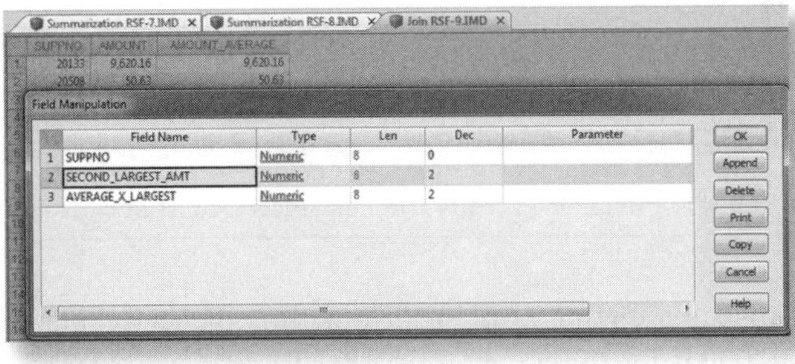

FIGURE 5.30 Renaming Fields to Identify the Second Largest Amount and the Average Excluding the Largest Amount

Step 11. Join the "Summarization RSF-4" database as the primary file with "Join RSF-9" database as the secondary file. "Summarization RSF-4" contains the largest or top amounts. Use the SUPPNO fields as Match Key Fields as shown in Figure 5.31. Select

FIGURE 5.31 Putting the Largest Amount, Second Largest Amount, and Average Amount Excluding the Largest Amount Fields Together

the "Matches only" join option. For the primary file include the SUPPNO, NO_OF_RECS, and AMOUNT fields. For the secondary file include the SECOND_LARGEST_AMT and AVERAGE_X_LARGEST fields. Name this file "Join RSF-11."

Step 12. Rename the NO_OF_RECS field to COUNT and the AMOUNT field to LARGEST_AMT as in Figure 5.32.

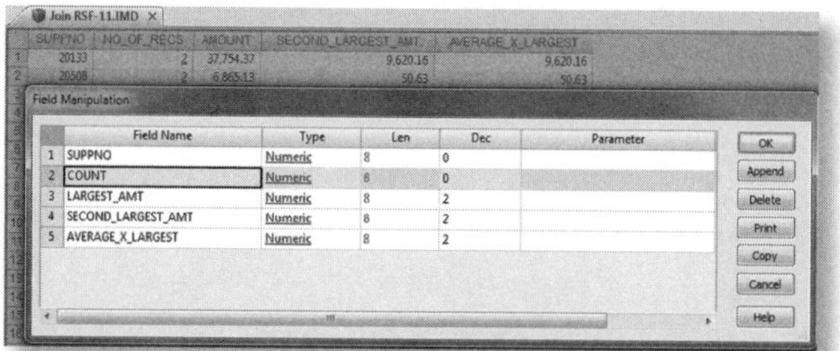

FIGURE 5.32 Rename Fields to Identify the Largest Amount and Count

Step 13. Append a virtual numeric field with two decimal places called RELATIVE_SIZE_FACTOR using the equation of LARGEST_AMT/SECOND_LARGEST_AMT as shown in Figure 5.33.

The final file, indexed by RELATIVE_SIZE_FACTOR in descending order, is shown in Figure 5.34. The auditor needs to decide above what RSF ratio further investigation is required. Knowing the average amounts without the largest amount included in the average calculation is useful for formulating the auditor's decision. It is suggested that RSF ratios above 2.50 should be reviewed. A note of significance is where the RSF ratio

FIGURE 5.33 Calculating the Relative Size Factor

	SUPPNO	COUNT	LARGEST_AMT	SECOND_LARGEST_AMT	AVERAGE_X_LARGEST	RELATIVE_SIZE_FACTOR ▾
1	20508	2	6,865.13	50.63	50.63	135.59
2	21395	2	48,399.72	7,106.92	7,106.92	6.81
3	92411	3	24,163.78	3,593.30	3,275.25	6.72
4	92241	2	56,227.23	9,351.19	9,351.19	6.01
5	21175	2	47,438.23	11,129.65	11,129.65	4.26
6	92311	2	60,355.21	14,425.71	14,425.71	4.18
7	20133	2	37,754.37	9,620.16	9,620.16	3.92
8	92211	3	57,998.57	16,700.56	16,374.40	3.47
9	21490	2	96,166.49	30,097.05	30,097.05	3.20
10	40502	2	86,441.66	29,990.31	29,990.31	2.88
11	60600	2	83,880.73	32,169.70	32,169.70	2.61
12	99999	79	52,845.00	22,829.04	2,573.86	2.31
13	21650	2	50,067.31	21,632.22	21,632.22	2.31
14	20535	7	78,262.98	34,259.55	17,358.36	2.28
15	92700	2	4,367.36	2,338.22	2,338.22	1.87
16	92231	2	42,026.88	24,308.55	24,308.55	1.73
17	30228	2	59,109.76	35,637.48	35,637.48	1.66
18	92221	3	74,625.32	47,232.67	25,705.68	1.58
19	40713	5	40,325.22	25,943.21	12,869.45	1.55
20	20532	3	37,418.72	26,340.30	21,822.55	1.42
21	92611	3	97,376.40	73,703.93	48,352.05	1.32

FIGURE 5.34 Resulting File Displaying the Relative Size Factor for Each Supplier

is equal to 10. This would likely be a data entry error of shifting the decimal place one over to the left. An example might be where monthly rental is $3,000 per month and the largest amount is $30,000, resulting in an RSF of 10.

The RSF test is a test for reasonableness within a specific grouping of data sets. It identifies outliers within the group where the amount is too small to be considered as an anomaly when the data set is taken as a whole.

SAME-SAME-SAME TEST

The purpose of the same-same-same (SSS) test is to identify abnormal duplications as potential indicators of errors or fraud.

This test is based on Chapter 12 of Mark J. Nigrini's book, *Forensic Analytics: Methods and Techniques for Forensic Accounting Investigations.*[8]

Application of this test assists in detecting duplicate expenses claimed, occurrences of the same payment to vendors made in error, multiple warranty claims, or duplicated service fees paid by private or government health plans.

IDEA has a Duplicate Key Detection option, as displayed in Figure 5.35. It can output duplicate records or its inverse of outputting records without duplicates. Up to eight fields may be selected by the auditor to match.

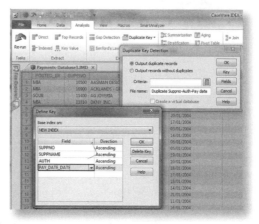

FIGURE 5.35   Duplicate Key Detection for Same Supplier Number, Supplier Name, Authorizing Individual, and Payment Date

From the payment data set, we perform the test where the supplier number, supplier name, the authorizing personnel, and the payment date are all the same.

The output in Figure 5.36 displays six records of three pairs that match the test criteria. Why are two separate checks made out to the same vendor on the same day? They were even authorized by the same people. If these are not errors, then, at the very least, they are inefficient. This file provides the auditor with records to further review.

	SUPPNO	SUPPNAME	AUTH	PAY_DATE_DATE	INVOICE_DATE_DATE	AMOUNT	INVOICE_DATE_TIME	INVOICE	CHEQUE
1	20133	BISHOP PUBLISHING INC.	HMV	04/02/2004	14/01/2004	37,754.37	00:00:00	100139	A52645
2	20133	BISHOP PUBLISHING INC.	HMV	04/02/2004	08/01/2004	9,620.16	00:00:00	TJ9729	A52646
3	20508	FOSSIL INC.	HMV	06/02/2004	17/01/2004	6,865.13	00:00:00	L-1221/55	A52651
4	20508	FOSSIL INC.	HMV	06/02/2004	18/01/2004	50.63	00:00:00	14598	A52652
5	92241	ROSS RIVER SERVICE CENTRE LTD.	WJT	25/02/2004	01/01/2004	56,227.23	00:00:00	GR150 97	B52156
6	92241	ROSS RIVER SERVICE CENTRE LTD.	WJT	25/02/2004	16/01/2004	9,351.19	00:00:00	871465BUZ	B52157

FIGURE 5.36   Results of the Duplicate Key Detection Test

 ## SAME-SAME-DIFFERENT TEST

The same-same-different (SSD) test is used to identify records with near duplicates for fields selected by the auditor. The auditor may select up to eight fields to match and one field that is excluded from the matching.

Mark Nigrini states, "The same-same-different test is a powerful test for errors and fraud. This test should be considered for every forensic analytics project." His experience has shown that, "This test always detects errors in accounts payable data" and "The longer the time period, the higher the chances of SSD detecting errors."[9]

One example that demonstrates the value of this test is in the detection of instances where a payment is made to a wrong vendor initially and then subsequently the correct vendor is properly paid (same invoice number, same amount, but different vendors). The auditor needs to follow-up whether the payment was recovered from the vendor who was paid incorrectly.

IDEA has a Duplicate Key Exclusion feature as shown in Figure 5.37.

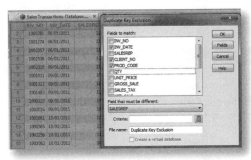

FIGURE 5.37 Duplicate Key Exclusion for Same Invoice Date, Client Number, and Product Code but Different Sales Representative

The built-in Duplicate Key Exclusion feature of IDEA is simple and easy to use. However, it is limited, as it does not display more than one exclusion. A manual approach can be employed. The output of this manual approach will be compared to the output of the Duplicate Key Exclusion feature at the end of this section.

For both methods, the fields that must match are invoice date (INV_DATE), client number (CLIENT_NO), and the product code (PROD_CODE). The field that must be different is the sales representative (SALESREP). The SSD test is applied to the "Sales Transactions" database.

Step 1. Summarize all fields, including the one that needs to be different (SALESREP) as shown in Figure 5.38. Call the new file "Summarization SSD-1."

Step 2. Use the Duplicate Key Detection feature of IDEA with defined key for all fields that must match being INV_DATE, CLIENT_NO, and PROD_CODE, as in Figure 5.39. Call the file "Duplicate SSD-2."

Step 3. Join using the "Sales Transactions" database as the primary file with the Join SSD-3 file as the secondary database. Match Key Fields should include the fields of INV_DATE, CLIENT_NO, PROD_CODE, and SALESREP, as displayed in Figure 5.40. Use the "Matches only" join option. This will give us all the transactions that relate to the SSD test rather than only the first transaction that IDEA's Duplicate Key Exclusion provides. Call this final file "Join SSD-3."

IDEA shows one unique exclusion and omits the rest when using Duplicate Key Exclusion, as shown in the top screen for record numbers 3 and 4 in Figure 5.41. By

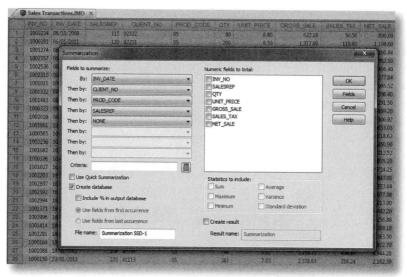

FIGURE 5.38 Summarize All the Fields to Be Tested That Include Both the Required Same Field and the Different Field

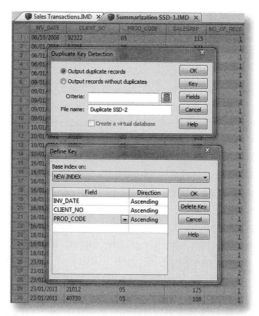

FIGURE 5.39 Find the Duplicates by Using Idea's Duplicate Key Detection for Fields That Must Be the Same

using summarization, duplicate key detection, and then joining the duplicate key detection to the original data set, you will see all the results relating to SSD as shown on the bottom screen for record numbers 5, 6, and 7.

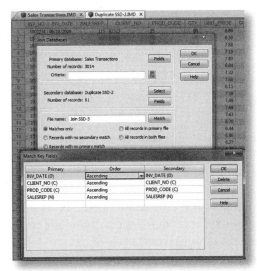

FIGURE 5.40 Putting Together the Files for the Same-Same-Different Test

Duplicate Key Exclusion.IMD ×

	INV_DATE	SALESREP	CLIENT_NO ▲	PROD_CODE	QTY	UNIT_PRICE	GROSS_SALE	SALES_TAX	NET_SALE
1	21/04/2011	102	21646	05	198	7.60	1,655.28	150.48	1,504.80
2	21/04/2011	125	21646	05	389	6.95	2,973.91	270.36	2,703.55
3	14/03/2011	105	30501	05	59	6.77	439.38	39.95	399.43
4	14/03/2011	125	30501	05	65	7.68	549.12	49.92	499.20
5	17/03/2011	104	30501	05	594	7.62	0.00	452.63	4,526.28
6	17/03/2011	105	30501	05	59	6.77	388.75	35.34	353.41
7	03/02/2011	102	30608	05	25	6.44	177.10	16.10	161.00
8	03/02/2011	105	30608	05	230	7.27	1,839.31	167.21	1,672.10
9	10/03/2011	105	30608	05	1235	7.25	9,849.13	895.38	8,953.75
10	10/03/2011	125	30608	05	35	7.95	306.08	27.83	278.25
11	14/07/2011	104	30608	05	150	6.22	1,026.30	93.30	933.00
12	14/07/2011	105	30608	05	167	6.21	1,140.78	103.71	1,037.07
13	01/08/2011	105	30608	05	450	7.62	3,771.90	342.90	3,429.00
14	01/08/2011	125	30608	05	35	7.95	230.62	20.97	209.65

Join SSD-3.IMD ×

	INV_DATE	SALESREP	CLIENT_NO	PROD_CODE	QTY	UNIT_PRICE	GROSS_SALE	SALES_TAX	NET_SALE
1	03/02/2011	102	30608	05	25	6.44	177.10	16.10	161.00
2	03/02/2011	105	30608	05	230	7.27	1,839.31	167.21	1,672.10
3	10/03/2011	105	30608	05	1235	7.25	9,849.13	895.38	8,953.75
4	10/03/2011	125	30608	05	35	7.95	306.08	27.83	278.25
5	14/03/2011	105	30501	05	1608	6.03	10,665.87	969.63	9,696.24
6	14/03/2011	105	30501	05	59	6.77	439.38	39.95	399.43
7	14/03/2011	125	30501	05	65	7.68	549.12	49.92	499.20
8	17/03/2011	104	30501	05	594	7.62	0.00	452.63	4,526.28
9	17/03/2011	105	30501	05	59	6.77	388.75	35.34	353.41
10	21/04/2011	102	21646	05	198	7.60	1,655.28	150.48	1,504.80
11	21/04/2011	125	21646	05	389	6.95	2,973.91	270.36	2,703.55
12	04/05/2011	113	60300	05	50	7.82	430.10	39.10	391.00
13	04/05/2011	118	60300	05	250	7.09	1,647.25	149.75	1,497.50
14	31/05/2011	119	92241	05	1400	6.13	9,440.20	858.20	8,582.00
15	21/05/2011	120	92241	05	692	7.60	5,852.62	532.15	5,321.48

FIGURE 5.41 Comparing the Built-In Duplicate Key Exclusion Test and the Manually Created Same-Same-Different Test

If a business system does not process orders in real time, this example may indicate customers attempting to split their orders to avoid exceeding their credit limit (same invoice date, same customer number, same product code, and different sales representatives).

 ## EVEN AMOUNTS

Even or rounded-dollar amounts do not normally occur at high-frequency rates. Therefore numbers that are rounded to tens, hundreds, and thousands may be considered as anomalies and some attention should be given to them.

While it is intuitive that high, even amounts paid should be reviewed, some low amounts may be subject to fraud or abuse. Take, for example, reimbursement of travel expenses. The organization may set maximum amounts for each category of reimbursement. These maximums would likely be in even-dollar amounts. Meals may be subject to certain maximums, such as lunch being set at a maximum of $20.00 and dinner at $50.00. Daily accommodations may be fixed at a maximum of $200.00. To ensure that the maximums are not abused, the claims should be checked against receipts. Valid claims should have receipts that show the maximum amount or are in excess of the maximum amount.

Even amounts need to be identified. This is simple to accomplish in IDEA. We have a large file consisting of payments that contains 2,066,536 records totaling $15,258,988,474.48. We want to identify amounts that are in the even tens of thousands. Using the criteria equation of (PAYMENT_AMOUNT % 10000) = 0 .AND. PAYMENT_AMOUNT < > 0, it takes mere seconds to obtain 1,799 matches of even tens of thousands totaling $402,920,00.00.

The "%" sign in the equation is not the percentage sign, but rather represents the MOD or modulus. The MOD operator is simply the remainder after a calculation. For example, 10 mod 3 would result in 1, which is the remainder of $10 \div 3 = 3$.

In our equation, the payment amount mod by 10,000 will give us a remainder. If the remainder is zero, then we would have even 10,000 amounts. The second condition of the equation of PAYMENT_AMOUNT < > 0 eliminates any amounts that were originally zero in the field. Zero divided by any amount (10,000 in our example) would always return a zero.

To obtain amounts of even tens our equation would be (PAYMENT_AMOUNT % 10) = 0 .AND. PAYMENT_AMOUNT < > 0.

For amounts of even hundreds, our equation would be (PAYMENT_AMOUNT % 100) = 0 .AND. PAYMENT_AMOUNT < > 0.

Finally, to obtain the more popular even thousand amounts, our equations would be (PAYMENT_AMOUNT % 1000) = 0 .AND. PAYMENT_AMOUNT < > 0. The formula is shown in the Equation Editor in Figure 5.42.

It seems that even tens of thousands are significant as shown in the results in Figure 5.43. While only 0.09 percent of the records matched, these records represent 2.64 percent of the total amounts. The results should be visually scanned and the appropriate payments should be reviewed in detail.

Keep in mind that many payment amounts are normally rounded, particularly amounts such as consulting fees or rent. These types of payments would be low-risk anomalies. A sharp eye should be focused on even amounts where rounding is not expected.

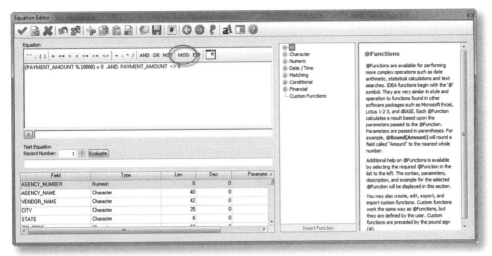

FIGURE 5.42 Isolating Even Tens of Thousands Amounts

FIGURE 5.43 Results of Applying the Even Tens of Thousands Amount Equation

CONCLUSION

This chapter familiarized you with the primary, advanced, and associated tests of Benford's Law. It provided you with an understanding of how it works and some suggested applications. Benford's Law is a good general test that can be applied to most data sets to test for excessive duplications that may be indicators of fraud. IDEA's built-in Benford's Law tests make it simple to use and the results are graphically displayed to give you an excellent visual overview of whether the data conforms to Benford's Law. The graphical view allows you to see how well the data conforms or how much nonconformity exists. It is a good first test to apply to data sets.

With the exception of the same-same-same test that is built into IDEA and known as Duplicate Key Detection, the other tests have to be performed manually. Step-by-step instructions are provided so the reader can apply these procedures. During the step-by-step instructions, the reader is exposed to little-known items, such as using the @FieldStatistics function to calculate Z-score, even amounts extractions using MOD to provide the results, using @Precno to fix a physical record number to each record, how the Duplicate Key Exclusion feature only provides one unique exclusion, and how the same-same-different test can overcome that limitation.

All the tests described in this chapter are powerful and useful to detect and highlight anomalies in data sets. Additional tests are presented in Chapter 6.

 NOTES

1. Mark J. Nigrini, *Forensic Analytics: Methods and Techniques for Forensic Accounting Investigations* (Hoboken, NJ: John Wiley & Sons, 2011).
2. Scott D. J. Graham, John Hasseldine, and David Paton, "Taylor & Francis Online: Statistical Fraud Detection in a Commercial Lobster Fishery," *New Zealand Journal of Marine and Freshwater Research* 43, no. 1 (2009).
3. Andreas Diekmann, "Not the First Digit! Using Benford's Law to Detect Fraudulent Scientific Data," Ideas, July 9, 2005, accessed January 28, 2014, http://ideas.repec.org/p/wpa/wuwpot/0507001.html.
4. Susumu Shikano and Verena Mack, "When Does the Second-Digit Benford's Law-Test Signal an Election Fraud? Facts or Misleading Test Results," Ideas, accessed January 28, 2014, http://ideas.repec.org/a/jns/jbstat/v231y2011i5-6p719-732.html.
5. Mark J. Nigrini, *Benford's Law: Applications for Forensic Accounting, Auditing, and Fraud Detection* (Hoboken, NJ: John Wiley & Sons, 2012).
6. Nigrini, *Forensic Analytics.*
7. Joseph T. Wells, *Principles of Fraud Examination*, 3rd ed. (Hoboken, NJ: John Wiley & Sons, 2011).
8. Nigrini, *Forensic Analytics.*
9. Ibid.

CHAPTER SIX

Advanced Data Analytical Tests

WHILE CORRELATION, TREND ANALYSIS, and times series analyses are considered advanced statistical methods, they are easy to apply within IDEA. These tests are explained and demonstrated in IDEA. Tests to establish relationships between two fields have their procedures shown step by step in this chapter. These advanced data analytical tests are grouped together as they all establish some form of relationship testing.

CORRELATION

A correlation is a relationship between two things or mathematical variables that tend to vary or move together. The data is represented by the letters x and y where x is the independent variable and y is the dependent variable. The independent variable x is usually described first. There is usually some logical connection between the two variables.

Many studies have been done on income levels of high school graduates, college, and university graduates and those with post-graduate degrees. The question in those studies is whether there is a connection or correlation between educational levels and income levels. Educational level would be x, the independent variable that would influence the income level variable of y, the dependent variable.

How much does the independent variable have influence over the dependent variable can be determined by calculating the correlation coefficient and is designated as r. A perfect linear correlation would have r equaling to 1 and a perfect negative correlation would have r equaling −1. The closer r is to 1 or −1, the stronger the correlation. Where there is no correlation, r would equal to 0.

There are three basic formulas for calculating r. The correlation coefficient can be calculated for the population, the sample, or the product moment.

The most common one is the product-moment correlation coefficient as shown.

$$r = \sum (xy)/\text{sqrt}\left[\left(\sum x^2\right) * \left(\sum y^2\right)\right]$$

Σ denotes the summation symbol, so the formula for the top part or numerator is to multiply the x variables by the y variables and then take the sum of those numbers. For the denominator, you square the x variables and take the sum of them. Do the same for the y variables and then multiple the resulting two sums. Apply the square root to the results and then divide the final results of the numerator by the final results of the denominator to obtain the correlation coefficient.

Since we already know how to calculate the Z-scores (or have IDEA calculate it for us), a simpler method of obtaining r would be to multiply the Z-scores of the x variables by the Z-scores of the y variables and then total up all the results. Take the total of the results and divide by the number of records less one.

The formula would be $r = \Sigma(Z_x * Z_y)/(n-1)$ where Z_x is the Z-score for the x variable and Z_y is the Z-score for the y variable. The letter n in the formula represents the number of records.

In general, the correlation coefficient, whether negative or positive, can be interpreted as:

.0 to .2	No correlation
.2 to .4	Weak correlation
.4 to .6	Moderate correlation
.6 to .8	Strong correlation
.8 to 1.0	Very strong correlation

The calculations of the correlation coefficients were shown for a better understanding of correlation. The auditor does not need to perform the calculations using the formulas, as IDEA has a built-in correlation feature that provides the correlation coefficient and you merely have to interpret the results.

Using a summarized monthly sales file from a POS system, we select Correlation from the Statistics area of IDEA. For demonstration purposes, the fields we correlate will be the HD_NETAMOUNT_SUM field, which is the sales amount before taxes, and the PAYAMOUNT_SUM_SUM_SUM field, which are amounts paid that include taxes. We will also include payments of cash only and payments of debit cards only for the correlation calculation as shown in Figure 6.1. In addition to the results being displayed, which can be exported to various file formats, you may optionally create an IDEA database of these results.

As expected, there is a perfect positive correlation of 1.000 between sales before taxes and payments. As sales go up or down, the sales tax moves accordingly, so the total payment by customers correlates to sales net of taxes.

There is a strong correlation between both the cash tender and the debit cards tender to the payment amounts of 0.710 and 0.792, respectively. There is no correlation between cash and debit cards payments as the correlation coefficient is 0.189. See Figure 6.2.

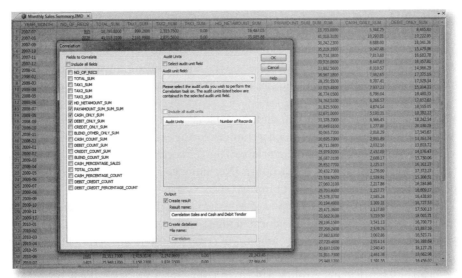

FIGURE 6.1   Applying the Advanced Statistical Analysis Correlation Feature of IDEA

	HD_NETAMOUNT_SUM	PAYAMOUNT_SUM_SUM_SUM	CASH_ONLY_SUM
PAYAMOUNT_SUM_SUM_SUM	1.000		
CASH_ONLY_SUM	0.706	0.710	
DEBIT_ONLY_SUM	0.796	0.792	0.189

Fields : HD_NETAMOUNT_SUM, PAYAMOUNT_SUM_SUM_SUM, CASH_ONLY_SUM, DEBIT_ONLY_SUM

FIGURE 6.2   Correlation Coefficient Results

While IDEA does not calculate the coefficient of determination, it can be done simply by squaring the correlation coefficient that is already calculated for you. The coefficient of determination, or r^2, tells us how much of the variation in one variable can be attributed to the variation of the other variable. This calculation when multiplied by 100 will be expressed in a percentage.

In our example of the correlation between cash tender and the payment amount of 0.710, 50.41 percent ($0.710 \times 0.710 \times 100$) of the variation can be attributed to the other variable.

One has to be mindful that even if the variables are calculated to have a strong correlation, there may not be a cause-and-effect relationship.

Are there direct cause-and-effect relations? That is, does x cause y or, in our previous example, does the level of education cause the income level? Maybe it is a reverse cause and effect where y causes x. That is, income levels determine your education level.

Possibly there is a third variable or a combination of several other variables that caused the relationship, such as networking relationships while in school that resulted in higher paying jobs. Maybe the whole relationship between the two variables was just a coincidence?

TREND ANALYSIS

Trend analysis is based on regression analysis. Regression analysis produces a line of best fit and predictions can be made based on the line. It is also known as the least square line, because the line passes through the distribution where the distance squared from the line is minimized.

Similar to that of correlation, the x variable can estimate or predict the y variable. That is, if x changes, then how much y changes can be estimated. For two numeric variables, you can predict y from the x variable if the the correlation coefficient is strong and there is a linear pattern for the variables. Normally you would want the r correlation coefficient to be better than plus or minus 0.60.

Unless there is perfect correlation, the prediction for the value of y, given x, is merely a prediction. It is a guess but an educated guess with some sound scientific basis. The prediction will be subject to some amount of error. The standard error of the estimate measures how much the predicted values deviate from the actual y values. IDEA uses the mean absolute percent error (MAPE) to calculate the accuracy of predictions. MAPE is the average of the percentage errors, is expressed in percentage terms, and works best with positive amounts. The MAPE number is the predicted line on the average that is away from the actual line in percentages. Low MAPE values mean that the past data has a good fit to the regression line and you can have more confidence in the data and prediction.

To use trend analysis in IDEA, the database needs at least one numeric field, and the field where trend analysis is to be applied cannot contain any bad data. The database cannot contain more than 65,536 records. The audit unit field cannot be the same field as the trend analysis field. In addition, the database should not contain seasonal data. If it contains seasonal data, then time series analysis should be selected over trend analysis. time series works similarly to trend analysis.

In our data file, we will perform trend analysis on the 12-month data from the debit card payments field of DEBIT_2010_2011 and generate 3 months of forecasts. It is not necessary to provide a reference field or audit units. Refer to Figure 6.3.

For debit card payments, it is trending slightly downward, and it is predicted that at the end of the three months, debit payments would drop to approximately $18,000 for that month as seen in Figure 6.4.

The MAPE is 5.36 percent, which provides high confidence as the reliability of the predictions.

In contrast to the debit card payments, cash payments are trending upward when we select CASH_2010_2011 as the field to trend.

There is less reliability in the prediction as the MAPE percentage is 23.17. It is predicted that at the end of the three months, cash payments would increase to approximately $14,500, as displayed in Figure 6.5. We discuss this increase more in Chapter 16 regarding zapper fraud.

We will perform a trend analysis showing a reference field and audit units. There are five branches and we will include all of them as audit units. The reference field of GLOBAL_AVERAGE_SALES is the average sales for the five stores broken down by months. We have eight years of data so each store would have 96 records (8 years × 12 months). We will generate forecasts for three months as shown in Figure 6.6.

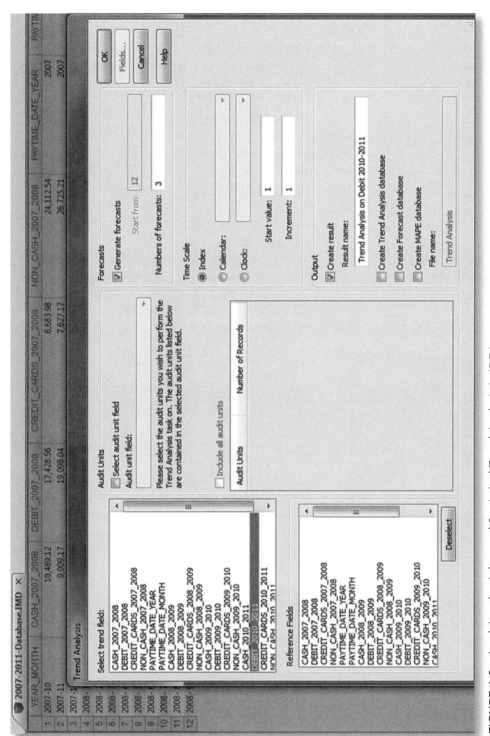

FIGURE 6.3 Applying the Advanced Statistical Trend Analysis in IDEA

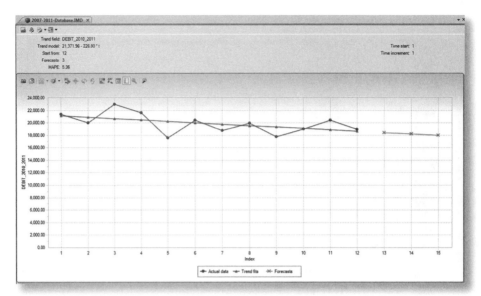

FIGURE 6.4 Trend Analysis Results of Debit Card Payments with Forecast of Three Months

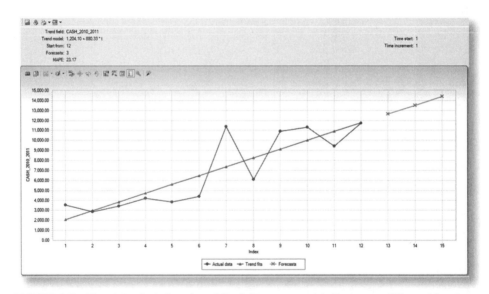

FIGURE 6.5 Trend Analysis Results of Cash Payments with Forecast of Three Months

Branch A outperformed the average of the five branches. The actual data is above the reference data line and shows good promise of trending upward in Figure 6.7. The prediction is sound as the MAPE is 5.26 percent.

By selecting all five branches as the audit unit, we can display other branches by choosing from the Audit unit pull-down menu. We will look at one more by selecting

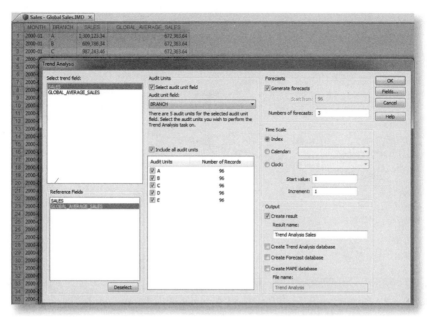

FIGURE 6.6 Applying Trend Analysis of Sales Referencing Global Average Sales for Each Branch

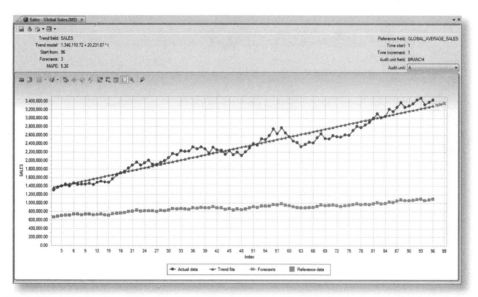

FIGURE 6.7 Results of Branch *A*'s Trend Analysis with Three-Months Forecast

branch *B* (see Figure 6.8). Branch *B* fits right in around the global average sales and is also trending up.

For data with seasonal values where there are higher values in certain months (or any other time units) and lower values in other months, the time series analysis option is more appropriate. In our example in Figure 6.9, we will use gas-heating costs as the

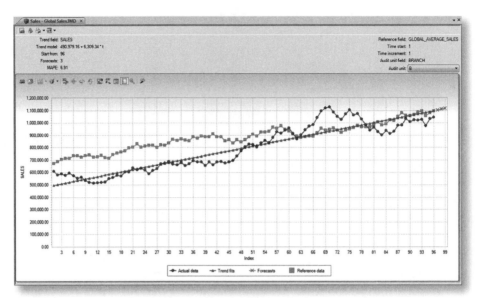

FIGURE 6.8 Results of Branch *B*'s Trend Analysis with Three-Month Forecast

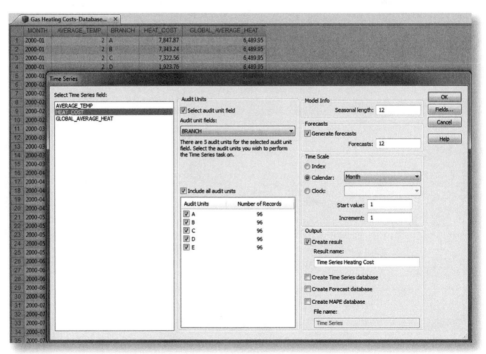

FIGURE 6.9 Applying Time Series Trend Analysis of Heating Costs for Each Branch with 12-Month Forecast

field for the time series and all five branches as the audit units. We ensure that we input the correct season length of 12 as our records are broken down by months. We will generate 12 months of forecasts.

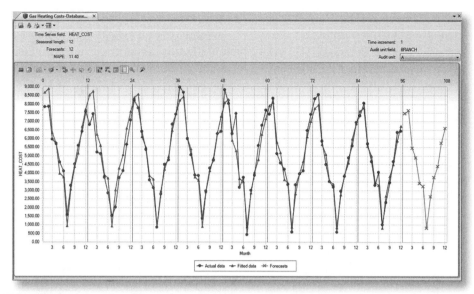

FIGURE 6.10 Results of Branch *A*'s Time Series Trend Analysis with 12-Month Forecast

From the chart in Figure 6.10, you can see that heating costs are higher in the winter months and lower in the summer months for branch *A*. The mean absolute percentage error of 11.40% is fairly reliable in terms of the forecast. You can also view the other branches by using the pull-down menus from the Audit unit area.

Trend analysis using IDEA is simple and the auditor need not be concerned with the complex formulas to calculate the regression line and the mean average percentage error.

GEL-1 AND GEL-2

The purpose of the GEL tests (GEL-1 and GEL-2) is to detect the relationship or link within the data file as potential indicators of fraud.

The GEL tests establish the link between two selected fields with the first field being the key field and the second field being the element factor over the entire data set.

GEL is short for the gestalt element link. *Gestalt* is defined by the online *Merriam-Webster* dictionary as:

> a structure, configuration, or pattern of physical, biological, or psychological phenomena so integrated as to constitute a functional unit with properties not derivable by summation of its parts.[1]

An example for using GEL tests is to detect bribery or improper relationships. Since most entities do not have access to the records of the payer company, their own data can be analyzed to detect improper relationship patterns.

The following GEL-1 example depicts testing of potential links between the sales representatives and their customers. A high GEL factor may be an indicator of an improper relationship or merely that certain sales representatives are assigned certain customers. A good understanding of the business practices and procedures is necessary to properly interpret the results.

GEL-1

The example uses the "Sales Transactions" database that contains the fields SALESREP (sales representative) and CLIENT_NO (client or customer number). We want to know the number of transactions each sales representative had with each client expressed as a ratio. The higher the GEL-1 ratio, the more transactions were done with the particular client that may indicate a special relationship.

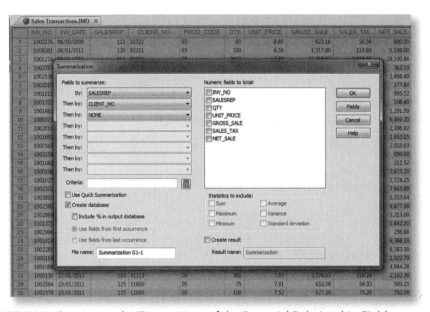

FIGURE 6.11 Summarize the Transactions of the Potential Relationship Fields

Step 1. Summarize by SALESREP and then CLIENT_NO and name the new file "Summarization G1-1." Note that the file name contains the step identification to keep tracking simpler as shown in Figure 6.11. This step creates a file that shows how many records or transactions there are for each sales representative by client.

Step 2. Append a field named REC_NO using the @Recno( ) function shown in Figure 6.12. Associating the record number is necessary to properly join the file together later.

Step 3. Obtain the highest number of records or transactions by sales representative. Use the Top Records Extraction feature to obtain the top-most record for NO_OF_RECS grouped by SALESREP as in Figure 6.13. Name the file "Top Records G1-3."

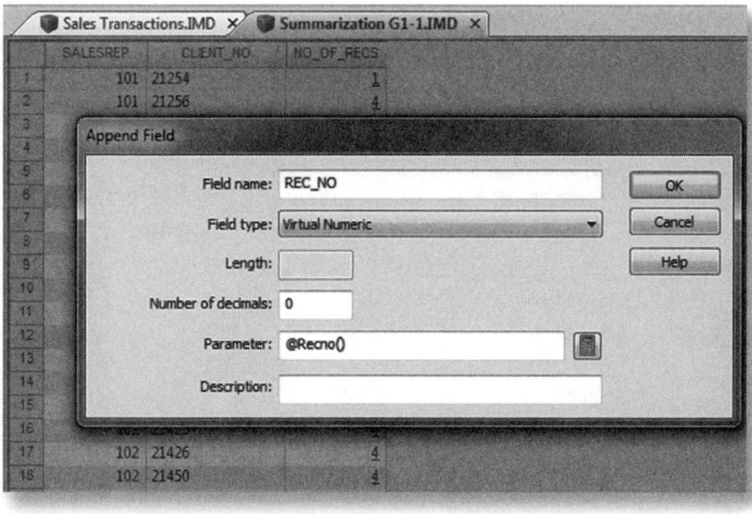

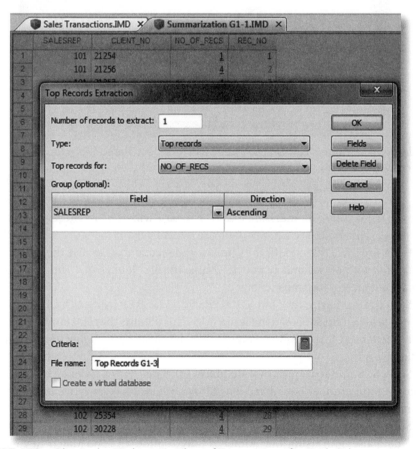

FIGURE 6.12 Create a Record Number Field

FIGURE 6.13 Obtain the Highest Number of Transactions for Each Sales
Representative

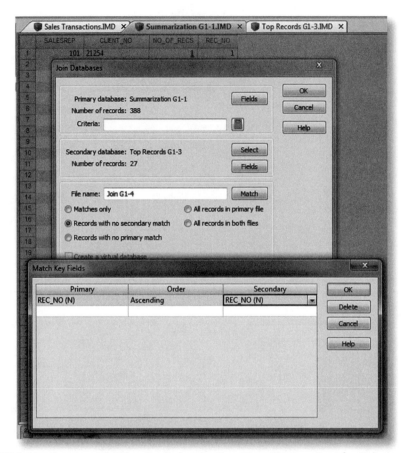

FIGURE 6.14 Create a File That Excludes the Top-Most Transactions for Sales Representatives

Step 4. Join the "Summarization G1-1" database with the "Top Records G1-3" database as the primary and secondary database respectively, as in Figure 6.14. The Match Key Fields are REC_NO for both the primary and secondary files. Use the match option of "Records with no secondary match." Name the file "Join G1-4." The result is those records that are not top transactions.

Step 5. Summarize the "Join G1-4" file by SALESREP using NO_OF_RECS as the numeric field to total as shown in Figure 6.15. This obtains the total number of records or transactions by SALESREP, excluding the top transactions. Name the file "Summarization G1-5."

Step 6. Summarize original database of "Sales Transactions" by SALESREP to obtain total number of transactions for each sales representative as displayed in Figure 6.16. Name this file "Summarization G1-6."

Step 7. Join as primary database, "Summarization G1-5" with the "Top Records G1-3" database. Join using the "Matches only" option and the Match Key Fields as SALESREP, as shown in Figure 6.17. We do not need all the fields from both the primary and secondary files. In fact, retaining all the fields would create confusion. By selecting

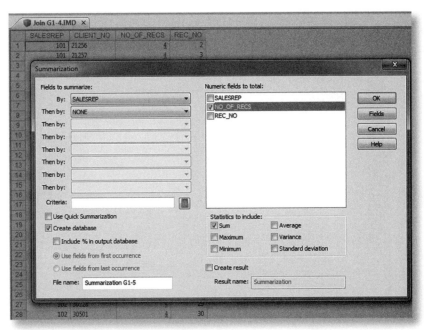

FIGURE 6.15 Obtain the Total Number of Transactions by Sales Representatives Excluding the Top-Most Transactions

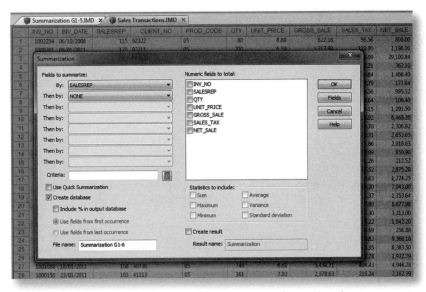

FIGURE 6.16 Obtain the Total Number of Transactions for Each Sales Representative from the Original Sales File

the Fields button for the primary file, choose the SALESREP field. Fields to include from the secondary file are NO_OF_RECS and CLIENT_NO. This results in a file that has the top transactions for each client. Name this file "Join G1-7."

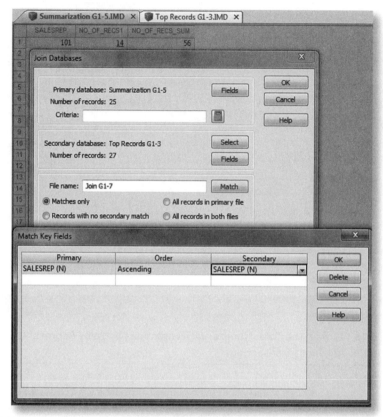

FIGURE 6.17 Create a File with the Top Transactions for Each Client

Step 8. Rename the field NO_OF_RECS to TRAN_PER_FREQ_CLIENT_NO to display the number of transactions with the sales representatives' most frequent clients. Refer to Figure 6.18.

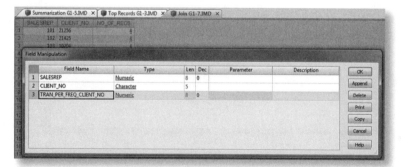

FIGURE 6.18 Identify the Number of Client Transactions by Renaming the Number of Records Field

Step 9. Make "Join G1-7" as the primary database and join it with "Summarization G1-6" as the secondary file using the "Matches only" option shown in Figure 6.19. The Match Key Fields is SALESREP. Include from the primary database all fields and only the NO_OF_RECS field from the secondary file. Name the file "Join G1-9." The resulting file will have total transactions and top-items transactions.

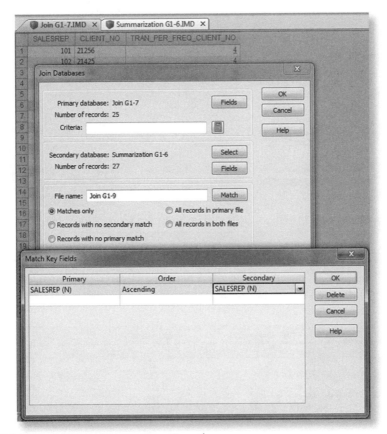

FIGURE 6.19 Put All the Transactions Together

Step 10. Rename the NO_OF_RECS field to TOTAL_FOR_SALESREP as in Figure 6.20.

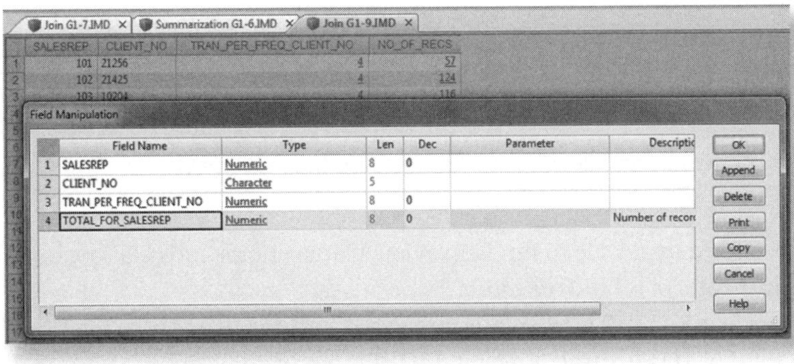

FIGURE 6.20 Rename the Number of Records Field to Identify the Total Transactions for Each Sales Representative

Step 11. There is one final step to obtain the ratio that we are looking for. Append or create a field called GEL_1 with four decimal places, using the equation of TRAN_PER_FREQ_CUSTOMER_NO/TOTAL_FOR_SALESREP as shown in Figure 6.21.

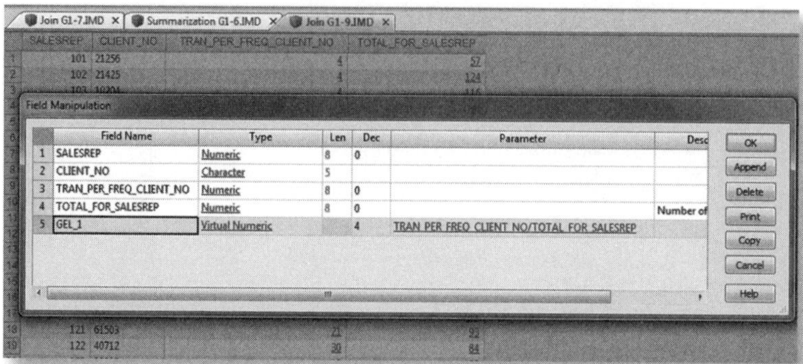

FIGURE 6.21 Create the GEL-1 Field and Perform the Calculation

The final file is shown in Figure 6.22 with the GEL_1 ratio indexed by descending order to display the highest to the lowest. A high GEL_1 ratio shows an overview of the link between the sales representative and clients.

Join G1-7.IMD | Summarization G1-6.IMD | Join G1-9.IMD

	SALESREP	CLIENT_NO	TRAN_PER_FREQ_CLIENT_NO	TOTAL_FOR_SALESREP	GEL_1
1	119	92241	93	96	0.9688
2	117	92326	93	99	0.9394
3	110	92431	143	167	0.8563
4	108	40730	132	164	0.8049
5	105	30608	120	160	0.7500
6	115	92323	57	96	0.5938
7	113	60300	54	105	0.5143
8	118	60300	48	111	0.4324
9	122	40712	30	84	0.3571
10	120	92100	39	114	0.3421
11	107	40312	36	120	0.3000
12	128	20914	15	51	0.2941
13	127	20954	27	105	0.2571
14	121	61503	21	93	0.2258
15	125	11600	27	138	0.1957
16	104	10201	28	164	0.1707
17	124	12203	12	72	0.1667
18	126	21139	21	153	0.1373
19	123	20005	12	93	0.1290

FIGURE 6.22 Resulting File with the GEL-1 Ratio Indexed by Descending Order

The auditor may decide to further review transactions and relationships for those with a GEL_1 ratio of 0.6000 or more.

For instance, SALESREP 105 falls into this criterion with a GEL_1 factor of 0.7500. He had a total of 160 transactions but 120 of them were with CLIENT_NO 30608. In other words, 75 percent of SALESREP 105 transactions or sales were with one customer. He only had 40 transactions with other customers. Further analysis is needed.

GEL-2

The GEL-2 test can provide additional information on specific sales representatives and their clients. In this example, we will continue to focus on sales representative 105.

Step 1. First, extract all records from the "Sales Transactions" database for sales representative 105. Use the equation or criterion of SALESREP = = 105, as in Figure 6.23. Name this file "G2-1."

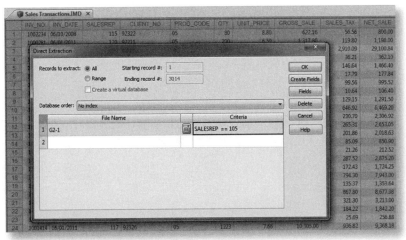

FIGURE 6.23 Create a File with All Transactions for Sales Representative Number 105

Step 2. Summarize by CLIENT_NO, in Figure 6.24, to obtain number of unique clients for this particular sales representative. Name the file "Summarization G2-2"; it should have the results shown in Figure 6.25.

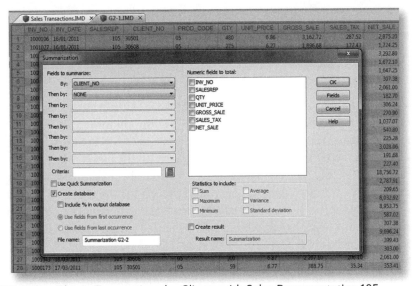

FIGURE 6.24 Obtain Transactions by Clients with Sales Representative 105

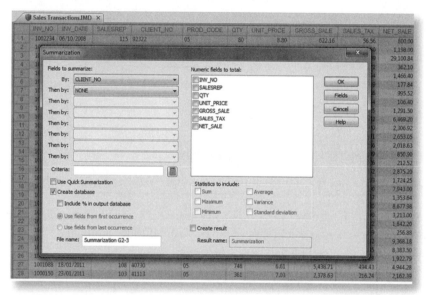

FIGURE 6.25 Resulting File of Transactions by Clients with Sales Representative 105

Step 3. Summarize the "Sales Transactions" database by CLIENT_NO to obtain the total transactions for each client as in Figure 6.26. Name this file "Summarization G2-3."

FIGURE 6.26 Create a File with Transactions by Clients from the Sales Transaction Database with All Sales Representatives

Step 4. Join the "Summarization G2-2" database as the primary database to the "Summarization G2-3" database as in Figure 6.27. The "Summarization G2-3" is the secondary database. Use the "Matches only" option and CLIENT_NO as the Match Key Fields to attach the total transactions per customers to the file. Name this file "GEL 2 Salesrep 105 G2-4." Having the sales representative number in the filename allows you to easily identify the sales representative you were applying the GEL-2 test to. Since the auditor decided that the GEL-1 ratio cut-off was 0.6000, individual GEL-2 tests of sales representatives 108, 110, 117, and 119 would be needed as they all exceeded the cut-off ratio as shown in Figure 6.22.

Step 5. Rename the NO_OF_RECS1 field to TOTAL_NO_OF_RECS as in Figure 6.28.

Step 6. Append the GEL_2 field with four decimal places using the equation of NO_OF_RECS/TOTAL_NO_OF_RECS to produce the GEL_2 ratio as seen in Figure 6.29.

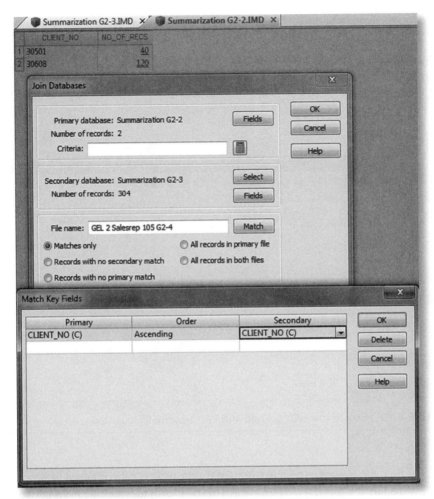

FIGURE 6.27   Put All the Information Together

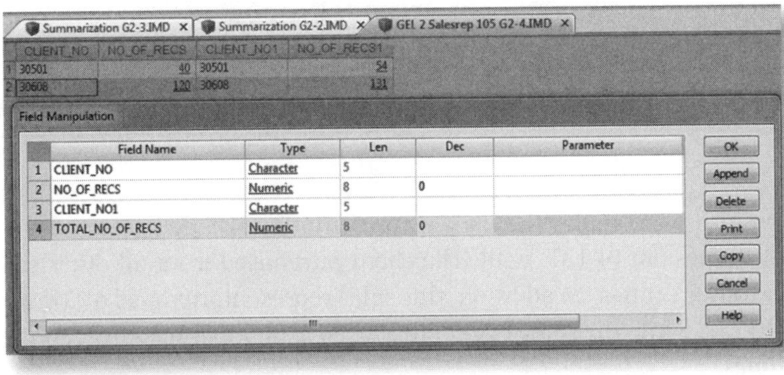

FIGURE 6.28   Identifying the Total Number of Records by Renaming the Additional Number of Records Field

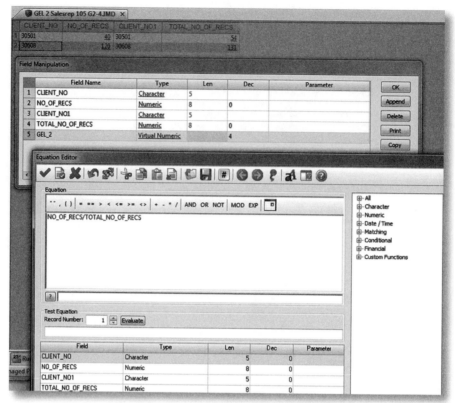

FIGURE 6.29 Create the GEL_2 Field and Perform the Calculation

The final file is shown in Figure 6.30, with the GEL_2 ratio indexed by descending order to display the highest to the lowest. This ratio provides specific links between the sales representative and his or her clients.

	CLIENT_NO	NO_OF_RECS	CLIENT_NO1	TOTAL_NO_OF_RECS	GEL_2
1	30608	120	30608	131	0.9160
2	30501	40	30501	54	0.7407

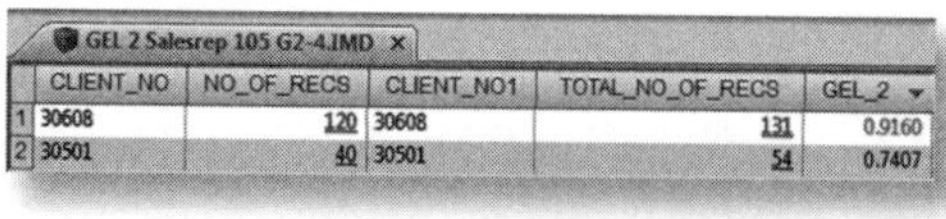

FIGURE 6.30 Resulting File with the GEL_2 Ratio Indexed by Descending Order

The resulting file shows that sales representative 105 dealt with client number 30608 120 times out of 131, while the client purchased from all other sales representatives only 11 times. In addition, this sales representative sold 40 times to client number 30501, while the same client purchased from all other sales representatives only 14 times.

Clearly, there is a strong business relationship between this sales representative and clients 30608 and 30501. Additional investigation is needed to determine whether this relationship is of benefit to the company or of benefit to the sales representative and the clients to the detriment of the company.

Additional steps can be added to this GEL-2 example that provide more information, such as gross sales amounts totals. The objective was to ensure that the reader understands the concept and steps without added complexities. An IDEAScript has been developed to automate the GEL-1 and GEL-2 processes that provide the additional relevant information shown in Figure 6.31. The IDEAScript is available on the companion website.

FIGURE 6.31   Final Result of the GEL-2 Test

Applying the two GEL tests against an accounts payable file and analyzing the Check Authorized By field and the Vendor field can indicate favorable status given to some vendors by the authorizing personnel. It may also provide an indication of a money-laundering or a disbursement scheme.

Applying the GEL-1 test to a corporate credit card file may reveal some red flags when the following field combinations are selected.

1. Employee ID versus general ledger account number.
2. Employee ID versus vendor ID (business name).
3. Employee ID versus vendor location (city, province/state, or country). Low GEL ratios should be reviewed.
4. Vendor ID versus employee ID.

The GEL-2 test can be then be run against the selected results above.

Using the GEL-1 test on a sales file from a point-of-sales system for EMPLOYEEID (or SERVERID) field with the order date field may indicate the suppression of sales invoices for certain employees. A low GEL ratio, where the number of transactions is low compared to total transactions for the day, should be analyzed by employing GEL-2 on specific EMPLOYEEID. Was the employee on a short shift, and did not serve many tables, or were there other unexplained anomalies that require investigation?

 CONCLUSION

This chapter outlines some advanced data analytical tests that provide relationship information. Correlation calculates how well or poorly two variables or data set fields move together in relationship to each other. Trend analysis shows how the trend line fits with the actual data and can make predictions based on the analysis. These two procedures are simple to apply as they are built into the IDEA software.

The two GEL tests were developed by Gee, Element, and Luciani to establish a relationship link between two fields within a data set. While the steps may be numerous, especially for the GEL-1 test, they are well worth doing as there is a potential for ferreting out previously unseen ties or relationships. The step-by-step procedures outlined allow the reader to understand what can be accomplished with the IDEA software and understand exactly how the GEL procedures work. An IDEAScript has been created to allow all these procedures to be processed automatically just by applying the script. Well-written scripts can be applied effectively even by the most novice of users. Further IDEAScript information is provided in Chapter 17.

Having outlined data analytical tests in detail in this chapter and in Chapter 5, we move on to specific fraud schemes and how data analytics can detect them.

 NOTE

1. *Merriam-Webster Dictionary*, "Gestalt," accessed April 19, 2014, www.merriam-webster .com/dictionary/gestalt.

CHAPTER SEVEN

7

Skimming and Cash Larceny

W HEN WE HEAR ABOUT skimming fraud in the news these days, it is usually related to the theft of credit or debit card information using an electronic device that skims or reads and stores customer credit card information from the magnetic stripe on the cards. With the advent of chip technology, where the customer has to enter a personal identification number (PIN) to complete a transaction, skimming magnetic stripes has moved on to skimming radio-frequency identification (RFID) tags information embedded in new credit cards. RFID transactions are for small currency transactions that need no signature or PIN.

When we speak about skimming, we are talking in the more traditional sense of removing cash prior to the cash being entered into the business system. This differs from cash larceny where the cash is stolen after it is recorded in the business system. Because of the recording processes, larceny is much simpler to detect than skimming as it leaves audit trails.

SKIMMING

Any employee who handles cash is in a position to skim. This includes bank tellers, sales staff, waitstaff, parking attendants, apartment managers, and others whose duties include the collection of cash from customers.

It is not only employees that may skim, but owners of the business have incentives to skim also. It may be to reduce obligations such as retaining sales taxes collected or to reduce income taxes or royalties payable. It may also be to create a slush fund to make unrecorded payments such as bribes.

Skimming can occur when cash is removed from the mail or from the cash register till. The simplest form is by just not entering the sale at all. Have you ever noticed that when you purchase a single item at grocery stores or fast-food stalls and the cash register was still opened from the last transactions, the cashier might not ring up your sale, take your cash, and give you change? You should carefully check your change, as you might also be short-changed, either on purpose or by accident, when the cashier has to do the math manually. Sales could also be recorded for a lesser amount than actually charged and the difference pocketed. Recording discounts or larger than normal discounts that are not offered to the customer also puts cash into the employee's pocket while still balancing with the cash register.

Excessive refunds, price adjustments, discounts, voids, and no-sale transactions should be reviewed carefully on an employee-by-employee basis as these transactions may be related to skimming.

A sophisticated, but less successful, form of not having the sale show up on the cash register tape includes removing the print ribbon temporarily; another scheme is to remove the after-hours sales recorded on register tapes and insert a fresh, blank roll for regular hours. While this may have worked in the past, modern cash registers or electronic cash registers have built in Z and X totals that cannot be accessed or reset without a physical key or access codes. Even if sales are not printed on the cash register tape, the amounts are still cumulated in the Z and X totals, as discussed in Chapter 16 on zapper fraud. These totals would not then reconcile to the amounts shown (or not shown) on the tape.

CASH LARCENY

Cash larceny can include both cash and other negotiable items such as checks. It can take place at the point of sales, during the bank deposit process, or during incoming payments for accounts receivable. Since the revenues are recorded on the books already, it takes additional efforts to cover up any significant amounts of larceny.

Small amounts taken from the cash register till are normally accepted by the organization and written off as cash shortages. This occurs in any type of organization that transacts in cash. There will always be some errors where the customers paid too much or too little by mistake. Customers may not know that they were given too much change or undercharged, but even if they are aware, they may not complain when it is in their favor.

Other forms of covering up may be taking the cash from someone else's cash register or reversing recorded sales as voids or refunds.

Proceeds from a sale can be retained by the employee if the employee can debit the accounts receivable of a fictitious account or another real account that is due to be written off as a bad debt. If the employee can have the equivalent amount taken offset by recording discounts of the same total amount, the books remain balanced. In cases where receipts for cash payments are issued but no receipts are issued for payment by checks, checks can be substituted for cash taken and the receipts register would still reconcile to the total.

CASE STUDY

We will use the sample sales files included with the IDEA software. There are sales for two separate years. The current year sales file is called "Sample—Detailed Sales" with 2011 transactions and the other is called "Sample—Detailed Previous Year" and contains transactions for 2010.

The files each have 10 fields, including an invoice date field, as shown in Figure 7.1. We may be performing analysis based on the month of the sale, so we append an eleventh field called MONTH, using the function and equation of @Month(INV_DATE) to isolate the month from within the invoice date field.

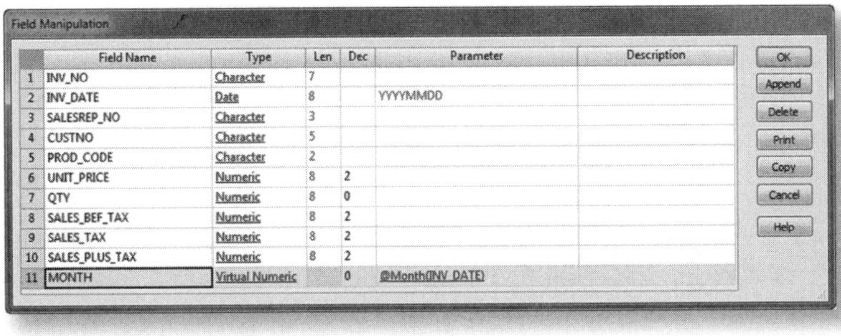

Field Manipulation

	Field Name	Type	Len	Dec	Parameter	Description
1	INV_NO	Character	7			
2	INV_DATE	Date	8		YYYYMMDD	
3	SALESREP_NO	Character	3			
4	CUSTNO	Character	5			
5	PROD_CODE	Character	2			
6	UNIT_PRICE	Numeric	8	2		
7	QTY	Numeric	8	0		
8	SALES_BEF_TAX	Numeric	8	2		
9	SALES_TAX	Numeric	8	2		
10	SALES_PLUS_TAX	Numeric	8	2		
11	MONTH	Virtual Numeric		0	@Month(INV_DATE)	

FIGURE 7.1 Fields for Both the 2011 and 2010 Sample Detailed Sales Files

A review of the field statistics for both years shows that there was only one negative sales amount in 2011 and no negative amounts in 2010. Also of interest was that in 2010, there were significant sales being done on the weekend and less so in 2011.

We can summarize each of the detailed sales files using various keys that will provide us with additional information. First we can summarize by the sale representative and total on the sales before taxes. We can then apply the Z-score, as discussed in Chapter 5, to see how far the total sales for each sales representative is away from the mean for each of the two years.

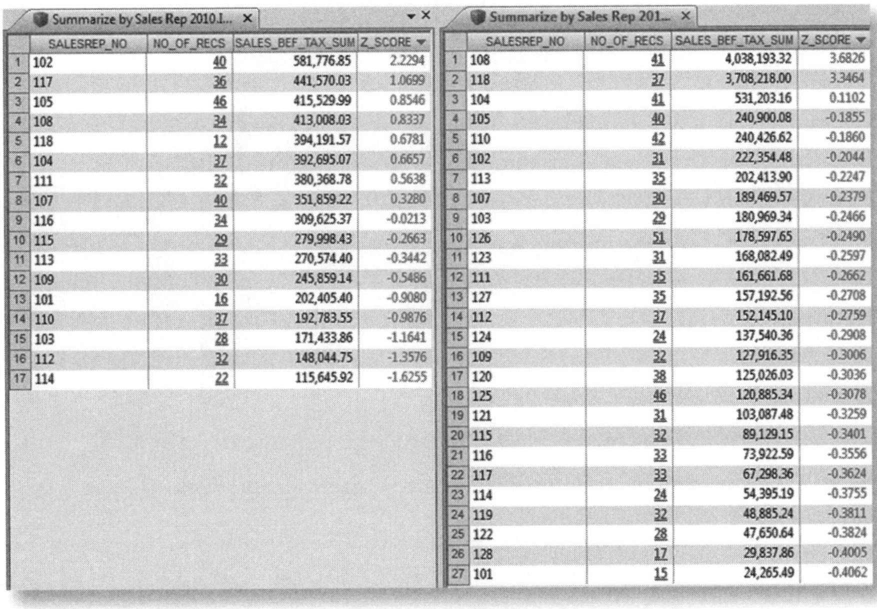

Summarize by Sales Rep 2010.I...

	SALESREP_NO	NO_OF_RECS	SALES_BEF_TAX_SUM	Z_SCORE
1	102	40	581,776.85	2.2294
2	117	36	441,570.03	1.0699
3	105	46	415,529.99	0.8546
4	108	34	413,008.03	0.8337
5	118	12	394,191.57	0.6781
6	104	37	392,695.07	0.6657
7	111	32	380,368.78	0.5638
8	107	40	351,859.22	0.3280
9	116	34	309,625.37	-0.0213
10	115	29	279,998.43	-0.2663
11	113	33	270,574.40	-0.3442
12	109	30	245,859.14	-0.5486
13	101	16	202,405.40	-0.9080
14	110	37	192,783.55	-0.9876
15	103	28	171,433.86	-1.1641
16	112	32	148,044.75	-1.3576
17	114	22	115,645.92	-1.6255

Summarize by Sales Rep 201...

	SALESREP_NO	NO_OF_RECS	SALES_BEF_TAX_SUM	Z_SCORE
1	108	41	4,038,193.32	3.6826
2	118	37	3,708,218.00	3.3464
3	104	41	531,203.16	0.1102
4	105	40	240,900.08	-0.1855
5	110	42	240,426.62	-0.1860
6	102	31	222,354.48	-0.2044
7	113	35	202,413.90	-0.2247
8	107	30	189,469.57	-0.2379
9	103	29	180,969.34	-0.2466
10	126	51	178,597.65	-0.2490
11	123	31	168,082.49	-0.2597
12	111	35	161,661.68	-0.2662
13	127	35	157,192.56	-0.2708
14	112	37	152,145.10	-0.2759
15	124	24	137,540.36	-0.2908
16	109	32	127,916.35	-0.3006
17	120	38	125,026.03	-0.3036
18	125	46	120,885.34	-0.3078
19	121	31	103,087.48	-0.3259
20	115	32	89,129.15	-0.3401
21	116	33	73,922.59	-0.3556
22	117	33	67,298.36	-0.3624
23	114	24	54,395.19	-0.3755
24	119	32	48,885.24	-0.3811
25	122	28	47,650.64	-0.3824
26	128	17	29,837.86	-0.4005
27	101	15	24,265.49	-0.4062

FIGURE 7.2 Summarized by Sales Representatives' Totals on Sales before Taxes with Z-Scores

Having set the view to vertically display the two files with the 2010 summary on the left side and the 2011 summary on the right side, as in Figure 7.2, we can see that, in 2011, ten additional sales representatives were hired. They were assigned the numbers of 119 to 128.

For 2010, the Z-scores on sales before taxes for each sales representative do not have exceptionally positive or negative swings away from the mean or center of the amounts. The sales representatives with high negative Z-scores can be examined for potential skimming and those with high positive Z-scores should be examined for potential commission fraud as discussed in Chapter 10. For 2011, sales representatives number 108 and 118 each have a high Z-score above 3.00, which is unexpected. These Z-scores were calculated on sales. To detect potential skimming or larceny, Z-scores should also be performed on refunds, price adjustments, voids, and returns where the information is available.

The two summarized files can be combined by using the Join feature of IDEA.

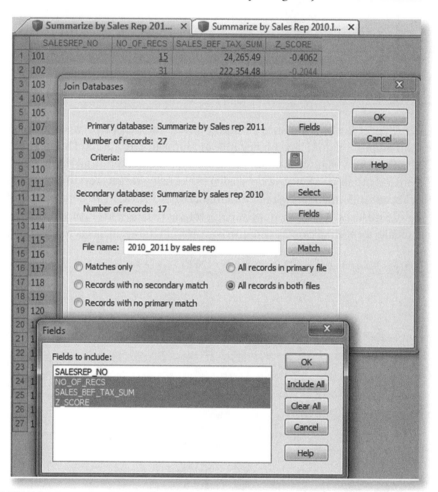

FIGURE 7.3 Preparing to Join the 2010 and 2011 Summarized Files by Sales Representatives

The primary file selected is the 2011 file with the 2010 file as the secondary file. For the secondary file, we will select all fields to bring in with the exception of the SALESREP_NO field as shown in Figure 7.3. IDEA will add a number 1 to the field name from the secondary file if it encounters an identical field name in the primary file. The fields can be renamed after the join to something more meaningful. We will match on the SALESREP_NO field.

	SALESREP_NO	NO_OF_RECS_2011	SALES_BEF_TAX_2011	Z_SCORE_2011	NO_OF_RECS_2010	SALES_BEF_TAX_2010	Z_SCORE_2010
1	101	15	24,265.49	-0.4062	16	202,405.40	-0.9080
2	102	31	222,354.48	-0.2044	40	581,776.85	2.2294
3	103	29	180,969.34	-0.2466	28	171,433.86	-1.1641
4	104	41	531,203.16	0.1102	37	392,695.07	0.6657
5	105	40	240,900.08	-0.1855	46	415,529.99	0.8546
6	107	30	189,469.57	-0.2379	40	351,859.22	0.3280
7	108	41	4,038,193.32	3.6826	34	413,008.03	0.8337
8	109	32	127,916.35	-0.3006	30	245,859.14	-0.5486
9	110	42	240,426.62	-0.1860	37	192,783.55	-0.9876
10	111	35	161,661.68	-0.2662	32	380,368.78	0.5638
11	112	37	152,145.10	-0.2759	32	148,044.75	-1.3576
12	113	35	202,413.90	-0.2247	33	270,574.40	-0.3442
13	114	24	54,395.19	-0.3755	22	115,645.92	-1.6255
14	115	32	89,129.15	-0.3401	29	279,998.43	-0.2663
15	116	33	73,922.59	-0.3556	34	309,625.37	-0.0213
16	117	33	67,298.36	-0.3624	36	441,570.03	1.0699
17	118	37	3,708,218.00	3.3464	12	394,191.57	0.6781
18	119	32	48,885.24	-0.3811	0	0.00	0.00
19	120	38	125,026.03	-0.3036	0	0.00	0.00
20	121	31	103,087.48	-0.3259	0	0.00	0.00
21	122	28	47,650.64	-0.3824	0	0.00	0.00
22	123	31	168,082.49	-0.2597	0	0.00	0.00
23	124	24	137,540.36	-0.2908	0	0.00	0.00
24	125	46	120,885.34	-0.3078	0	0.00	0.00
25	126	51	178,597.65	-0.2490	0	0.00	0.00
26	127	35	157,192.56	-0.2708	0	0.00	0.00
27	128	17	29,837.86	-0.4005	0	0.00	0.00

FIGURE 7.4   Results of the Join

We had renamed the fields to include the year for ease of identification as displayed in Figure 7.4. By using the chart feature, a visual comparison would give us better insights.

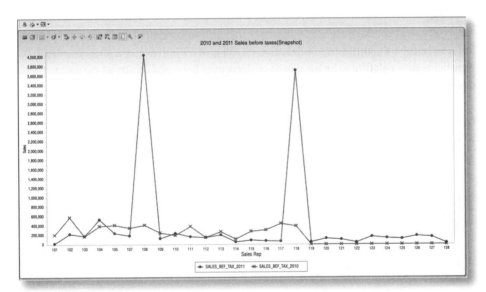

FIGURE 7.5   Chart Comparing Sale Representative Sales for 2010 and 2011

Sales differences between the two years can be easily compared. It is obvious from Figure 7.5 that the two most significant changes were for sales representative 108 and 118. We can also see the less-startling spread between the two years of the other sales representatives. Some sales representatives may need to be reviewed in more detail as to why the change in increased or decreased sales.

Another chart of interest would be the number of records or transactions comparison of each sales representative for the two years.

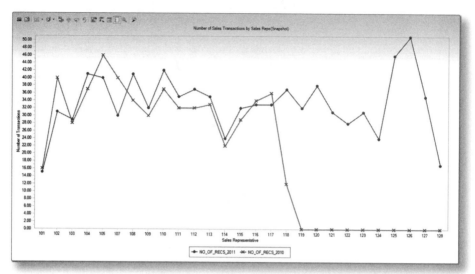

FIGURE 7.6 Comparison of the Number of Sales by Sales Representatives for 2010 and 2011

Sales representative 108 did not have a significant increase in the number of sales, whereas sales representative 118 not only had an improvement in the number of sales but also in the total amount of sales, as seen in Figure 7.6. If desired, you can create two new fields that calculate the increases or decreases between the two years. One can be done for the number of records and the other on the sales amounts.

Since we had created a month field in the detailed sales database, we can create a new file by first summarizing on the SALESREP_NO field and then by the MONTH field totaling on the SALES_BEF_TAX field. The results can be viewed using IDEA's Pivot Table feature.

Sample-Detailed Sales.IMD | Summarize by rep and mont...

Drop Page Fields Here

Sum: SALES_ MONTH

SALESR	1	2	3	4	5	6	7	8	9	10	11	12	Total
101			7,176.02	2,198.33	2,995.00	7,894.82	431.28		1,874.87			1,695.17	24,265.49
102	7,313.79	35,850.15	43,827.41	149.75	4,929.77	1,164.56	3,538.70	21,414.25	98,835.00	3,594.00	1,647.25	89.85	222,354.48
103	10,338.74		101,231.00	8,080.51	9,379.80	4,181.02	15,118.76	898.50	21,719.74	7,104.14	2,467.88	449.25	180,969.34
104	3,929.44	1,497.50	19,695.12	11,400.28	44,371.09	6,337.42	16,107.11		2,725.45	275,288.53	149,036.58	814.64	531,203.16
105	299.50	8,460.96	15,709.72	6,840.58	28,629.69	13,806.95	6,517.12	7,589.33	135,267.91	16,610.27	1,168.05		240,900.08
107	22,282.80		1,557.40	179.70	4,905.74	8,697.48	19,605.27	2,396.00		20,144.37	85,812.74	23,888.07	189,468.57
108		1,605.32	3,899,925.00	1,994.67	7,182.01	12,573.01	40,875.76	12,453.21	4,762.05	8,350.06	45,776.73	2,695.50	4,038,193.32
109		700.83	52,855.66	12,309.45	365.39	5,900.15	37,497.40	11,572.68	1,209.98	4,869.87	634.94		127,916.35
110		4,234.93	664.89	1,880.86	39,036.83	9,793.65	33,010.89	12,537.07	16,370.67	110,102.19	5,253.23	7,541.41	240,426.62
111	898.50	6,201.22	9,503.40		7,307.80	2,252.24	85,847.41	7,026.27		16,484.48	8,302.14	17,838.22	161,661.68
112	1,090.18	850.58		62,230.11	4,097.16	6,690.83	26,510.84	4,091.17	11,081.50	1,635.27	33,268.46	599.00	152,145.10
113		6,493.16		15,010.94	30,231.53	1,186.02	12,990.91	6,589.00	8,799.31	112,151.99	53.91	8,907.13	202,413.90
114	15,603.95	4,857.89		14,118.43	1,371.71	2,485.85	4,450.57	47.92	4,276.86	3,168.71		4,013.30	54,395.19
115		479.20	2,461.89	14,929.70		4,841.91	26,223.55	6,319.45	8,326.10	12,027.92	2,090.51	11,428.92	89,129.15
116	4,318.79	18,329.40	1,976.70	3,755.73	3,462.22	11.98	4,756.06	13,124.09	299.50	2,114.47	1,371.71	20,401.94	73,922.59
117	634.94		1,245.92	21,012.92		1,293.84	6,356.10	12,171.68	6,091.83	14,034.57	1,904.82	2,551.74	67,298.36
118	1,257.90	3,611.97	3,692.60	2,713.47	3,444.25		3,552,175.74	2,701.49	4,396.66	10,943.73	18,940.38	104,339.81	3,708,218.00
119		3,894.35	2,737.43	3,450.24	527.12	4,690.17	8,571.69	13,297.80	4,702.15	1,862.89	3,114.80	2,036.60	48,885.24
120		13,932.74	1,952.74	5,145.41	10,251.93	4,133.10	23,510.46	10,159.04	4,193.00	16,041.22	10,057.21	25,649.18	125,026.03
121		1,497.50	1,030.28	13,303.05	25,729.48	1,419.63	26,110.41	3,555.95	27,733.70	2,533.77		173.71	103,067.48
122	1,138.10	3,438.26	3,378.36	3,743.75	3,767.71	16,316.95	2,911.14		5,690.50	545.09	6,720.78		47,650.64
123		66,788.50	3,008.88	13,872.84	4,258.89	3,501.38	3,809.64			53,955.89	3,629.94	15,256.53	168,082.49
124	9,404.30	772.71		71,706.29	1,498.09		6,316.84	3,042.92	1,126.12	26,308.08	13,339.73	4,025.28	137,540.36
125	2,755.40	209.65	36,651.49	8,499.00	5,605.51	3,927.86	16,957.69	341.43	1,605.32	19,946.70	13,615.27	10,770.02	120,885.34
126		15,867.51	4,193.00	17,247.67	27,488.50	7,325.77	12,620.53	14,381.99	65,833.45	6,714.79	4,648.24	2,276.20	178,597.65
127	3,354.40	1,198.00		32,075.32	8,270.31		10,332.75	35,963.96	55,215.82	5,450.90	3,671.87	1,659.23	157,192.56
128		246.05	3,062.10	7,439.58	5,031.60	431.28	419.30	407.32	5,564.71	1,245.92		5,990.00	29,837.86
Total	84,620.73	201,018.38	4,217,537.01	355,288.58	284,139.13	130,857.87	4,003,573.92	202,082.52	497,702.20	753,229.82	416,527.17	275,090.70	11,421,668.03

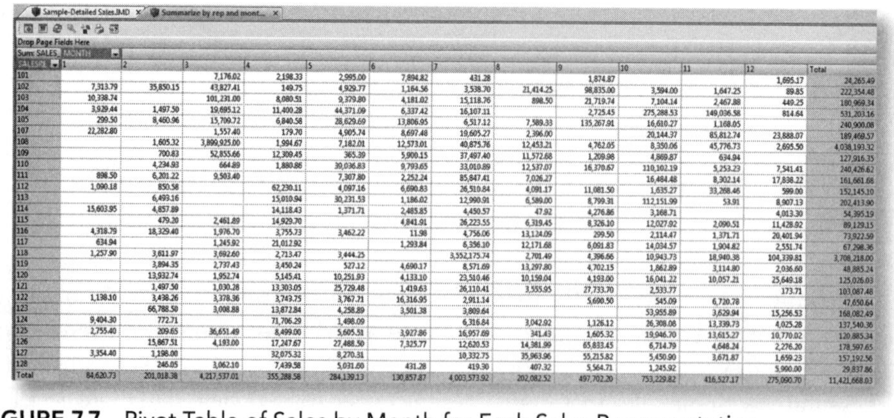

FIGURE 7.7 Pivot Table of Sales by Month for Each Sales Representative

Figure 7.7 allows us to see how much each sales representative sold month to month. It is also simple to compare sales representatives. The information can be filtered by sales representatives so only those of interest are displayed. By selecting the dropdown box headed as SALESRE at the upper left corner in Figure 7.7, you can uncheck those that you do not wish to be displayed. Similarly, from the MONTH dropdown box, you can select only those months you wish displayed.

Another view to explore would be by sales representatives as compared to products. First we summarize the 2011 file by the SALESREP_NO field and then by the PROD_CODE field totaling on the SALES_BEF_TAX field. Once completed, use the pivot table to view by product numbers as in Figure 7.8.

SALESREP_NO	01	02	03	04	05	06	Total
101					24,265.49		24,265.49
102		337.35	3,233.80	42,276.00	176,507.33		222,354.48
103			4,288.30		176,681.04		180,969.34
104			2,249.60	301,322.19	93,473.95	134,157.42	531,203.16
105			10,193.50	126,828.00	103,878.58		240,900.08
107			1,335.70		164,353.62		189,469.57
108				22,829.04	115,439.28	3,899,925.00	4,038,193.32
109				47,560.50	80,355.85		127,916.35
110					240,426.62		240,426.62
111	11,231.36	1,479.15	5,272.50	62,885.55	80,793.12		161,661.68
112	21,119.84				131,025.26		152,145.10
113			5,659.15	52,845.00	143,909.75		202,413.90
114					54,395.19		54,395.19
115			7,908.75	3,170.70	78,049.70		89,129.15
116					73,922.59		73,922.59
117			4,499.20		62,799.16		67,298.36
118			1,476.30		170,289.71	3,536,451.99	3,708,218.00
119			1,827.80		47,057.44		48,885.24
120			9,103.85	12,894.18	103,028.00		125,026.03
121			8,014.20		95,073.28		103,087.48
122			2,390.20		45,260.44		47,650.64
123			4,569.50	15,853.50	147,659.49		168,082.49
124		2,387.40	773.30		134,379.66		137,540.36
125			11,142.55		109,742.79		120,885.34
126			14,833.30	57,178.29	106,586.06		178,597.65
127			3,515.00	7,821.06	145,856.50		157,192.56
128		3,062.10	246.05		26,529.71		29,837.86
Total	32,351.20	7,266.00	102,532.55	777,244.26	2,931,739.61	7,570,534.41	11,421,668.03

FIGURE 7.8 Products Sold by Each Sales Representative for 2011

This pivot table view allows us to see that all representatives sold product number 05 but only a few sold product number 06 and product number 01. Again, sales representatives 108 and 118 stand out but this time we know that it is because of selling product 06. It is also an anomaly that only one other sales representative, number 104, had made sales of product 06 but at significantly lower totals than the other two representatives. This could be a red flag of larceny or possibly the other two representatives are involved in a commission scheme.

More analysis is needed and a good place to start would be to use the same pivot table for the 2010 years as a comparison, displayed in Figure 7.9.

Comparing the 2010 sales to the 2011 sales, product numbers 01, 02, and 03 dropped in 2011 while product numbers 04, 05, and 06 increased. Commission rates for each product should be examined to ensure that a sales representative maximizing their commissions was not detrimental to the organization sales strategy. We also note

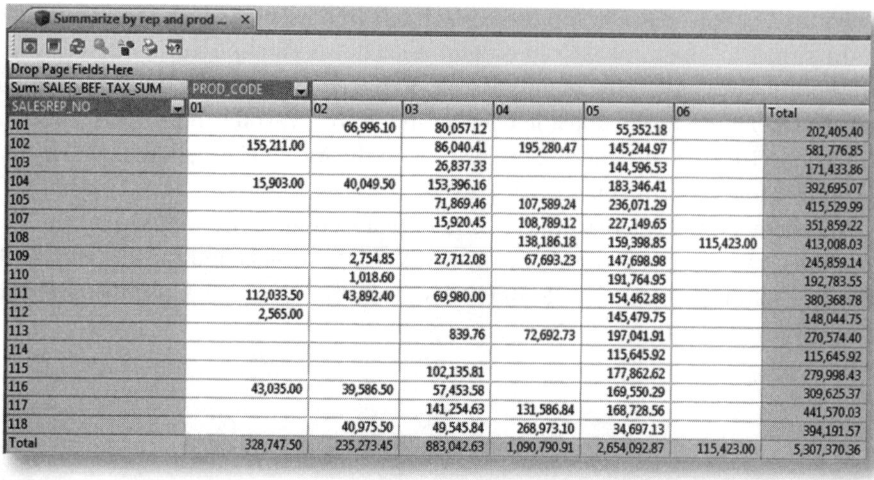

Sum: SALES_BEF_TAX_SUM SALESREP_NO	01	02	03	04	05	06	Total
101		66,996.10	80,057.12		55,352.18		202,405.40
102	155,211.00		86,040.41	195,280.47	145,244.97		581,776.85
103			26,837.33		144,596.53		171,433.86
104	15,903.00	40,049.50	153,396.16		183,346.41		392,695.07
105			71,869.46	107,589.24	236,071.29		415,529.99
107			15,920.45	108,789.12	227,149.65		351,859.22
108				138,186.18	159,398.85	115,423.00	413,008.03
109		2,754.85	27,712.08	67,693.23	147,698.98		245,859.14
110		1,018.60			191,764.95		192,783.55
111	112,033.50	43,892.40	69,980.00		154,462.88		380,368.78
112	2,565.00				145,479.75		148,044.75
113			839.76	72,692.73	197,041.91		270,574.40
114					115,645.92		115,645.92
115			102,135.81		177,862.62		279,998.43
116	43,035.00	39,586.50	57,453.58		169,550.29		309,625.37
117			141,254.63	131,586.84	168,728.56		441,570.03
118		40,975.50	49,545.84	268,973.10	34,697.13		394,191.57
Total	328,747.50	235,273.45	883,042.63	1,090,790.91	2,654,092.87	115,423.00	5,307,370.36

FIGURE 7.9 Products Sold by Each Sales Representative for 2010

that in 2010, only sales representative 108 sold product number 06 as opposed to two additional representatives selling the same product in 2011.

Might the increased sales for product 06 or any product be a result of heavy price discounting? Recall that one way to cover up larceny is to offset money taken by recording equivalent discounts. On the assumption that the UNIT_PRICE field is net of discounts, an easy way of determining whether any items are sold below regular prices or discounts given would be to summarize the 2011 detailed sales file by PROD_CODE. Select the UNIT_PRICE_SUM field to be totaled and averaged. It is optional to select the SALES_BEF_TAX to be totaled and averaged.

If the UNIT_PRICE_AVERAGE field amount for a product is the same as the unit prices visually tested in the detailed sales file, then you know that there were no sales for that product at below the regular sales price. An example is shown in Figure 7.10.

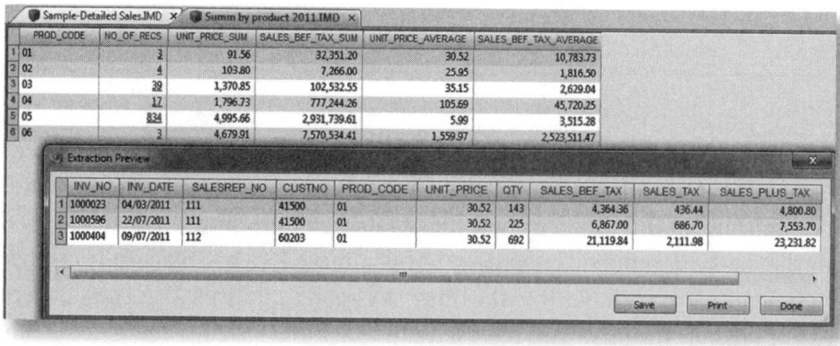

	PROD_CODE	NO_OF_RECS	UNIT_PRICE_SUM	SALES_BEF_TAX_SUM	UNIT_PRICE_AVERAGE	SALES_BEF_TAX_AVERAGE
1	01	3	91.56	32,351.20	30.52	10,783.73
2	02	4	103.80	7,266.00	25.95	1,816.50
3	03	39	1,370.85	102,532.55	35.15	2,629.04
4	04	17	1,796.73	777,244.26	105.69	45,720.25
5	05	834	4,995.66	2,931,739.61	5.99	3,515.28
6	06	3	4,679.91	7,570,534.41	1,559.97	2,523,511.47

	INV_NO	INV_DATE	SALESREP_NO	CUSTNO	PROD_CODE	UNIT_PRICE	QTY	SALES_BEF_TAX	SALES_TAX	SALES_PLUS_TAX
1	1000023	04/03/2011	111	41500	01	30.52	143	4,364.36	436.44	4,800.80
2	1000596	22/07/2011	111	41500	01	30.52	225	6,867.00	686.70	7,553.70
3	1000404	09/07/2011	112	60203	01	30.52	692	21,119.84	2,111.98	23,231.82

FIGURE 7.10 Results of Summarizing by Product, Totaling, and Averaging on the Unit Price for 2011

A quick examination assures you that no sales representative sold any products at other than the listed prices. Similarly, an analysis for 2010 determined the same results. It is only noted that there were price increases for all products in 2011. Increased prices are a good example of why not only dollar values should be included in any analysis, but also the number of transactions should be included, as in Figure 7.6.

There are many other tests that can be performed that may produce unusual results that can be investigated, such as:

- Write-offs of accounts receivable that are inappropriate, either due to frequency, amounts, or contravening write-off policies of the organization.
- Extract partial payments that reduce overdue customer accounts receivable that may be booked to avoid attention resulting from routine aging analysis of accounts receivable.
- Review accounts receivable in a credit balance position. Any unusual results should be traced to the postings to ensure that they were proper, as they may be associated with larceny.
- Apply trend analysis to those fulltime employees with low sales and high discounts.
- For service employees, analyze low hours booked, as this may be an indication of working and charging the customers directly. At the very least, inefficiencies in the operations would be revealed.
- Compare selling prices, net of discounts and adjustments, by different sales locations. Correlation can simplify the comparison process.

The best tests are those that employ other databases, especially those from other business systems. Examples of independent databases that can be compared to accounting system data follow.

- Compare sales returns and other adjustments, such as voids, to the inventory database. Periodic verification of physical inventory needs to be done in order for this test to be effective.
- Match access logs to the accounts receivable module of the accounting system to employees who are in sales.
- Extract computer or access-card logs for nonbusiness hour access to the sales location or to the accounting system.
- Compare the POS or cash register system information to cash-receipt reports. Reconciliation will show any discrepancies and high numbers of small differences are suspicious.
- Compare purchases made by debit and credit cards and refunds. Extract and review transactions where customers made the purchase on one card but had it refunded to different debit or credit cards.
- Compare sales prices to the cost of goods in the inventory system and extract out items sold at below cost that are not considered obsolete. A percentage below expected gross margins of products may also be used.

CONCLUSION

Every organization that accepts cash payments is susceptible to skimming and cash larceny. Cash is the most vulnerable to fraud as it is the most liquid of all assets.

Employees may handle large sums of cash, which makes it tempting for a fraudster to retain some of it for personal use. Misappropriation of any other asset, such as inventory, requires that the goods be converted to cash before the fraudster can enjoy the results. Conversion involves extra steps, which means extra risks for the fraudster.

With technology these days, skimming can occur faster and result in larger losses. It is no longer as simple as an apartment manager not recording that an apartment has been rented out and keeping the rent money collected. Some of today's fraudsters have a high degree of IT skills that help them to perpetrate fraud or in covering up fraudulent transactions. There are a number of cases where managers and managing shareholders would use software programs called zappers to delete sales so they can defraud their employer or silent partners/shareholders along with the taxation authorities. Since the sales are only temporarily recorded in the point-of-sales system and deleted before being entered into the accounting system, this type of fraud can be considered as skimming. Further discussion of zapper fraud is in Chapter 16.

## CHAPTER EIGHT

Billing Schemes

BILLING SCHEMES ARE PERPETRATED on the business through the accounts payable department. Businesses incur liabilities through the normal course of business that must be settled within a certain time period. Almost all expenditures made by the company are processed by accounts payable. The majority of the payments would be for trade payable and expense payable accounts. Trade payables are for the purchases of goods that are normally recorded as inventory and as part of the cost of goods sold. Expenses payable are those spent for purchases of goods or services that are normally expensed. Travel and entertainment expenses are also typically handled by accounts payable.

Payments flow through the system in the same manner, whether they are legitimate or fraudulent. Since so many transactions go through accounts payable and are the largest outlay for most organizations, you need to be vigilant to detect bogus payments. Not only is fraud of concern, but errors and inefficient payment processing are also issues, and all are costly to organizations just the same. Errors may be duplicate payments made or unnecessary charges paid for. Inefficient processing may include unnecessary payments for late payment interest or fees, discounts for earlier payment not taken, or individual payments of multiple invoices to the same provider during the same period.

There are a number of ways to run a billing scheme. The costliest to the organization are those where the corrupt employee forms a company for the purpose of receiving illegitimate payments. The company is formed so that the transaction flows are the same as a legitimate business, but the company has not provided goods or services invoiced to the targeted business. Normally the fraudulent invoices would be for services, as services eliminate involving the receiving department for goods. Where the billing of goods is involved, collusion from the receiving department or warehouse is needed to verify the receipt of fictitious shipments. However, there would be an inventory issue that needs to be covered by means of falsifying inventory counts or by setting up a method of writing the goods off. For goods, the intermediary scheme is simpler and less risky to implement. The corrupt purchasing employee, rather than purchasing directly from the vendor, would have his own intermediary company make the purchase and resell it to the employer at inflated prices.

A company is formed; a bank account is set up; and sometimes a post office box is used to receive the payments. When a false invoice is submitted to the organization, the corrupt employee, if in the right position, would authorize the payment of the invoice. If the employee cannot authorize the payment, then he or she may bring it to someone who is overly trusting to sign the authorization. Alternatively, the corrupt employee could just forge an authorization signature. Once the first payment goes through the accounts payable system, subsequent payments are simpler. The vendor by then is already added to the vendor master file as a supplier. Where there are strong controls over adding new vendors to the master file, the fraudster can form a company with the name similar to that of an existing vendor. An inactive vendor still on the vendor master file would be preferred so that only the address where the payment is to be sent needs to be changed.

Where there are strong controls over the automated flow of payments, there may be weak controls over manual payments. The corrupt employee will cause some deliberate error in the payment process so that the process is disrupted and manual intervention is necessary. This allows an opportunity for the employee to take control of the payment process to their benefit.

There are also overpayments, duplicate payments, and paying the wrong vendor schemes. These schemes involve making deliberate errors and paying legitimate vendors excess funds. The corrupt employee calls and asks those vendors to return the check or the excessive payment back directly to them for conversion to their own account.

Schemes that have the organization purchase goods benefiting the corrupt employee may be personal items paid for by the organization or supplies used for the corrupt employee's side business or for resale. These are not goods that the organization requires in their regular business operations so it is not classified as theft. The corrupt employee caused the organization to pay for items not needed so it is considered a billing scheme. If the employee cannot authorize the purchases, then the fraudster has to take additional steps, such as getting a supervisor to sign a purchase requisition so a purchase order can be sent to the vendor. Signatures can be forged and purchase orders can be inserted into the purchasing cycle depending on the corrupt employee's position in the organization.

 ## DATA AND DATA FAMILIARIZATION

For accounts payable data analytical tests, we will mainly be using a large data set downloaded from the state of Oklahoma's website.[1] The data set is the state of Oklahoma Vendor Payments Fiscal Year 2013, which contains over 2 million records from the different agencies in Oklahoma. There are 29 fields, of which 15 are relevant to our discussion:

- AGENCY_NUMBER
- AGENCY_NAME
- VENDOR_NAME: There are no vendor numbers in this file and some of the names are redacted and replaced with the words Protected Information

- VOUCHER_ID
- VOUCHER_TYPE
- VOUCHER_DESCRIPTION
- INVOICE_ID
- INVOICE_DATE: The dates are in three different formats as a character field; the author normalized the dates and then converted the character field to a date field called INVOICE_DATE_2
- TRANSACTION_TYPE
- PAYMENT_DATE: The dates are in three different formats as a character field; the author normalized the dates and then converted the character field to a date field called PAYMENT_DATE_2
- ACCOUNT
- EXPENDITURE_DESCRIPTION
- PAYMENT_AMOUNT
- PURCHASE_ORDER_CONTRACT_NUMBER
- PURCHASE_ORDER_CONTRACT_ITEM_DESCRIPTION

Where this payment file is not appropriate for demonstration purposes, the sample files that are included with the IDEA software or IDEA course material will be used.

To get an overall view of the data contents of the "State Vendor Payments" file, we review the field statistics. Of the numeric fields, only the PAYMENT_AMOUNT field provides any interest, as shown in Figure 8.1.

We note that all 2,066,536 records have valid values in this field but 34,388 of them contain the amount of zero. There is a wide spread among the data amounts, ranging from a negative $5,996,550.22 to a positive value of $48,907,078.15. To obtain a better insight of the amounts, you should perform a stratification of the PAYMENT_AMOUNT field.

More interesting are the field statistics for the INVOICE_DATE_2 and the PAYMENT_DATE_2 fields.

We can see that the INVOICE_DATE_2 field contains 76,461 errors and that there are issues with date inputs, as can be seen in both the record number of the earliest and of the latest dates as displayed in Figure 8.2.

The PAYMENT_DATE_2 field appears to be reliable. There are no data errors and the dates seem to be in line with what is expected. Of special interest are the 41 payments made on Sundays and the 64 payments made on Saturdays.

Both the INVOICE_DATE_2 and the PAYMENT_DATE_2 fields contain zero or were originally blank in these fields of 17,919 and 30,742 respectively.

Summarizing on TRANSACTION_TYPE tells us that our main focus should be on type P, as they appear to be payments actually made. See Figure 8.3.

From the review of the data the following are noted:

- B—The voucher type for all the records is JRNL with PAYMENT_AMOUNT as zero; it seems that these are journal entries
- C—Contains both positive and negative amounts in the PAYMENT_AMOUNT field

Numeric Statistics	PAYMENT_AMOUNT
Net Value	15,258,988,474.48
Absolute Value	15,805,432,151.44
# of Records	2,066,536
# of Zero Items	34,388
Positive Value	15,532,210,312.96
Negative Value	-273,221,838.48
# of Positive Records	1,877,972
# of Negative Records	154,176
▶ # of Data Errors	0
# of Valid Values	2,066,536
Average Value	7,383.85
Minimum Value	-5,996,550.22
Maximum Value	48,907,078.15
Record # of Min	1,242,836
Record # of Max	2,014,794
Sample Std Dev	131,442.62
Sample Variance	17,277,161,279.29
Pop Std Dev	131,442.58
Pop Variance	17,277,152,918.84
Pop Skewness	141.634253
Pop Kurtosis	31,897.005489

FIGURE 8.1   Field Statistics of Payment Amount

- H—Contains negative amounts and are noted as Regular Voucher
- P—Paid amounts
- R—Refunds
- W—Negative amounts

We are not sure of all the coding as the data file was downloaded from an Internet public source.

From the "State Vendor Payments" file, we can extract to a new file called "Payments trans type P" by using the equation of TRANSACTION_TYPE = P.

Date Statistics	INVOICE_DATE_2	PAYMENT_DATE_2
# of Valid Values	1,972,156	2,035,794
# of Zero Items	17919	30742
# of Records	2,066,536	2,066,536
▶ # of Data Errors	76461	0
Earliest Date	03/05/0213	02/07/2012
Latest Date	01/01/9202	27/09/2013
Record # of Earliest	1750996	16127
Record # of Latest	1250454	939
Most Common Day	Wednesday	Wednesday
Most Common Month	October	October
Items in January	169724	179723
Items in February	154776	161881
Items in March	160048	162822
Items in April	168407	170052
Items in May	174859	186306
Items in June	160447	166808
Items in July	158674	149149
Items in August	181202	187233
Items in September	158659	158071
Items in October	184218	192590
Items in November	155364	162217
Items in December	145778	158942
Items on Sunday	42026	41
Items on Monday	234753	208366
Items on Tuesday	234970	273490
Items on Wednesday	895266	951760
Items on Thursday	250570	330209
Items on Friday	255334	271864
Items on Saturday	59237	64

FIGURE 8.2　Field Statistics of Dates

	TRANSACTION_TYPE	NO_OF_RECS	PAYMENT_AMOUNT_SUM
1	B	17919	0.00
2	C	10131	-30,782,957.22
3	H	545	-7,489,033.02
4	P	2035663	15,299,912,602.11
5	R	76	-256,169.85
6	W	2202	-2,395,967.54

FIGURE 8.3 Transaction Types

 BENFORD'S LAW TESTS

We can check to see if the data set conforms to Benford's Law. For Benford's Law, we will test on where TRANSACTION_TYPE are *P* or payments and on positive values.

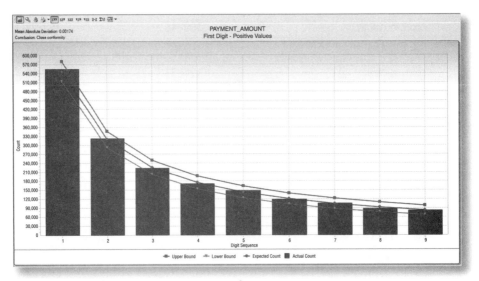

FIGURE 8.4 Benford's Law First Digit Test for Payment Amounts

For the high-level first digit test, the resulting graph shows high conformity in Figure 8.4. We can then select the first two digits for a better precision analysis.

There is acceptable conformity in Figure 8.5. While it is not unusual for the first two digits test for all the digit pairs not to meet the expected count, on the whole the data set conforms. However, it would be prudent to examine some of the contents of the highly suspicious and suspicious numbers.

For the last two digits test shown in Figure 8.6, there is close conformity for almost all the numbers with the exception of 0 and 50, which in reality is normal, especially for numbers ending with zero.

Since the data set as a whole conforms we can accept the Benford's Law results or we can apply the tests on specific individual agencies. If a specific agency is selected for a

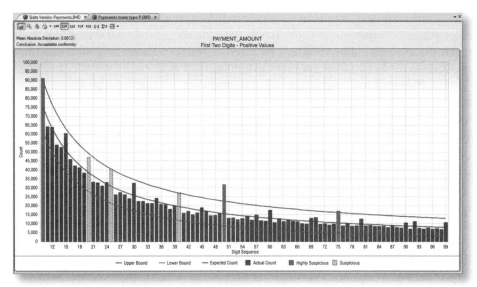

FIGURE 8.5 Benford's Law First Two Digits Test on Payment Amounts

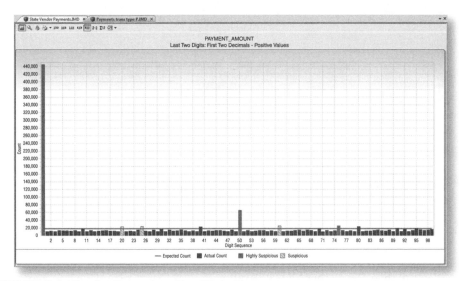

FIGURE 8.6 Benford's Law Last Two Digits Test

detail review, then all the general tests can be reapplied just to the payments associated with that specific agency.

RELATIVE SIZE FACTOR TEST

This data set contains many high-dollar-payment amounts. There are 1,590 records where the paid amounts were $1 million or more. To see these high-dollar records, we simply index the PAYMENT_AMOUNT field in descending order. The largest amount of almost $49 million was paid to a Protected Information vendor name. Many of the top amounts exceeding $20 million were paid to JPMorgan Chase Bank for the purchases of securities and other investments. It is unlikely in our general review that these high-dollar amounts would be of significant interest, unless we were auditing investment transactions or focusing on payments to banks.

What we are interested in are unusually high payments to individual vendors. We could employ the Top Records feature of IDEA to extract a user-specified number of the top-most amounts for each vendor. However, we would have to examine all the vendors. There are many vendors in this payment file. Our objective is to review, by vendors, where the largest amount paid is significantly higher than the next highest amount. High differences can signify errors or fraud.

To make reviewing details easier, in the resulting Relative Size Factor test file, we use the Defined Action Field feature on the VENDOR_NAME linked to the payment file. We can then just click on any of the vendor names to obtain an extraction preview for the selected vendor. As an example, we will look at the transactions of the incredibly high RSF ratio of the first vendor displayed. All records had payments of $3.00 each while the largest records showed a payment of $42,500.00, shown in Figure 8.7.

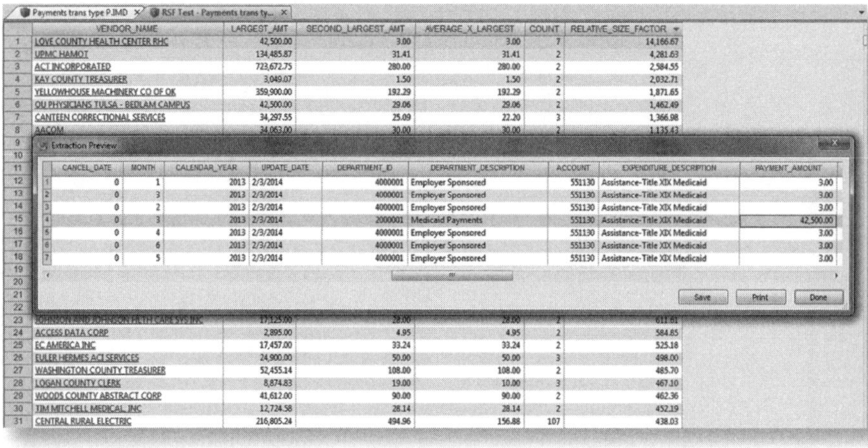

FIGURE 8.7 Relative Size Factor Test of Payments by Vendor Names

You can then select other high-RSF ratios, such as Central Rural Electric in record number 31, to examine in more detail. There were 107 transactions with average amounts of $156.88 if the largest number of $216,805.24 was excluded.

Z-SCORE

Applying the Z-score test on the entire payment file and indexing the Z_SCORE field by descending order, we can see from the score how much the amount deviates from the center amount shown in Figure 8.8.

While useful, the Z-score test is more effective when applied to certain classes such as on a specific agency or specific vendor.

#	DEPARTMENT_ID	DEPARTMENT_DESCRIPTION	ACCOUNT	EXPENDITURE_DESCRIPTION	PAYMENT_AMOUNT	Z_SCORE	FUND_CODE	FUND_DESCRIPTION	CLASS_FI
1	9404040	FAP Loans	562160	Trans-Invest.Fds-Master Cust.	48,907,078.15	369.5156	1000	General Fund - No Divisions	
2	200001	Dedicated Revenue	561230	Purchase of Sec & Other Invest	37,144,264.29	280.6285	6000	Pension Trust Funds	
3	2000001	Medicaid Payments	551130	Assistance-Title XIX Medicaid	35,643,606.00	269.2886	1000	General Fund - No Divisions	
4	7100001	Agency 760 Sub-Activity Code	561230	Purchase of Sec & Other Invest	32,424,181.12	244.9606	9000	Higher Educ Component Unit	
5	2000001	Medicaid Payments	551130	Assistance-Title XIX Medicaid	30,745,133.00	232.2726	1000	General Fund - No Divisions	
6	9600001	District 1	554120	Approved Program Reimbursement	30,400,573.43	229.6689	1000	General Fund - No Divisions	
7	9904040	Emer Grants To Gov't Entities	562160	Trans-Invest.Fds-Master Cust.	30,255,609.00	228.5735	1000	General Fund - No Divisions	
8	200001	Dedicated Revenue	561230	Purchase of Sec & Other Invest	29,682,093.49	224.2396	6000	Pension Trust Funds	
9	200001	Dedicated Revenue	561230	Purchase of Sec & Other Invest	29,332,528.33	221.5981	6000	Pension Trust Funds	
10	200001	Dedicated Revenue	561230	Purchase of Sec & Other Invest	28,922,797.95	218.5019	6000	Pension Trust Funds	
11	200001	Dedicated Revenue	561230	Purchase of Sec & Other Invest	28,460,583.97	215.0092	6000	Pension Trust Funds	
12	7100001	Agency 760 Sub-Activity Code	561230	Purchase of Sec & Other Invest	26,405,038.06	200.1583	9000	Higher Educ Component Unit	
13	7999999	Clearing and ASA Department	563110	Employee With.-Withh.Payable	23,748,322.89	179.4004	1603	Escrow Funds	
14	200001	Dedicated Revenue	561230	Purchase of Sec & Other Invest	23,551,851.99	177.9157	6000	Pension Trust Funds	
15	200001	Dedicated Revenue	561230	Purchase of Sec & Other Invest	22,572,325.10	170.5138	6000	Pension Trust Funds	
16	200001	Dedicated Revenue	561230	Purchase of Sec & Other Invest	21,680,723.79	163.7763	6000	Pension Trust Funds	
17	200001	Dedicated Revenue	561230	Purchase of Sec & Other Invest	21,256,859.85	160.5733	6000	Pension Trust Funds	
18	1000003	Indigent Care	515860	Gen.Medical-Surgical Hospitals	21,180,413.00	159.9956	8000	Business-Type Component Units	
19	2000001	Medicaid Payments	551130	Assistance-Title XIX Medicaid	21,180,413.00	159.9956	1000	General Fund - No Divisions	
20	1000003	Indigent Care	515860	Gen.Medical-Surgical Hospitals	20,856,394.00	157.5471	8000	Business-Type Component Units	
21	2000001	Medicaid Payments	551130	Assistance-Title XIX Medicaid	20,856,394.00	157.5471	1000	General Fund - No Divisions	
22	200001	Dedicated Revenue	561230	Purchase of Sec & Other Invest	20,843,260.40	157.4479	6000	Pension Trust Funds	

FIGURE 8.8 Z-Score Test of All Payments

Let's summarize by vendor to select some to apply the Z-score test to. The new summarize file is named "Summarize by Vendor—Payment."

Since we do not have vendor numbers and are relying on vendor names, in Figure 8.9, we note that there may be issues with how the names are entered. This should be kept in mind when applying additional tests later. For instance, record 158 and 159 are likely the same vendor. Similarly, records 189 and 190 are the same vendor.

We will combine the vendors A Better Life Home Care with A Better Life Homecare and then apply Z-score to both as if they were one vendor. The new file can be called "A better life home care—combined."

You can see how the Z_SCORE1 field calculated on the combined vendor deviates from the center much more than when the Z_SCORE field was calculated against the entire payment data set in Figure 8.10. The full payment data set had very large numbers in both the negative and positive directions that made our vendor maximum of $27,496.22 seem irrelevant.

EVEN DOLLAR AMOUNTS

Even dollar values paid are usually of interest whether they are journal entries or actual payments by various tender types such as checks or electronic fund transfers. Most liabilities are not of even amounts and some payments include taxes, which make even amounts more unusual. We can do analysis on those that are of even hundreds, thousands, or tens of thousands. Using the payment file, we extract amounts that are in even thousands of dollars for review using the equation of

(PAYMENT_AMOUNT % 1000) = 0 .AND. PAYMENT_AMOUNT < > 0

	VENDOR_NAME	NO_OF_RECS	PAYMENT_AMOUNT_SUM
156	A B C RURAL HEALTH CLINIC	113	184,093.50
157	A B SCIEX LLC	5	39,156.30
158	A BETTER LIFE HOME CARE	105	113,017.99
159	A BETTER LIFE HOMECARE	112	1,195,820.83
160	A BETTER SIGN COMPANY	5	363.00
161	A BETTER SMILE PC	102	680,791.62
162	A C C T	1	2,879.00
163	A C T	3	7,328.00
164	A CHANCE TO CHANGE FOUNDATION	188	125,009.49
165	A CHILD S DREAM DAY CARE, INC.	5	13,745.41
166	A DAIGGER & CO INC	1	1,800.00
167	A DAIGGER & COMPANY INC	4	389.24
168	A Daigger & Co Inc *	15	1,405.18
169	A E C SERVICES INC	5	1,628.74
170	A E S INSURANCE BROKERS	1	421.00
171	A EUGENE REYNOLDS PHD	14	6,800.00
172	A F POTTS LUMBER SALES	2	53,823.81
173	A FAR CRY, INC	2	6,000.00
174	A FINE SHINE	2	4,179.00
175	A GOOD ROAD	1	45.00
176	A GREAT START LEARNING CENTER	8	59,219.79
177	A HEART AFTER KIDS DAYCARE AND	3	4,639.23
178	A HEATH PHOTO	2	1,656.00
179	A KEVIN YOUNG EYECARE CENTER INC	52	69,090.80
180	A LADY'S DAY OUT	1	250.00
181	A LEARNING CENTER	12	67,221.55
182	A M BEST COMPANY	1	168.95
183	A M HOME DIAGNOSTICS INC	22	3,821.66
184	A MARLENE *WEST	3	287.10
185	A MAX SIGNS CO INC	2	1,812.50
186	A MOTHERS TOUCH CHILD DEV	12	82,326.79
187	A NEW BEGINNING WOMEN'S HEALTHCARE	69	44,236.77
188	A NEW DAY COUNSELING, INC.	70	412,376.26
189	A NEW LEAF	57	239,421.18
190	A NEW LEAF INC	94	536,801.34

FIGURE 8.9 Summarizing by Vendors' Names

The % is not a percentage but instead represents Mod or modulus in the equation editor. Modulus returns the remainder when one number is divided by another. For example, where 7 mod 2, the remainder is 1 (7 divided by 2 = 3 with a remainder of 1). Where 8 mod 2 divides evenly, the remainder is zero. For our even thousand equation, if our amount divided by 1,000 has a remainder of zero, then it matches the first part of

Payments trans type P.IMD | A better life home care - co...

	ACCOUNT	EXPENDITURE_DESCRIPTION	PAYMENT_AMOUNT	Z_SCORE1	Z_SCORE	FUND_CODE	FUND_DESCRIPTION
1	551130	Assistance-Title XIX Medicaid	27,496.22	2.5061	0.1510	1000	General Fund - No Divisions
2	551130	Assistance-Title XIX Medicaid	23,904.27	2.0868	0.1238	1000	General Fund - No Divisions
3	551130	Assistance-Title XIX Medicaid	23,729.62	2.0664	0.1225	1000	General Fund - No Divisions
4	551130	Assistance-Title XIX Medicaid	23,645.39	2.0565	0.1219	1000	General Fund - No Divisions
5	551130	Assistance-Title XIX Medicaid	22,998.01	1.9810	0.1170	1000	General Fund - No Divisions
6	551130	Assistance-Title XIX Medicaid	22,950.62	1.9754	0.1166	1000	General Fund - No Divisions
7	551130	Assistance-Title XIX Medicaid	22,647.66	1.9400	0.1143	1000	General Fund - No Divisions
8	551130	Assistance-Title XIX Medicaid	22,570.65	1.9311	0.1138	1000	General Fund - No Divisions
9	551130	Assistance-Title XIX Medicaid	22,363.55	1.9069	0.1122	1000	General Fund - No Divisions
10	551130	Assistance-Title XIX Medicaid	22,162.71	1.8834	0.1107	1000	General Fund - No Divisions
11	551130	Assistance-Title XIX Medicaid	21,957.91	1.8595	0.1091	1000	General Fund - No Divisions
12	551130	Assistance-Title XIX Medicaid	21,957.32	1.8594	0.1091	1000	General Fund - No Divisions
13	551130	Assistance-Title XIX Medicaid	21,881.51	1.8506	0.1086	1000	General Fund - No Divisions
14	551130	Assistance-Title XIX Medicaid	21,868.43	1.8491	0.1085	1000	General Fund - No Divisions
15	551130	Assistance-Title XIX Medicaid	21,598.39	1.8175	0.1064	1000	General Fund - No Divisions
16	551130	Assistance-Title XIX Medicaid	21,572.72	1.8145	0.1062	1000	General Fund - No Divisions
17	551130	Assistance-Title XIX Medicaid	21,534.12	1.8100	0.1059	1000	General Fund - No Divisions
18	551130	Assistance-Title XIX Medicaid	21,525.98	1.8091	0.1059	1000	General Fund - No Divisions
19	551130	Assistance-Title XIX Medicaid	21,475.64	1.8032	0.1055	1000	General Fund - No Divisions
20	551130	Assistance-Title XIX Medicaid	21,449.81	1.8002	0.1053	1000	General Fund - No Divisions
21	551130	Assistance-Title XIX Medicaid	21,381.64	1.7922	0.1048	1000	General Fund - No Divisions
22	551130	Assistance-Title XIX Medicaid	21,356.27	1.7893	0.1046	1000	General Fund - No Divisions
23	551130	Assistance-Title XIX Medicaid	21,299.55	1.7826	0.1042	1000	General Fund - No Divisions
24	551130	Assistance-Title XIX Medicaid	21,263.27	1.7784	0.1039	1000	General Fund - No Divisions
25	551130	Assistance-Title XIX Medicaid	21,261.05	1.7781	0.1039	1000	General Fund - No Divisions
26	551130	Assistance-Title XIX Medicaid	21,224.62	1.7739	0.1036	1000	General Fund - No Divisions
27	551130	Assistance-Title XIX Medicaid	21,099.76	1.7593	0.1026	1000	General Fund - No Divisions
28	551130	Assistance-Title XIX Medicaid	21,090.20	1.7582	0.1026	1000	General Fund - No Divisions
29	551130	Assistance-Title XIX Medicaid	20,971.10	1.7443	0.1017	1000	General Fund - No Divisions
30	551130	Assistance-Title XIX Medicaid	20,966.98	1.7438	0.1016	1000	General Fund - No Divisions
31	551130	Assistance-Title XIX Medicaid	20,954.44	1.7424	0.1015	1000	General Fund - No Divisions
32	551130	Assistance-Title XIX Medicaid	20,934.32	1.7400	0.1014	1000	General Fund - No Divisions
33	551130	Assistance-Title XIX Medicaid	20,773.24	1.7212	0.1002	1000	General Fund - No Divisions
34	551130	Assistance-Title XIX Medicaid	20,754.36	1.7190	0.1000	1000	General Fund - No Divisions
35	551130	Assistance-Title XIX Medicaid	20,724.96	1.7156	0.0998	1000	General Fund - No Divisions
36	551130	Assistance-Title XIX Medicaid	20,719.19	1.7149	0.0998	1000	General Fund - No Divisions
37	551130	Assistance-Title XIX Medicaid	20,555.94	1.6958	0.0985	1000	General Fund - No Divisions

FIGURE 8.10 Z-Score of Payments to a Specific Vendor

our equation. We have the second part of the equation to exclude where amounts were zero. This eliminates excessive irrelevant records.

Payments trans type P.IMD | A better life home care - com... | EVEN_THOUSANDS.IMD

	DEPARTMENT_ID	DEPARTMENT_DESCRIPTION	ACCOUNT	EXPENDITURE_DESCRIPTION	PAYMENT_AMOUNT	FUND_CODE	FUND_DESCRIPTION	CLASS_FIELD	CLASS_DESCRIPTION
1	2000001	Medicaid Payments	551130	Assistance-Title XIX Medicaid	10,450,000.00	1000	General Fund - No Divisions	34000	CMIA Programs Disbursing Fund
2	2000001	Medicaid Payments	551130	Assistance-Title XIX Medicaid	10,450,000.00	1000	General Fund - No Divisions	34000	CMIA Programs Disbursing Fund
3	2000001	Medicaid Payments	551130	Assistance-Title XIX Medicaid	10,450,000.00	1000	General Fund - No Divisions	34000	CMIA Programs Disbursing Fund
4	2000001	Medicaid Payments	551130	Assistance-Title XIX Medicaid	10,450,000.00	1000	General Fund - No Divisions	34000	CMIA Programs Disbursing Fund
5	6100001	Endowment Trust (Chairs)	562120	Trsf to Treasury Fund-ONUS	9,000,000.00	9000	Higher Educ Component Unit	70700	Endowment Fund
6	6100001	Endowment Trust (Chairs)	562120	Trsf to Treasury Fund-ONUS	9,000,000.00	9000	Higher Educ Component Unit	70700	Endowment Fund
7	6100001	Endowment Trust (Chairs)	562120	Trsf to Treasury Fund-ONUS	9,000,000.00	9000	Higher Educ Component Unit	70700	Endowment Fund
8	6100001	Endowment Trust (Chairs)	562120	Trsf to Treasury Fund-ONUS	9,000,000.00	9000	Higher Educ Component Unit	70700	Endowment Fund
9	6100001	Endowment Trust (Chairs)	562120	Trsf to Treasury Fund-ONUS	9,000,000.00	9000	Higher Educ Component Unit	70700	Endowment Fund
10	6100001	Endowment Trust (Chairs)	562120	Trsf to Treasury Fund-ONUS	9,000,000.00	9000	Higher Educ Component Unit	70700	Endowment Fund
11	6100001	Endowment Trust (Chairs)	562120	Trsf to Treasury Fund-ONUS	9,000,000.00	9000	Higher Educ Component Unit	70700	Endowment Fund
12	6100001	Endowment Trust (Chairs)	562120	Trsf to Treasury Fund-ONUS	9,000,000.00	9000	Higher Educ Component Unit	70700	Endowment Fund
13	6100001	Endowment Trust (Chairs)	562120	Trsf to Treasury Fund-ONUS	9,000,000.00	9000	Higher Educ Component Unit	70700	Endowment Fund
14	6100001	Endowment Trust (Chairs)	562120	Trsf to Treasury Fund-ONUS	9,000,000.00	9000	Higher Educ Component Unit	70700	Endowment Fund
15	7000011	Education Stabilization	555120	Pmts-Local Gov't-Pub Sch Ed	8,000,000.00	1000	General Fund - No Divisions	21000	Multiyr Edu Dist Stab Revl Fnd
16	9400001	Highway Projects	548110	Principal Payments-Bond Debt	6,500,000.00	1300	State Transportation Fund	34000	CMIA Programs Disbursing Fund
17	6100001	Endowment Trust (Chairs)	562120	Trsf to Treasury Fund-ONUS	6,000,000.00	9000	Higher Educ Component Unit	70700	Endowment Fund
18	9400001	Highway Projects	548110	Principal Payments-Bond Debt	5,200,000.00	1300	State Transportation Fund	34000	CMIA Programs Disbursing Fund
19	6100001	Endowment Trust (Chairs)	562120	Trsf to Treasury Fund-ONUS	5,000,000.00	9000	Higher Educ Component Unit	70700	Endowment Fund
20	6100001	Endowment Trust (Chairs)	562120	Trsf to Treasury Fund-ONUS	5,000,000.00	9000	Higher Educ Component Unit	70700	Endowment Fund
21	6100001	Endowment Trust (Chairs)	562120	Trsf to Treasury Fund-ONUS	5,000,000.00	9000	Higher Educ Component Unit	70700	Endowment Fund
22	6100001	Endowment Trust (Chairs)	562120	Trsf to Treasury Fund-ONUS	5,000,000.00	9000	Higher Educ Component Unit	70700	Endowment Fund
23	7000710	State Share Reimbursement	551130	Assistance-Title XIX Medicaid	5,000,000.00	1000	General Fund - No Divisions	19301	GRF - Duties
24	6700004	Contract Com&Econ Dev-Comm Dev	555110	Pmts-Local Gov't-Gen Govt	4,400,000.00	1000	General Fund - No Divisions	40500	Okla. DHS-LIHEAP
25	7000710	State Share Reimbursement	551130	Assistance-Title XIX Medicaid	4,200,000.00	1000	General Fund - No Divisions	57601	Duties
26	7000710	State Share Reimbursement	551130	Assistance-Title XIX Medicaid	4,200,000.00	1000	General Fund - No Divisions	57601	Duties
27	2100001	Children and Family Services	553180	Settlemnts-Pd to/thru Attorney	4,000,000.00	1000	General Fund - No Divisions	32300	Fy13 Human Services Disb Fund
28	2000001	Medicaid Payments	551130	Assistance-Title XIX Medicaid	3,850,000.00	1000	General Fund - No Divisions	34000	CMIA Programs Disbursing Fund
29	2000001	Medicaid Payments	551130	Assistance-Title XIX Medicaid	3,850,000.00	1000	General Fund - No Divisions	34000	CMIA Programs Disbursing Fund
30	2000001	Medicaid Payments	551130	Assistance-Title XIX Medicaid	3,850,000.00	1000	General Fund - No Divisions	34000	CMIA Programs Disbursing Fund
31	2000001	Medicaid Payments	551130	Assistance-Title XIX Medicaid	3,850,000.00	1000	General Fund - No Divisions	34000	CMIA Programs Disbursing Fund
32	2000001	Medicaid Payments	551130	Assistance-Title XIX Medicaid	3,850,000.00	1000	General Fund - No Divisions	34000	CMIA Programs Disbursing Fund
33	9139928	Purchase of Property	561130	Employee Reimb.-Non-Travel	3,800,000.00	9000	Higher Educ Component Unit	47600	Reg Of OU Stud Facil Rev Bonds

FIGURE 8.11 Even Thousand Amounts in the Payment File

The result of this analysis contains 13,827 records in Figure 8.11. You can quickly scroll through some of the larger records both to get a sense of what is included and to see if there are any transactions of interest. Since we have so many transactions that meet our even thousand dollar amount criteria, we can employ sampling techniques to obtain a smaller representative sample of these records. For any general analysis that results in too many records to review in detail that cannot be further reduced by additional criteria, the sampling techniques outlined in Chapter 4 may be used.

 ## SAME-SAME-SAME TEST

The same-same-same test can be used with various combinations of fields that all must match before outputting the results. In our example test, we wish to see if there are any transactions that were paid by the same agency to the same vendor on the same date for the same invoice identification number along with the identical payment amounts.

We can use the same fields of AGENCY_NAME, VENDOR_NAME, PAYMENT_DATE_2, INVOICE_ID, and PAYMENT_AMOUNT.

We specify the same agency name as different agencies may pay on the same date to the same vendor although it is unlikely that the invoice ID would be the same.

We will do a same-same-different test using different agencies for the same matches afterward.

	AGENCY_NAME	VENDOR_NAME	PAYMENT_DATE_2	INVOICE_ID	PAYMENT_AMOUNT	TRANSACTION_TYPE
62	ATTORNEY GENERAL	OFFICE OF MANAGEMENT & ENTERPRISE SVCS	03/04/2013	0003130005	457.02	P
63	ATTORNEY GENERAL	OFFICE OF MANAGEMENT & ENTERPRISE SVCS	03/04/2013	0003130005	457.02	P
64	ATTORNEY GENERAL	OFFICE OF MANAGEMENT & ENTERPRISE SVCS	04/04/2013	FC00000233	10,066.19	P
65	ATTORNEY GENERAL	OFFICE OF MANAGEMENT & ENTERPRISE SVCS	04/04/2013	FC00000233	10,066.19	P
66	ATTORNEY GENERAL	OFFICE OF MANAGEMENT & ENTERPRISE SVCS	12/04/2013	FC00000307	10,066.19	P
67	ATTORNEY GENERAL	OFFICE OF MANAGEMENT & ENTERPRISE SVCS	12/04/2013	FC00000307	10,066.19	P
68	ATTORNEY GENERAL	OFFICE OF MANAGEMENT & ENTERPRISE SVCS	17/04/2013	EB00001702	88.69	P
69	ATTORNEY GENERAL	OFFICE OF MANAGEMENT & ENTERPRISE SVCS	17/04/2013	EB00001702	88.69	P
70	ATTORNEY GENERAL	OFFICE OF MANAGEMENT & ENTERPRISE SVCS	22/04/2013	0004130005	673.57	P
71	ATTORNEY GENERAL	OFFICE OF MANAGEMENT & ENTERPRISE SVCS	22/04/2013	0004130005	673.57	P
72	ATTORNEY GENERAL	OFFICE OF MANAGEMENT & ENTERPRISE SVCS	16/05/2013	EB00001804	235.29	P
73	ATTORNEY GENERAL	OFFICE OF MANAGEMENT & ENTERPRISE SVCS	16/05/2013	EB00001804	235.29	P
74	ATTORNEY GENERAL	OFFICE OF MANAGEMENT & ENTERPRISE SVCS	16/05/2013	FC00000352	10,066.19	P
75	ATTORNEY GENERAL	OFFICE OF MANAGEMENT & ENTERPRISE SVCS	16/05/2013	FC00000352	10,066.19	P
76	ATTORNEY GENERAL	OFFICE OF MANAGEMENT & ENTERPRISE SVCS	20/06/2013	0005130005	1,150.19	P
77	ATTORNEY GENERAL	OFFICE OF MANAGEMENT & ENTERPRISE SVCS	20/06/2013	0005130005	1,150.19	P
78	ATTORNEY GENERAL	OKLAHOMA BAR ASSOCIATION	18/12/2012	12/10/2012	275.00	P
79	ATTORNEY GENERAL	OKLAHOMA BAR ASSOCIATION	18/12/2012	12/10/2012	275.00	P
80	ATTORNEY GENERAL	OKLAHOMA BAR ASSOCIATION	18/12/2012	12/10/2012	275.00	P
81	ATTORNEY GENERAL	OKLAHOMA BAR ASSOCIATION	18/12/2012	12/10/2012	825.00	P
82	ATTORNEY GENERAL	OKLAHOMA BAR ASSOCIATION	18/12/2012	12/10/2012	825.00	P

FIGURE 8.12 Same-Same-Same Test Applied to the Payment File for Same Agencies, Vendors, Payment Dates, Invoice IDs, and Payment Amount Transactions

To our surprise, we got 51,743 records or 2.5 percent of the 2,066,536 total records as duplicates in Figure 8.12. There may be some duplicate payments to the vendors given that identical invoice identification numbers were paid. Some invoice identification numbers used the invoice date as the reference and some records in the INVOICE_ID field are blank.

We can further reduce the duplicate records for review by filtering, using a criteria equation of

INVOICE_ID < > " " .AND. PAYMENT_AMOUNT < > 0

Looking at records where the invoice identification numbers are populated with amounts not equaling zero brings our duplicate records down to 27,733 or 1.3 percent.

On the other hand, after some investigation, you may decide that those transactions without the invoice identification numbers are higher-risk payments. Regardless, even if fraud or errors are not present, the processing of what appears to be individual payments is inefficient.

 ## SAME-SAME-DIFFERENT TEST

Now we will see if there are any transactions in different agencies that paid the same vendor with the same invoice identification number on the same day using the same amount.

We can use the same fields of VENDOR_NAME, PAYMENT_DATE_2, INVOICE_ID, and PAYMENT_AMOUNT but different AGENCY_NUMBER.

Any matching records would be either duplicate payments or portion of payments allocated by the contracting agency to other agencies.

AGENCY_NUMBER	AGENCY_NAME	VENDOR_NAME	PAYMENT_DATE_2	PAYMENT_AMOUNT	INVOICE_ID	TRANSACTION_TYPE
1000	OKLAHOMA STATE UNIVERSITY	ALDINGER CO	14/01/2013	100.00	C-121015-0269	P
1100	OSU-EXPERIMENT STATION	ALDINGER CO	14/01/2013	100.00	C-121015-0269	P
1100	OSU-EXPERIMENT STATION	ALDINGER CO	14/01/2013	100.00	C-121015-0269	P
1600	OSU-TULSA	ANIXTER INC	20/09/2012	2,101.05	105-490465	P
77300	OSU-COLLEGE OF OSTEOPATHIC MED.	ANIXTER INC	20/09/2012	2,101.05	105-490465	P
1000	OKLAHOMA STATE UNIVERSITY	B&C BUSINESS PRODUCTS INC	16/01/2013	42.50	176414.	P
1200	OSU-EXTENSION DIVISION	B&C BUSINESS PRODUCTS INC	16/01/2013	42.50	176414.	P
1000	OKLAHOMA STATE UNIVERSITY	BLALARK,KAYLA GENE	23/04/2013	3.00	0054236	P
1200	OSU-EXTENSION DIVISION	BLALARK,KAYLA GENE	23/04/2013	3.00	0054236	P
1000	OKLAHOMA STATE UNIVERSITY	BLALARK,KAYLA GENE	21/05/2013	3.00	0055476	P
1200	OSU-EXTENSION DIVISION	BLALARK,KAYLA GENE	21/05/2013	3.00	0055476	P
1000	OKLAHOMA STATE UNIVERSITY	BLALARK,KAYLA GENE	11/06/2013	3.00	0056624	P
1200	OSU-EXTENSION DIVISION	BLALARK,KAYLA GENE	11/06/2013	3.00	0056624	P
1000	OKLAHOMA STATE UNIVERSITY	BRENDA *SHEIK	09/11/2012	16.50	0047323	P
1200	OSU-EXTENSION DIVISION	BRENDA *SHEIK	09/11/2012	16.50	0047323	P
1000	OKLAHOMA STATE UNIVERSITY	BRENDA *SHEIK	09/11/2012	150.00	0047323	P
1200	OSU-EXTENSION DIVISION	BRENDA *SHEIK	09/11/2012	150.00	0047323	P
1600	OSU-TULSA	CBORD GROUP	21/09/2012	224.40	CTR034674	P
77300	OSU-COLLEGE OF OSTEOPATHIC MED.	CBORD GROUP	21/09/2012	224.40	CTR034674	P
1000	OKLAHOMA STATE UNIVERSITY	COWBOY JOURNAL	17/06/2013	333.33	152-009	P
1100	OSU-EXPERIMENT STATION	COWBOY JOURNAL	17/06/2013	333.33	152-009	P
1600	OSU-TULSA	COWBOY SPORTS PROPERTIES LLC	27/09/2012	20,000.00	274-175386-091	P
77300	OSU-COLLEGE OF OSTEOPATHIC MED.	COWBOY SPORTS PROPERTIES LLC	27/09/2012	20,000.00	274-175386-091	P
1600	OSU-TULSA	COWBOY SPORTS PROPERTIES LLC	10/12/2012	3,750.00	274-179098-111	P
77300	OSU-COLLEGE OF OSTEOPATHIC MED.	COWBOY SPORTS PROPERTIES LLC	10/12/2012	3,750.00	274-179098-111	P
1100	OSU-EXPERIMENT STATION	DAVID *LALMAN	05/03/2013	20.00	0050667	P
1200	OSU-EXTENSION DIVISION	DAVID *LALMAN	05/03/2013	20.00	0050667	P
1100	OSU-EXPERIMENT STATION	DELL MARKETING LP	24/10/2012	119.69	XFXMWRFP4	P
1200	OSU-EXTENSION DIVISION	DELL MARKETING LP	24/10/2012	119.69	XFXMWRFP4	P
1300	OSU-TECHNICAL BRANCH, OKMULGEE	EDUCAUSE	07/08/2012	924.00	09131:EMULT1	P
1600	OSU-TULSA	EDUCAUSE	07/08/2012	924.00	09131:EMULT1	P
1000	OKLAHOMA STATE UNIVERSITY	EMRICK'S VAN & STORAGE	14/08/2012	5,000.00	273815	P
1100	OSU-EXPERIMENT STATION	EMRICK'S VAN & STORAGE	14/08/2012	5,000.00	273815	P
1100	OSU-EXPERIMENT STATION	ESKIMO JOE'S PROMOTIONAL GROUP	07/09/2012	200.03	24359	P
1200	OSU-EXTENSION DIVISION	ESKIMO JOE'S PROMOTIONAL GROUP	07/09/2012	200.03	24359	P
1000	OKLAHOMA STATE UNIVERSITY	FENTON'S OFFICE MART	13/09/2012	1,975.76	298658-0	P
1100	OSU-EXPERIMENT STATION	FENTON'S OFFICE MART	13/09/2012	1,975.76	298658-0	P

FIGURE 8.13 Same-Same-Different Test for Same Vendors, Payment Dates, Invoice IDs, and Payment Amount but with Different Agencies

After filtering the field, PAYMENT_AMOUNT < > 0, we have 174 records out of 182 as displayed in Figure 8.13.

OSU headings are different departments within Oklahoma State University that are not really different agencies. Some of the transactions should be verified that they are indeed proper allocations to different departments within the university rather than duplicate payments in error.

 ## PAYMENTS WITHOUT PURCHASE ORDERS TEST

If it is the policy of the state to require purchase orders from vendors before goods or services can be contracted, we can look for payments where there is no corresponding purchase order recorded. Some vendors have standing order contracts with the organization that are preapproved so the cumbersome procurement process does not have to be done for each individual purchase.

We start by determining the number of transactions where there are payments of any amount that do not have a purchase order. The payment amount minimum can be adjusted later in accordance with the organization's policy or for materiality.

Using the file "Payments trans type P" and the equation of PURCHASE_ORDER_ CONTRACT_NUMBER = = " " .AND. PAYMENT_AMOUNT < > 0.00, we extract a new file and name it "Payments without Purchase Order." The resulting file of 1,597,436 records—over 78 percent of the original file— has too many records to review.

We look to the field statistics in Figure 8.14 of the PAYMENT_AMOUNT of this file to obtain a better understanding of what steps to take next.

There are 138,196 records making up the negative value of $210,162,202.50 or an average negative amount of $1,520. Removing the credits from the file would not significantly increase the overall average of $7,465.23 due to the proportion of the positive amounts versus the negative amounts.

We can perform a number of summarizations to potentially get an idea of where the no-purchase-order issue is occurring. Possible summarization examples might be individually or in combination by the VENDOR_NAME, ACCOUNT, AGENCY_NUM-BER, VOUCHER_TYPE, or FUND_CODE fields.

We may also consider using the Top Records Extraction feature of IDEA to look at a specified number of highest-dollar amounts for certain categories. We can see from the field statistics that the largest amount is $48,907,078.15. It seems likely that there are large numbers of high-dollar-value payments.

We will summarize by AGENCY_NUMBER and total on the PAYMENT_AMOUNT field. It is useful to include the AGENCY_NAME field in the output along with the average payment amount by agency as shown in Figure 8.15. This file should be called "Summarize by Agency wo PO."

Observe the payment averages in descending order in Figure 8.16, and note that the Capitol Improvement Authority (agency number 10500) had the highest average payment amounts where there were no purchase orders. Extracting to preview those 17 transactions, we see that the expenditures were mainly for bond debt.

Numeric Statistics	PAYMENT_AMOUNT
Net Value	11,925,230,034.19
Absolute Value	12,345,554,439.19
# of Records	1,597,436
# of Zero Items	0
Positive Value	12,135,392,236.69
Negative Value	-210,162,202.50
# of Positive Records	1,459,240
# of Negative Records	138,196
# of Data Errors	0
# of Valid Values	1,597,436
Average Value	7,465.23
Minimum Value	-977,208.31
Maximum Value	48,907,078.15
Record # of Min	273,011
Record # of Max	1,558,424
Sample Std Dev	137,976.54
Sample Variance	19,037,524,328.46
Pop Std Dev	137,976.49
Pop Variance	19,037,512,410.91
Pop Skewness	143.292616
Pop Kurtosis	31,594.509442

FIGURE 8.14 Field Statistics of the File of Payments without Purchase Orders

We can also summarize by VENDOR_NAME, totaling on the payment amounts, and include a payment average calculation. Name this new file "Summarize by Vendor wo PO."

In this case, one of the areas we may want to devote some attention to is infrequent payments to vendors that have no purchase orders associated with the payments. We

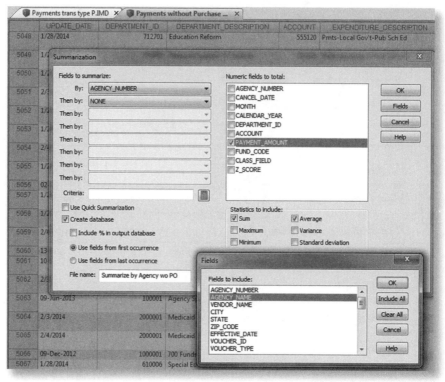

FIGURE 8.15 Summarize by Agency for Total and Average Payment Amounts

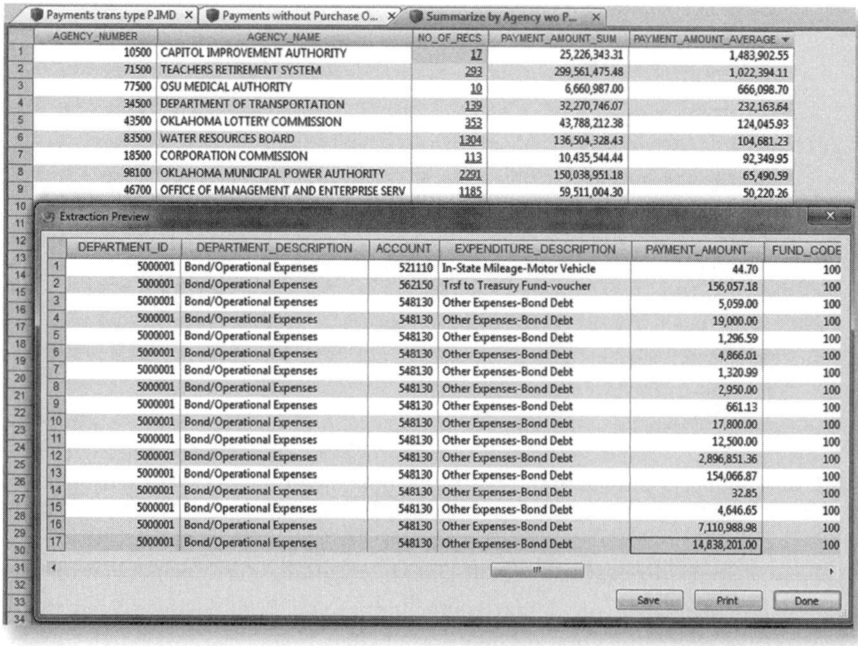

FIGURE 8.16 Result of the Summarization by Agency with Average Payments Displayed in Descending Order

index by NO_OF_RECS and then by PAYMENT_AMOUNT_SUM to display the screen in Figure 8.17.

	VENDOR_NAME	NO_OF_RECS▲	PAYMENT_AMOUNT_SUM ▼	PAYMENT_AMOUNT_AVERAGE
1	CHILDRENS RIGHTS	1	4,000,000.00	4,000,000.00
2	Broken Arrow MA	1	3,378,579.00	3,378,579.00
3	FLINTCO INC.	1	3,086,486.95	3,086,486.95
4	OKLAHOMA YOUTH EXPOSITION INC	1	2,000,000.00	2,000,000.00
5	MIDWEST REGIONAL MEDICAL CENTER LLC	1	1,691,384.51	1,691,384.51
6	FAIRBANKS MORSE ENGINE	1	1,565,735.85	1,565,735.85
7	TULSAIR BEECHCRAFT INC	1	1,422,500.00	1,422,500.00
8	Transfer to BancFirst Reserve Fund	1	1,313,851.20	1,313,851.20
9	AMBLING UNIVERSITY DEVELOPMENT GROUP LLC	1	1,210,189.90	1,210,189.90
10	Enid MA	1	1,166,388.64	1,166,388.64
11	CHESAPEAKE ENERGY CORPORATION	1	1,065,521.23	1,065,521.23
12	TIAACREF	1	755,435.00	755,435.00
13	CHRIS QUISENBERRY	1	662,956.51	662,956.51
14	Laverne PWA	1	605,502.85	605,502.85
15	College Assn.of Liability Management	1	561,894.64	561,894.64
16	BANK OF OKLAHOMA N A	1	555,012.00	555,012.00
17	MANKILLER PROJECT LLC	1	552,627.88	552,627.88
18	Logan RWD #1 - reissued 3/1/13	1	551,943.00	551,943.00
19	CHILD ABUSE NETWORK	1	551,898.86	551,898.86
20	CHILD ABUSE RESPONSE CENTER INC	1	551,898.86	551,898.86
21	Eufaula PWA	1	523,984.63	523,984.63
22	Lone Grove WSTA	1	522,788.94	522,788.94
23	Lawton WA	1	475,059.35	475,059.35
24	THE RESTORATION CORPORATION	1	442,966.35	442,966.35
25	Longtown RW&SD #1	1	393,551.66	393,551.66
26	THOMSON REUTERS SCI INC	1	350,383.00	350,383.00
27	Adair MA-failed to draw green funds earl	1	332,000.00	332,000.00
28	MCINTOSH CO PUBLIC FACILITIES AUTHORITY	1	328,050.00	328,050.00
29	Wagoner #4	1	311,279.84	311,279.84
30	Muskogee MA	1	311,220.00	311,220.00
31	HOME RUN MOVIE LLC	1	304,140.00	304,140.00
32	Citizens Bank of Edmond	1	300,000.00	300,000.00
33	DEPT. OF CENTRAL SERVICES	1	294,604.00	294,604.00
34	Bartlesville MA	1	288,844.17	288,844.17
35	ATTACHMATE WRQ	1	287,960.00	287,960.00
36	THUNDERHEAD.COM	1	275,857.00	275,857.00

FIGURE 8.17 Summarize by Vendor with Totals and Average Payment Amounts without Any Purchase Orders

We can see there are a number of one-off payments to vendors that are significant in dollar amounts. Given that our file has 76,678 records, it would be difficult to examine all the transactions and it would be inconvenient to scroll or perform a criteria view for low numbers of transactions by vendor.

We can perform a Top Records Extraction for the top five amounts based on the dollar values and grouped by the number of records, as seen in Figure 8.18. We limit our review to those vendors that had five or fewer transactions. The file should be called "Top Records Payment Sum by Records." This will give us only a maximum of 25 transactions that we should audit in detail to ensure compliance with policies and procedures. We also want to ensure the validity and accuracy of the payments.

Depending on the audit focus and resources, you may wish to increase the top 5 amounts selected to 10, which still would be a reasonable number to audit and can be printed out on a single page.

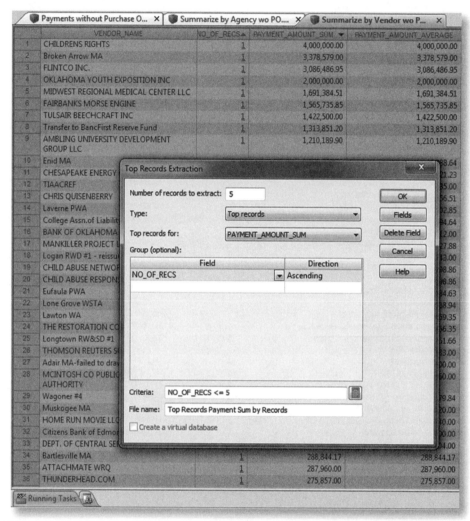

FIGURE 8.18 Obtaining the Top Five Payment Amounts of Vendors Transacted with Frequency of Five Times or Less

As an example, if we click on the number 1 to the right of the vendor Children's Rights of the first record in Figure 8.19, IDEA displays the details. The agency that paid Children's Rights was the Department of Human Services, Children and Family Services department. The expenditure description noted that it was a settlement paid to or through the attorney general. As the amount was significant to the tune of $4 million, this transaction should clearly be reviewed by the auditors for appropriateness. It may be possible that this transaction was already selected and examined as an anomaly through other tests, such as the even thousand amount test.

	VENDOR_NAME	NO_OF_RECS	PAYMENT_AMOUNT_SUM	PAYMENT_AMOUNT_AVERAGE
1	CHILDRENS RIGHTS	1	4,000,000.00	4,000,000.00
2	Broken Arrow MA	1	3,378,579.00	3,378,579.00
3	FLINTCO INC.	1	3,086,486.95	3,086,486.95
4	OKLAHOMA YOUTH EXPOSITION INC	1	2,000,000.00	2,000,000.00
5	MIDWEST REGIONAL MEDICAL CENTER LLC	1	1,691,384.51	1,691,384.51
6	UNIVERSITY HOSPITAL AUTHOR	2	42,036,807.00	21,018,403.50
7	DEUTSCHE BANK TRUST CO.	2	2,338,150.00	1,169,075.00
8	GUIDEWIRE SOFTWARE INC	2	1,990,092.00	995,046.00
9	Workplace Solutions, LLC dba	2	998,315.86	499,157.93
10	US ARMY CORP OF ENGINEERS	2	996,389.84	498,194.92
11	ST JOHN MEDICAL CENTER INC	3	6,473,746.51	2,157,915.50
12	INTEGRIS SOUTHWEST MEDICAL CENTER	3	2,944,738.19	981,579.40
13	COTTON ELECTRIC	3	1,736,814.74	578,938.25
14	CHRISTIANSEN AVIATION INC	3	1,578,108.00	526,036.00
15	TIAA/CREF	3	1,420,000.00	473,333.33
16	AHS HILLCREST MEDICAL CENTER LLC	4	22,327,202.95	5,581,800.74
17	INTEGRIS SOUTHWEST MEDICAL CENTER INC	4	7,912,879.17	1,978,219.79
18	Oklahoma City WUT	4	2,105,746.35	526,436.59
19	ELSEVIER BV - USE NEW TIN	4	1,511,976.82	377,994.21
20	HARMON ELECTRIC ASSOCIATION INC	4	1,460,707.06	365,176.77
21	DEPT OF MENTAL HEALTH - OBH	5	40,133,334.00	8,026,666.80
22	Tulsa MUA	5	11,372,392.00	2,274,478.40
23	OSU MEDICAL CENTER	5	8,777,026.34	1,755,405.27
24	CEDAR RIDGE HOSPITAL	5	6,568,932.35	1,313,786.47
25	Moore PWA	5	5,898,668.56	1,179,733.71

FIGURE 8.19 Results of the Top Five Payment Amounts of Vendors Transacted with Frequency of Five Times or Less

LENGTH OF TIME BETWEEN INVOICE AND PAYMENT DATES TEST

This test may reveal unusually quick payments to certain vendors or slow payments that result in interest charges or early-payment discounts not taken.

Using the "State Vendor Payments" file, a DATE_DIFFERENCE field is created by using the @Age function in IDEA. This function calculates the differences in days between two date fields.

This equation should be used:

@Age(PAYMENT_DATE_2, INVOICE_DATE_2)

With over 2 million records in this file, we can stratify the date difference results into a number of bands from 0 to 120 days, as displayed in Figure 8.20.

Stratum #	>= L Limit	< U Limit	# Records	(%) # Records	PAYMENT_AMOUNT	(%) PAYMENT_AMOUNT
1	0	1	826,000	39.97	7,961,856,450.29	52.18
2	1	5	225,892	10.93	1,991,826,798.68	13.05
3	5	10	156,141	7.56	1,059,622,752.54	6.94
4	10	15	195,147	9.44	731,120,867.81	4.79
5	15	20	131,589	6.37	628,678,590.74	4.12
6	20	30	206,589	10.00	1,046,345,438.93	6.86
7	30	60	219,671	10.63	955,384,128.22	6.26
8	60	90	54,644	2.64	245,402,332.40	1.61
9	90	120	21,877	1.06	76,569,162.41	0.50
	Lower limit exceptions:		2,728	0.13	409,282,004.46	2.68
	Upper limit exceptions:		26,248	1.27	152,899,948.00	1.00
	Totals:		2,066,536	100.00	15,258,988,474.48	100.00

FIGURE 8.20 Results of Stratification Payment and Invoice Date Differences

From the stratification, we note that 826,000 payments were made on the same day as the invoice date. Testing of a sample of these transactions should be done. There were also 2,728 payments that were made before the invoice date, which is highly unusual. However, from the outset of reviewing this file, we had identified that the invoice date contains many input errors. Obvious errors should be dismissed and remaining anomalies should be reviewed.

Since we are looking at payment dates, this would be a good time to extract and review the 41 payments that were made on Sundays and the 64 payments that were made on Saturdays, as identified in our initial review of the field statistics for the date fields in Figure 8.2.

We can create a new field using the @Workday function that returns the number 1 if the payment date falls on a weekday or conversely returns a zero if the date falls on a weekend day. We can set the criteria or extraction to output only transactions falling on the weekend where the field contains a zero. In the event that some agencies or departments process payments on Saturdays, it would be better to segregate the two weekend days. We can use the @Dow or date of week function. This function will return, based on a date field, 1 for Sunday, 2 for Monday . . . and 7 for Saturday.

First we append a new numeric field to the "State Vendor Payments" file called DOW using the equation of

@Dow(PAYMENT_DATE_2)

We then extract to a file called "Saturday and Sunday Payments," where DOW = 1 .OR. DOW = 7.

Since the file now contains a reasonable 105 records, we can clearly see in Figure 8.21 that the original INVOICE_DATE field had a number of blanks that gave us an error message relating to those blanks.

By filtering out the error or bad data, we end up with eight transactions that were paid on Sunday (DOW = 1) and 13 payments made on Saturday (DOW = 7), as displayed in Figure 8.22.

According to the invoice date, most of these 21 payments were made by the Water Resources Board agency over a year after the invoice data. Three minor payments were made by Murray State College on one particular Sunday.

 ## SEARCH FOR POST OFFICE BOX

A common test is to look for the usage of postal box numbers as the mailing address for check payments. The theory is that legitimate vendors should have physical locations and regular civic addresses. Vendors that use post office boxes raise red flags of potential fraud. It may be employees of the organization who set up payments to a vendor that they have a vested interest in and want to conceal the arrangement. It may also be a vehicle to receive payments where no such business actually exists. It is more difficult to trace the principals behind a post office than a standard address. However, small service providers may legitimately be using post office boxes, so this area is something to review that may result in some false-positive red flags of fraud.

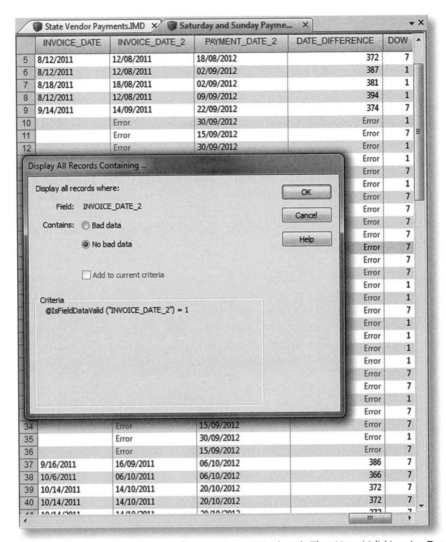

FIGURE 8.21 Isolating Good Data of Payments on Weekends That Have Valid Invoice Dates

	AGENCY_NAME	VENDOR_NAME	PAYMENT_AMOUNT	INVOICE_DATE	INVOICE_DATE_2	PAYMENT_DATE_2	DATE_DIFFERENCE	DOW
1	WATER RESOURCES BOARD	Owasso PWA	8,001.90	7/11/2011	11/07/2011	21/07/2012	376	7
2	WATER RESOURCES BOARD	Fort Gibson UA	95,866.00	6/23/2011	23/06/2011	22/07/2012	395	1
3	WATER RESOURCES BOARD	Beggs PWA	186,288.01	7/22/2011	22/07/2011	05/08/2012	380	1
4	WATER RESOURCES BOARD	Owasso PWA	618.00	8/8/2011	08/08/2011	18/08/2012	376	7
5	WATER RESOURCES BOARD	Inola PWA	204,039.39	8/12/2011	12/08/2011	18/08/2012	372	7
6	WATER RESOURCES BOARD	COMCD	17,624.91	8/12/2011	12/08/2011	02/09/2012	387	1
7	WATER RESOURCES BOARD	Beggs PWA	79,744.49	8/18/2011	18/08/2011	02/09/2012	381	1
8	WATER RESOURCES BOARD	COMCD	12,105.02	8/12/2011	12/08/2011	09/09/2012	394	1
9	WATER RESOURCES BOARD	Okemah UA	106,197.00	9/14/2011	14/09/2011	22/09/2012	374	7
10	WATER RESOURCES BOARD	Yale WST	127,725.85	9/16/2011	16/09/2011	06/10/2012	385	7
11	WATER RESOURCES BOARD	BancFirst - Owasso arra bond refund	1,975.00	10/6/2011	06/10/2011	06/10/2012	366	7
12	WATER RESOURCES BOARD	Bixby PWA	120,820.03	10/14/2011	14/10/2011	20/10/2012	372	7
13	WATER RESOURCES BOARD	Yale WST	57,051.70	10/14/2011	14/10/2011	20/10/2012	372	7
14	WATER RESOURCES BOARD	Inola PWA	227,816.65	10/14/2011	14/10/2011	20/10/2012	372	7
15	WATER RESOURCES BOARD	Lawton WA	475,059.35	11/4/2011	04/11/2011	10/11/2012	372	7
16	WATER RESOURCES BOARD	Okmulgee MA	101,284.33	11/3/2011	03/11/2011	10/11/2012	373	7
17	WATER RESOURCES BOARD	Moore PWA	1,644,555.49	11/4/2011	04/11/2011	10/11/2012	372	7
18	WATER RESOURCES BOARD	Yale WST	117,107.60	11/28/2011	28/11/2011	01/12/2012	369	7
19	MURRAY STATE COLLEGE	PROTECTED INFORMATION	219.22	14-Mar-2013	14/03/2013	17/03/2013	3	1
20	MURRAY STATE COLLEGE	PROTECTED INFORMATION	82.50	14-Mar-2013	14/03/2013	17/03/2013	3	1
21	MURRAY STATE COLLEGE	PROTECTED INFORMATION	92.24	14-Mar-2013	14/03/2013	17/03/2013	3	1

FIGURE 8.22 Results of Filtering Out Bad Data for Payments Made on Weekend Dates

Using IDEA's Search feature, we can enter various formats representing post office boxes in the address field of a vendor master file. In this case we will use the "Sample-Suppliers" file that was included with the software and search the SUPPLIER_ADDR field. The case-insensitive entry of po* tells the program to return matches for anything beginning with the letters po regardless of whether it is in uppercase or lowercase or in combination. The asterisk (*) is a wildcard character that represents all characters. While not used in this example, the question mark (?) represents exactly any one character. For the term po*, it returns items such as post, postal, po, poles, police, potatoe1234, and so on. If we had used the question mark of po?, it would return exactly three characters beginning with the two letters, such as pod, po8, pot, and pop.

We can also include p.o.* with the Boolean operator of OR, so the search can return either situation of items with or without periods, as shown in Figure 8.23. The OR matches either condition and is used rather than AND, which must meet both conditions before returning any results.

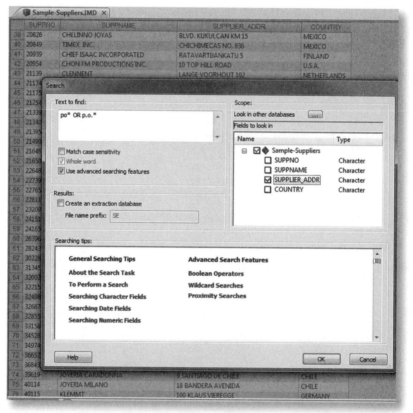

FIGURE 8.23 Searching for Post Office Boxes in Supplier Addresses

There were no post office boxes in our file, but it did pick up a street name that began with the letters "PO," confirming that the search criteria worked and that it is case insensitive, as shown in the results of our search in Figure 8.24.

MATCH EMPLOYEE ADDRESS TO SUPPLIER

Using the vendor master file and the employee master file, we wish to look for any addresses that are common in both files. We note that the supplier file has the addresses in all uppercase while the employee file does not, so we need to use the @Upper function to convert the field in the employee file to match that in the supplier file.

First, create a field in both files called ADDRESS_CHECK; it takes the first part of the field and removes control characters, punctuation, and spaces. In our example, we use the equation of @Strip(@Left(SUPPLIER_ADDR, 10)) in the "Sample-Suppliers" file, as shown in Figure 8.25. The equation takes the first 10 characters from the left of the SUPPLIER_ADDR field and removes any spaces, control characters, or punctuation.

	SUPPNO	SUPPNAME	SUPPLIER_ADDR	COUNTRY
39	20826	CHELINNO JOYAS	BLVD. KUKULCAN KM 15	MEXICO
40	20849	TIMEX INC.	CHICHIMECAS NO. 836	MEXICO
41	20939	CHIEF ISAAC INCORPORATED	RATAVARTIJANKATU 5	FINLAND
42	20954	CHON FM PRODUCTIONS INC.	10 TOP HILL ROAD	U.S.A.
43	21139	CLENNENT	LANGE VOORHOUT 102	NETHERLANDS
44	21174	SWISS ARMY INC.	46 CHEZ MOQUERAT	FRANCE
45	21175	CORPORATE EXPRESS	36-977 KING ST.	HONDURAS
46	21254	COTE D'OR	86400 LIZANT	FRANCE
47	21339	CRESTLINE COACH LTD.	No. 52, 14TH WEI ROAD	CHINA
48	21340	CROWN PUBLICATIONS INC.	16 SHENYANG ROAD	CHINA
49	21395	D A TOWNLEY & ASSOCIATES LTD	100 SHANGHAI	CHINA
50	21490	BULOVA INC.	SOMBRERETE X TEOTIHUACAN X JORDAN	MEXICO
51	21646	DHL CUSTOMS BROKERAGE LTD	C1425EOF BUENOS AIRES	ARGENTINA
52	21650	DIALOG CORPORATION	CALZADA CARDO S/N 8	MEXICO
53	22648	DIVERSIFIED TRANSPORTATION LTD	HIDALGO NO. 4	MEXICO
54	22739	DONNELY	MUSEUMPLEIN 19	NETHERLANDS
55	22765	DUBWEAR INC	DHR MOD UKAIR	ITALY
56	22811	EI EDUCATION INTERNATIONAL LTD	VIA PONZIO 34/5	ITALY
57	23209	EINKAUF GMBH & CO KG	16 MAGDALENA	GERMANY
58	24151	ELECTRICAL SHOP LTD	165 ADELAIDE TERRACE	AUSTRALIA
59	24165	EQUITRAC CORPORATION	45 MUGYO-DONG JUNG-KU	KOREA
60	26396	FA. BLÜMEL	1900 BILLEKEM	GERMANY
61	28243	FA. HOIDES	96 KAROLINE SCHAUER	GERMANY
62	30228	FABRICA TOSONI	CORDOBA 5824	ARGENTINA
63	31345	FINEX SC	55 BUENOS AIRES	ARGENTINA
64	32002	GATUVIA JOYERIA	9 BOULEVARD SAN JUAN BOSCO	HONDURAS
65	32215	GENEVE	6 AVENIDA RAMON CRUZ	HONDURAS
66	32408	GRANTIG AG	1 DER SENDROTE	GERMANY

Sample-Suppliers.IMD

Search Results

	DATABASE	RECORD_NUMBER	FIELD_NAME	TEXT
1	Sample-Suppliers	56	SUPPLIER_ADDR	VIA PONZIO 34/5

FIGURE 8.24 Results of the Search for Post Office Boxes in Supplier Addresses

We do the same when adding the ADDRESS_CHECK field in the "Employees" file, but we also include the @Upper function to convert all the results into uppercase. We use the formula of @Upper(@Strip(@Left(ADDRESS,10))), as displayed in Figure 8.26.

With the "Sample-Suppliers" file as the primary file and the "Employees" file as the secondary file and using the match option of "Matches only," we join the two files , which

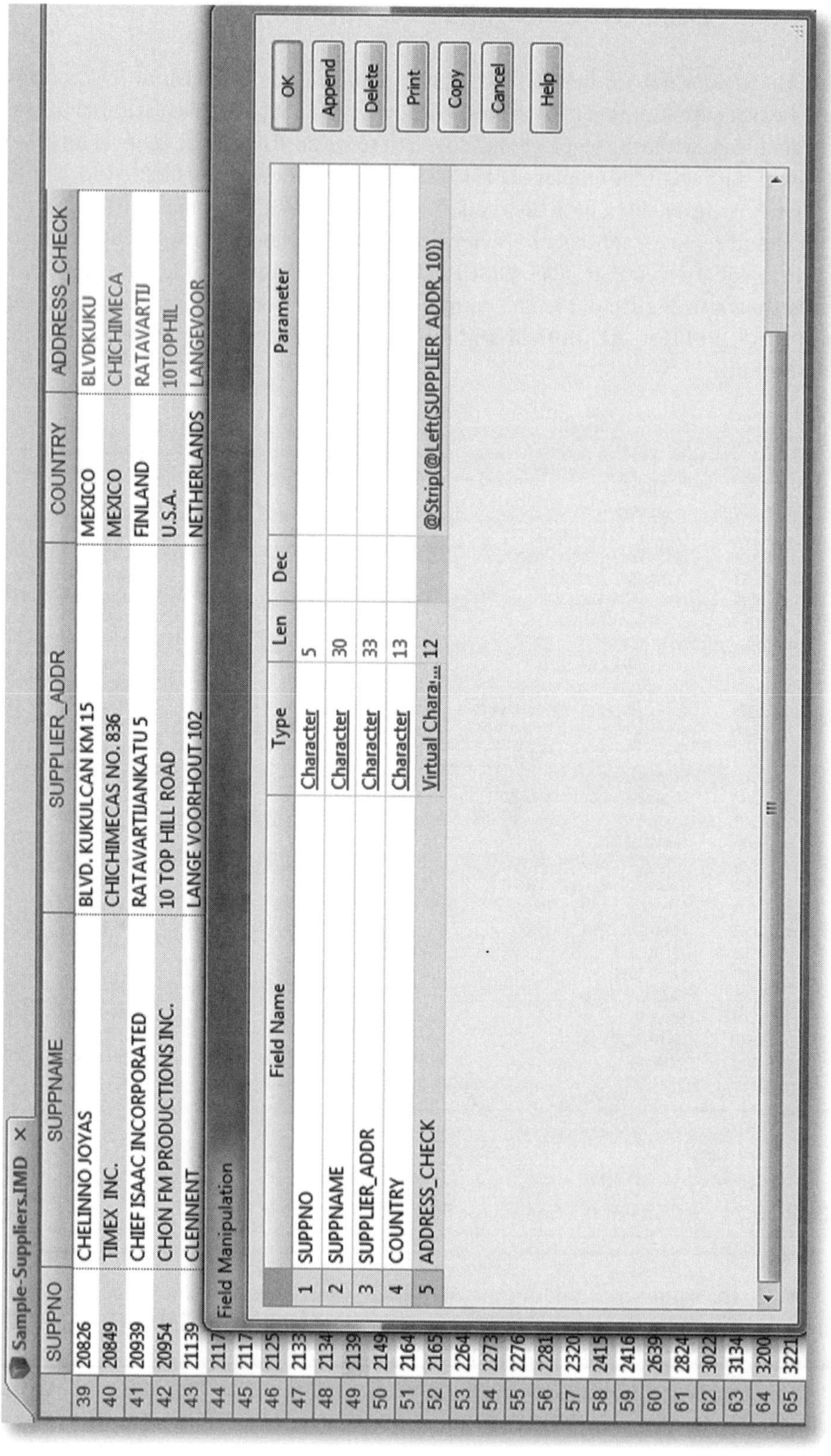

FIGURE 8.25 Preparing the Supplier File for Address Checks

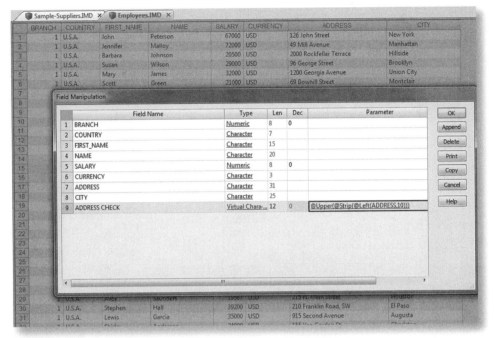

FIGURE 8.26 Preparing the Employees File for Address Checks

results in a new file called "Employees with same address as Vendor." Our match keys are the newly appended fields of ADDRESS_CHECK, as used in Figure 8.27.

Only one record matches in both the primary and secondary file. Supply number 92611 has the same address as one of the employees in Figure 8.28.

It was not necessary to have the ADDRESS_CHECK field from the primary file or from the secondary file field to be included in the output file. They were included here for demonstration purposes. When IDEA encounters an existing field name, it adds a 1 to the end of the first duplicated field name, such as ADDRESS_CHECK1.

Additional field matches may be performed on phone numbers, fax numbers, e-mail addresses, contact names, and other information common in both vendor and employee master files.

 ## DUPLICATE ADDRESSES IN VENDOR MASTER

Using Duplicate Key Detection we can test for different vendors that have common addresses. In our vendor master file of "Sample-Suppliers," we will output duplicate records from the ADDRESS_CHECK field to a file called "Duplicate Address Check," as shown in Figure 8.29.

The results in Figure 8.30 show a match of the same address in the SUPPLIER_ADDR field, but look at the country field—it is clear that the same street name exists in different countries. More difficult false positives to distinguish are matches to the same street address that houses a number of businesses. Suite or unit numbers that are

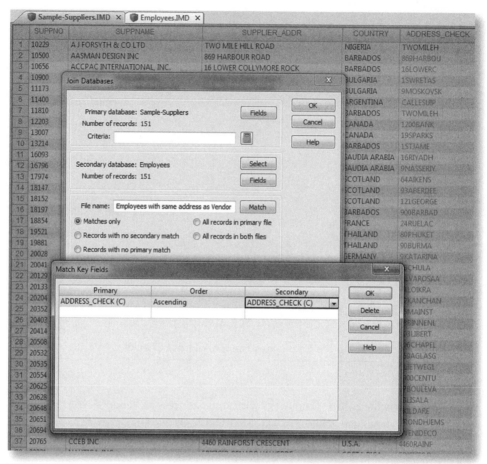

FIGURE 8.27   Matching the Addresses of the Supplier File with the Employee File

SUPPNO	SUPPNAME	SUPPLIER_ADDR	COUNTRY	ADDRESS_CHECK	FIRST_NAME	NAME	ADDRESS	ADDRESS_CHECK1
1 92611	MORRIS GOLD INC	345 PERRY HILL RD.	U.S.A.	345PERRY	Julie	Morris	345 Perry Hill Road	345PERRY

FIGURE 8.28   Results of the Address Matching Test

different may actually be different businesses or the same business. Even if it is the same business, it is not necessarily a fraud issue as a corporation may have several divisions performing different business services or performing identical business services under different names to give the appearance of competition.

 ## PAYMENTS TO VENDORS NOT IN MASTER

To ensure that the organization deals with approved vendors, purchase orders and payments need to be from the vendor master file except in unusual circumstances or for low-dollar transactions.

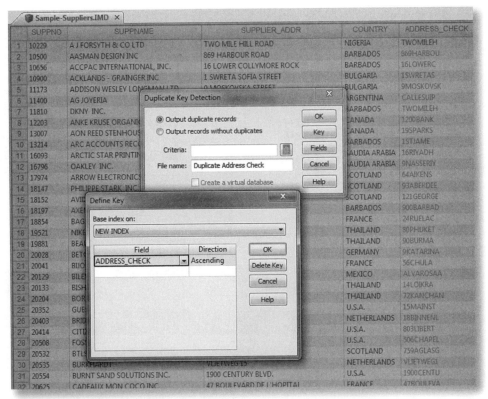

FIGURE 8.29 Testing for Different Suppliers with Same Addresses

FIGURE 8.30 Results of Testing for Different Suppliers with Same Addresses

We can test for payments made to vendors that were not in the vendor master file. Using the "Payments" file as the primary file and the "Sample-Suppliers" file as the secondary file, and the match key as SUPPNO, we can create a new file to output the results to called "Payments to Suppliers Not in Master." The Join option of "Records with no secondary match" is used in Figure 8.31. This means that only suppliers that are in the primary "Payments" file but not in the "Sample-Suppliers" file are displayed.

One record in Figure 8.32 clearly needs investigation. An amount of $14,370.05 was paid to supplier number 20536. This supplier was not in the vendor master list and may not have been approved to do business with the company. More likely, it was once in the vendor master list but since removed, as the organization no longer wished to continue its business relationship. It is also interesting that the person who authorized

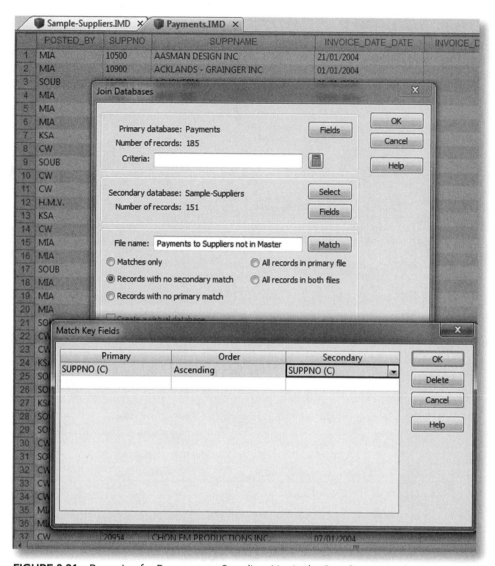

FIGURE 8.31 Preparing for Payments to Suppliers Not in the Supplier or Vendor Master File

the payment is the same person who posted the payment. The internal control of segregation of duties failed here and places this transaction as a high-fraud-risk transaction. While on the subject of approvals, record number 11 did not have an authorizing person noted in the AUTH field. An additional test that can be performed in the "Payments" file is to extract payment with no authorization using the equation

$$AUTH == ``\ "$$

Supplier number 9999 is normally for onetime transactions that do not necessitate adding the vendor to the vendor master file. High-dollar transactions in this category should be reviewed for validity and also whether policies and procedures were adhered to.

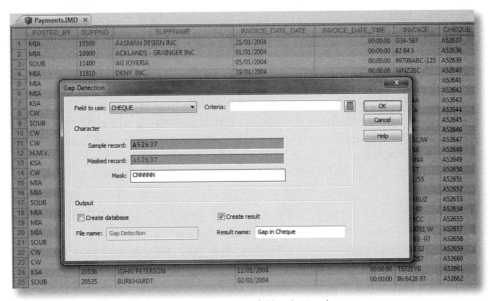

	POSTED_BY	SUPPNO	SUPPNAME	INVOICE_DATE_DATE	INVOICE_DATE_TIME	INVOICE	CHEQUE	PAY_DATE_DATE	PAY_DATE_TIME	PURCH_ORDE	AUTH	AMOUNT
1	KSA	20536	JOHN PETERSON	11/01/2004	00:00:00	T5721VB	A52661	10/02/2004	00:00:00	100084400	KSA	14,370.05
2	CW	99999	TOOL PRECISIONS	31/12/2004	00:00:00	T5730VB	B52171	29/02/2004	00:00:00	100089400	VMH	3,773.70
3	CW	99999	CASH & CO	31/12/2004	00:00:00	PPN98787	B52172	01/03/2004	00:00:00	100089500	V.S.T	1,844.92
4	CW	99999	WITCH PRODUCTS	31/12/2004	00:00:00	3501050	B52173	01/03/2004	00:00:00	100089600	H.M	71.88
5	MIA	99999	WINCHESTER	31/12/2004	00:00:00	9724644	B52174	01/03/2004	00:00:00	100089700	CB	808.65
6	ERIC	99999	O KAY YAHS	31/12/2004	00:00:00	54977/10	B52175	03/03/2004	00:00:00	100089800	H.M.V.	71.88
7	SOUB	99999	FIXES	31/12/2004	00:00:00	7899449	B52176	03/03/2004	00:00:00	100089900	VMH	3,427.62
8	MIA	99999	DENISE BENT	31/12/2004	00:00:00	659818	B52177	03/03/2004	00:00:00	100090000	H.M.V.	197.67
9	MIA	99999	PENNY CILLIN	31/12/2004	00:00:00	BUR1350-G	B52178	03/03/2004	00:00:00	100090100	WJT	1,329.78
10	UUU	99999	DRACELL	31/12/2004	00:00:00	35220DUF	B52179	03/03/2004	00:00:00	100090200	BC	5,432.93
11	UUU	99999	TREVOR WILLS	31/12/2004	00:00:00	IN/1146/97	B52180	03/03/2004	00:00:00	100090300		8,859.90
12	DES	99999	NELLIE DUNN	31/12/2004	00:00:00	LBQ-687-XY	B52181	03/03/2004	00:00:00	100090400	HMV	485.19
13	WJT	99999	WANDA FARR	31/12/2004	00:00:00	GR158 97	B52182	03/03/2004	00:00:00	100090500	WJT	341.43
14	SOUB	99999	FIXES	31/12/2004	00:00:00	7899449	B52183	03/03/2004	00:00:00	100090600	HMV	-1,994.67
15	WJT	99999	FARMER	31/12/2004	00:00:00	47/952	B52184	03/03/2004	00:00:00	100090700	BC	7,804.97
16	WJT	99999	MILESTONE FORD	31/12/2004	00:00:00	G34-569	B52185	04/03/2004	00:00:00	100090800	VH	22,829.04
17	WJT	99999	LINDA HAND	31/12/2004	00:00:00	147870CTR	B52186	05/03/2004	00:00:00	100090900	HMV	1,916.80
18	WJT	99999	POLLY GUNN	31/12/2004	00:00:00	WNZ36C	B52187	06/03/2004	00:00:00	100091000	VST	4,300.82
19	KSA	99999	P GREEN	31/12/2004	00:00:00	1651 1OU-97	B52188	06/03/2004	00:00:00	100091100	HMV	1,383.69
20	WJT	99999	LUKE HAIR	31/12/2004	00:00:00	54640	B52189	06/03/2004	00:00:00	100091200	HMV	2,995.00
21	UUU	99999	DICK TATE	31/12/2004	00:00:00	97 2044.29J	B52190	06/03/2004	00:00:00	100091300	HMV	5,306.99
22	H.M.V.	99999	RAY	31/12/2004	00:00:00	261199FF	B52191	06/03/2004	00:00:00	100091400	HMV	4,762.05
23	DES	99999	MICROCOMPUTERS	31/12/2004	00:00:00	51524	B52192	06/03/2004	00:00:00	100091500	BC	2,096.50

FIGURE 8.32   Results of Payments to Suppliers Not in the Supplier or Vendor Master File

GAP DETECTION OF CHECK NUMBER SEQUENCES

The check-numbering system is alphanumeric rather than the standard numeric-sequencing convention. When we do a gap detection to see if there are any checks missing, the IDEA software recognizes the contents of the selected CHEQUE field and automatically sets a mask before performing the gap detection process, as shown in Figure 8.33.

FIGURE 8.33   Preparing for Gap Detection of Check Numbers

The result shows that there is one missing check from the sequence in Figure 8.34. Check A52656 should be located to see if it was marked as void. Failing that, bank reconciliations or bank statements should be reviewed to ensure they were not used for a payment that was not recorded in the "Payments" database.

	From: CHEQUE		To: CHEQUE			Number
⊟ A52656			A52656		1	
	A52656					
			Total number of items detected		1	
			Total number of gaps detected		1	

FIGURE 8.34   Results of Gap Detection of Check Numbers

If there is a code to distinguish manual checks from automated checks, the manual check payments should be extracted and reviewed. Manual checks are not the norm and manual checks provide more opportunities for errors or fraud. Sometimes, deliberate errors are made, forcing the payment out of the automated system so that the fraudster can take control over that particular payment.

CONCLUSION

Billing schemes are costly. Once the fraudster implements the scheme, it is repetitive and appears in the organization's business systems as a normal business expense. A legitimate payment is made to settle for the services or goods that the organization believes it received. The payment could be paid to a fictitious company that did not provide value for the payment. The payments could be paid to a legitimate company but diverted to the fraudster. Just because a check is written for a vendor and signed, it does not mean it reached the proper vendor.

Due to the large outflow of funds through the accounts payable department, auditors tend to include verifying payments as part of their audit plan. Also included would be a review and testing of the internal controls for payments. Data analytics will help in both the verification and control testing. Anomalies found may expose fraud or weaknesses in the system.

NOTE

1. "State of Oklahoma Vendor Payments Fiscal Year 2013," accessed February 19, 2014, https://data.ok.gov/Finance-and-Administration/State-of-Oklahoma-Vendor-Payments-Fiscal-Year-2013/aykr-xnjm.

## CHAPTER NINE

Check-Tampering Schemes

A CHECK IS A CONTRACT TO PAY THE HOLDER of the check to be negotiated through a financial institution. It is the instrument by which the payor provides directions to the financial institution to provide the funds to the payee. In the event that the financial institution does not make the payment for any reason such as insufficient funds in the account or due to an error on the check, the check continues to be acknowledgment of the obligation of debt by the payor.

Even with today's technology, with more and more payments being made electronically online, the physical hardcopy checks will remain as the business currency for some time to come. The sheer volume of business payments still made by check today will maintain this as the preferred method of payment. The traditional check-tampering fraud schemes will continue to exist as long as check payments exist. Electronic-payment systems open the door to new types of fraud that must be guarded against. Many organizations use both traditional checks and electronic transfer payments. It is not unusual that an organization would use electronic direct deposits for their payroll and checks as payments for everything else. It is also not unusual for a business to use a hybrid system for receiving payments. Checks sent into the organization are scanned and then deposited electronically into their account. The original checks are maintained for a period of time pursuant to the agreement with their financial institution before being destroyed.

In the United States, the Automated Clearing House (ACH) electronic network clears electronic payments between financial institutions. The Electronic Payments Association (NACHA) manages ACH's governance, development, and administration.

In Canada, the Canadian Payments Association (CPA) operates the clearing and settlement of both electronic payments and checks.

Payments made electronically by organizations require access to the system that requires a user identification and password. Some systems include a security or authentication token—a hardware device used to log into payment systems. A secret personal identification number (PIN) must first be entered into the token. If the PIN is correct, then the token displays a number that allows the user to access the system. The number changes frequently and the token must be used for each log-in.

In order to manipulate payments, the fraudster needs to gain access to the payment system. Once this difficulty is overcome, the fraudster does not have to be concerned with some aspects that are associated with traditional check-tampering schemes that may necessitate producing counterfeit or altered checks, gaining access to physical checks, forging or obtaining authorizing signatures, and the endorsement of the checks.

The fraudster may have authorized access to the payment system so, while making legitimate payments, they can also make electronic payments to their own benefit. Passwords may also be obtained by coworkers who spy ("shoulder surf") by watching an authorized user enter their password. If an authorized user leaves his computer momentarily while still logged into the payment system, a coworker may seize the opportunity to make payments or changes.

Outsiders may target an authorized employee with a spear-phishing e-mail. Spear phishing is the sending of a spoofed e-mail that appears to come from a trusted source. The message content seems reasonable and logical when it instructs the recipient to click on the embedded link. The link downloads spyware or a key logger that later captures the target's login information. A less sophisticated version of the spoofed e-mail asks the target to log into a bogus website that requires the employee's user name and password.

Once that information is available to the fraudster they have unfettered access and the payment system is compromised.

 ## ELECTRONIC PAYMENTS FRAUD PREVENTION

The opportunities for fraud with electronic payments can be mitigated if procedures and internal controls are in place and adhered to. Some of these prevention methods are listed here.

- Institute a dual-control system where one employee initiates payments while a different employee has to approve and release the payments.
- Do not permit the sharing of banking log-in access.
- Do not permit offsite log-in access.
- Ensure that the organization has a firewall installed along with up-to-date anti-spyware and antivirus software.
- Log off the payment system when not in use. This should be done even if it is just for a short break.
- Never open attachments or click on links in unsolicited e-mails.
- Do not use a link to access the payment system even if it is included in e-mails that appear to be from the financial institution.
- Organizations should use a separate computer for accessing the payment system. Both e-mail and other web browsers should be disabled on it.
- Employ options available from the financial institution to help detect and prevent fraud, such as blocks and filters.
- Review and reconcile accounts regularly for unauthorized payments.

When one avenue for fraud is closed off, the fraudster may move on to other areas. Typically, it would be in an area that they are familiar with. This move can be from the more traditional payment schemes to electronic-payment fraud. Alternatively, it can be from electronic payments to check-tampering fraud.

 ## CHECK TAMPERING

In order to perpetrate this fraud, a check is needed along with an authorized signature that can be cashed or converted by the fraudster. To continue with the fraud, previous frauds may need to be concealed.

Obtaining Checks

Checks are needed before check tampering can occur. Checks can be obtained in many ways, including:

- The employee may have direct access to checks as part of their duties.
- Blank checks can be stolen. The checks may be taken from the bottom of the box to avoid or delay detection.
- Void or slightly damaged checks can be used if these are not disposed of securely.
- Checks may be counterfeited.
- Checks could be handed over to the fraudster who is a trusted employee or whose duties include delivery of checks as part of the payment process.
- Returned checks can be stolen for fraudulent purposes.

Obtaining an Authorized Signature

Authorized signatures need to be signed on the checks. Financial institutions would return checks that have blanks in the signature space. Signatures may be obtained in the following ways:

- The employee is authorized to sign checks as part of his or her duties.
- The employee gains access to and uses the automated check-signing machine.
- The signature can be forged either by hand or with the aid of a photocopying machine.
- A fraudulent check can be slipped in with a batch of legitimate checks for signature.

The Payee

Checks can be made out in favor of the fraudster, an accomplice, shell company, or even cash. They can also be made out to legitimate vendors to pay for personal items. Checks made payable to the fraudster, while easy to cash, are also easier to detect.

If checks are already prepared, the payee name can be altered and replaced with the fraudster's name. Amounts can be also changed. Modification of the existing name by adding additional letters to the end of the payee line or setting up shell companies with similar names of legitimate vendors facilitate the conversion of checks to be cashed.

If the fraudster has access to the payments system in updating or changing vendor names, this can be done just prior to a check being issued and then changed back afterward. Addresses may also be changed at the same time to divert the check to the fraudster or an accomplice.

If the check is made out to a third party, then the fraudster would have to forge the endorsement also. Having matching identification may be an issue for the fraudster.

Concealing the Deed

Check-tampering schemes are usually perpetrated by those who have the opportunities. They are usually involved in the reconciliation of the check register to the bank statements. They are the ones who are supposed to match the canceled checks to the register. It is the lack of internal controls that allows the fraudster to carry on with the scheme.

Canceled checks can be destroyed to hide evidence that they were made payable to the employee. The entries in the check register are falsified to list the name of a legitimate vendor or simply not recorded in the register. One way to balance the check register to the bank statement is to combine the amounts of the check made out to the employee with a legitimate payment to a vendor. Suppose the vendor was paid $7,000 by check and a separate check of $3,000 was made out to the employee. Both would be listed as a single amount of $10,000 against the legitimate vendor name in the register.

Altered checks returned with the bank statement can be re-altered back to the original payee. Based on the same invoice, a second check can be issued to the original payee so that the vendor would not call to see what happened to their payment.

If the fraudster has control over issuing checks, then they can issue themselves a check and cover up the fraud with falsified supporting documents.

There are numerous ways to cover up check-tampering fraud depending on the internal controls in place and whether the procedures are followed or not.

 DATA ANALYTICAL TESTS

Using the sample payment file included with the IDEA software, a number of tests can be demonstrated.

Of major concern would be the same person authorizing the check and also performing the posting of payment to books.

In the sample payment file we note that POSTED_BY field data of initials is consistent while the AUTH field sometimes contains periods after the initials and sometimes not. We first normalize the AUTH field by creating a new field called AUTHORIZE using the equation of @Strip(AUTH), which removes spaces, punctuations, and control characters from the field, as shown in Figure 9.1.

From the test, we find that there were five transactions that were authorized and posted by the same person, as shown in Figure 9.2. One of the five transactions had no entries of who authorized the payment or who posted the payment. All of these transactions must be reviewed in greater detail.

Since we are now aware that the system permits blank entries, we need to extract out all transactions that are blank in either the POSTED_BY field or the AUTHORIZED

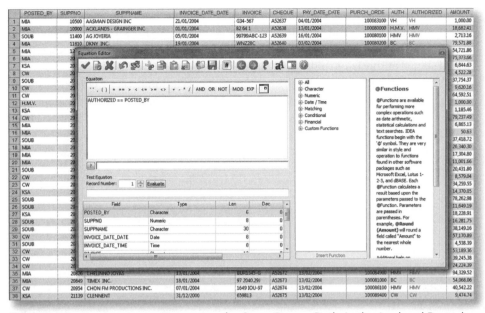

FIGURE 9.1 Preparation to Determine the Same Person Both Authorized and Posted the Transaction

	POSTED_BY	SUPPNO	SUPPNAME	INVOICE_DATE_DATE	INVOICE	CHEQUE	PAY_DATE_DATE	PURCH_ORDE	AUTH	AUTHORIZED	AMOUNT
1	KSA	20536	JOHN PETERSON	11/01/2004	T5721VB	A52661	10/02/2004	100084400	KSA	KSA	14,370.05
2	CW	40713	MACKENZIE PETROLEUM LTD.	03/01/2004	IN 6438 97	B52135	18/02/2004	100084800	CW	CW	40,325.22
3	CW	92411	SAAN STORES LTD.	11/01/2004	IN 6446 97	B52163	27/02/2004	100088600	CW	CW	24,163.78
4		92611	MORRIS GOLD INC	31/12/2004	BUR1351-G	B52211	10/03/2004	100093400			23,000.16
5	WJT	99999	WANDA FARR	31/12/2004	GR158 97	B52182	03/03/2004	100090500	WJT	WJT	341.43

FIGURE 9.2 Results Where the Same Person Authorized and Posted the Transactions

field. This is a good example where the results from one test lead to the need of applying additional tests based on the output.

We can use the equation of AUTHORIZED = = " " .OR. POSTED_BY = = " " to meet both these conditions. The results are displayed in Figure 9.3.

	POSTED_BY	SUPPNO	SUPPNAME	INVOICE_DATE_DATE	INVOICE	CHEQUE	PAY_DATE_DATE	PURCH_ORDE	AUTH	AUTHORIZED	AMOUNT
1		92611	MORRIS GOLD INC	31/12/2004	BUR1351-G	B52211	10/03/2004	100093400			23,000.16
2	UUU	99999	TREVOR WILLS	31/12/2004	IN/1146/97	B52180	03/03/2004	100090300			8,859.90
3	JEN	99999	JENNIFER MALLOY	31/12/2004	000509CJW	B52202	09/03/2004	100092500			4,091.17

FIGURE 9.3 Results of Where There Are Blank Entries for the POSTED_BY Field or the AUTHORIZED Field

Two additional transactions are discovered to have been posted with no authorization. In addition to reviewing these transactions, determination of how the system allowed this is necessary. Is there a programming error at the stage where processing of transactions is allowed, even when all fields are not populated? Possibly, the system does not proceed without all the fields completed but allows for modification of these two fields later on. If this is the case, then reliance cannot be placed on the test results shown in Figure 9.2. The fraudster merely has to change one of the fields so it does not show that the same person both authorized and posted the transactions. The potential of this cover-up scheme requires sampling and testing of the invoices and viewing the actual signed authorizing and posting initials.

To determine whether there are any missing check numbers, we can perform gap detections as shown in Chapter 8 in Figure 8.33. In addition to gaps, we are interested to know whether there were payments using out-of-sequence checks, that is, check numbers that are out of sequence in relation to the date. We simply index the PAY_DATE_DATE field and then the CHEQUE field, and visually scan for out-of-sequence transactions, as in Figure 9.4.

	INVOICE_DATE_DATE	INVOICE	PAY_DATE_DATE ▲	CHEQUE ▲	PURCH_ORDE	AUTH	AUTHORIZED	AMOUNT
3	05/01/2004	99799ABC-123	16/01/2004	A52639	100080100	HMV	HMV	2,713.16
4	19/01/2004	WNZ28C	03/02/2004	A52640	100080200	BC	BC	79,571.88
5	09/01/2004	AZ278	03/02/2004	A52641	100080300	WJT	WJT	54,721.86
6	20/01/2004	81340	03/02/2004	A52642	100082800	BC	BC	75,373.66
7	17/01/2004	971004A	04/02/2004	A52643	100080900	CB	CB	6,844.63
8	03/01/2004	10000 A	04/02/2004	A52644	100082500	BC	BC	4,522.28
9	14/01/2004	100139	04/02/2004	A52645	100082100	HMV	HMV	37,754.37
10	08/01/2004	TJ9729	04/02/2004	A52646	100082000	HMV	HMV	9,620.16
11	05/01/2004	000496CJW	04/02/2004	A52647	100089900	H.M.V.	HMV	64,592.51
12	19/01/2004	G34-568	04/02/2004	A52648	100083200	VH	VH	1,000.00
13	10/01/2004	2828 BNA	06/02/2004	A52649	100083300	WJT	WJT	1,185.46
14	18/01/2004	566698T	06/02/2004	A52650	100086000	BC	BC	79,237.49
15	17/01/2004	L-1221/55	06/02/2004	A52651	100082200	HMV	HMV	6,865.13
16	18/01/2004	14598	06/02/2004	A52652	100090000	HMV	HMV	50.63
17	14/01/2004	871456BUZ	06/02/2004	A52653	100081900	WJT	WJT	37,418.72
18	21/01/2004	GR132 97	06/02/2004	A52654	100080400	HMV	HMV	26,340.30
19	11/01/2004	5745MCC	07/02/2004	A52655	100081800	HMV	HMV	17,304.80
20	16/01/2004	BC 469701 W	08/02/2004	A52657	100083700	H.M.V.	HMV	11,001.66
21	12/01/2004	CS - 563 -97	08/02/2004	A52658	100084500	H.M.V.	HMV	20,431.80
22	09/01/2004	FR-963 32	09/02/2004	A52659	100084300	HMV	HMV	8,579.04
23	01/01/2004	117- 2287	10/02/2004	A52660	100083600	HMV	HMV	34,259.55
24	11/01/2004	T5721VB	10/02/2004	A52661	100084400	KSA	KSA	14,370.05
25	02/01/2004	IN 6428 97	10/02/2004	A52662	100084600	CW	CW	78,262.98

FIGURE 9.4 Indexed by Date and Check Number

If the CHEQUE field was a numeric field rather than a character field, we take an additional step after the index to identify every out-of-sequence transaction. We can append a new field using the equation of @If(@GetNextValue("CHEQUE") – CHEQUE = 1, 10, 11).

The equation takes the next value in the CHEQUE field, subtracts the current check value, and if the difference is 1, the number 10 is returned in the new field. If the difference is not 1, then the number 11 is displayed in the new field. All items with 11 are transactions not in sequence.

Payments based on an invoice that was diverted and then subsequently properly paid can be detected by using the Duplicate Key Exclusion test. We look for the same invoice number along with the same amount, but with different vendor names. In our sample payment file, there were no records that matched our criteria. We can also test for transactions of payments made to the same vendor with the same invoice number but with different amounts. These transactions could be payments made to the vendor in error or could be used as a mechanism for check-tampering fraud.

Our example test for the same supplier number along with the same invoice number but with different payment amounts is shown in Figure 9.5.

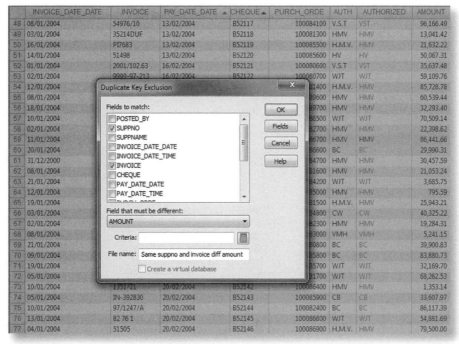

FIGURE 9.5 Duplicate Key Exclusion Test for Different Amounts Paid to the Same Supplier Base on the Same Invoice Number

Our test results in 10 records that match the criteria, as shown in Figure 9.6.

	POSTED_BY	SUPPNO	SUPPNAME	INVOICE_DATE_DATE	INVOICE	PAY_DATE_DATE	CHEQUE	PURCH_ORDE	AUTH	AUTHORIZED	AMOUNT
1	DES	99999	DENISE BENT	31/12/2004	147873CTR	19/03/2004	C51003	100095500	VMH	VMH	144.34
2	KSA	99999	DENISE BENT	31/12/2004	147873CTR	24/03/2004	C51010	100096200	VMH	VMH	251.58
3	MIA	99999	A RAID	31/12/2004	21569	10/03/2004	B52207	100093000	HMV	HMV	790.68
4	ERIC	99999	A RAID	31/12/2004	21569	09/03/2004	B52204	100092700	WJT	WJT	52,845.00
5	MIA	99999	TRUCKSTOP	31/12/2004	232 A2Z	15/03/2004	B52227	100095000	WJT	WJT	-1,198.00
6	SOUB	99999	TRUCKSTOP	31/12/2004	232 A2Z	13/03/2004	B52223	100094600	HMV	HMV	5,738.42
7	SOUB	99999	FIXES	31/12/2004	7899449	03/03/2004	B52183	100090600	HMV	HMV	-1,994.67
8	SOUB	99999	FIXES	31/12/2004	7899449	03/03/2004	B52176	100089900	VMH	VMH	3,427.62
9	WJT	99999	POLLY GUNN	31/12/2004	WNZ36C	06/03/2004	B52195	100091800	CB	CB	-695.50
10	WJT	99999	POLLY GUNN	31/12/2004	WNZ36C	06/03/2004	B52187	100091000	VST	VST	4,300.82

FIGURE 9.6 Results of the Duplicate Key Exclusion Test

Other Analytical Tests

Other analytical tests that can be done in which the data file contains additional fields include:

- Extract and review checks made out to cash, as these are of higher risk for fraud.
- Extract void checks and test for accuracy, as they may actually be cashed and just coded as void.
- Extract and review all payments of zero amounts, as the actual amounts may be higher or the amount may be changed from zero later on.

- Payments without purchase orders, as shown in Figure 8.17 in Chapter 8, should be reviewed. These could be further summarized by vendor, authorizer, and poster or in any combination.
- Summarize debit memos by vendor, authorizer, and poster or in any combination.
- Join payment system employee access log information for the authorizer or poster with the check register/payment database or electronic payment database.
- Extract and review journal entries or adjustments impacting the bank accounts.

In our example payment file, there is a MEMO field. We can check for any adjustments by using the search feature of IDEA to look for variations of the word adjustments.

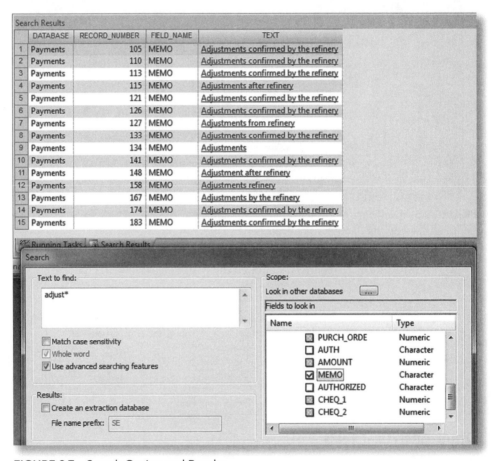

FIGURE 9.7 Search Option and Results

We had used the wildcard character of * after the word *adjust*, as this would find words such as *adjust, adjusted, adjustment*, and *adjustments* in both uppercase and lowercase or in combination. Our search resulted in 15 matches, as seen in Figure 9.7. To access the record details we can click on the underlined words in the TEXT search-result field.

 **CONCLUSION**

Some critical tests cannot be done by analyzing data alone or reviewing internal documents. Statements should be obtained from vendors, including those with zero balances, and compared to accounts payable. Data analytics can assist by using sampling to reduce the number of confirmations with vendors. Online bank balances and reconciliation should be reviewed on a regular basis. This is especially necessary with electronic-payment systems. The bank transactions details can be downloaded and then, by using the Join feature of IDEA, you can output those transactions that do not match with the check register database.

Fraudulent schemes are evolving rapidly, especially in the area of electronic payments. When the fraudster takes over an organization's electronic-payment system, instead of sending payments directly to the shell company they control, they can add another layer of complexity that makes detection more difficult. If the fraudster has taken over the payment systems of other organizations at the same time, they can have one organization pay the other legitimate organization first, and then have the second organization pay the fraudsters. This makes the electronic payments appear to be normal business-related transactions.

The risk of being victim of fraudulent schemes can be reduced by good internal controls that should not be circumvented. Successful check-tampering schemes rely heavily on the lack of separation of duties and lax internal controls.

CHAPTER TEN

Payroll Fraud

PAYROLL FRAUD IS WHEN an organization pays an employee or a fictitious employee for services not performed. We are referring to fraudulent payments schemes as opposed to abuse where employees are taking excessive personal time for personal surfing of Internet social media sites, making phone calls, e-mailing, and texting.

Fraudulent payment schemes fall under three main categories: ghost employees, falsified overtime or hours worked, and fraud related to commissions.

Ghost employees may be an actual or fictitious person. Fictitious ghost employees never existed in the organization. Someone with the authority or computer access hires employees by putting in the appropriate documentation or bypassing controls to create new employees in the payroll system. Setting up these nonexistent people with names similar to actual employees increases the chances of avoiding detection. Those classified as temporary or casual workers are at higher risk of being ghost employees who are fictitious. These workers usually have a high-turnover rate and are difficult to track after they leave the organization, making the fraud hard to detect. Further, actual people who at one time worked for the organization may unwittingly be used as part of the payroll fraud. An example would be a supervisor authorizing pay for one or two pay cycles before the employee actually started work. Another method would be failing to remove a terminated employee from the payroll. Participants of payroll schemes include those on the payroll who do not need to show up for work (typically in remote locations), and those that have some type of relationship to the person in authority, such as a family member. These ghost employees may have limited or no duties at all but are being paid the same as or more than fulltime employees with similar job titles.

It was mentioned that situations where temporary workers are employed have a higher-than-normal risk for ghost employees due to the high-turnover rate. Other situations that lend themselves to the risk of ghost employees include:

- Hiring of foreign workers where the fraudster can allege that the workers returned to their native countries if questioned.
- The organization is large and remote locations make oversight more difficult.
- Highly decentralized and independent divisions that have their own payroll systems.
- Divisions managed by someone with a high degree of authority.
- The division has large numbers of employees at entry-level jobs, such as call centers.
- Direct deposit pay setup for employees where the regular hiring procedures were bypassed.
- Any changes to the payroll master file, such as modifying direct deposit routing, that can be done without other checks and balances.

Whether the ghost employees are fictitious or real, the payroll–payment cycle requires that they must be added to the payroll master file with relevant information, such as hourly wage rates or salary amounts. The time-tracking system must be provided with information, such as vacation days taken for salary staff and hours worked for hourly employees. The pay must be issued and then delivered to the ghost employee or accomplice by way of direct deposit or physical delivery.

Falsified overtime or hours worked likely occur in every organization. Employees may be responsible for inputting their hours worked and filing overtime claims. It is a simple matter to add extra time when doing this. Small additions may not be noticed by the authorizing supervisor. When the authorizing supervisor is lax or when there is collusion with the supervisor, larger amounts can be defrauded. Time documents may also be falsified by forging an authorizing signature or altered after approval. If authorization is through a computerized time system, the fraudster may have access to the password. This is especially true if the fraudster or accomplice works in the payroll department.

While salaried employees who are entitled to overtime can use the falsified overtime-hours scheme, those that cannot claim overtime must increase their salary rate as a way to pocket undeserved extra funds. They need access to the payroll master file to change their rate of pay. More likely, there would be collusion with an employee who has access to change salary amounts or, in the case of hourly employees, the hourly rate. These employees, given the opportunity, would likely be involved in expense-reimbursement schemes, as discussed in Chapter 11.

Commission fraud usually involves falsely increasing sales made by the employee. Prices of items sold can be internally increased or the commission rate increased to increase the amount of commissions. Like wage-rate increases, commission-rate changes need access to the payroll master file that can be accomplished by collusion.

Where the commission rate structure is such that after exceeding a certain quota, a higher rate is applied to all sales made during the year, there is motivation to push higher sales through. Bonuses paid after meeting a set quota may have a similar effect. Sales made near year-end should be reviewed, as sales can be booked and then canceled after the year-end. There could be overselling to the customers with promises of a liberal return policy for unused or unsold merchandise. The salesperson may be providing customers with unauthorized benefits or generous payment terms. At times, it may be worthwhile for the salesperson to generate the sale to a cooperative customer and then personally reimburse or kick back some or the entire amount to the customer if the resulting bonus or the increase in commission rate is higher than the reimbursed amount.

DATA AND DATA FAMILIARIZATION

Our case study will use real-life payroll data from the State of Oklahoma Payroll—Q1 2012 through to Q4 2012.[1] An EMPLOYEE_ID field was added to the original data to be displayed in place of the actual employee names.

The data is used to demonstrate how to find anomalies. All data contains anomalies. Most anomalies either just occur or are contributed to by the business system. Most anomalies are not fraudulent, but one must be aware that anomalies are red flags of potential fraud. Most anomalies are also explainable and normal, but the anomalies need to be investigated to arrive at conclusions. We do not have sufficient information and we cannot follow the audit trail to form a conclusion as to whether any of the exceptions identified are errors or fraud.

We do not have a payroll master file associated with the Oklahoma payroll data. However, when obtaining payroll master file data, the following fields should be requested at the minimum:

- Employee name (last and first)
- Employee number
- Social Security number or Social Insurance number
- Address
- Phone number
- Hire date
- Bank information for direct deposits
- Employee classification code
- Rate of pay (both hourly and salary)
- Pay rate history
- Overtime hourly rate
- Commission rate
- Payroll codes (withholding taxes, health, and other benefits, etc.)
- Addition/modification field with associated date and who authorized it

The quarterly payroll data files were downloaded in comma-separated values (CSV format). When importing these four files for each year into IDEA, note that the first visible row is field names, so ensure that you place a checkmark to select this. The CSV file contains three fields that are dates. IDEA automatically assigned them to be character fields. For each of the three fields, ensure that you change the field type to "Date" and include the correct date mask of DD-MMM-YY, as entered in Figure 10.1. This will avoid the need to change from character fields to date fields within IDEA.

Once you have imported the first file (e.g., 1st Quarter), a record definition file or RDF is automatically created by IDEA and saved in the Import Definitons.ILB folder under the project folder. Subsequent identical CSV files can be imported using this record definition. You do not have to make any changes to those date fields that were initially selected by IDEA as character fields, as these were already defined in the record definition file.

FIGURE 10.1   Preparing the Date Fields for File Import

Once you have the four 2012 quarters imported into IDEA, use the Append files feature and create a file called "Payroll 2012" that contains records for all four quarters. The "Payroll 2012" file contains the fields displayed in Figure 10.2.

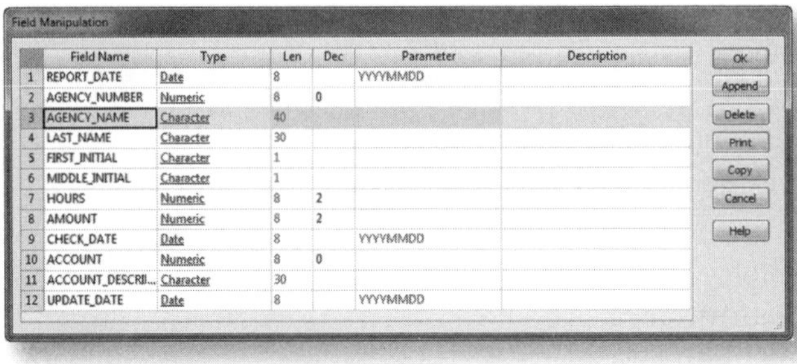

FIGURE 10.2   "Payroll 2012" Fields

The data set does not contain an employee number or identification number. To uniquely identify the employee for features such as summarization, join, or extractions, we need to include three fields individually: LAST_NAME, FIRST_INITIAL, and MIDDLE_INITIAL. As we probably need to do this many times, some advance data preparation can save us work and time. We can append a new field called NAME using the equation of LAST_NAME + " " + FIRST_INITIAL + " " + MIDDLE_INITIAL. This concatenates the three name-related fields into one by last name, a space before the first initial, and another space before the middle initial. We can now just select the NAME field when applying our analytical tests. For the purposes of this case study, an EMPLOYEE_ID field is created and the contents generated are based on the new NAME field. We will be using the EMPLOYEE_ID field for display purposes.

Data Familiarization Steps

We should look at the field statistics in Figure 10.3 to get an idea of what the data holds for us.

Numeric Statistics	AGENCY_NUM...	HOURS	AMOUNT	ACCOUNT
▶ Net Value	83,212,350,300	149,516,181.46	3,271,506,329.46	919,400,940,160
Absolute Value	83,212,350,300	149,726,343.48	3,275,859,990.32	919,400,940,160
# of Records	1,798,710	1,798,710	1,798,710	1,798,710
# of Zero Items	0	250,464	198,142	0
Positive Value	83,212,350,300	149,621,262.47	3,273,683,159.89	919,400,940,160
Negative Value	0	-105,081.01	-2,176,830.43	0
# of Positive Records	1,798,710	1,540,613	1,592,971	1,798,710
# of Negative Records	0	7,633	7,597	0
# of Data Errors	0	0	0	0
# of Valid Values	1,798,710	1,798,710	1,798,710	1,798,710
Average Value	46,262.24	83.12	1,818.81	511,144.62
Minimum Value	1,000	-276.00	-40,304.44	511,110
Maximum Value	98,000	1,888.00	442,165.09	514,440
Record # of Min	3	863,433	204,035	1
Record # of Max	1,041,488	1,113,741	508,296	41,046
Sample Std Dev	29,382.20	69.65	2,809.65	55.96
Sample Variance	863,313,933.63	4,851.78	7,894,144.05	3,131.21
Pop Std Dev	29,382.20	69.65	2,809.65	55.96
Pop Variance	863,313,453.66	4,851.78	7,894,139.66	3,131.21
Pop Skewness	-0.240205	0.429300	22.978214	-54.211791
Pop Kurtosis	-1.413242	-0.045529	2,195.543336	1,347,827.536849

FIGURE 10.3 Numeric Field Statistics for the "Payroll 2012" Data Set

The only numeric fields of interest are the HOURS field and the AMOUNT field. There are 1,798,710 records. In the HOURS field, there are 250,464 zero items. Zero items are expected in this field. However, the AMOUNT field contains 198,142 zero items. We are now aware that we may have to exclude zero amounts in our future equations to obtain the proper count results.

Next, we examine the field statistics for the date fields in Figure 10.4.

The REPORT_DATE earliest and latest records appear to be monthly reports and the date ranges are as expected. The CHECK_DATE has some records that are outside of the 2012 calendar year that may require investigation. IDEA provides the record number of the earliest and latest date for ease of location. We can just click on the earliest date record number of 103,278 and the record will be displayed for us. In this case, the October 31, 2011, date of payment appears to be a payroll recovery of negative $2,500.00. It is interesting to note that no payments were made on any Saturdays but 84 payments were issued on Sundays. If we were to click on the 84 in Items on Sunday under the CHECK_DATE field, we would see the results displayed as in Figure 10.5.

Upon examination, we determined that the payments on Sundays were all made by the same agency for salaries. All 84 records had blanks in the LAST_NAME field. While the last name may have been removed for privacy reasons before the payroll information was released on the website, this could also be a control issue with the payroll system. Due to the fact that the payments were all made by a single agency on Sundays and the last-name field had no information, these items should be queried. We will later perform a test to determine how many records in the entire data set have blank last names.

For the moment, we will continue with the overview of our data set.

Date Statistics	REPORT_DATE	CHECK_DATE	UPDATE_DATE
# of Valid Values	1,798,710	1,798,710	1,798,710
# of Zero Items	0	0	0
# of Records	1,798,710	1,798,710	1,798,710
# of Data Errors	0	0	0
Earliest Date	31/01/2012	31/10/2011	03/02/2012
Latest Date	31/12/2012	11/01/2013	18/01/2013
Record # of Earliest	1	103278	79205
Record # of Latest	1614296	1661045	1797295
Most Common Day	Friday	Friday	Wednesday
Most Common Month	November	November	December
Items in January	118028	120009	184415
Items in February	131128	128882	38824
Items in March	137288	138133	47388
Items in April	136739	131689	47751
Items in May	138922	136537	50576
Items in June	142568	153350	44364
Items in July	130056	128967	38256
Items in August	138572	134489	27705
Items in September	175892	167577	31814
Items in October	178362	174849	9929
Items in November	186740	201839	10402
Items in December	184415	182389	1267286
Items on Sunday	175892	84	27705
Items on Monday	321154	117126	240790
Items on Tuesday	248084	145125	92115
Items on Wednesday	309490	207431	815191
Items on Thursday	138922	120792	582670
Items on Friday	325312	1208152	40239
▶ Items on Saturday	279856	0	0

FIGURE 10.4   Date Field Statistics for the "Payroll 2012" Data Set

FIGURE 10.5   Items on Sunday of the CHECK_DATE Field

We can summarize ACCOUNT by totaling and averaging on the HOURS and AMOUNT fields. Select to also display the ACCOUNT_DESCRIPTION field.

	ACCOUNT	ACCOUNT_DESCRIPTION	NO_OF_RECS	HOURS_SUM	AMOUNT_SUM	HOURS_AVERAGE	AMOUNT_AVERAGE
1	511110	Sals-Regular Pay	775244	85,616,733.10	1,875,111,720.71	110.44	2,418.74
2	511120	Sals-Regular Pay Legislature	1778	304,384.00	5,730,978.59	171.19	3,223.27
3	511130	Sals-Non-Reg Pay	348908	13,212,283.26	169,402,536.39	37.87	485.52
4	511140	Sals-H.Ed Teaching Pay	47676	7,333,121.16	235,736,929.23	153.81	4,944.56
5	511150	Sals-H.Ed Prof.(Non-Teach) Pay	131924	18,511,779.89	596,928,819.60	140.32	4,524.79
6	511160	Sals-H.Ed Non-Prof. Pay	254415	16,967,890.92	242,510,007.57	66.69	953.21
7	511170	Sals-H.Ed Other Teach Pay	45405	1,684,327.95	50,482,766.84	37.10	1,111.83
8	511210	Longevity Pay-State Employees	28647	0.00	37,633,944.04	0.00	1,313.71
9	511220	Longevity Pay-H.Ed	257	36,099.00	327,343.56	140.46	1,273.71
10	511230	Individ.Incent.Pay-Safety Awds	450	0.00	583,854.26	0.00	1,297.45
11	511250	Unit Incentive Pay	270	0.00	570,127.07	0.00	2,111.58
12	511270	Overtime Wages	86789	1,414,481.65	31,647,896.17	16.30	364.65
13	511280	Holiday Pay - Payroll Only	9499	112,690.18	1,561,617.53	11.86	164.40
14	511290	Pay Differential	45166	3,593,594.62	4,630,403.18	79.56	102.52
15	511300	Education Loan Reimb Incentive	7	0.00	30,922.00	0.00	4,417.43
16	511310	Terminal Leave	5982	710,147.77	15,977,192.00	118.71	2,670.88
17	511390	Cafeteria Plan - Other	2	2.00	878.40	1.00	439.20
18	511400	Compensation - Brd-Com Members	1033	18,007.01	96,351.79	17.43	93.27
19	511430	Employee Exp.Allow-Reportable	14471	638.95	2,043,350.84	0.04	141.20
20	511440	Signing Incent.Pln Pmts Non DP	436	0.00	300,747.67	0.00	689.79
21	511450	Cont.Svc.Incentive Plan Pmts	312	0.00	166,650.00	0.00	534.13
22	514420	Retirement Pmts OPERS-Payroll	15	0.00	31,292.02	0.00	2,086.13
23	514440	Retirement Pmts-HEd-Payroll	24	0.00	0.00	0.00	0.00

FIGURE 10.6 Summarize by the Account Field

There are 23 account types for the entire data set in Figure 10.6. Because account 511140 indicates teaching pay, it can be concluded that not all of the 23 account types will be used by all the different agencies as not all agencies would employ educators.

We can determine the number of agencies by summarizing on AGENCY_NUMBER, totaling and averaging on the HOURS and AMOUNT fields; we should also display the AGENCY_NAME field.

	AGENCY_NUMBER	AGENCY_NAME	NO_OF_RECS	HOURS_SUM	AMOUNT_SUM	HOURS_AVERAGE	AMOUNT_AVERAGE
1	1000	OKLAHOMA STATE UNIVERSITY	226318	16,645,389.39	399,682,769.84	73.55	1,766.02
2	2000	OKLAHOMA ACCOUNTANCY BOARD	131	20,857.60	519,342.17	159.22	3,964.44
3	2200	OKLAHOMA ABSTRACTORS BOARD	38	6,249.50	115,103.26	164.46	3,029.03
4	2500	OKLAHOMA MILITARY DEPARTMENT	5441	732,192.32	12,021,229.92	134.57	2,209.38
5	3000	ALCOHOLIC BEV. LAWS ENFORCE.	592	78,218.76	1,932,995.76	132.13	3,265.20
6	3900	BOLL WEEVIL ERADICATION ORG.	149	21,128.25	432,111.28	141.80	2,900.08
7	4000	DEPARTMENT OF AGRICULTURE	5904	837,704.98	15,472,277.44	141.89	2,620.64
8	4100	WESTERN OKLA. STATE COLLEGE	5124	387,905.55	7,483,135.37	75.70	1,460.41
9	4500	OKLA. BD. OF ARCHITECTS	63	6,276.00	172,505.64	99.62	2,738.18
10	4700	INDIGENT DEFENSE SYSTEM	1393	218,926.75	6,397,153.47	157.16	4,592.36
11	4900	ATTORNEY GENERAL	2296	351,017.10	10,053,097.73	152.88	4,378.53
12	5500	STATE ARTS COUNCIL	182	27,489.95	636,401.85	151.04	3,496.71
13	6000	OKLAHOMA AERONAUTICS COMMISSION	140	21,471.65	565,452.82	153.37	4,038.95
14	6500	STATE BANKING DEPARTMENT	546	86,713.50	3,419,524.54	158.82	6,262.87
15	9000	OFFICE OF STATE FINANCE	20107	1,682,932.82	42,435,319.45	83.70	2,110.47
16	9200	TOBACCO SETTLEMENT ENDMT TRUST	167	27,165.18	773,100.40	162.67	4,629.34
17	10000	CAMERON UNIVERSITY	19583	1,271,963.48	26,592,495.44	64.95	1,357.94
18	10800	CARL ALBERT STATE COLLEGE	6988	583,073.50	9,879,869.06	83.44	1,413.83
19	11700	COMMERCIAL PET BREEDERS BOARD	20	2,879.63	59,942.37	143.98	2,997.12
20	12000	UNIV. OF CENTRAL OKLA.	50768	3,162,881.51	76,167,238.68	62.30	1,500.30
21	12500	DEPARTMENT OF MINES	629	64,208.66	1,451,577.13	102.08	2,307.75
22	12700	COMMISSION ON CHILDREN AND YOUTH	406	51,516.79	1,208,970.19	126.89	2,977.76
23	13100	DEPARTMENT OF CORRECTIONS	124255	9,038,833.68	167,406,142.31	72.74	1,347.28

FIGURE 10.7 Summarize by Agency Number

The resulting file contains 159 records with each record representing an agency. We can see the number of records for each agency. The number of records represents the number of transactions. For example, record 23 shows agency number 13100, which is the Department of Corrections; it had 124,255 payroll transactions totaling $167,406,142.31. The average payment amount is $1,347.28. However, during our examination of the field statistics there were a number of zero amounts. If the Department of Corrections had some zero amounts in their payments, then the average shown in Figure 10.7 is lower than the actual average due to zero amounts that are counted as valid records.

Before we summarize by employee to determine how many employees were on the state's payroll, let us see how many transaction results there are in which the employees' last name field is blank.

We can use the criteria of LAST_NAME = = " " to achieve this, as shown in Figure 10.8.

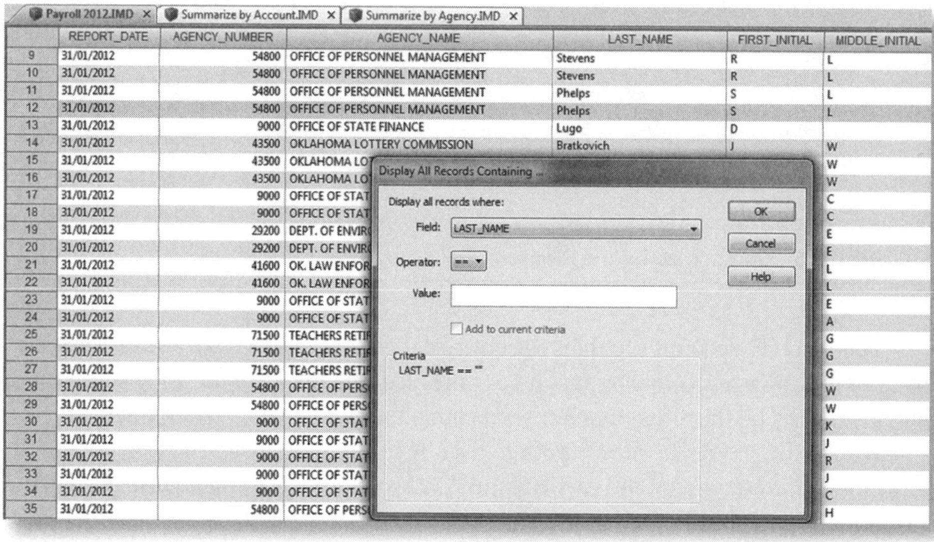

FIGURE 10.8   Determining How Many Records Have No Last Names Entered

The procedure returned 42,831 records where the last-name field was blank. Again, this could have been deliberately redacted for privacy reasons before making the data public. If these blanks occurred in the original data, the auditors would question some of the transactions and must determine whether there are weaknesses in the payroll system.

By summarizing by the EMPLOYEE_ID field and totaling and averaging on HOURS and AMOUNT fields, the resulting number of records provides us with an indication of how many employees are in the data set.

The resulting file contains 126,598 records, as displayed in Figure 10.9. Normally we can accept this number as the number of state employees on the payroll in 2012, if the employee ID was included in the original file and not generated. However, since the blank last-name fields affect the generated employee IDs, the number of unique employees may be a few less than shown.

	EMPLOYEE_ID	NO_OF_RECS	HOURS_SUM	AMOUNT_SUM	HOURS_AVERAGE	AMOUNT_AVERAGE
126582	00000099984-SH	4	352.00	12,500.00	88.00	3,125.00
126583	00000099985-SH	8	417.00	3,023.25	52.13	377.91
126584	00000099986-SH	8	1,384.00	35,701.36	173.00	4,462.67
126585	00000099987-SH	6	1,033.00	31,341.00	172.17	5,223.50
126586	00000099988-SH	1	48.00	1,123.10	48.00	1,123.10
126587	00000099989-SH	5	205.00	1,479.01	41.00	295.80
126588	0000009999-Bar	4	671.99	9,351.02	168.00	2,337.76
126589	00000099990-SH	8	1,384.00	88,082.68	173.00	11,010.34
126590	00000099991-SH	6	831.00	24,275.47	138.50	4,045.91
126591	00000099992-SH	6	1,023.00	34,052.76	170.50	5,675.46
126592	00000099993-SH	8	90.00	2,373.60	11.25	296.70
126593	00000099994-SH	23	1,841.00	28,661.20	80.04	1,246.14
126594	00000099995-SH	7	1,211.00	42,815.61	173.00	6,116.52
126595	00000099996-SH	12	2,046.00	78,518.76	170.50	6,543.23
126596	00000099997-SH	3	357.00	2,591.88	119.00	863.96
126597	00000099998-SH	9	217.00	1,564.20	24.11	173.80
126598	00000099999-SH	6	729.00	19,322.82	121.50	3,220.47

FIGURE 10.9 Summarized by Employee ID

We have a good idea of what we face within the payroll data file. We can now formulate appropriate data analytical tests to perform.

DATA ANALYSIS

If we were familiar with the payroll system and did audits of various agencies previously, we would perform some of the general data analytical tests outlined in Chapter 5, such as Z-score and Benford's Law. From the results of the general tests, we can decide to perform a review of the entire state's payroll transactions or focus a detail audit of the higher-risk agencies as determined by the general tests.

Since this is our first encounter with the payroll data, we will focus on both general and specific tests for agency number 13100, the Department of Corrections. This agency was selected for demonstration purposes mainly as it contains suitable amounts of records for testing purposes.

We perform a direct extraction from the "Payroll 2012" file using the equation of AGENCY_NUMBER = 13100. From our usual review of the field statistics, we find that there are 124,255 records with 11,117 containing zero in the AMOUNT field. This is expected as the "Payroll 2012" file contained zero amounts and our new "Department of Corrections—13100" file is a subset of that file. There are no unusual earliest or latest date issues in the date statistics. No payments were made on either Saturdays or Sundays. All of our subsequent tests will be from the "Department of Corrections—13100" file or files created from it.

Blank Contents in the Last-Name Field

Since we know that the Payroll 2012 file had 42,831 records where the last-name field was blank and we also know that some records have zero in the AMOUNT field, we should determine if any of these blank last names are in the agency that we are focusing on. Using the equation criteria of LAST_NAME == " " .AND. AMOUNT < > 0.00, we find 23 records. These 23 transactions—consisting of regular, nonregular, overtime, and longevity pay—should be examined in more detail.

We will perform similar summarizations as we had done for the "Payroll 2012" file and more. Summarize by the ACCOUNT field, totaling on HOURS and AMOUNT fields, and selecting the ACCOUNT_DESCRIPTION to display, we obtain the information displayed in Figure 10.10.

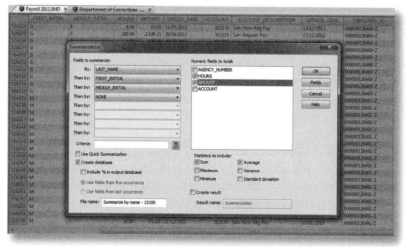

	ACCOUNT	NO_OF_RECS	HOURS_SUM	AMOUNT_SUM	ACCOUNT_DESCRIPTION
1	511110	65113	8,030,453.45	143,610,276.44	Sals-Regular Pay
2	511130	26570	187,864.85	3,828,803.50	Sals-Non-Reg Pay
3	511210	3419	0.00	4,439,592.31	Longevity Pay-State Employees
4	511270	22105	585,218.61	12,721,309.99	Overtime Wages
5	511280	5531	63,853.17	962,910.29	Holiday Pay - Payroll Only
6	511290	710	87,397.25	163,496.66	Pay Differential
7	511310	638	84,046.35	1,471,664.45	Terminal Leave
8	511430	66	0.00	48,667.00	Employee Exp.Allow-Reportable
9	511440	103	0.00	159,421.67	Signing Incent.Pln Pmts Non DP

FIGURE 10.10 Summarizing by Account Provides Us with Nine Types of Payroll Payments for the Department of Corrections

We will summarize by name, as in Figure 10.11, to determine the number of employees at this agency and also total their hours and payment amounts with averages. For illustration purposes, instead of using our preprepared NAME field, we will summarize using the three related name fields to show the timesavings that our NAME (or EMPLOYEE_ID) field provides to us. We also need to select the EMPLOYEE_ID field to display in our results.

FIGURE 10.11 Summarize by Name Totaling and Averaging on Hours and Amounts

We can see that of the 23 transactions that had blanks in the last name, it was likely for just one employee, so focus can be kept at a minimum for this agency. There were actually 24 records (7 plus 17) but one has zero in the AMOUNT field. There are a total of 4,707 records that includes the two blank last names. The highlight spaces option is turned on within IDEA. You can see that the number of entered blank spaces differs in the first two records in Figure 10.12. IDEA treats these different blanks as unique records. If we had summarized only on the NAME (or EMPLOYEE_ID) field, we would have had only 4,706 records. This example highlights that not all blank spaces are equal; they are blank in different ways.

	LAST_NAME	FIRST_INITIAL	MIDDLE_INITIAL	NO_OF_RECS	EMPLOYEE_ID	HOURS_SUM	AMOUNT_SUM	HOURS_AVERAGE	AMOUNT_AVERAGE
1	....	N	H	7	000000326-NH	976.00	13,413.12	139.43	1,916.16
2	....	N	H	17	000000326-NH	1,106.25	15,636.31	65.07	919.78

FIGURE 10.12 Results of Summarizing by Name Totaling and Averaging on Hours and Amounts

High Number of Payments

We normally look at the employees who received the highest payments, so we index by descending order the AMOUNT_SUM field. Later on in the chapter, we can stratify payments by various payment types to see the number of payments in each range.

	FIRST_INITIAL	MIDDLE_INITIAL	NO_OF_RECS	EMPLOYEE_ID	HOURS_SUM	AMOUNT_SUM ▼	HOURS_AVERAGE	AMOUNT_AVERAGE
1	D	L	18	000000110273-S	2,086.50	189,117.00	115.92	10,506.50
2	D	E	19	000000103867-S	2,072.00	183,600.04	109.05	9,663.16
3	R	.	20	00000011710-Bh	2,085.00	171,911.92	104.25	8,595.60
4	H	G	18	00000078312-Me	2,068.00	171,062.04	114.89	9,503.45
5	R	T	18	00000030893-Do	2,068.00	170,626.04	114.89	9,479.22
6	L	H	19	000000114687-T	2,079.00	170,425.92	109.42	8,969.79
7	J	T	17	00000054620-Ho	2,076.00	169,999.92	122.12	10,000.00
8	J	C	18	000000114737-T	2,088.00	156,524.04	116.00	8,695.78
9	G	E	18	00000058756-Jo	2,088.00	156,500.04	116.00	8,694.45
10	P	B	18	00000042237-Ge	2,082.50	156,062.04	115.69	8,670.11
11	J	B	19	00000076541-Mc	2,082.00	155,249.92	109.58	8,171.05
12	J	B	18	00000074761-Ma	2,062.00	151,625.96	114.56	8,423.66
13	R	L	18	00000037251-Fi	2,085.00	151,625.96	115.83	8,423.66
14	L	D	18	00000013459-Bo	2,088.00	151,312.32	116.00	8,406.24
15	S	D	57	00000059024-Jo	6,262.32	149,502.19	109.87	2,622.85
16	J	D	130	00000015005-Br	7,339.25	146,951.43	56.46	1,130.40
17	B	L	18	00000078564-Me	2,081.00	142,500.00	115.61	7,916.67
18	W	A	18	00000024532-Co	2,066.00	142,250.00	114.78	7,902.78
19	W	.	18	00000021742-Ch	2,076.00	142,062.00	115.33	7,892.33
20	M	.	18	00000054568-Jo	2,085.25	141,626.00	115.85	7,868.11
21	R	L	18	000000122551-W	2,060.50	140,725.45	114.47	7,818.08
22	M	D	30	00000021172-Ca	3,275.00	138,848.09	109.17	4,628.27
23	D	M	61	00000058517-Jo	4,586.00	138,655.29	75.18	2,273.04
24	J	W	18	00000058926-Jo	2,085.00	135,709.00	115.83	7,539.39
25	J	D	100	000000123262-W	6,523.96	127,158.96	65.24	1,271.59

FIGURE 10.13 Payments from Highest to Lowest by Employee

While high dollar amounts are of interest, even more interesting are the high number of records in record numbers 15, 16, 23, and 25 in Figure 10.13. A high number of records represents a high number of payments. Even recognizing the fact that there may be some zero amounts that would increase the number of records, this seems excessive. To get a better idea of the extent of the high number of payments, we can index the NO_OF_RECS field in descending order, as in Figure 10.14.

Why are these employees receiving payments so frequently? Why is the number of their hours so high? It is expected that the average employee will have a little over 2,000 hours per year excluding overtime. We will perform more precise analyses by looking at the different types of payments later. For now, a quick visual review of the details of the top-record employees shows potential duplicated payments. Using the "Department of Corrections—13100" file, we can perform a Duplicate Key Detection to quantify the quick review.

	FIRST_INITIAL	MIDDLE_INITIAL	NO_OF_RECS	EMPLOYEE_ID	HOURS_SUM	AMOUNT_SUM	HOURS_AVERAGE	AMOUNT_AVERAGE
1	J	D	130	00000015005-Br	7,339.25	146,951.43	56.46	1,130.40
2	J	D	100	000000123262-W	6,523.96	127,158.96	65.24	1,271.59
3	R	L	100	000000121376-W	4,836.00	72,515.34	48.36	725.15
4	J	M	100	000000104242-S	4,596.50	83,582.25	45.97	835.82
5	J	L	93	00000023685-Co	5,065.50	77,407.68	54.47	832.34
6	T	G	91	000000104258-S	5,276.00	76,837.52	57.98	844.37
7	R	M	91	0000003692-And	4,575.50	81,832.17	50.28	899.25
8	L	M	87	000000123735-W	4,293.75	77,612.87	49.35	892.10
9	B	J	81	000000123187-W	4,639.25	66,415.69	57.27	819.95
10	S	E	79	00000091537-Pu	4,780.40	67,870.90	60.51	859.13
11	M	D	79	00000083254-Ni	4,796.00	69,297.53	60.71	877.18
12	M	D	78	000000104195-S	4,484.69	79,859.76	57.50	1,023.84
13	J	K	78	00000067970-Le	4,606.00	79,390.28	59.05	1,017.82
14	P	L	76	00000090934-Po	5,048.25	41,159.82	66.42	541.58
15	T	N	75	000000106215-S	3,903.25	29,903.16	52.04	398.71
16	K	S	74	000000110319-S	4,553.50	45,159.60	61.53	610.26
17	M	E	73	00000095010-Re	4,041.95	42,408.67	55.37	580.94
18	N	F	73	00000061689-Ke	4,861.50	39,388.56	66.60	539.57
19	S	R	71	000000113563-T	3,176.63	43,627.14	44.74	614.47
20	M	D	71	00000075074-Ma	4,271.75	38,895.11	60.17	547.82
21	B	D	71	00000069483-Lo	4,749.00	44,514.57	66.89	626.97
22	D	V	71	00000025796-Cr	4,434.95	63,096.24	62.46	888.68
23	S	L	71	0000009793-Bar	4,170.25	60,439.17	58.74	851.26
24	C	F	71	0000009068-Bak	5,461.00	84,176.72	76.92	1,185.59
25	J	R	70	000000121761-W	3,957.75	40,177.26	56.54	573.96
26	J	G	70	000000114980-T	4,311.75	62,070.32	61.60	886.72
27	C	L	70	00000080316-Mo	4,798.00	74,370.98	68.54	1,062.44
28	M	K	70	00000061563-Ke	4,240.25	70,287.26	60.58	1,004.10
29	M	.	69	000000108091-S	3,226.00	54,361.52	46.75	787.85

FIGURE 10.14 Number of Payments from Highest to Lowest by Employee

Duplicate Key Detection

There are many keys that we can use where all the keys must be the same before the records are matched. In this example, we wish to see payroll payments paid on the same day to the same employee for the same payroll type, as in Figure 10.15. The same payroll type (ACCOUNT field) eliminates any matches where the employee was paid their regular salary and something else, such as overtime.

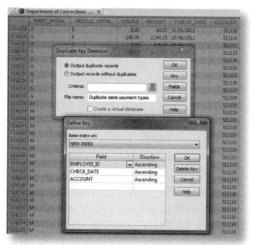

FIGURE 10.15 Preparing the Duplicate Key Detection for Same Employee ID, Same Payment Date, and Same Type of Payments

There were 2,195 records that matched our duplicate selections in Figure 10.16. Some of the duplicates are clearly valid, such as reversing a pay made in error processed on the same date. Since we lack real employee numbers (we generated the employee ID by name), it is possible that there are a number of employees with the same last name and same first and middle initials. Regardless, these duplicate payments must be reviewed in more detail to clear the anomalies that may be potential fraud.

	FIRST_INITIAL	MIDDLE_INITIAL	HOURS	AMOUNT	CHECK_DATE	ACCOUNT	ACCOUNT_DESCRIPTION	UPDATE_DATE	EMPLOYEE_ID
2168	P	A	184.00	2,832.63	31/10/2012	511110	Sals-Regular Pay	13/12/2012	0000009154-Bak
2169	P	A	184.00	4,178.39	31/10/2012	511110	Sals-Regular Pay	13/12/2012	0000009154-Bak
2170	P	A	152.00	2,446.36	30/11/2012	511110	Sals-Regular Pay	13/12/2012	0000009154-Bak
2171	P	A	152.00	3,608.61	30/11/2012	511110	Sals-Regular Pay	13/12/2012	0000009154-Bak
2172	P	A	24.00	386.27	30/11/2012	511130	Sals-Non-Reg Pay	13/12/2012	0000009154-Bak
2173	P	A	24.00	569.78	30/11/2012	511130	Sals-Non-Reg Pay	13/12/2012	0000009154-Bak
2174	P	A	152.00	2,562.86	31/12/2012	511110	Sals-Regular Pay	07/01/2013	0000009154-Bak
2175	P	A	152.00	3,780.45	31/12/2012	511110	Sals-Regular Pay	07/01/2013	0000009154-Bak
2176	P	A	16.00	269.77	31/12/2012	511130	Sals-Non-Reg Pay	07/01/2013	0000009154-Bak
2177	P	A	16.00	397.94	31/12/2012	511130	Sals-Non-Reg Pay	07/01/2013	0000009154-Bak
2178	R	C	276.00	17,625.00	29/06/2012	511110	Sals-Regular Pay	12/12/2012	0000009396-Bal
2179	R	C	-276.00	-17,625.00	29/06/2012	511110	Sals-Regular Pay	12/12/2012	0000009396-Bal
2180	C	D	62.06	883.80	12/01/2012	511110	Sals-Regular Pay	12/12/2012	00000094842-Ra
2181	C	D	0.00	0.00	12/01/2012	511110	Sals-Regular Pay	12/12/2012	00000094842-Ra
2182	M	A	160.00	2,170.08	29/06/2012	511110	Sals-Regular Pay	12/12/2012	0000009512-Bar
2183	M	A	-160.00	-2,170.08	29/06/2012	511110	Sals-Regular Pay	12/12/2012	0000009512-Bar
2184	C	F	120.00	1,708.92	12/04/2012	511110	Sals-Regular Pay	12/12/2012	00000096133-Ri
2185	C	F	0.00	0.00	12/04/2012	511110	Sals-Regular Pay	12/12/2012	00000096133-Ri
2186	C	D	0.00	0.00	21/11/2012	511110	Sals-Regular Pay	13/12/2012	00000096327-Ri
2187	C	D	0.00	0.00	21/11/2012	511110	Sals-Regular Pay	07/01/2013	00000096327-Ri
2188	C	D	11.00	336.91	21/11/2012	511270	Overtime Wages	13/12/2012	00000096327-Ri
2189	C	D	-11.00	-336.91	21/11/2012	511270	Overtime Wages	07/01/2013	00000096327-Ri
2190	J	C	53.82	693.19	12/04/2012	511110	Sals-Regular Pay	12/12/2012	00000097371-Ro
2191	J	C	57.23	746.37	12/04/2012	511110	Sals-Regular Pay	12/12/2012	00000097371-Ro
2192	M		48.00	566.18	12/01/2012	511110	Sals-Regular Pay	12/12/2012	00000098149-Ru
2193	M		0.00	0.00	12/01/2012	511110	Sals-Regular Pay	12/12/2012	00000098149-Ru
2194	J	D	168.00	2,296.26	29/02/2012	511110	Sals-Regular Pay	12/12/2012	0000009826-Bar
2195	J	D	-168.00	-2,296.26	29/02/2012	511110	Sals-Regular Pay	12/12/2012	0000009826-Bar

FIGURE 10.16 Results of the Duplicate Key Detection for Same Employee ID, Same Payment Date, and Same Type of Payments

Additional duplicate key detection or same-same-same tests that can be done include these matches:

- Same employee, same payment date, same payment type, and same amounts.
- Same employee, same payment date, and same hours.
- Same employee, same payment date, same payment type, and same hours.

Payments on Last Day of the Month

When we viewed the payment dates, it was apparent that most transactions for regular pay took place at the end of the month or the last Friday of the month when the last day of the month falls on a weekend. This agency does not process payments on the weekends.

We can prepare the "Department of Corrections—13100" file to break down the CHECK_DATE field into days, months, and year for potential analyses tests involving days or months.

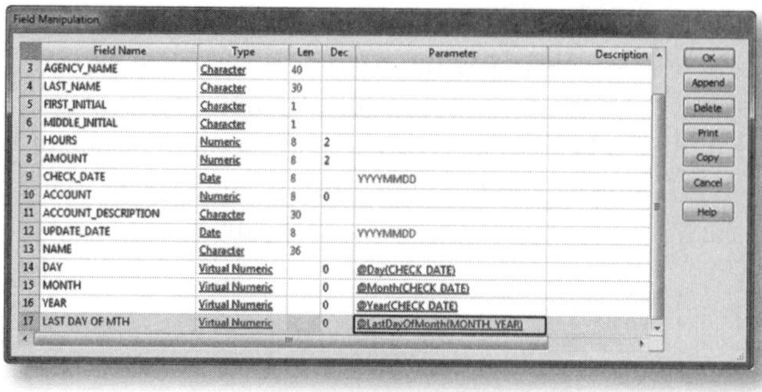

FIGURE 10.17   Appending Date-Related Fields

We can append a number of fields without having IDEA apply them until the OK button is selected. In Figure 10.17, we create the DAY, MONTH, and YEAR field names and enter the related @function equations. For each of the fields, we enter the CHECK_ DATE field as the reference field to extract the information from. In the last field, the @ LastDayOfMonth function returns the last day of the month. Note that the reference fields are those that have just been defined but not yet applied. IDEA allows the usage of these new fields. If we wish to test if payments were made on the last day of the month, we need to take into consideration where the last day of the month falls on a weekend. In those cases, payments are made the Friday before the weekend. We should consider the possibility that the Friday before the weekend might be a holiday.

We append a new field called PAID_LAST_DAY_OF_MTH with the equation of

$$@\,\mathrm{If}((LAST\_DAY\_OF\_MTH\text{-}3) < DAY,1,2)$$

The field would return the number 1 if the last day of the month field minus three days to account for the weekend and one holiday is a smaller number than the day of the payment. If the condition does not match, then the field would display the number 2 to represent not paid on the last day of the month. This would be good to see when we are reviewing payments for regular salaries, which are normally paid once a month at the end of the month.

Analyzing Files by Payment Type

We will do a Key Value Extraction that will create separate databases for each of the account numbers. In this case, we will select the ACCOUNT_DESCRIPTION field as the key instead of the account number so that the file name displays the payment type. This saves us from having to cross reference the account number with the description. We enter as the prefix for each of the output databases "Account = ".

Once we select the ACCOUNT_DESCRIPTION field as the key, IDEA automatically identifies that there are nine unique keys and lists them. You can remove the checkmark beside each of the keys you do not wish to create a separate database for. For this example, leave the default of all keys selected, as in Figure 10.18.

Once we select the OK button the nine files are created, as displayed in the File Explorer shown in Figure 10.19.

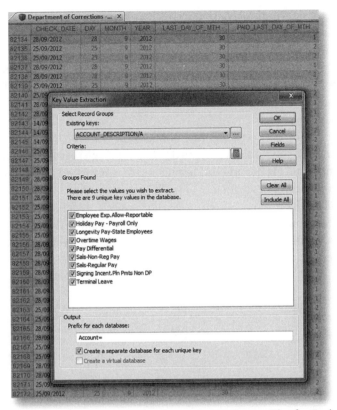

FIGURE 10.18 Preparing to Use Key Value Extraction to Create Files for Each Type of Pay

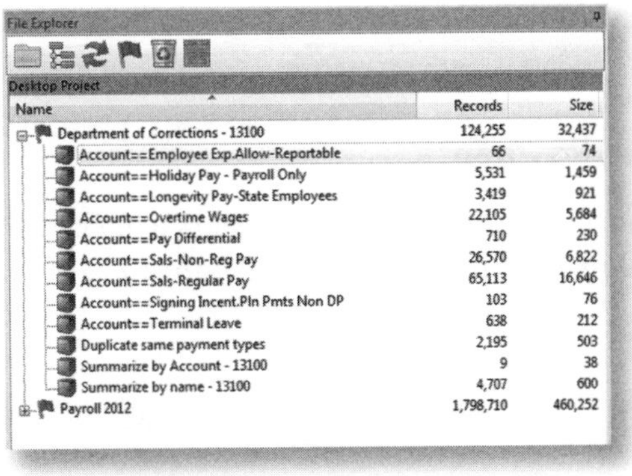

FIGURE 10.19 File Explorer Displaying the Files Created Using Key Value Extraction

Regular Salary Payments

The regular pay salary file has 65,113 records, as shown in Figure 10.19. We can open this file to examine it in more detail. We expect that since these are regular salary payments, most of the 65,113 transactions occur at the end of the month.

We can apply a criteria of PAID_LAST_DAY_OF_MTH = 2 to display 18,431 records where payment was not made at the end of the month.

Adding a new field called DAY_OF_WEEK, using the equation of @Dow(CHECK_DATE) returns a number representing the day of the week. The number 1 is Sunday, 2 is Monday, . . . and 7 represents Saturday. This allows us to see if there are any patterns as to which day of the week payments not made at the end of the month took place.

Detail testing of some of the payments made other than on the last day of the month should be done. We should also look into the details of high regular salary payments. To determine the cutoff for the amount to review, we can stratify the amounts to see the range of regular salary payments.

The bulk of the number of regular salary payments falls between $2,000 and $4,000. These comprise over 75 percent of the dollar value. All of the 16 payments of over $15,000 in the upper limit exceptions should be reviewed and some of the 240 payments from $10,000 to $15,000 should also be examined. Refer to Figure 10.20.

Account=-Sals-Regular Pay.I...

Totalled on: AMOUNT

Stratum #	>= L Limit	< U Limit	# Records	(%) #	AMOUNT	(%) AMOUNT
1	0.00	1,000.00	17,587	27.01	1,624,051.98	1.13
2	1,000.00	2,000.00	3,555	5.46	6,409,257.36	4.46
3	2,000.00	3,000.00	26,085	40.06	64,667,844.69	45.03
4	3,000.00	4,000.00	12,837	19.71	43,577,058.66	30.34
5	4,000.00	5,000.00	2,945	4.52	12,907,905.04	8.99
6	5,000.00	7,500.00	1,331	2.04	7,704,010.92	5.36
7	7,500.00	10,000.00	435	0.67	3,652,255.45	2.54
8	10,000.00	15,000.00	240	0.37	2,957,533.77	2.06
		Lower limit exceptions:	82	0.13	-139,309.90	-0.10
		Upper limit exceptions:	16	0.02	249,768.47	0.17
		Totals:	65,113	100.00	143,610,276.44	100.00

FIGURE 10.20 Stratification of Regular Salary Payments

Overtime Wages Payments

We created a separate file of overtime wages as shown in Figure 10.19. We can stratify this file on the payment amounts, resulting in Figure 10.21.

Account::Sals-Regular Pay.I... Account=-Overtime Wages...

Totalled on: AMOUNT

Stratum #	>= L Limit	< U Limit	# Records	(%) # Records	AMOUNT	(%) AMOUNT
1	0.00	500.00	13,153	59.50	2,427,893.57	19.09
2	500.00	1,000.00	4,487	20.30	3,211,973.50	25.25
3	1,000.00	2,000.00	3,427	15.50	4,840,210.85	38.05
4	2,000.00	3,000.00	892	4.04	2,079,022.35	16.34
5	3,000.00	4,000.00	53	0.24	169,083.83	1.33
6	4,000.00	5,000.00	2	0.01	9,365.07	0.07
		Lower limit exceptions:	91	0.41	-16,239.18	-0.13
		Upper limit exceptions:	0	0.00	0.00	0.00
		Totals:	22,105	100.00	12,721,309.99	100.00

FIGURE 10.21 Stratification of Overtime Wage Payments

While the amounts paid are interesting, the hours should even be more interesting. We set the criteria of HOURS < > 0 to eliminate the zero amounts before performing the stratification.

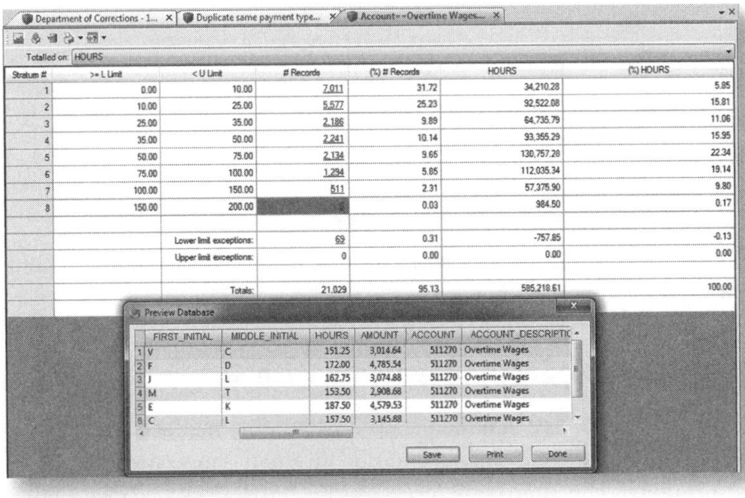

FIGURE 10.22   Stratification of Overtime Wage Hours

We see that there are six records with excessive overtime hours of between 150 and 200 hours. By clicking on the 6 we display these records that need further auditing, as in Figure 10.22. Examination of some of the other high hours should also be done.

Signing Incentive Plan Payments

This file contains only 103 records and can be visually scanned. However, it is simple to perform a Duplicate Key Detection by name to see if any employee was paid a signing incentive twice. There were 74 records that had more than one payment for the same employee. Some of the matching records had negative payment amounts that offset a payment. In this case, we are better off summarizing by employee ID instead of using the Duplicate Key Detection method on a single key. Summarizing will give us the number of records or transactions, and totaling on the amount will give us a zero amount if an identical negative and positive amount was recorded for the same employee. Only those with more than one record should be displayed. The criteria of NO_OF_RECS > 1 can be used.

We have 35 people who had more than one record, with 3 of the 35 having a net amount of zero, as seen in Figure 10.23. The question is why are these employees paid more than once for signing incentives? These may be red flags of fraud or, more likely, signing incentives are paid over several months. We can be comforted that if we did a Duplicate Key Detection using the EMPLOYEE_ID field and the CHECK_DATE field, it would result in no duplicates of payments on the same date that were paid to the same person. The procedures and policies of signing incentives should be reviewed.

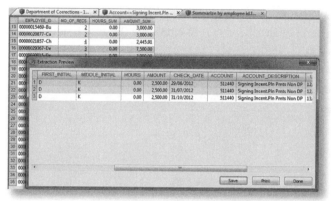

FIGURE 10.23 Result of Summarization by Employee ID Totaling on Payment Amounts with More Than One Record

Comparing Regular Salary Payments with Other Payment Types

We are looking for employees that have regular salary payments but received no holiday pay. Not receiving holiday pay may be an indicator of a ghost employee.

We summarize the regular salary file by EMPLOYEE_ID and obtain 4,657 unique employees. We also summarize the holiday pay file by EMPLOYEE_ID, resulting in 1,631 unique employees. Join the two resulting summarized files by selecting the regular salary file as the primary file and the holiday pay file as the secondary file. Use "Records with no secondary match" as the type of Join to create a new file called "Regular Salary But No Holiday Pay" and match on the EMPLOYEE_ID field. The result is that 3,026 employees are paid regular salary but do not have any holiday pay. This is unusual, but the employees may be new employees who are not yet entitled to vacation pay. We can test this further by taking the "Regular Salary But No Holiday Pay" file and seeing if these employees were paid longevity pay. If there are matches, then it is unlikely that the matched employees are new since they are receiving longevity pay.

We summarize the longevity pay file by EMPLOYEE_ID. This results in 3,281 unique employee names that received longevity pay. Use the "Regular Salary But No Holiday Pay" file as the primary file and the summarized longevity pay file as the secondary file. Select the Join option of "Matches only" and match on the EMPLOYEE_ID field. We end up with 2,150 records where the employees received a regular salary, no holiday pay, but yet received longevity pay during the year. This unusual circumstance must be explored during the audit process.

We shall create a new file called "Last Pay of the Year by Employee ID" from the regular salary database. The objective is to identify the last regular salary payment for the year for each employee. Using the Top Records Extraction feature, we extract one record of the top-most (latest date) CHECK_DATE field and group by the EMPLOYEE_ID field as shown in Figure 10.24.

We are interested in analyzing the terminal leave pay dates with the last regular pay date for the year to see if any employees were still getting a regular paycheck after 31 days of being paid their terminal leave amount.

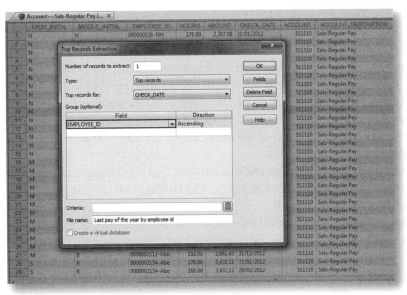

FIGURE 10.24 Obtaining the Last Pay Date for the Year

We should summarize the terminal leave file of 638 records by EMPLOYEE_ID in the event some employees received more than 1 terminal leave pay. Ensure that you select the CHECK_DATE as a field to include. Call this file "Summarize by ID Terminal Leave" as shown in Figure 10.25. The resulting file contained 622 unique names with 15 employees receiving more than 1 terminal leave pay. The reason the 15 employees were paid terminal leave more than once should be explored.

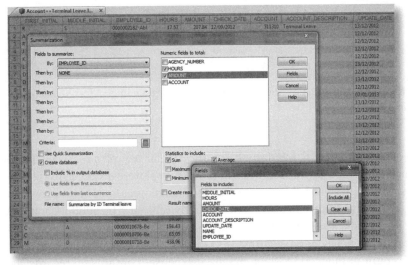

FIGURE 10.25 Summarize the Terminal Leave File

Once the new file is created, rename the CHECK_DATE field to TERMINAL_CHECK_DATE so we can differentiate the terminal payment date from the last regular payment date of the year when we join the file.

Join the "Last Pay of the Year by Employee ID" file as the primary file with the "Summarize by ID Terminal leave" file as the secondary file. Match by the EMPLOYEE_ID fields from both files and select "Matches only" as the Join option. Ensure that you select the TERMINAL_CHECK_DATE field for the secondary file and leave the default fields selected for the primary file. Call the new file "Last regular pay and terminal pay."

Append the DATE_DIFFERENCE field to the "Last regular pay and terminal pay" file using the equation @Age(CHECK_DATE, TERMINAL_CHECK_DATE). This calculates the number of days between the regular paycheck date and the terminal paycheck date. It is conceivable that it would take a month for the employee to get the last regular paycheck after receiving the terminal paycheck. We can use the criteria of DATE_DIFFERENCE > 31 to isolate employees still receiving a regular paycheck after 31 days.

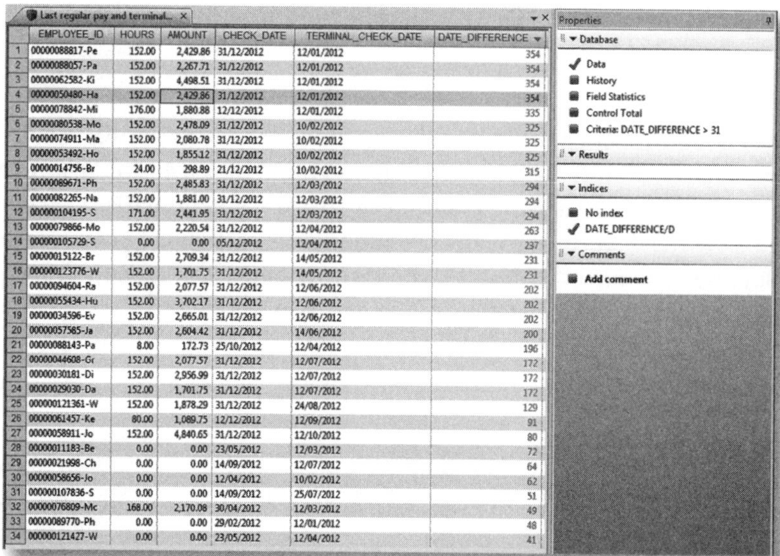
Last regular pay and terminal...

	EMPLOYEE_ID	HOURS	AMOUNT	CHECK_DATE	TERMINAL_CHECK_DATE	DATE_DIFFERENCE
1	00000088817-Pe	152.00	2,429.86	31/12/2012	12/01/2012	354
2	00000088057-Pa	152.00	2,267.71	31/12/2012	12/01/2012	354
3	00000062582-Ki	152.00	4,498.51	31/12/2012	12/01/2012	354
4	00000050480-Ha	152.00	2,429.86	31/12/2012	12/01/2012	354
5	00000078842-Mi	176.00	1,880.88	12/12/2012	12/01/2012	335
6	00000080538-Mo	152.00	2,478.09	31/12/2012	10/02/2012	325
7	00000074911-Ma	152.00	2,080.78	31/12/2012	10/02/2012	325
8	00000053492-Ho	152.00	1,855.12	31/12/2012	10/02/2012	325
9	00000014756-Br	24.00	298.89	21/12/2012	10/02/2012	315
10	00000089671-Ph	152.00	2,485.83	31/12/2012	12/03/2012	294
11	00000082265-Na	152.00	1,881.00	31/12/2012	12/03/2012	294
12	000000104195-S	171.00	2,441.95	31/12/2012	12/03/2012	294
13	00000079866-Mo	152.00	2,220.54	31/12/2012	12/04/2012	263
14	000000105729-S	0.00	0.00	05/12/2012	12/04/2012	237
15	00000015122-Br	152.00	2,709.34	31/12/2012	14/05/2012	231
16	000000123776-W	152.00	1,701.75	31/12/2012	14/05/2012	231
17	00000094604-Ra	152.00	2,077.57	31/12/2012	12/06/2012	202
18	00000055434-Hu	152.00	3,702.17	31/12/2012	12/06/2012	202
19	00000034596-Ev	152.00	2,665.01	31/12/2012	12/06/2012	202
20	00000057585-Ja	152.00	2,604.42	31/12/2012	14/06/2012	200
21	00000088143-Pa	8.00	172.73	25/10/2012	12/04/2012	196
22	00000044608-Gr	152.00	2,077.57	31/12/2012	12/07/2012	172
23	00000030181-Di	152.00	2,956.99	31/12/2012	12/07/2012	172
24	00000029030-Da	152.00	1,701.75	31/12/2012	12/07/2012	172
25	000000121361-W	152.00	1,878.29	31/12/2012	24/08/2012	129
26	00000061457-Ke	80.00	1,089.75	12/12/2012	12/09/2012	91
27	00000058911-Jo	152.00	4,840.65	31/12/2012	12/10/2012	80
28	00000011183-Be	0.00	0.00	23/05/2012	12/03/2012	72
29	00000021998-Ch	0.00	0.00	14/09/2012	12/07/2012	64
30	00000058656-Jo	0.00	0.00	12/04/2012	10/02/2012	62
31	000000107836-S	0.00	0.00	14/09/2012	25/07/2012	51
32	00000076809-Mc	168.00	2,170.08	30/04/2012	12/03/2012	49
33	00000089770-Ph	0.00	0.00	29/02/2012	12/01/2012	48
34	000000121427-W	0.00	0.00	23/05/2012	12/04/2012	41

FIGURE 10.26 Employees Still Receiving a Regular Paycheck After Receiving Terminal Pay

We see that 34 employees are still on the regular payroll after receiving their terminal pay for over 31 days in Figure 10.26. Some employees are receiving paychecks for almost a year afterward. It is possible that these employees had left the agency, received their terminal pay, and then were subsequently rehired. The auditor should examine these 34 records closer. Even if these were not fraudulent, there may be contraventions of the rehiring policy or procedures.

Account number 511430 for employee expenses contains 66 records, as shown in Figure 10.10. We can test to see if anyone is receiving an employee expense who is not receiving a regular salary. First we summarize the employee expense file by EMPLOYEE_ID to determine whether these are isolated payments or payments to a few employees.

Account==Employee Exp.Allo... | Summarize employee expen...

	EMPLOYEE_ID	NO_OF_RECS	AMOUNT_SUM
1	00000010678-Be	6	3,000.00
2	00000015399-Br	4	3,326.09
3	00000022519-Ch	12	9,000.00
4	00000033703-El	1	750.00
5	00000062526-Ki	12	9,000.00
6	00000078234-Me	12	9,000.00
7	00000080520-Mo	1	1,090.91
8	00000080893-Mu	9	6,750.00
9	00000083071-Ne	9	6,750.00

Extraction Preview

	FIRST_INITIAL	MIDDLE_INITIAL	HOURS	AMOUNT	CHECK_DATE	ACCOUNT	ACCOUNT_DESCRIPTION	L
1	J	L	0.00	750.00	31/01/2012	511430	Employee Exp.Allow-Reportable	12,
2	J	L	0.00	750.00	29/02/2012	511430	Employee Exp.Allow-Reportable	12,
3	J	L	0.00	750.00	30/03/2012	511430	Employee Exp.Allow-Reportable	12,
4	J	L	0.00	750.00	30/04/2012	511430	Employee Exp.Allow-Reportable	12,
5	J	L	0.00	750.00	31/05/2012	511430	Employee Exp.Allow-Reportable	12,
6	J	L	0.00	750.00	29/06/2012	511430	Employee Exp.Allow-Reportable	12,
7	J	L	0.00	750.00	31/07/2012	511430	Employee Exp.Allow-Reportable	12,
8	J	L	0.00	750.00	31/08/2012	511430	Employee Exp.Allow-Reportable	12,
9	J	L	0.00	750.00	28/09/2012	511430	Employee Exp.Allow-Reportable	13,
10	J	L	0.00	750.00	31/10/2012	511430	Employee Exp.Allow-Reportable	13,
11	J	L	0.00	750.00	30/11/2012	511430	Employee Exp.Allow-Reportable	13,
12	J	L	0.00	750.00	31/12/2012	511430	Employee Exp.Allow-Reportable	07,

Save | Print | Done

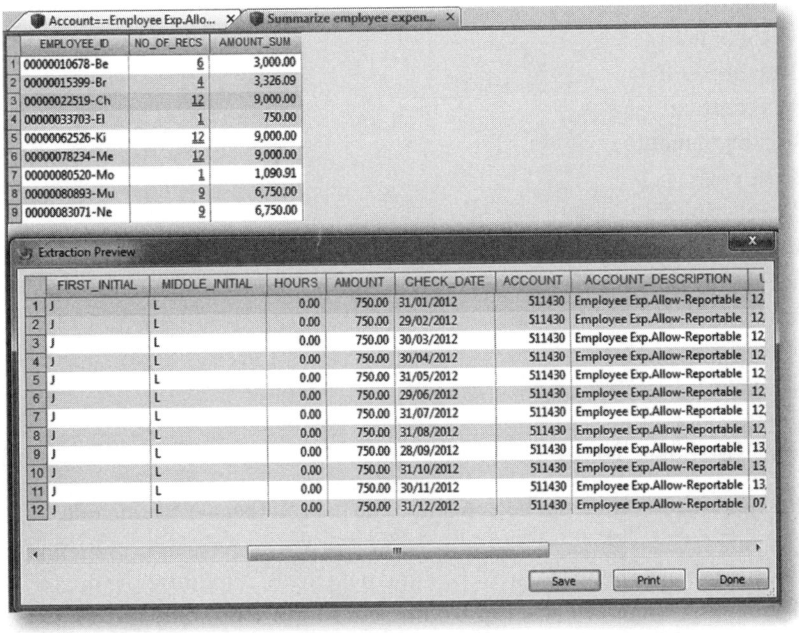

FIGURE 10.27 Results of Summarizing Employee Expenses by Employee

There were only nine employees who received employee expenses in Figure 10.27. A quick examination of some of the contents suggests that $750 per month is typical. We can test to ensure that all nine employees also received regular salaries.

Using either the "Account = = Sals-Regular Pay" file or its file that was summarized by employee ID as the primary file, we can join the newly created summarized employee expense file as the secondary file. Use the Join option of "Records with no primary match." Any records resulting may mean that someone who is not a regular employee is getting employee expenses. There were no records resulting from the join, so we do not have to investigate this test any further.

Similar testing can be performed with the "Account = = Sals-Regular Pay" file by joining it with the "Account = = Pay Differential" file and the "Account = = Sals-Non-Reg Pay" file.

THE PAYROLL REGISTER

Our case study file is not a true payroll register but rather a payroll payment data file. Payroll registers contain information such as:

- Payment date
- Pay period

- Employee identification
- Name
- Daily hours worked
- Vacation hours sick hours
- Holiday hours
- Personal hours
- Overtime hours
- Total regular pay
- Reimbursements
- Gross pay
- Taxes withheld
- Mandatory government withholdings
- Health, dental, and life insurance premiums
- Pension plan contributions
- Other deductions
- Net pay

Payroll Register Tests

Ghost employee tests that can be applied to the payroll register file include:

- Low percentages between gross pay and net pay. To maximize the net pay amount of the ghost employee, a setup would be for high withholding exemption status to minimize tax withholding and minimal participation for benefits that require contributions.
- Manually processed checks that require intervention so changes may be made.

Testing the Payroll Register File against Other Data Files

- Payments made outside of the starting or ending employment date recorded in the payroll master file.
- Payments made to employees not in the payroll master file.
- Differences in pay rates between the payroll register and the payroll master file.
- Employee coded as an active employee with no payments in the payroll register. This employee account may be reserved for use for future payroll fraud.
- Payments to hourly employees who are not in the time-recording system.
- Time system hours that do not match the payroll register hours.
- Payments made to employees not in system logs, such as computer logs, access card entry logs, or telephone usage logs.

 ## PAYROLL MASTER AND COMMISSION TESTS

There are a number of tests that can be applied against the payroll master file to detect red flags of potential fraud. Payroll master files should always be obtained. Suggested commission payment tests are also listed.

Payroll Master File Tests

- Apply duplicate key detection on employee direct deposit bank information.
- Apply duplicate key detection on employee contact information field.
- Search for post office boxes as employee addresses.
- Identify blank fields for employee information.
- Identify frequent address changes.
- Review payroll codes added or changed.
- Identify employees with no changes in vacation or sick leave balances.
- Identify employees with little or no voluntary deductions for health insurance, life insurance, and retirement benefits.
- Identify those with no pay increases or excess increases in pay history.
- Review employees coded as temporary or casual as they are higher risk. Include those paid through employment agencies.
- The payroll master file employee addresses can be tested to vendor addresses, as in the example in Chapter 8 on billing schemes.

Commission Payment Tests

- Test for excessive commissions by selecting high amounts (say top 10 percent) or high number of commission payments.
- Correlate commissions paid to sales by salesperson. There should be a perfect or near-perfect correlation ratio. However, if there were canceled sales, refunds, or returns that did not adjust for commissions already paid, then the correlation ratio would be lower.
- Correlate commission payments to travel and entertainment expenses.
- Perform a duplicate key detection test on the sales file for duplicate invoices processed and test for the same amount on the same date by the same salesperson for the same customer.
- Match sales with normally dormant accounts from the customer master file that had sales during the last two months of the year.
- Perform the relative size factor test on sales by employees.
- Extract sales made to customers not in the customer master.

 ## CONCLUSION

Payroll expense is one of the largest outlays of every organization. Due to the large amounts and high number of employees in large organizations, fraudulent payments may slip through the payroll system. Good internal controls, such as segregation of duties, mitigate the risk of these schemes. Also add best practices, such as investigating all returned mail of government-required wage information such as W-2 tax forms in the United States and T-4 tax forms in Canada. The returned mail may be because the employee or former employee moved without providing a forwarding address. There is also the potential that this may be a ghost employee. Having independent parties meet each employee for various reasons periodically confirms the existence of the employee. The meetings could be in the form of performance appraisals or confirmation of human resource information, such as beneficiary or dependants' names.

A nonintrusive test that can be done by the payroll or human resources department is to validate U.S. social security numbers (SSN) or Canadian social insurance numbers (SIN).

Verification of SSN is available online at the Social Security Number Verification Service.[2] If there is a concern about the validity of an SIN, Service Canada's Social Insurance Registration Office can be contacted.[3]

The SIN last digit is a checksum digit and is based on the Luhn algorithm. The social insurance numbers in the payroll master can be tested for format validity using its checksum digit.

Canadian business numbers (HST/GST) and credit card numbers also use checksum based on the Luhn algorithm. The Luhn algorithm will be discussed in Chapter 17 on automation and IDEAScript.

It should also be recognized that not all types of payroll fraud or abuse can be detected from analyzing data unless you have a specific target for investigation. Without focusing on all the data associated with a certain employee, it would be difficult to detect misusing the employee's time for personal activities or for political campaigns. There are usually no records kept for these activities, making the use of data analytics difficult.

 ## NOTES

1. "Data | State of Oklahoma," accessed March 7, 2014, https://data.ok.gov.
2. "The Social Security Number Verification Service," accessed March 20, 2014, www.ssa .gov/employer/ssnv.htm.
3. "Information for Employers—Service Canada," accessed March 20, 2014, www.service-canada.gc.ca/eng/sin/employers/responsibilities.shtml.

## CHAPTER ELEVEN

Expense Reimbursement Schemes

THE MOST COMMON TYPE OF EXPENSE reimbursement paid by organizations to employees is for travel and entertainment expenses. Also popular are purchase cards or procurement cards, a form of company charge cards that are issued to employees. It is often used for, but not restricted to, buying low-value goods and services to avoid the cost of red tape or processing cost associated with the normal procurement procedures. The company normally pays purchase-card bills, so it is not specifically expense reimbursement to an employee's out-of-pocket costs. However, discussions of purchase cards traditionally fall under the expense reimbursement scheme category.

Travel and entertainment expenses are incurred at every level of employment, whether they are for sales, training, meetings, or attending conferences. Typically, those that incur the highest travel and entertainment expenses would be those in sales-related functions and executives of the company.

Detection relies on review and analysis of the expenses, followed by a detailed audit of the expense reports and supporting documents. Analysis can only point out anomalies that must be followed up by a thorough review of source documents. Similarly, sampling techniques can only select transactions which need to be audited in detail. Fraud would unlikely be uncovered unless the sample happened to pull out a transaction to audit by chance. The smaller the sample, the lower the opportunity there is to detect travel and entertainment fraud.

Analysis can initially be done on historical, budget, or other employee comparisons for an overview. These analyses may display unusual items or patterns. One must be familiar with the company's travel policy and procedures in order to distinguish between acceptable or improper expense claims.

Improper expense claims include:

- Personal items
- Expenses that never materialized or were subsequently canceled
- Fake or altered receipts

How fraudulent expense reimbursements are perpetrated is typically broken down into four categories:

1. Overstated Expense Reimbursements

■ Overstated expenses are those items incurred as legitimate business expenses, but are over-claimed by the employee. Receipts are altered or created to support the expense actually spent but for amounts exceeding the actual payment by the employee. The employee may have stayed at a lower-price hotel or used lower-cost transportation and then created receipts showing higher-priced methods of transportation or accommodation.

■ Another way to overstate reimbursements is to purchase a higher-cost item, return it, and then purchase a similar but lower-cost item. For example, the cost of a direct-flight ticket may be more expensive than one with a stopover. Purchasing two tickets and then returning for a refund of the higher-priced ticket results in the employee having both receipts. Similarly, a flight may be booked weeks in advance at a reasonable cost. An expensive last-minute flight booked on the same flight may also be done and then refunded to achieve the same effect of additional cash for the employee when the expense claim is submitted to the company.

2. Mischaracterized Expense Reimbursements

■ Expense reimbursements are for business-related purposes only. Receipts may be submitted for business reimbursement when in fact the expenditures were of a personal nature. The fraud is simple to do as receipts are easily available and it is only necessary for the employee to mischaracterize or reclassify the personal expense as a business expense. At times, the dates of the expenditures claimed as business may not coincide with a legitimate business trip.

In an audit report released by the Parliament of Canada, titled "Review of Senator Wallin's Travel Expense and Living Allowance Claims," Senator Wallin was found to have claimed $90,323 in travel for non-Senate business, citing 79 examples.[1]

While the report lists a number of audit findings, only the expense mischaracterization categories from the audit report are highlighted here:

The amount related to non-Senate business from these claims totaled $90,323, as they fell into one or more of the following:

■ Travel claim was reimbursed by Senator Wallin as she deemed the claim was for personal business.

■ Travel claim was for private business commitments made prior to Senator Wallin's appointment to the Senate (Senator Wallin has indicated that she understood that these costs were to be covered).

■ Travel claim included amounts related to returning to Ottawa from private business activities.

■ Travel claim related to speaking or other events that were non-Senate related.

■ Travel claim related to partisan-related activity, such as fundraising.

3. Multiple Reimbursements

- Multiple reimbursements fraud is simple in that the same expenses are claimed more than once, so the employee may be reimbursed two or more times. At the very basic level is submitting the charge card receipt for reimbursement and then submitting the charge card bill for the same item for reimbursement. It may be that the charge was on a company credit or purchase card that the company pays but the employee, using the card receipt, would claim for a reimbursement that the employee never originally paid for in the first place. Staff at a more senior level in charge of several budgets may submit the same expenses to each of the budgets for multiple reimbursements.

4. Fictitious Expense Reimbursements

- This type of fraud requires a bit of work and artistic skills since receipts have to be created. With personal computers and ease of use of sophisticated software, making counterfeit or realistic-looking receipts becomes easier. In fact, there are websites that will create legitimate looking receipts for you. One such website, Sales Receipt Store (www.salesreceiptstore.com), can provide fake hotel receipts, fake ATM receipts, and can design other types of receipts for you for novelty and stage use.[2] They can even be printed on thermal paper that many businesses still use. The home page of the website is shown in Figure 11.1.

FIGURE 11.1 Novelty Receipts Website Home Page

Source: Sales Receipt Store, www.salesreceiptstore.com.

Sample receipts from the novelty website are displayed in Figure 11.2.

FIGURE 11.2 Sample Receipts from the Novelty Website

Source: Sales Receipt Store, www.salesreceiptstore.com.

To obtain false receipts, sometimes it is a simple matter of just asking the server at a restaurant or the taxi driver for blank receipts. Many are happy to accommodate. There are even restaurants that have a glass jar out for customers to leave unwanted receipts that other customers may take from.

False receipts are a worldwide problem. A *New York Times* article dated August 3, 2013, describes the openness and prevalence of the trade in false receipts in China. "Signs posted throughout this city advertise all kinds of fake receipts: travel receipts, lease receipts, waste material receipts and value-added tax receipts."[3]

It is not just restricted to employees defrauding the company of a few hundred dollars. The stakes are much, much higher. The *New York Times* article also notes that, "GlaxoSmithKline is still trying to figure out how four senior executives at its China operation were able to submit fake receipts to embezzle millions of dollars."

Detecting false or altered receipts is a significant challenge. Unless the quality of the fake receipts is so poor it can be spotted upon visual inspection, there is no way to really know whether the receipts are valid, short of confirming it with the issuing third parties. Even then, the receipts may be legitimate but were issued to someone else who had no need of them.

Data analytics can help isolate unusual patterns or outliers of expense reimbursement and P-Card transactions. Resources can then be applied to the suspicious transactions for additional investigation.

DATA AND DATA ANALYSIS

We will use real-life data obtained on the Internet in order to demonstrate some of the steps used to analyze data for outliers and anomalies. The analysis results provide the auditor with a good starting point to narrow down transactions to a manageable level for further review.

While we only have access to the data set and not any backup or source documents, it is not possible to confirm any speculation or hypothesis resulting from the anomalies obtained from the analysis. The data is accessible to anyone with Internet access; the Ontario Government maintains it in an archived expense claim area.[4] With much government oversight open to public scrutiny, it is unlikely that there are any fraudulent transactions contained in the data set. Nevertheless, the data highlights the fact that all data contains some sort of anomalies and the auditor must be very aware of false positives. The auditor should reserve any conclusion until source documents are examined and possibly confirmed by issuing parties.

The data was downloaded in the CSV-delimited format and unmodified in any way with the exception of the name field being replaced with an employee number field.

The fields in the data set are shown Figure 11.3.

	Field Name	Type	Len	Dec
1	EMPLOYEE_NO	Character	8	
2	START_DATE	Date	8	
3	END_DATE	Date	8	
4	AIR_FARE	Numeric	8	2
5	OTHER_TRANSPORTATION	Numeric	8	2
6	ACCOMMODATION	Numeric	8	2
7	MEALS	Numeric	8	2
8	INCIDENTALS	Numeric	8	2
9	SUBTOTAL	Numeric	8	2
10	HOSPITALITY	Numeric	8	2
11	OTHER_EXPENSES	Numeric	8	2
12	TOTAL	Numeric	8	2
13	DESTINATION	Character	153	
14	MINISTRY	Character	42	
15	POSITION	Character	41	
16	PURPOSE	Character	241	

FIGURE 11.3 Fields of the Travel Expenses Database

The first step is to browse the data to become familiar with the contents of contained in each field. We then review the field statistics (not shown) for both the date and numeric fields. For the date-field statistics, we see that there are 2,800 records in the entire database, with the earliest date being October 30, 2009, and the latest date being March 31, 2011.

For the numeric-field statistics, the critical information is that there are no negative values in any of the amount fields. The total field sums to $1,995,498.35 and there are a number of records that contain zero in other numeric fields.

Since we have the fields START_DATE and END_DATE available to us, we can calculate the difference between the two dates and call the field DATE_DIFF. This will provide us with the time span of the travel claim. We must be familiar with the procedures regarding the date entry of these dates. Is it mandatory that the employee enter these dates and that the receipts must fall within the dates in order for the claim to be processed? What if the END_DATE is blank? Does the computer system apply the START_DATE there, as it appears to be a mandatory field? It is expected that there will be some keypunch errors, too. We do not know how the system works so we must maintain an open mind if we come across any anomalies when using the DATE_DIFF field in our analysis.

Days Traveled

Create a field called DATE_DIFF using the equation of

$$@Age(END\_DATE, START\_DATE)$$

There are 78 records with DATE_DIFF. The ones with differences of more than 60 suggest that those records contain claims where the employee traveled over 60 days. These may have errors in either the START_DATE or END_DATE, or have errors in both. It may be possible that several claims over a spread of time were combined into one claim. A review of the source documents and receipts can easily clear this up.

Various analyses can be done using the DATE_DIFF field. Using the criteria of DATE_DIFF $= = 0$, 972 records were obtained, which means that 972 of the 2,800 claims/records were for travel that started and ended on the same day. Conversely, 1,828 of the records showed travels of 1 day or more.

Same Day Traveled with Accommodation Charges

To obtain transactions where there are accommodation costs and both the start and end of the travel claim are on the same date, we extract the records using this formula:

$$DATE\_DIFF = = 0 .AND. ACCOMMODATION > 0$$

There were 124 records obtained as shown in Figure 11.4.

Same Day Traveled with Flight Charges

To obtain transactions where there are airfare costs and both the start and end of the travel claim are on the same date, we extract the records using this formula:

$$DATE\_DIFF = = 0 .AND. AIR\_FARE > 0$$

	EMPLOYEE_NO	START_DATE	END_DATE	DATE_DIFF	AIR_FARE	OTHER_TRANSPORTATION	ACCOMMODATION	MEALS	INCIDENTALS	SUBTOTAL	HOSPITALITY	OTHER_EXP
1	1453	17/12/2009	17/12/2009	0	2,978.57	0.00	114.45	0.00	0.00	3,093.02	0.00	
2	1410	25/03/2010	25/03/2010	0	0.00	0.00	127.60	0.00	0.00	127.60	0.00	
3	1003	07/04/2010	07/04/2010	0	0.00	0.00	117.52	0.00	0.00	117.52	0.00	
4	1027	07/04/2010	07/04/2010	0	0.00	0.00	165.90	0.00	0.00	165.90	0.00	
5	1467	07/04/2010	07/04/2010	0	74.00	173.00	165.90	0.00	0.00	412.90	0.00	
6	1029	08/04/2010	08/04/2010	0	0.00	0.00	336.51	0.00	0.00	336.51	0.00	
7	1247	12/04/2010	12/04/2010	0	399.08	74.90	143.71	0.00	0.00	617.69	0.00	
8	1440	12/04/2010	12/04/2010	0	425.28	52.80	168.37	0.00	0.00	646.45	0.00	
9	1309	13/04/2010	13/04/2010	0	0.00	0.00	113.00	0.00	0.00	113.00	0.00	
10	1473	14/04/2010	14/04/2010	0	670.98	138.74	117.52	20.81	122.79	1,070.84	0.00	
11	1144	16/04/2010	16/04/2010	0	0.00	0.00	115.50	0.00	0.00	115.50	0.00	
12	1286	21/04/2010	21/04/2010	0	874.67	0.00	96.04	31.25	0.00	1,001.96	0.00	
13	1111	22/04/2010	22/04/2010	0	0.00	0.00	97.90	0.00	0.00	97.90	0.00	
14	1178	22/04/2010	22/04/2010	0	0.00	0.00	97.90	0.00	0.00	97.90	0.00	
15	1439	22/04/2010	22/04/2010	0	0.00	0.00	97.90	0.00	0.00	97.90	0.00	
16	1092	03/05/2010	03/05/2010	0	432.84	0.00	102.30	0.00	0.00	535.14	0.00	
17	1359	03/05/2010	03/05/2010	0	0.00	83.54	93.50	90.61	0.00	267.65	0.00	
18	1158	06/05/2010	06/05/2010	0	1,025.13	104.00	107.80	43.20	0.00	1,280.13	0.00	
19	1206	06/05/2010	06/05/2010	0	1,030.31	45.24	174.02	70.86	0.00	1,320.43	0.00	
20	1459	10/05/2010	10/05/2010	0	0.00	144.00	120.91	0.00	0.00	264.91	0.00	
21	1031	12/05/2010	12/05/2010	0	0.00	72.60	108.90	0.00	0.00	181.50	0.00	
22	1037	12/05/2010	12/05/2010	0	371.38	56.00	184.86	0.00	0.00	612.24	0.00	
23	1240	17/05/2010	17/05/2010	0	0.00	0.00	168.30	20.00	0.00	188.30	0.00	
24	1019	19/05/2010	19/05/2010	0	453.55	0.00	224.87	0.00	0.00	678.42	0.00	
25	1106	27/05/2010	27/05/2010	0	0.00	0.00	108.90	18.39	0.00	127.29	0.00	
26	1266	30/05/2010	30/05/2010	0	0.00	0.00	168.37	7.67	0.00	176.04	0.00	
27	1111	03/06/2010	03/06/2010	0	336.04	0.00	121.00	0.00	0.00	457.04	0.00	
28	1178	03/06/2010	03/06/2010	0	326.36	13.75	121.00	0.00	0.00	461.11	0.00	
29	1359	03/06/2010	03/06/2010	0	0.00	0.00	82.95	0.00	0.00	82.95	0.00	
30	1106	05/06/2010	05/06/2010	0	488.51	0.00	198.00	0.00	0.00	686.51	0.00	
31	1359	10/06/2010	10/06/2010	0	0.00	0.00	101.83	0.00	0.00	101.83	0.00	
32	1413	14/06/2010	14/06/2010	0	0.00	0.00	124.30	20.79	0.00	145.09	0.00	
33	1020	15/06/2010	15/06/2010	0	285.38	28.55	283.68	25.70	0.00	623.31	0.00	
34	1065	15/06/2010	15/06/2010	0	0.00	0.00	283.68	0.00	0.00	283.68	0.00	
35	1413	15/06/2010	15/06/2010	0	0.00	0.00	283.68	43.74	14.65	342.07	0.00	
36	1413	15/06/2010	15/06/2010	0	0.00	0.00	271.11	0.00	0.00	271.11	0.00	
37	1422	15/06/2010	15/06/2010	0	263.17	58.00	283.68	0.00	0.00	604.85	0.00	
38	1438	16/06/2010	16/06/2010	0	0.00	0.00	174.06	0.00	0.00	174.06	0.00	
39	1410	23/06/2010	23/06/2010	0	0.00	0.00	384.41	0.00	0.00	384.41	0.00	

FIGURE 11.4 Results of Accommodations with No Overnight Travel

There were 311 records obtained.

Same Day Traveled with Both Flight and Accommodation Charges

Where the start and end dates are on the same day that contains airfare amounts and accommodation costs, we extract the matching records with this formula:

DATE_DIFF = 0 .AND. AIR_FARE > 0 .AND. ACCOMMODATION > 0

There are 273 records outputted.

Traveled Overnight with Both Flight and Accommodation Charges

Where the start and end dates are not on the same day that contains airfare amounts and accommodation costs, we extract the matching records with this formula:

DATE_DIFF > 0 .AND. AIR_FARE > 0 .AND. ACCOMMODATION > 0

There are 116 records outputted.

Traveled Overnight with Flight but No Accommodation Charges

From the travel expense data set, we can look for travel claims that were for more than the same day with an airfare expense but not accommodations.

	EMPLOYEE_NO	START_DATE	END_DATE	DATE_DIFF	AIR_FARE	ACCOMMODATION	OTHER_TRANSPORTATION	MEALS	INCIDENTALS
1	1037	17/01/2010	20/01/2010	3	1,305.44	0.00	0.00	39.42	84.03
2	1462	08/02/2010	26/03/2010	46	410.78	0.00	29.00	0.00	0.00
3	1003	26/03/2010	28/03/2010	2	481.18	0.00	48.50	22.60	0.00
4	1099	26/03/2010	26/05/2010	61	463.67	0.00	119.82	0.00	0.00
5	1389	01/04/2010	19/04/2010	18	900.48	0.00	186.67	0.00	0.00
6	1376	08/04/2010	10/05/2010	32	1,923.97	0.00	389.58	0.00	41.25
7	1330	13/04/2010	07/06/2010	55	558.60	0.00	147.28	0.00	0.00
8	1352	14/04/2010	18/06/2010	65	264.95	0.00	116.72	0.00	0.00
9	1274	16/04/2010	07/06/2010	52	1,657.37	0.00	0.00	119.05	75.00
10	1353	18/04/2010	12/05/2010	24	381.23	0.00	119.75	0.00	0.00
11	1065	22/04/2010	28/04/2010	6	1,309.25	0.00	55.00	0.00	0.00
12	1287	05/05/2010	09/05/2010	4	302.53	0.00	320.72	0.00	0.00
13	1047	06/05/2010	07/05/2010	1	1,286.46	0.00	148.08	0.00	19.83
14	1205	06/05/2010	07/05/2010	1	333.04	0.00	35.00	0.00	0.00
15	1280	06/05/2010	11/05/2010	5	1,030.31	0.00	35.00	50.36	0.00
16	1283	06/05/2010	06/10/2010	153	416.06	0.00	30.00	48.94	0.00
17	1174	10/05/2010	11/05/2010	1	703.33	0.00	117.84	6.27	0.00
18	1158	18/05/2010	19/05/2010	1	344.84	0.00	40.00	0.00	0.00
19	1476	19/05/2010	15/06/2010	27	337.28	0.00	0.00	0.00	0.00
20	1462	20/05/2010	14/10/2010	147	1,416.07	0.00	48.00	0.00	0.00

FIGURE 11.5   Overnight Travel with Flight without Accommodations

Using this formula, 116 records matched, as displayed in Figure 11.5.

DATE_DIFF > 0 .AND. AIR_FARE > 0 .AND. ACCOMMODATION = 0

Top-10 Flight Charges with No Accommodation Charge and Traveled Overnight

	EMPLOYEE_NO	START_DATE	END_DATE	DATE_DIFF	AIR_FARE	OTHER_TRANSPORTATION	ACCOMMODATION	MEALS	INCIDENTALS	SUBTOTAL	HOSPITALITY	OTHER_EXPENSES	TOTAL
1	1069	07/11/2010	04/03/2011	117	9,411.19	0.00	0.00	0.00	0.00	9,411.19	0.00	0.00	9,411.19
2	1297	14/12/2010	16/02/2011	64	3,724.19	85.50	0.00	0.00	0.00	3,809.69	0.00	0.00	3,809.69
3	1328	09/07/2010	23/07/2010	14	2,488.40	405.00	0.00	0.00	0.00	2,893.40	0.00	57.75	2,951.15
4	1084	12/09/2010	14/10/2010	32	2,209.45	0.00	0.00	11.25	56.50	2,277.20	0.00	0.00	2,277.20
5	1376	08/04/2010	10/05/2010	32	1,923.97	389.58	0.00	0.00	41.25	2,354.80	0.00	0.00	2,354.80
6	1482	08/09/2010	09/09/2010	1	1,889.36	82.00	0.00	0.00	0.00	1,971.36	0.00	0.00	1,971.36
7	1162	26/05/2010	28/05/2010	2	1,788.65	0.00	0.00	0.00	0.00	1,788.65	0.00	0.00	1,788.65
8	1354	24/11/2010	25/11/2010	1	1,696.10	183.39	0.00	0.00	0.00	1,879.49	0.00	0.00	1,879.49
9	1160	23/11/2010	03/12/2010	10	1,695.67	268.80	0.00	0.00	0.00	1,964.47	0.00	0.00	1,964.47
10	1274	16/04/2010	07/06/2010	52	1,657.37	0.00	0.00	119.05	75.00	1,851.42	0.00	0.00	1,851.42

FIGURE 11.6   Top-10 Airfare Amounts

Here are examples of the top-10 highest airfare claims where there are no accommodations and the employees did not return home on the same day. From the "Travel Expenses" database, we extract to a new file using the equation of DATE_DIFF > 0 .AND. AIR_FARE > 0 .AND. ACCOMMODATION=0. We then index on the AIR_FARE field by descending order for us to be able to review the top-10 or any of the 116 resulting records, as shown in Figure 11.6.

Another method to arrive at the top-10 flight costs that match our criteria is to use the results from Figure 11.5, apply the Top Records Extraction option of IDEA to them, and input 10 as the number of records to extract for the AIR_FARE field. This illustrates, again, that there are many ways to arrive at the same audit objectives within IDEA. It is a matter of personal choice of which methods and which equations are preferred.

Some of these resulting records need to be audited by going to the expense report and the attached receipts to answer the anomalies. It is up to the auditor's professional judgment as to which records to examine based on cut-off amounts, sampling, or even intuition.

Z-Score Tests

We can summarize the data set on various fields that shows the total and average for each of the summarized fields. The Z-score can be calculated against the average to see how far each average is away from the center or norm. The summarization and Z-score totaling on the sum and average can be applied to these examples.

Summarize by the EMPLOYEE_NO field and sum and average the TOTAL field. Append or create a Z-score field and index the Z-score in descending order to potentially review high Z-scores. The resulting file has 10 records above the score of 3.0 that should be audited in detail, as shown in Figure 11.7.

	EMPLOYEE_NO	NO_OF_RECS	TOTAL_SUM	TOTAL_AVERAGE	Z_SCORE ▼
1	1142	1	8,822.02	8,822.02	11.2110
2	1303	1	5,297.57	5,297.57	6.3603
3	1212	17	68,527.87	4,031.05	4.6172
4	1372	2	7,978.93	3,989.47	4.5600
5	1366	17	60,407.99	3,553.41	3.9598
6	1069	3	9,890.28	3,296.76	3.6066
7	1392	5	15,761.34	3,152.27	3.4077
8	1422	7	21,347.43	3,049.63	3.2665
9	1046	1	2,963.01	2,963.01	3.1472
10	1413	12	34,816.94	2,901.41	3.0625
11	1418	4	10,977.72	2,744.43	2.8464

Travel Expenses.IMD × *Summ Employee.IMD* ×

FIGURE 11.7 High Z-Score of Average Amounts

A review of the PURPOSE field for the record with a score of 11.2110 notes that employee 1142 took a trip to China, resulting in the high-average cost that deviates significantly from the center amount. The second record, for employee 1303, also incurred high-average costs, with a score of 6.3603, due to a trip to Israel. The auditor may wish to confirm the validity of the business reason for the trips.

Z-scores can be used with other groupings to test for deviations. We can look at the different divisions or ministries. Summarize by the ministry field, then sum and average the total field. Append or create a Z-score field, and index the Z-score in descending order to review potentially high Z-scores. A comparison can be seen of average total travel expenses among the various ministries.

Z-scores can be applied to multiple groups or keys also. We can summarize first by the POSITION field, second by the MINISTRY field, and third by the EMPLOYEE_NO field and sum and average the TOTAL field. Comparison by the employees' position in each of the ministries and then by individual employees can be done. Later on, we can enhance this analysis by applying the relative size factor (RSF) test on it.

For higher-level analysis, summarization can be applied just to the POSITION field so that travel for classes of job positions or classifications can be compared. To further refine this, summarize by the POSITION field and by the MINISTRY field to provide a comparison of the same jobs in different ministries.

Pivot Table View

By using the Pivot Table feature of IDEA, other high-level summarization views are easily available. If you wish to see the total of each expense category by employee, simply drag the desired fields into the data area, as in Figure 11.8.

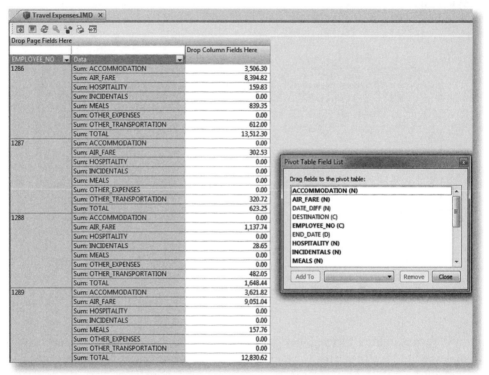

FIGURE 11.8   Pivot Table View of Total Expenses by Employees, by Type

Top Record Extractions

The highest total dollar values, or highest dollar values by any category, can be obtained by using the Top Record Extraction feature. The examples in Figure 11.9 were from selecting the top-10 records for the AIR_FARE field and the top-most records for the ACCOMMODATION field. The IDEA software automatically sequences the selected field top records from the highest to lowest.

Same-Same-Same Tests

Duplicate Key Detection is used to look for unusual duplicate items that may be signs of error or fraud.

	EMPLOYEE_NO	START_DATE	END_DATE	DATE_OFF	AIR_FARE	OTHER_TRANSPORTATION	ACCOMMODATION	MEALS	INCIDENTALS	SUBTOTAL	HOSPITALITY	OTHER_EXPENSES	TOTAL
1	1366	24/01/2011	02/02/2011	9	11,810.57	0.00	3,692.74	206.06	0.00	15,709.37	0.00	0.00	15,709.37
2	1063	25/10/2010	04/11/2010	10	11,079.20	46.44	2,453.48	0.00	133.88	13,713.00	0.00	0.00	13,713.00
3	1422	28/10/2010	04/11/2010	7	9,512.93	78.50	1,584.94	24.28	10.86	11,211.51	0.00	0.00	11,211.51
4	1413	28/10/2010	04/11/2010	7	9,482.42	77.00	1,586.72	82.53	130.69	11,359.36	0.00	0.00	11,359.36
5	1069	07/11/2010	04/03/2011	117	9,411.19	0.00	0.00	0.00	0.00	9,411.19	0.00	0.00	9,411.19
6	1289	28/10/2010	04/11/2010	7	9,051.04	0.00	2,673.41	157.76	0.00	11,882.21	0.00	0.00	11,882.21
7	1366	27/10/2010	28/11/2010	32	8,040.25	0.00	2,334.46	72.22	0.00	10,446.93	0.00	0.00	10,446.93
8	1386	21/09/2010	02/10/2010	11	7,244.71	42.66	2,061.47	0.00	110.00	9,458.84	0.00	0.00	9,458.84
9	1142	28/10/2010	03/11/2010	6	7,230.93	0.00	1,557.82	33.27	0.00	8,822.02	0.00	0.00	8,822.02
10	1112	19/06/2010	24/06/2010	5	7,169.48	0.00	1,608.52	0.00	0.00	8,778.00	0.00	0.00	8,778.00

	EMPLOYEE_NO	START_DATE	END_DATE	DATE_OFF	AIR_FARE	OTHER_TRANSPORTATION	ACCOMMODATION	MEALS	INCIDENTALS	SUBTOTAL	HOSPITALITY	OTHER_EXPENSES	TOTAL
1	1241	07/05/2010	16/06/2010	40	1,495.24	46.00	5,560.96	163.98	399.96	7,666.14	0.00	0.00	7,666.14
2	1473	30/04/2010	21/06/2010	52	2,346.90	63.00	4,980.96	230.85	289.38	7,911.09	0.00	0.00	7,911.09
3	1418	23/01/2011	03/02/2011	11	3,727.09	86.03	4,174.41	197.18	0.00	8,184.71	0.00	0.00	8,184.71
4	1473	20/10/2010	09/11/2010	20	3,069.35	65.00	4,106.35	217.42	0.00	7,458.12	0.00	0.00	7,458.12
5	1241	20/10/2010	03/11/2010	14	2,478.92	0.00	4,069.04	146.98	159.49	6,854.43	0.00	0.00	6,854.43
6	1303	19/05/2010	26/05/2010	7	1,204.44	118.14	3,868.19	24.89	81.91	5,297.57	0.00	0.00	5,297.57
7	1089	24/12/2010	03/02/2011	41	2,501.74	75.00	3,700.54	192.64	109.81	6,579.73	0.00	0.00	6,579.73
8	1366	24/01/2011	02/02/2011	0	11,810.57	0.00	3,692.74	206.06	0.00	15,709.37	0.00	0.00	15,709.37
9	1445	24/01/2011	02/02/2011	9	3,020.18	0.00	3,633.96	196.36	53.47	6,903.97	0.00	0.00	6,903.97
10	1403	19/10/2010	04/11/2010	16	5,850.43	1.71	3,537.34	289.28	99.36	9,778.12	0.00	0.00	9,778.12

FIGURE 11.9 Top-10 Amounts for Each Category Example

We use this feature on the "Travel Expenses" data set to extract transactions that contain the same START_DATE for the same EMPLOYEE_NO in their travel claims. This process produced 122 records. An examination of these records shows us that the typical reason for duplicate matches is because airfare is inputted into one line and accommodations in another line. Other expenses could be mixed in either line for the same travel claim. Employee 1277 appears to have the travel claims posted with the going to the destination in one record and the return flight in another record. For this employee the data shows two claims of accommodations where there does not appear to be an overnight stay based on the start and end dates of the travel claim. Refer to Figure 11.10.

	EMPLOYEE_NO	START_DATE	END_DATE	DATE_OFF	AIR_FARE	OTHER_TRANSPORTATION	ACCOMMODATION	MEALS	INCIDENTALS	SUBTOTAL	HOSPITALITY	OTHER_EXPENSES	TOTAL
51	1277	14/10/2010	15/10/2010	1	1,255.80	0.00	124.30	14.69	0.00	1,394.79	0.00	0.00	1,394.79
52	1277	14/10/2010	14/10/2010	0	679.13	0.00	0.00	0.00	0.00	679.13	0.00	0.00	679.13
53	1277	06/11/2010	08/11/2010	0	0.00	0.00	118.65	0.00	0.00	118.65	0.00	0.00	118.65
54	1277	08/11/2010	08/11/2010	0	1,245.15	0.00	0.00	0.00	0.00	1,245.15	0.00	0.00	1,245.15
55	1277	03/12/2010	03/12/2010	0	313.31	0.00	134.47	0.00	0.00	447.78	0.00	0.00	447.78
56	1277	03/12/2010	03/12/2010	0	1,135.85	0.00	0.00	0.00	0.00	1,135.85	0.00	0.00	1,135.85
57	1277	03/02/2011	03/02/2011	0	125.43	0.00	0.00	0.00	0.00	125.43	0.00	0.00	125.43
58	1277	03/02/2011	03/02/2011	0	347.43	0.00	0.00	0.00	0.00	347.43	0.00	0.00	347.43
59	1292	05/10/2010	06/10/2010	1	578.39	125.00	0.00	8.75	0.00	712.14	0.00	0.00	712.14
60	1292	05/10/2010	05/10/2010	0	0.00	24.00	0.00	0.00	0.00	24.00	0.00	0.00	24.00
61	1294	12/04/2010	13/04/2010	1	2,987.51	87.00	219.08	18.00	0.00	3,311.59	0.00	0.00	3,311.59
62	1294	12/04/2010	12/04/2010	0	0.00	0.00	0.00	8.21	0.00	8.21	0.00	0.00	8.21
63	1302	08/11/2010	29/11/2010	21	0.00	66.80	185.32	40.00	0.00	292.12	0.00	0.00	292.12
64	1302	08/11/2010	05/01/2011	58	0.00	33.00	0.00	0.00	0.00	33.00	0.00	0.00	33.00
65	1304	07/11/2010	09/11/2010	2	0.00	334.58	221.48	78.97	0.00	635.03	0.00	0.00	635.03
66	1304	07/11/2010	09/11/2010	2	1,281.84	0.00	0.00	0.00	0.00	1,281.84	0.00	0.00	1,281.84
67	1314	31/05/2010	31/05/2010	0	0.00	55.41	0.00	0.00	33.75	89.16	0.00	0.00	89.16
68	1314	31/05/2010	11/06/2010	11	319.18	54.00	0.00	0.00	0.00	373.18	0.00	0.00	373.18
69	1322	17/12/2010	17/12/2010	0	33.90	0.00	0.00	0.00	0.00	33.90	0.00	0.00	33.90
70	1322	17/12/2010	17/12/2010	0	602.57	0.00	0.00	0.00	0.00	602.57	0.00	0.00	602.57

FIGURE 11.10 Same Employee with Same Start Date Claims

Performing Duplicate Key Detection on EMPLOYEE_NO and AIR_FARE where AIR_FARE is greater than zero produced six records. We need to specify that AIR_FARE is greater than zero or that it is not equal to zero, as there are many records that do not contain any airfare amounts. The three matched pairs for the same employees were claimed for different dates, but the airfares were the same, as they were for the same destination.

Similarly, this method can be used on EMPLOYEE_NO and ACCOMMODATION, where ACCOMMODATION is greater than 0 and produced 97 records. For employee 1089, there is only one airfare charged but two identical accommodation amounts in Figure 11.11. The auditor must consider whether the average stay of $196 per night is reasonable in London, UK, or is double the amount ($393 per night) more reasonable? There are also identical amounts for other transportation and meals in each of the records. Source documents must be reviewed to confirm whether there are any duplicated posting errors.

EMPLOYEE_NO	START_DATE	END_DATE	DATE_DIFF	AIR_FARE	OTHER_TRANSPORTATION	ACCOMMODATION	MEALS	INCIDENTALS	SUBTOTAL	HOSPITALITY	OTHER_EXPENSES	TOTAL	
1089	17/07/2010	22/07/2010	5	0.00	109.80	1,767.96	44.50	0.00	1,922.26	0.00	0.00	1,922.26	London, United Kin
1089	17/07/2010	26/07/2010	9	2,158.82	109.80	1,767.96	44.50	0.00	4,081.08	0.00	0.00	4,081.08	London, UK
1092	04/08/2010	06/08/2010	2	762.86	84.00	214.70	22.49	0.00	1,084.05	0.00	216.17	1,300.22	Thunder Bay, ON
1092	30/11/2010	02/12/2010	2	586.80	56.00	214.70	0.00	0.00	857.50	60.00	0.00	917.50	Thunder Bay, ON
1111	16/08/2010	17/08/2010	1	0.00	0.00	168.37	0.00	0.00	168.37	0.00	0.00	168.37	Windsor, ON
1111	17/08/2010	17/08/2010	0	1,105.20	0.00	0.00	168.37	0.00	1,273.57	0.00	0.00	1,273.57	Windsor, ON
1139	08/11/2010	09/11/2010	1	0.00	180.40	123.17	19.64	0.00	323.21	0.00	0.00	323.21	London, ON
1139	23/03/2011	24/03/2011	1	0.00	61.60	123.17	20.00	0.00	204.77	0.00	0.00	204.77	Barrie, ON
1143	21/10/2010	24/10/2010	3	467.50	104.01	522.06	17.50	0.00	1,111.07	0.00	0.00	1,111.07	Ottawa, ON
1143	24/03/2011	27/03/2011	3	648.07	117.05	522.06	54.76	0.00	1,341.94	0.00	0.00	1,341.94	Ottawa, ON
1190	26/01/2011	27/01/2011	1	0.00	41.64	150.29	33.77	0.00	225.70	0.00	0.00	225.70	Toronto, ON
1190	09/03/2011	10/03/2011	1	0.00	54.64	150.29	53.98	0.00	258.91	0.00	0.00	258.91	Toronto, ON
1190	20/10/2010	21/10/2010	1	0.00	40.51	180.80	47.64	0.00	268.95	0.00	0.00	268.95	Toronto, ON
1190	25/10/2010	26/10/2010	1	0.00	60.51	180.80	49.92	0.00	291.23	0.00	0.00	291.23	Toronto, ON
1190	26/05/2011	27/05/2011	1	0.00	60.51	192.02	57.02	0.00	309.55	0.00	0.00	309.55	Toronto, ON
1190	13/06/2010	14/06/2010	1	0.00	40.51	192.02	38.25	0.00	270.78	0.00	0.00	270.78	Toronto, ON
1190	04/01/2011	06/01/2011	2	0.00	93.28	300.58	110.93	0.00	504.79	0.00	0.00	504.79	Toronto, ON
1190	19/01/2011	20/01/2011	1	0.00	10.00	300.58	70.72	0.00	381.30	0.00	0.00	381.30	Toronto, ON
1190	22/02/2011	24/02/2011	2	0.00	93.28	300.58	104.63	0.00	498.49	0.00	0.00	498.49	Toronto, ON
1190	23/03/2011	25/03/2011	2	0.00	63.28	300.58	77.17	0.00	441.03	0.00	0.00	441.03	Toronto, ON
1200	23/08/2010	24/08/2010	1	422.53	35.00	174.02	8.75	0.00	640.30	0.00	0.00	640.30	Ottawa, ON
1200	23/09/2010	19/11/2010	57	110.74	88.00	174.02	0.00	0.00	372.76	0.00	0.00	372.76	Ottawa, ON

FIGURE 11.11   Same Employee with Same Accommodation Amounts

When the "Duplicate Employee Accommodation" data set is indexed by the EMPLOYEE_NO, START_DATE, and ACCOMMODATION fields, records 82 and 83 show two airfare amounts, but with two identical accommodations amounts of $526.92. Both the airfare and accommodation amounts in Figure 11.12 require additional scrutiny.

EMPLOYEE_NO	START_DATE	END_DATE	DATE_DIFF	AIR_FARE	OTHER_TRANSPORTATION	ACCOMMODATION	MEALS	INCIDENTALS	SUBTOTAL	HOSPITALITY	OTHER_EXPENSES	TOTAL	
1334	19/10/2010	20/10/2010	1	414.16	0.00	174.02	0.00	0.00	588.18	0.00	0.00	588.18	Ottawa, ON
1334	19/11/2010	21/11/2010	2	423.88	136.60	174.02	11.25	0.00	745.75	0.00	0.00	745.75	Ottawa, ON
1334	13/12/2010	14/12/2010	1	140.33	169.17	174.02	25.26	0.00	508.78	0.00	33.75	542.53	Ottawa and Sudbur
1360	25/02/2010	26/02/2010	1	0.00	49.81	119.90	0.00	105.91	275.62	0.00	0.00	275.82	Widnsor, ON
1360	18/03/2010	22/03/2010	4	0.00	81.72	119.90	12.15	68.60	282.37	0.00	0.00	282.37	Windsor, On
1360	07/04/2010	12/04/2010	5	0.00	110.36	125.50	7.77	70.57	314.20	0.00	0.00	314.20	Sarnia, Windsor, ON
1360	16/04/2010	23/04/2010	7	0.00	86.39	125.50	0.00	31.54	243.43	0.00	0.00	243.43	Windsor, ON
1360	09/06/2010	14/06/2010	5	0.00	74.25	125.50	9.32	83.22	292.29	0.00	0.00	292.29	Windsor, ON
1360	04/11/2010	05/11/2010	1	0.00	82.54	123.17	29.56	81.15	316.42	0.00	0.00	316.42	Windsor, On
1360	30/11/2010	01/12/2010	1	0.00	156.01	123.17	11.41	0.00	290.59	0.00	0.00	290.59	Windsor, On
1360	09/12/2010	10/12/2010	1	0.00	84.62	123.17	13.66	58.53	279.98	0.00	0.00	279.98	Windsor, On
1377	10/06/2010	11/08/2010	1	637.60	70.00	124.30	20.00	0.00	851.90	0.00	0.00	851.90	Thunder Bay, ON
1377	23/10/2010	24/10/2010	1	579.97	65.60	124.30	0.00	0.00	769.87	0.00	0.00	769.87	Webequie, ON
1413	03/08/2010	06/08/2010	3	660.41	77.00	526.92	0.00	0.00	1,264.33	0.00	0.00	1,264.33	Winnipeg, MB
1413	03/08/2010	06/08/2010	3	1,347.95	0.00	526.92	0.00	0.00	1,874.87	0.00	0.00	1,874.87	Winnipeg, MB
1423	29/08/2010	30/08/2010	1	281.96	63.00	135.60	5.88	0.00	486.44	0.00	0.00	486.44	Webequie and Ogol
1423	23/10/2010	24/10/2010	1	543.81	51.00	135.60	0.00	0.00	730.41	0.00	0.00	730.41	Webequie, ON
1443	14/11/2010	15/11/2010	1	1,049.26	195.50	157.07	40.00	0.00	1,441.83	0.00	0.00	1,441.83	Toronto, ON
1443	21/11/2010	22/11/2010	1	1,342.95	134.00	157.07	18.86	0.00	1,652.88	34.83	0.00	1,687.71	Toronto, ON

FIGURE 11.12   Display of Indexing by Employee, Travel Start Date, and Accommodations

Same-Same-Different Test

The Duplicate Key Exclusion or same-same-different test should also be applied. When looking for the same EMPLOYEE_NO with the same END_DATE but different START_DATE, 50 records are produced, as in Figure 11.13. The auditor may wish to examine why some of these may have occurred.

SSDT - Travel Expenses.IMD

	EMPLOYEE_NO	START_DATE	END_DATE	AIR_FARE	OTHER_TRANSPORTATION	ACCOMMODATION	MEALS	INCIDENTALS	SUBTOTAL	HOSPITALITY	OTHER_
1	1013	09/11/2010	10/11/2010	0.00	45.88	0.00	0.00	18.11	63.99	0.00	
2	1013	10/11/2010	10/11/2010	433.55	37.50	0.00	0.00	0.00	471.05	0.00	
3	1013	22/01/2011	24/01/2011	0.00	101.70	0.00	0.00	17.42	119.12	0.00	
4	1013	24/01/2011	24/01/2011	0.00	82.61	0.00	0.00	0.00	82.61	0.00	
5	1018	28/01/2011	07/02/2011	765.41	0.00	0.00	0.00	0.00	765.41	0.00	
6	1018	07/02/2011	07/02/2011	875.35	0.00	0.00	0.00	0.00	875.35	0.00	
7	1022	04/11/2010	09/11/2010	0.00	89.09	0.00	0.00	43.97	133.06	0.00	
8	1022	08/11/2010	09/11/2010	720.39	74.39	127.69	0.00	0.00	922.47	0.00	
9	1022	07/02/2011	11/02/2011	0.00	71.86	0.00	0.00	19.70	91.56	0.00	
10	1022	10/02/2011	11/02/2011	928.62	152.49	108.48	29.32	11.51	1,230.42	0.00	
11	1053	07/02/2011	01/03/2011	204.53	0.00	0.00	0.00	0.00	204.53	0.00	
12	1053	01/03/2011	01/03/2011	0.00	38.00	0.00	0.00	0.00	38.00	0.00	
13	1060	14/01/2011	16/01/2011	563.04	51.35	268.94	56.89	0.00	940.22	0.00	
14	1060	16/01/2011	16/01/2011	0.00	61.65	0.00	0.00	0.00	61.65	0.00	
15	1069	07/11/2010	04/03/2011	9,411.19	0.00	0.00	0.00	0.00	9,411.19	0.00	
16	1069	03/03/2011	04/03/2011	0.00	89.24	179.67	0.00	0.00	268.91	0.00	
17	1088	27/09/2010	28/09/2010	482.20	87.50	0.00	49.99	0.00	619.69	0.00	
18	1088	28/09/2010	28/09/2010	0.00	0.00	196.62	0.00	0.00	196.62	0.00	
19	1111	16/08/2010	17/08/2010	0.00	0.00	168.37	0.00	0.00	168.37	0.00	
20	1111	17/08/2010	17/08/2010	1,105.20	0.00	168.37	0.00	0.00	1,273.57	0.00	
21	1128	24/02/2011	01/03/2011	1,164.63	167.68	158.19	31.29	0.00	1,521.79	0.00	
22	1128	28/02/2011	01/03/2011	511.91	139.07	168.37	0.00	0.00	819.35	0.00	
23	1208	24/11/2010	26/11/2010	0.00	85.02	339.00	16.31	0.00	440.33	0.00	
24	1208	26/11/2010	26/11/2010	0.00	65.21	0.00	0.00	0.00	65.21	0.00	
25	1232	11/01/2011	12/01/2011	0.00	8.00	145.77	0.00	0.00	153.77	0.00	
26	1232	12/01/2011	12/01/2011	0.00	15.00	0.00	0.00	0.00	15.00	0.00	
27	1242	22/02/2011	24/03/2011	0.00	150.50	0.00	0.00	0.00	150.50	0.00	
28	1242	04/03/2011	24/03/2011	0.00	407.27	993.38	219.29	0.00	1,619.94	0.00	
29	1247	04/08/2010	14/09/2010	0.00	32.00	0.00	0.00	0.00	32.00	0.00	
30	1247	14/09/2010	14/09/2010	0.00	0.00	0.00	0.00	0.00	0.00	48.51	
31	1252	09/03/2011	25/03/2011	0.00	150.00	0.00	0.00	0.00	150.00	0.00	
32	1252	25/03/2011	25/03/2011	0.00	0.00	0.00	0.00	0.00	0.00	35.03	
33	1334	23/07/2010	27/07/2010	1,026.61	403.71	477.14	0.00	59.70	1,967.16	121.60	
34	1334	27/07/2010	27/07/2010	1,564.60	0.00	0.00	0.00	0.00	1,564.60	0.00	
35	1334	13/12/2010	14/12/2010	140.33	169.17	174.02	25.26	0.00	508.78	0.00	
36	1334	14/12/2010	14/12/2010	568.63	0.00	0.00	0.00	0.00	568.63	0.00	
37	1367	02/05/2010	15/06/2010	0.00	21.00	0.00	0.00	0.00	21.00	0.00	
38	1367	14/06/2010	15/06/2010	294.37	28.00	174.02	0.00	0.00	496.39	0.00	

FIGURE 11.13 Same Employees with Same End-Claim Dates

Even Amounts Tests

Even amounts are always a curiosity. Typically, in an accounts payable file, we would probably look for even thousands, such as $25,000, $43,000, $108,000, and so on. For a travel expense file with smaller amounts we look for even hundreds.

Using the criteria view, nine records of OTHER_TRANSPORTATION amounts are displayed in Figure 11.14 with the equation of

(OTHER_TRANSPORTATION % 100) = 0 .AND. OTHER_TRANSPORTATION < > 0

Travel Expenses.IMD

	EMPLOYEE_NO	START_DATE	END_DATE	DATE_DIFF	AIR_FARE	OTHER_TRANSPORTATION	ACCOMMODATION
1	1152	07/05/2010	18/06/2010	42	0.00	100.00	0.00
2	1174	13/06/2010	17/06/2010	4	0.00	100.00	0.00
3	1335	15/08/2010	17/08/2010	2	0.00	500.00	0.00
4	1174	12/09/2010	12/09/2010	0	0.00	100.00	0.00
5	1440	05/10/2010	05/10/2010	0	712.58	100.00	0.00
6	1470	16/12/2010	16/12/2010	0	1,160.34	100.00	0.00
7	1126	11/01/2011	11/01/2011	0	0.00	200.00	0.00
8	1286	19/01/2011	20/01/2011	1	2,550.10	200.00	158.20
9	1126	23/03/2011	23/03/2011	0	0.00	200.00	0.00

FIGURE 11.14 Even Hundreds Amounts

Employee 1126 noted that the charge was for a Presto card. Presto cards are use with public transportation services that can be loaded up with funds. It should be determined whether the excessive top-up amount would be used for government business or for personal use. Note that other even amounts are unusual and that employee 1126 and 1174 both made similar claims before.

Applying the following criteria for the ACCOMMODATION field, two records of $100.00 and $300.00 are displayed for Employee 1012 and 1377 respectively.

$$(\text{ACCOMMODATION} \% 100) = 0 \text{ .AND. ACCOMMODATION} <> 0$$

Applying the following criteria for the MEAL field, two records of $100.00 each are displayed for employees 1012 and 1465. Note that employee 1012 also previously claimed $100.00 for accommodations. Travel policies must be reviewed to determine whether these are permissible per-diem allowances.

$$(\text{MEALS} \% 100) = 0 \text{ .AND. MEALS} <> 0$$

Daily Averages Tests

Flight costs to and from a destination normally do not vary incrementally with the number of days spent at the destination, with the possible exception of a reduced cost if staying over a Saturday night. For accommodations, meals, incidentals, and other expenses, the more overnight stays, the larger the costs would be. On the assumption that we can rely on the accuracy of the start and end dates of the travel trip (we know that we cannot place this reliance in a number of cases), we can use the start and end date differences to calculate averages for some of these expense categories.

The daily averages for accommodation, meals, and incidentals can be created by appending the fields ACCOMMOD_AVG, MEALS_AVG, and INCIDENTALS_AVG respectively, using the following equation.

$$@\text{If(DATE\_DIFF} > 0, \text{ACCOMMODATION/DATE\_DIFF, ACCOMMODATION)}$$

Applying the calculations resulted in the 70 records shown in Figure 11.15, with over $300 as the average per day. The largest accommodation daily average was $1,131.20. There is a need for a detailed review of large averages.

Our equation looks for travel claims of one day or more and then divides the accommodation amount by the number of days. If the travel claim is for the same day, then the equation returns the accommodation amount.

Similarly, you can calculate the averages for meals and also for incidentals.

$$@\text{If(DATE\_DIFF} > 0, \text{MEALS/DATE\_DIFF, MEALS)}$$

Applying the calculations resulted in 14 records with over $100 as the average per day. The largest daily average for meals was $458.11.

$$@\text{If(DATE\_DIFF} > 0, \text{INCIDENTALS/DATE\_DIFF, INCIDENTALS)}$$

Applying the calculations resulted in 31 records with over $50 as the average per day. The largest incidentals daily average was $520.62.

EMPLOYEE_NO	START_DATE	END_DATE	DATE_DIFF	AIR_FARE	OTHER_TRANSPORTATION	ACCOMMODATION	ACCOMMOD_AVG	MEALS	MEALS_AVG	INCIDENTALS	INCIDENTALS_AVG
1340	26/06/2010	27/06/2010	1	0.00	0.00	1,131.20	1,131.20	5.47	5.47	0.00	0.00
1112	08/12/2010	09/12/2010	1	1,181.17	0.00	834.90	834.90	0.00	0.00	0.00	0.00
1109	14/08/2010	14/08/2010	0	0.00	66.67	673.48	673.48	0.00	0.00	0.00	0.00
1392	02/10/2010	04/10/2010	2	4,856.40	0.00	1,336.10	668.05	0.00	0.00	0.00	0.00
1410	22/10/2010	24/10/2010	2	1,196.75	105.88	1,330.92	665.46	151.96	75.98	14.68	7.34
1139	22/08/2010	23/08/2010	1	589.13	22.40	653.14	653.14	0.00	0.00	0.00	0.00
1277	24/08/2010	25/08/2010	1	365.35	0.00	644.10	644.10	62.50	62.50	0.00	0.00
1325	02/10/2010	04/10/2010	2	1,955.14	29.20	1,262.58	631.29	28.17	14.09	0.00	0.00
1350	12/10/2010	12/10/2010	0	0.00	80.00	614.58	614.58	0.00	0.00	0.00	0.00
1372	19/05/2010	23/05/2010	4	1,444.36	5.54	2,416.58	604.15	27.35	6.84	139.01	34.75
1157	15/06/2010	16/06/2010	1	319.46	30.00	593.36	593.36	28.58	28.58	0.00	0.00
1227	17/06/2010	19/06/2010	2	2,272.51	0.00	1,178.73	589.37	0.00	0.00	0.00	0.00
1303	19/05/2010	26/05/2010	7	1,204.44	118.14	3,868.19	552.60	24.89	3.56	81.91	11.70
1218	15/08/2010	15/08/2010	0	0.00	61.02	505.11	505.11	0.00	0.00	0.00	0.00
1209	21/09/2010	23/09/2010	2	593.90	134.50	925.76	462.88	0.00	0.00	0.00	0.00
1366	29/03/2011	30/03/2011	1	987.43	0.00	438.16	438.16	27.48	27.48	0.00	0.00
1294	08/12/2010	10/12/2010	2	583.04	0.00	858.18	429.09	0.00	0.00	0.00	0.00
1366	17/07/2010	21/07/2010	4	5,952.74	0.00	1,685.30	421.33	75.35	18.84	0.00	0.00
1453	08/12/2010	10/12/2010	2	506.69	0.00	830.90	415.45	0.00	0.00	0.00	0.00
1366	24/01/2011	02/02/2011	9	11,810.57	0.00	3,692.74	410.30	206.06	22.90	0.00	0.00
1482	08/11/2010	08/11/2010	0	0.00	0.00	409.14	409.14	0.00	0.00	0.00	0.00
1001	06/02/2011	06/02/2011	0	0.00	0.00	408.50	408.50	0.00	0.00	0.00	0.00
1220	25/05/2010	26/05/2010	1	0.00	0.00	404.49	404.49	0.00	0.00	0.00	0.00
1445	24/01/2011	02/02/2011	9	3,020.18	0.00	3,633.96	403.77	196.36	21.82	53.47	5.94
1480	06/02/2011	06/02/2011	0	0.00	0.00	395.50	395.50	0.00	0.00	0.00	0.00

FIGURE 11.15 Average Accommodation Amounts

Having average expenses data is an excellent way to see if any of the results are out of the ordinary.

Relative Size Factor Test

The RSF test is a test for reasonableness within a specific grouping of data sets, such as employee number or job position. It identifies outliers within the group where the amount is too small to be considered as an anomaly when the entire "Travel Expenses" data set is taken as a whole.

We can apply the RSF test on the total amount based on each of the three separate groupings of EMPLOYEE_NO, POSITION, and then MINISTRY. After a review of these three distinct data sets, we can decide whether to apply additional tests on separate expenditure categories, such as accommodations, instead of the total amounts.

Running the test on the "Travel Expenses" data set by EMPLOYEE_NO and on the TOTAL field produced 50 records with the RSF ratio of more than 4.00 in Figure 11.16. By using the Define Action Field feature on the EMPLOYEE_NO linked to the "Travel Expenses" file, we can now just click on any employee number to display the detail records. High-RSF ratios should be examined, as the largest amount by employee is so much out of line from the employee's second-highest value. The AVERAGE_X_LARGEST, or average excluding the largest amount, gives you a sense of normal contents without having to review the detailed records.

The three records for employee 1069 are displayed in Figure 11.17 when the link is clicked.

Employing the RSF test by POSITION on the TOTAL field shows small RSF ratios, with only two positions exceeding a ratio of 4.00. This can be visualized as shown in the graph in Figure 11.18. The graph is produced with the RSF IDEAScript that shows a maximum of the top-50 ratios. We have 23 records in this case so all 23 are displayed.

	EMPLOYEE_NO	LARGEST_AMT	SECOND_LARGEST_AMT	AVERAGE_X_LARGEST	COUNT	RELATIVE_SIZE_FACTOR ▼
1	1275	934.55	11.00	11.00	2	84.96
2	1168	1,424.31	26.30	26.30	2	54.16
3	1264	985.31	20.00	20.00	2	49.27
4	1069	9,411.19	268.91	239.55	3	35.00
5	1057	1,885.92	55.23	44.80	4	34.15
6	1171	606.41	19.00	18.50	3	31.92
7	1401	1,088.52	42.57	42.57	2	25.57
8	1289	11,882.21	526.92	237.10	5	22.55
9	1257	350.47	20.00	20.00	2	17.52
10	1272	356.35	22.50	19.50	4	15.84
11	1452	259.73	17.00	17.00	2	15.28
12	1120	1,255.55	83.00	83.00	2	15.13
13	1402	2,373.88	157.07	157.07	2	15.11
14	1117	819.87	54.85	54.85	2	14.95
15	1050	835.40	56.15	56.15	2	14.88
16	1295	1,079.02	78.30	78.30	2	13.78
17	1414	699.57	50.80	50.80	2	13.77
18	1006	632.33	48.80	30.80	3	12.96
19	1094	1,710.19	140.70	140.70	2	12.15
20	1049	1,199.36	107.93	92.03	3	11.11

FIGURE 11.16   Relative Size Factor Test Results

	EMPLOYEE_NO	START_DATE	END_DATE	AIR_FARE	OTHER_TRANSPORTATION	ACCOMMODATION	MEALS	INCIDENTALS	SUBTOTAL	HOSPITALITY	OTHER_EXPENSES	TOTAL
1	1069	07/11/2010	04/03/2011	9,411.19	0.00	0.00	0.00	0.00	9,411.19	0.00	0.00	9,411.19
2	1069	08/11/2010	09/11/2010	0.00	0.00	210.18	0.00	0.00	210.18	0.00	0.00	210.18
3	1069	03/03/2011	04/03/2011	0.00	89.24	179.67	0.00	0.00	268.91	0.00	0.00	268.91

FIGURE 11.17   Drill-Down Display of Employee Number 1069

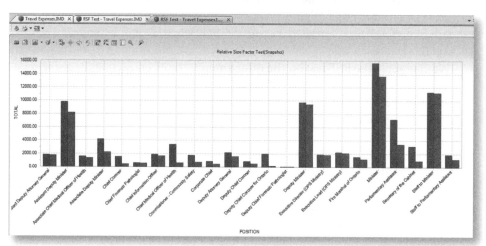

FIGURE 11.18   Graphic Display of Relative Size Factor Pairs of the Largest and Second-Largest Amounts

We can also employ the RSF test by MINISTRY on the TOTAL field that shows small RSF ratios with all ministries. With the exception of 5 records that have an RSF ratio of 15.32 at Small Business and Consumer Services, 4.72 at International Trade and Investment, 4.10 at Tourism and Culture, 4.06 at Citizenship and Immigration, and 3.00 at Energy and Infrastructure, the balance of the 33 records shows RSF ratios of less than 3.00.

Other RSF tests can be done using the summarized file based on POSITION, MINISTRY, and EMPLOYEE_NO that is summed and averaged on the total field. We can apply the RSF test to the TOTAL_AVERAGE amount by either the ministry field or the position field. This will provide us with highest averages versus the next-highest averages across ministries or for those holding the same positions across ministries.

The RSF test for averages of ministries has six records with RSF ratios of greater than 2.00. This is shown in Figure 11.19.

	MINISTRY	LARGEST_AMT	SECOND_LARGEST_AMT	AVERAGE_X_LARGEST	COUNT	RELATIVE_SIZE_FACTOR
1	Small Business and Consumer Services	1,557.98	101.69	101.69	3	15.32
2	Natural Resources	4,031.05	1,489.15	593.98	17	2.71
3	Tourism and Culture	2,111.75	800.69	512.82	12	2.64
4	Community and Social Services	2,582.75	1,174.69	490.70	16	2.20
5	Research and Innovation	2,381.20	1,136.88	587.86	19	2.09
6	Health and Long Term Care	2,744.43	1,331.77	453.30	28	2.06
7	Energy and Infrastructure	3,296.76	1,892.79	673.72	26	1.74

FIGURE 11.19   Relative Size Factor for Ministry Averages

The RSF test can lead us to abnormally high expenditures within each category. This test allows the auditor to focus on those transactions that may require additional attention.

Comparison Based on Audit Unit

Extractions may combine several steps and several tests. Suppose you wish to analyze the travel of those holding the position of assistant deputy minister in all of the different ministries. From the "Travel Expenses" database, extract where:

POSITION = = "Assistant Deputy Minister"

This results in 987 records, which is too many to examine if we were to look at further details. We can summarize this file by EMPLOYEE_NO and sum and average the TOTAL field. This gives us 129 records, which means that there are 129 assistant deputy ministers from all the ministries. Other tests may be applied against this file. For instance, we can use the Z-score test to see which assistant deputy ministers have total average spending that deviates from the center or norm the most, as shown in Figure 11.20.

Those with the highest Z-scores may be of interest for further explorations. For the sake of completeness, the auditor may wish to examine a few records that deviate in the other direction with negative Z-scores. We can view these at the bottom of the same analysis, as in Figure 11.21.

Travel Outside of the Country Test

We would like to examine travel outside of the country in more detail. As such, Canadian travel within and to other provinces needs to be eliminated.

Our "Travel Expenses" file's DESTINATION field contents are entered inconsistently. Our goal is to reduce the number of records that we have to review. It is not expected that

	EMPLOYEE_NO	NO_OF_RECS	TOTAL_SUM	TOTAL_AVERAGE	Z_SCORE ▼
1	1212	17	68,527.87	4,031.05	6.0013
2	1418	4	10,977.72	2,744.43	3.6879
3	1307	1	2,078.82	2,078.82	2.4911
4	1075	3	6,120.94	2,040.31	2.4219
5	1208	26	46,560.07	1,790.77	1.9732
6	1251	2	3,437.16	1,718.58	1.8434
7	1403	16	24,916.83	1,557.30	1.5535
8	1083	1	1,530.76	1,530.76	1.5057
9	1037	19	29,050.90	1,528.99	1.5025
10	1443	22	33,251.76	1,511.44	1.4710

FIGURE 11.20 Total and Average Travel Spending by Assistant Deputy Ministers

123	1163	3	337.36	112.45	-1.0444
124	1388	3	323.80	107.93	-1.0525
125	1272	4	414.84	103.71	-1.0601
126	1405	1	99.75	99.75	-1.0672
127	1051	1	64.48	64.48	-1.1306
128	1131	1	54.69	54.69	-1.1482
129	1394	3	64.00	21.33	-1.2082

FIGURE 11.21 Low Travel Spending by Assistant Deputy Ministers

the resulting file will be perfect by containing only foreign travel destinations. Sample contents of the DESTINATION field are displayed in Figure 11.22.

We first append the PROVINCE field using a reasonable character-field length (say 20) by using the equation of

$$@Split(DESTINATION, " ", ",", " ", 1, 1)$$

to pull out contents, from right to left to the first comma encountered in the DESTINA-TION field.

From a cursory visual scan of the data within the destination field, we know that using this equation will pull out most of the Canadian destinations.

@Match(PROVINCE, "ON", "On", "Ontario", "Ottawa ON", "ON.", "ON;", "PQ", "QC", "Quebec", "Quebec City", "Toronto", "Toronto ON" , "Montreal", "SK", "Saskatchewan", "NB", "NL", "Newfoundland", "NS", "Nova Scotia", "AB", "Alberta", "BC", "B.C.", "MB", "Manitoba", "NWT", "YT", "PEI")

Using the equation, we extract to a new file called "Known Provinces."

Use the Join feature with the "Travel Expenses" file as the primary file and "Known Provinces" as the secondary file with the Records with no secondary match option; this

	TOTAL	DESTINATIC
1	177.50	Toronto, ON
2	11.17	Toronto, ON
3	34.95	Toronto, ON
4	24.00	Toronto
5	722.31	Downsview, ON
6	17.34	Toronto, ON
7	3,093.02	Whitehorse, YT
8	358.50	St. Catharines, ON
9	68.50	Toronto, ON
10	177.25	Toronto, ON; Peterborough, ON; Guelph, ON
11	24.11	Toronto, ON
12	16.78	Toronto, ON
13	1,428.89	Brussels, Belgium
14	34.00	Toronto, ON
15	284.70	Toronto, ON
16	332.25	Fort Frances, Atikokan, Rainy River, ON
17	2,473.04	Denver, Colorado (USA)
18	487.18	Ottawa, Toronto, London, Lindsay, ON
19	162.75	Windsor/Toronto, ON
20	1,221.05	Brockville, Toronto, Sudbury, Ottawa, Bracebridge, ON
21	439.78	Toronto, Ottawa, ON
22	141.11	Toronto ON
23	128.59	Toronto, ON; Guelph, ON; Peterborough, ON

(Window title: Travel Expenses.IMD)

FIGURE 11.22 Destination Field Sample Contents

provides us with non-Canadian travel destinations. The match fields for both primary and secondary files would be PROVINCE.

Summarize the new joined file by province to obtain approximately 140 records. The number of records may differ depending on the length of the PROVINCE field that was initially defined in the first step.

To manually flag the records to review, we can append a field called FOREIGN, using the field type multistate. The parameter of 1 for the multistate field will provide us with a checkmark in each record. By clicking the checkmark once, the checkmark changes to an X. Additional clicks change the field contents to ?, and then blank, and then cycles again. Refer to Figure 11.23.

Extracting to a new file where FOREIGN= = 1 produces a file with only checkmarks. There are approximately 66 records remaining that are considered foreign travel. The exact number of remaining records is dependent on how the PROVINCE field content is interpreted by the auditor. Details of each travel-claim record can be viewed by clicking on the appropriate NO_OF_RECS field content to drill down to details. This file is now suitable to pass on to another member of the audit team for additional work.

Summ by Province for Forei...

	PROVINCE	NO_OF_RECS	FOREIGN
1		2	✔
2	B.C	1	✘
3	Beirut	1	✔
4	Belgium	5	✔
5	Brantford	1	✘
6	Brazil	2	✔
7	British Columbia	1	✘
8	CO	2	✔
9	China	6	✔
10	Colorado (USA)	1	✔
11	Cyprus	1	✔
12	D.C.	1	✔
13	DC	3	✔
14	DC USA	1	✔
15	DC United States	1	✔
16	Durham ON & York ON	1	✘
17	England	2	✔
18	Fort Hope	1	✘
19	Geneva	1	✔
20	Germany	4	✔
21	Huntsville ON and T	1	✘
22	IL	2	✔
23	IL US	1	✔

FIGURE 11.23 Selecting Non-Canadian Locations

Our "Travel Expenses" data set contains text fields of PURPOSE and DESTINATION. We can use the Search feature to located words in these two fields that may be of interest to us. As an example, the following terms, if they are in the data set, may require a review.

> "first class" OR pass OR routine OR misc* OR golf* OR fish OR fishing OR curling OR hockey OR gift OR present OR donation OR charit* OR club OR personal OR vacation OR holiday OR soccer OR baseball OR party OR vegas OR hawaii OR disney OR boat OR olympic* Or nhl OR "Green Fees" NOT "Holiday Inn"

We used the word *pass* as we know from previous reviews that 10 flight pass(es) had been purchased and claimed. Where travel claims are not descriptive and the words *routine* or *miscellaneous* are used, it may be a red flag for ineligible expenses. The last two words using the operator NOT exclude the words *Holiday Inn* from the search of the word *holiday*. The Search feature allows for a wildcard character such as *. The asterisk represents matching any text. For misc*, it would flag words including *misc, miscellaneous, Miscigan* (Michigan entered incorrectly), and so on.

Applying the text search words example on the "Travel Expenses" file produces 258 records, of which most contain the words *routine expenses*. If we remove the term *routine* from our search, we get the more manageable result of 21 records, as shown in Figure 11.24.

	DATABASE	RECORD_NUMBER	FIELD_NAME	TEXT
1	Travel Expenses	755	DESTINATI...	Kleinberg, Windsor, Ottawa, Vaughan, Oakville, Huttonville, St. Catherines, Lond on, Waterloo, Oshawa, Brantford, Kingston, ON and Detroit, Miscigan
2	Travel Expenses	755	PROVINCE	Miscigan
3	Travel Expenses	1029	PURPOSE	World Junior Baseball Championship/Healthy Communities Fund Announcement/Meeting with Nan regarding the HCF/Meeting with Local PHU
4	Travel Expenses	1030	PURPOSE	World Junior Baseball Championship/Healthy Communities Fund Announcement/Meeting with Nan regarding the HCF/Meeting with Local PHU
5	Travel Expenses	1031	PURPOSE	World Junior Baseball Championship/Healthy Communities Fund Announcement/Meeting with Nan regarding the HCF/ Meeting with Local PHU
6	Travel Expenses	1032	PURPOSE	World Junior Baseball Championship/Healthy Communities Fund Announcement/Meeting with Nan regarding the HCF/ Meeting with local PHU
7	Travel Expenses	1276	PURPOSE	Gift for Consul Corps official dinner
8	Travel Expenses	1360	PURPOSE	Miscellaneous Parking
9	Travel Expenses	1895	PURPOSE	To present at the L'Association Quebecoise d'Etablissements de Sante et de Servi ces Sociaux (AQESSS) Finance Seminar
10	Travel Expenses	1898	PURPOSE	Travel for Gold Medal Plates Charitable Dinner
11	Travel Expenses	1986	PURPOSE	Purchase Flight Pass - ten credits for future flights
12	Travel Expenses	2235	PURPOSE	Advanced the Premier's visit to the Rotary Club of Hamilton
13	Travel Expenses	2263	PURPOSE	Provided operational assistance to the Premier during a presentation given at th e Rotary Club of Hamilton
14	Travel Expenses	2316	PURPOSE	Travel for a Deputy Minister's meeting and participation at the Ontario 2011 Spe cial Olympics.
15	Travel Expenses	2324	PURPOSE	Travel for Fort William Historical Park Special Olympics.
16	Travel Expenses	2378	PURPOSE	Providing operational support to the Premier during a speech to the Rotary Club in Sault Ste Marie
17	Travel Expenses	2400	PURPOSE	To meet with British Columbia provincial officials and Vancouver Organizing Comm ittee for the 2010 Olympic and Paralymic Winter Games (VANOC).
18	Travel Expenses	2402	PURPOSE	To provide technical support for Premier and staff at Rotary Club of Sault Ste M arie.
19	Travel Expenses	2408	PURPOSE	Provided Media support to Premier at Rotary Club meeting in Sault Ste Marie
20	Travel Expenses	2446	PURPOSE	Purchase Flight Pass ten credits to be used for future flights
21	Travel Expenses	2479	PURPOSE	Provided media support to Premier McGuinty at speech to the London Chamber of Co mmerce/Canadian Club of London and media interview

FIGURE 11.24 Text Search Terms Result

Other Potential Tests

There are numerous other tests that are useful for auditing travel expenses and reimbursements. As seen from the previous examples, the tests are subject to the availability of the data sets, what fields are available, and how the fields are populated. We saw that the quality of the date entries is not always the best. We saw that the DESTINATION field is not consistent and we had to perform a number of steps to reduce the records to an acceptable level to review. Even then, the resulting data could not be made perfect and we had to visually filter out irrelevant ones.

A high-level test that could have been performed is Benford's Law by EMPLOYEE_ NO. However, to do so would require extracting all records for each employee into separate files and then applying Benford's Law. Using an IDEAScript, we can do this with ease. While we would normally prefer Benford's Law first two digits test, for a low number of records (based on each employee) the first digit test is more appropriate here.

If the destination field was reliable, we could better analyze the reasonableness of airfare, accommodations, and meals by using tests such as the RSF. We could also extract specific destination cities for more detailed analysis to compare expenses by employees who travel to the same cities.

Some business systems for travel claims have a dropdown menu of popular hotel chains and fields that must be populated. If this is the case, analysis can be done based on hotels to detect high-price accommodations and employees who do not use corporate discount rates or discounted weekend rates. Internal auditors are not always looking only for fraud, but also to ensure efficiencies and adherence to company travel policies.

Data sets from other business systems are invaluable for anomaly detection. Having the employee vacation data file from the human resource systems allows you to extract dates that match when an employee is on vacation to expense claims with dates during the vacation period. The travel advance data set should be matched against the travel claim data to ensure that any advances are netted against claim amounts owed to the employee or the employer.

Purchase Cards

For purchase cards (also known as purchasing cards or P-Cards), data from the credit card companies includes four-digit merchant category codes (MCC) that classify goods and services. Joining the MCC to the purchase card transactions file allows for the detection of potential personal purchases. One of the many places to obtain the merchant category code is from Citibank (www.citibank.com/transactionservices/home/sa/a2/gsasmartpay2/dod/docs/MCC_Codes10012010.xls).

An example of a purchase card data file joined by the MCC numbers to the merchant category descriptions is shown in Figure 11.25.

	DATE_TIME	EMPLOYEE_ID	VENDOR	AMOUNT	MCC	DESCRIPTION1
547	23/08/2013	00041-XXXX	SG DNA TECH	42.80	5199	Non-durable Goods, Not Elsewhere Classified
548	19/08/2013	00041-XXXX	LOWES #	28.17	5200	Home Supply Warehouse Stores
549	16/08/2013	00041-XXXX	LOCKHEEED SUPPL	30.57	5251	Hardware Stores
550	13/08/2013	00041-XXXX	HOME HARDWARE	24.15	5251	Hardware Stores
551	01/08/2013	00041-XXXX	INTERNATIONAL MAR	31.96	5411	Grocery Stores, Supermarkets
552	01/08/2013	00041-XXXX	WM SUPERCENTER#	49.32	5411	Grocery Stores, Supermarkets
553	09/08/2013	00041-XXXX	WM SUPERCENTER#	278.41	5411	Grocery Stores, Supermarkets
554	16/08/2013	00041-XXXX	WM SUPERCENTER#	16.94	5411	Grocery Stores, Supermarkets
555	19/08/2013	00041-XXXX	DISCOUNT TIRES	236.00	5532	Automotive Tire Stores
556	26/08/2013	00041-XXXX	NAPA AUTO PARTS	141.56	5533	Automotive Parts, Accessories Stores
557	20/08/2013	00041-XXXX	WWW.NEWEGG.COM	155.46	5732	Electronic Sales
558	22/08/2013	00041-XXXX	MCDONALD'S F	52.39	5814	Fast Food Restaurants
559	23/08/2013	00041-XXXX	MICROLAB LLC	146.00	5912	Drug Stores and Pharmacies
560	16/08/2013	00041-XXXX	Amazon.com	67.72	5942	Book Stores
561	19/08/2013	00041-XXXX	Amazon.com	149.51	5942	Book Stores
562	06/08/2013	00041-XXXX	Amazon.com	415.63	5942	Book Stores
563	13/08/2013	00041-XXXX	Amazon.com	132.03	5942	Book Stores
564	10/08/2013	00041-XXXX	OFFICE DEPOT #	397.26	5961	Mail Order Houses Including Catalog Order Stores, Book/Record Clubs (No longer p
565	23/08/2013	00041-XXXX	BINVITROGEN	236.75	5964	Direct Marketing - Catalog Merchant
566	06/08/2013	00041-XXXX	GRAPH EDITIONS	240.00	5964	Direct Marketing - Catalog Merchant
567	22/08/2013	00041-XXXX	B & G PHOTO-VIDEO	1,150.15	5969	Direct Marketing - Not Elsewhere Classified
568	19/08/2013	00041-XXXX	SPECIALTY STORE SERVICES	665.39	5969	Direct Marketing - Not Elsewhere Classified
569	05/08/2013	00041-XXXX	FLOWERS AND GIFT SHOP	65.95	5992	Florists
570	07/08/2013	00041-XXXX	LAUNDRY SVCS	19.14	7296	Clothing Rental - Costumes, Formal Wear, Uniforms
571	15/08/2013	00041-XXXX	FEDEXOFFICE	123.51	7338	Quick Copy, Reproduction and Blueprinting Services
572	12/08/2013	00041-XXXX	ZAP CONSULTING	495.00	7392	Management, Consulting, and Public Relations Services
573	23/08/2013	00041-XXXX	B&E BUSINESS PRODUCTS	527.76	7399	Business Services, Not Elsewhere Classified
574	28/08/2013	00041-XXXX	CLARK & CARR SECURITY	95.31	7399	Business Services, Not Elsewhere Classified
575	13/08/2013	00041-XXXX	EPOCH LIFE SCIENCE INC	202.00	7399	Business Services, Not Elsewhere Classified

FIGURE 11.25 Purchase Card Data File Joined to the Merchant Category Descriptions

There is increased usage of P-Cards by organizations as they look to efficiency in reducing procurement costs. Within organizations, the use of P-Cards is encouraged so more and more employees are using them. The combination of increased volume of usage and the sometimes insufficient or lax approval process opens a path to potential fraud. Personal benefits can be derived at the expense of the organization.

Many data analysis tests can be used to identify unusual items or situations that require further investigation as they may indicate potential fraud. The analysis should start with the transaction file that contains the detailed purchases that are combined to the merchant category descriptions, as shown in Figure 11.25.

Some potential tests include:

- Matching nonbusiness merchant category codes to the P-Card data. This can be done either from a list that is maintained by the organization of category codes that are not normally relevant to the business or from an accumulated list of business-related merchant categories.
- Suppose the organization maintains a list of codes that are normal for their business. Use the Join feature in IDEA with the P-Card data as the primary file and the MCC file as the secondary file. Set the join option of "No match" in secondary file to obtain a new file that contains transactions that have nonbusiness merchant category codes and new codes.
- Perform a text search using specific key words associated with nonbusiness transactions. Include the vendor name field as part of the search in addition to the description field.
- Test for prolific users of P-Cards who occupy similar job titles or descriptions. This can be done by summarizing by user and totaling on the purchase amount; Z-score results can also be added to the totals or averages. Also view this file indexed by descending order on the number of records to identify high-usage frequency in addition to the high-dollar values.
- Isolate transactions that occur on weekends and holidays or any other dates when employees are expected to be off. This includes joining a vacation schedule data file to look for purchases during the time when vacation was taken. The @Workday or @Dow functions in IDEA can simply provide you with transactions that took place on weekends.
- Multiple transactions should be reviewed. Duplicate Key Detection can be used to identify identical transactions billed in error or where one transaction is business related and the other is for personal use. Duplicate Key Exclusion or the same-same-different test can be used to identify possible split transactions of large purchase amounts that fall under the per-transaction limit. The P-Card purchase file can be joined to the travel and entertainment claim file to detect any duplicate transactions that were paid by the organization on the P-Card and directly to the employee by way of travel and entertainment claims.
- Analyze the P-Card master file for additions or modifications. Modifications may indicate changes to increase credit limits and then go back to normal. Also ensure there are proper deletions from the master file of employees who no longer work for the organization. Test the records of those employees who have unusually high credit limits.

 ## CONCLUSION AND AUDIT TRAIL

It is clear from the case study that many tests can be proactively used to identify anomalies of travel expenses and other reimbursement claims. Data analytics can increase the scope of the audit by testing every transaction in the data sets. The tests provide the auditor with starting points to focus on and reduce the large volume of transactions and records to a more manageable level that can be examined in more detail. Anomalies can only be classified as fraud once they are ascertained by evidence; otherwise the anomalies are just anomalies. Statistically, there are some anomalies in every data set. The auditor must determine whether they are false positives or in fact fraud. The only possible way to do so is to take the list of inconsistent results and follow the audit trail. From the list, the travel claims need to be reviewed along with source documents such as receipts. Suspicious items can then be pulled for additional investigation, including third-party confirmation if necessary. However, once even a single item is identified as fraudulent, the auditor should go back to the data sets and extract all records associated with the fraud, whether it is a specific employee or fraud in a specific category. If, for example, it was discovered that an employee provided a false hotel receipt for reimbursement, the audit should not only focus on that employee, but also be expanded to review accommodation expenses as a whole in more detail. The auditor needs to assure himself that it is unlikely that any other employee is involved in the same type of scheme. In addition, it is logical to expand the audit of that specific employee to other travel expense categories such as airfare and meals. Of course, other areas outside of travel reimbursement for the employee should also be reviewed for red flags of potential fraud.

 NOTES

1. Deloitte LLP, "Review of Senator Wallin's Travel Expense and Living Allowance Claims," accessed August 2013, www.parl.gc.ca/Content/SEN/Committee/411/ciba/rep/Deloitte_SenWallin-e.PDF.
2. "Sales Receipts," accessed January 23, 2014, www.salesreceiptstore.com/.
3. David Barboza, "Coin of Realm in China Graft—Phony Receipts," *New York Times*, August 3, 2013, www.nytimes.com/2013/08/04/business/global/coin-of-realm-in-china-graft-phony-receipts.html?partner=rss&emc=rss&_r=2&pagewanted=all&.
4. "Travel and Hospitality Expenses Home—Ontario.ca," accessed January 24, 2014, www.gov.on.ca/en/expense_claim/index.htm.

CHAPTER TWELVE

Register Disbursement Schemes

REGISTER DISBURSEMENT SCHEMES INVOLVE fraudulent refunds and fraudulent voids where these false entries allow the removal of funds from the cash register or point-of-sales system.

Register disbursement schemes differ from the skimming and cash larceny schemes discussed in Chapter 7, where funds are removed from the cash register before being recorded and leave no record of the transactions.

 ## FALSE REFUNDS AND ADJUSTMENTS

False refunds are when no actual return of goods or pricing adjustments are made—they are merely recorded. This allows cash to be taken from the register while the cash still balances to the register records. Instead of cash, refunds can be made to the fraudster's credit card or an accomplice's card. Refunding to credit cards avoids other people or surveillance cameras from seeing the fraudster take cash from the register and pocketing the money.

False refunds overstate the inventory of the goods. Since there are no goods actually returned to inventory, there will be inventory shortages. Some level of inventory shortages are expected and accepted as the cost of doing business but excessive and regular shortages are a cause for concern. Inventory may not be counted on a regular basis or the fraudster is involved with the inventory count. If the fraudster participates in the count, he can falsify the recording of the true situation. False price adjustments would not have any inventory issues.

There are some ingenious forms of register disbursement schemes perpetrated by employees. One example involves price guarantees. Customers are offered a refund of the price difference if the purchased item goes on sale within 30 days of purchase. The customer must bring in their receipt that has a barcode for scanning to qualify for the difference refund. Employees are very well aware of what will be going on sale next and if a customer purchases an item that will be going on sale soon, they might photocopy the receipt or take a picture of the barcode with their camera-capable smartphone. Most customers are not aware of the sale or do not bother going back to the store for the sales-price difference. The employee waits until near the end of the 30 days and then uses a copy of the barcode to generate the price-guarantee refund for him- or herself. Cash register or point-of-sale system records will still reconcile with the cash on hand.

 ## FALSE VOIDS

A legitimate sale is made and then the fraudster voids the sale. Funds received from the sale can then be appropriated by the fraudster. Typical controls for voids mandate that the original receipt should be attached to the voided sales. The salesperson can withhold the sales receipt from the customer to include with the voided sales records. If internal control is lax, lack of the original receipts can be overlooked during the daily sales reconciliation process. Normally managers are supposed to approve voids but may fail to do so. Some managers sign almost anything or may be colluding with the employee in the register scheme. Signatures are easily forged as little attention is given to comparing signatures. False voids create similar inventory problems just as the false return of goods does; inventory is lower than that recorded in the books.

 ## CONCEALMENT

While book inventory is higher than the actual in-stock inventory levels, these types of schemes are not usually accompanied with a concealment scheme. Small inventory differences are usually ignored as some shrinkage is expected.

Keeping the refunds, voids, and adjustments below certain levels may avoid review. The fraudster would have to have a number of these fraudulent transactions to total to any significant amounts, based on the low individual-transaction amounts.

Fraudsters may destroy various types of documentation, not to conceal the fraud but to conceal who the fraudster is. Missing records makes identifying the fraudster much more difficult.

 ## DATA ANALYTICAL TESTS

Our case study will use two dBase files from the IDEA training course to demonstrate some practical tests. The "ED-Sales-2010-L4.DBF" file and the "ED-Sales-2011-L4.DBF" file are imported into IDEA and named "Sales-2010" and "Sales-2011" respectively. These files represent one location of a quick-service or fast-food hamburger chain.

Data Familiarization

There are 18 fields in each of the files as outlined in Figure 12.1.

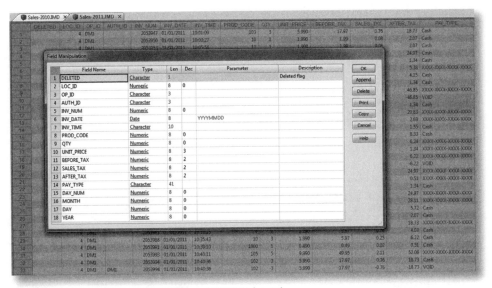

FIGURE 12.1 Fields of the 2010 and 2011 Sales Files

Since the data was imported into IDEA from a dBase file, the first field is always the DELETED field with a length of one.

For both the "Sales-2011" file and the "Sales-2010" file, separately create three files, summarized by:

- The register operator (OP_ID)
- The person authorizing the transaction (AUTH_ID)
- The tender payment type (PAY_TYPE)

The fields to total in each summarization include the BEFORE_TAX, SALES_TAX, and AFTER_TAX fields.

For 2011, sales summarized by OP_ID are shown on the right side of Figure 12.2 and sales summarized by AUTH_ID are displayed on the left side of the figure.

AUTH_ID	NO_OF_RECS	BEFORE_TAX_SUM	SALES_TAX_SUM	AFTER_TAX_SUM		OP_ID	NO_OF_RECS	BEFORE_TAX_SUM	SALES_TAX_SUM	AFTER_TAX_SUM
1		148884	1,999,456.15	116,551.67	2,116,015.09	1 DM1	71118	766,881.06	44,678.05	811,562.25
2 AH2	4847	-93,196.17	-5,413.20	-98,609.37		2 TM3	86737	1,063,549.29	62,049.53	1,125,602.95
3 DM1	3523	-63,543.72	-3,682.42	-67,226.14						
4 TM3	601	-12,285.91	-728.47	-13,014.38						

FIGURE 12.2 Summarization of the 2011 Sales by Authorizer and Summarized by Register Operator

The results of the summarization by PAY_TYPE are shown in Figure 12.3 for the years 2011 and 2010.

Summarize by pay type 2011... ✕

	PAY_TYPE	NO_OF_RECS	BEFORE_TAX_SUM	SALES_TAX_SUM	AFTER_TAX_SUM
1	$1 off King Burger Combo	998	-998.00	-59.88	-1,057.88
2	50% off King Burgers	406	-1,827.00	-109.62	-1,932.56
3	50% off Princess Burgers	194	-582.00	-34.92	-614.98
4	50% off Queen Burgers	127	-508.00	-30.48	-537.21
5	Buy 1 Prince Combo Get One FREE coupon	56	-391.44	-23.52	-414.96
6	Buy 1 Princess Combo Get One FREE coupon	48	-287.52	-17.28	-304.80
7	Buy 1 Queen Combo Get One FREE coupon	149	-1,190.51	-71.52	-1,262.03
8	Cash	83801	929,045.38	54,236.35	983,281.73
9	Ed's Football Game - Touchdown	179	-8,950.00	-537.00	-9,487.00
10	Thank God it's Fry-day - Free Fry Upgrade	280	-350.00	-22.40	-372.40
11	VOID	8971	-169,025.80	-9,824.09	-178,849.89
12	XXXX-XXXX-XXXX-XXXX	62646	1,085,495.24	63,221.94	1,148,717.18

Summarize by pay type 2010.1... ✕

	PAY_TYPE	NO_OF_RECS	BEFORE_TAX_SUM	SALES_TAX_SUM	AFTER_TAX_SUM
1	$1 off King Burger Combo	959	-959.00	-57.54	-1,016.54
2	50% off King Burgers	345	-1,552.50	-93.15	-1,642.20
3	50% off Princess Burgers	209	-627.00	-37.62	-662.53
4	50% off Queen Burgers	109	-436.00	-26.16	-461.07
5	Buy 1 Prince Combo Get One FREE coupon	56	-391.44	-23.52	-414.96
6	Buy 1 Princess Combo Get One FREE coupon	53	-317.47	-19.08	-336.55
7	Buy 1 Queen Combo Get One FREE coupon	115	-918.85	-55.20	-974.05
8	Cash	146949	2,522,602.88	146,982.08	2,669,584.96
9	Ed's Football Game - Touchdown	137	-6,850.00	-411.00	-7,261.00
10	Thank God it's Fry-day - Free Fry Upgrade	255	-318.75	-20.40	-339.15
11	VOID	9384	-175,752.32	-10,248.63	-186,000.95
12	XXXX-XXXX-XXXX-XXXX	62964	1,089,881.38	63,533.51	1,153,414.89

FIGURE 12.3 Summarized by Payment Type for 2011 and Summarized for 2010

A review of the payment type information for both years shows three significant areas of concern.

- Void transactions are significant, totaling $175,752 from 9,384 transactions in 2010. In 2011, there were 8,971 transactions totaling $169,025. Further analysis needs to be done to determine whether these are valid voids or part of a register disbursement scheme. Voided amounts may be legitimate sales where customers received their fast-food order but with the employee retaining the funds. Void entries are recorded to conceal the fraud and balance the point-of-sale (POS) system records with the payment tenders in the till. Inventory is not overstated as there could be significant spoilage within the fast-food industry.
- Redemption of "Ed's Football Game–touchdown" coupons has a high total compared to other coupons or special discounts. The amount obtained by dividing the dollar value by the number of transactions is $50 for each of the two years. For a fast-food restaurant, a $50 discount seems high.
- Cash sales before taxes dropped from $2,522,602 in 2010 to $929,045 in 2011. The corresponding number of transactions also dropped. This is the most significant issue at hand. It is not likely to be due to a decline in sales as credit card sales, represented by the blanked out card numbers of "XXXX-XXXX-XXXX-XXXX," did not

decline significantly. Cash-sale reductions do not appear to be caused by additional voided sales, as voided sales fell slightly in 2011. This issue is not discussed in this chapter. Cash-sales fraud is outlined in Chapter 7 ("Skimming and Cash Larceny") and in Chapter 16 ("Zapper Fraud").

Void Tests

To perform the analysis on void payment types, extract from the "Sales-2011" database where the field PAY_TYPE = = "VOID" to create a new file called "Voids 2011." Perform the same extraction for the "Sales-2010" database to create a new file called "Voids 2010."

Summarize each of the new void files by MONTH, totaling on the BEFORE_TAX field. Add the appropriate year to the end of each file's NO_OF_RECS and BEFORE_TAX fields, as shown in Figure 12.4.

MONTH	NO_OF_RECS_2011	BEFORE_TAX_SUM_2011		MONTH	NO_OF_RECS_2010	BEFORE_TAX_SUM_2010
1	865	-18,451.30	1	1	811	-17,554.70
2	665	-14,105.19	2	2	631	-13,162.91
3	734	-15,726.33	3	3	1410	-29,530.35
4	833	-17,615.17	4	4	844	-17,790.06
5	767	-15,985.66	5	5	758	-16,198.42
6	744	-16,188.92	6	6	792	-17,713.23
7	505	-5,143.95	7	7	548	-5,420.85
8	409	-4,241.08	8	8	537	-5,532.87
9	938	-13,851.20	9	9	880	-12,266.01
10	961	-13,898.47	10	10	771	-11,158.77
11	798	-16,278.71	11	11	645	-12,996.47
12	752	-17,539.82	12	12	757	-16,427.68

FIGURE 12.4 Voids Summarized by Month for Years 2011 and 2010

To obtain a better comparison of the voids between the two years, the two annual monthly files can be combined and charted.

Using the "Summarized Voids by Month 2010" as the primary file and the "Summarized Voids by Month 2011" as the secondary file, select the MONTH field as the match field in both files. Include the default of all the fields from the primary file and the NO_OF_RECS_2011 and BEFORE_TAX_SUM_2011 fields from the secondary file. Select the join option of "Matches only." Refer to the options selected in Figure 12.5.

The result of the join and the preparation to chart the results are in Figure 12.6.

The chart is shown in Figure 12.7.

The visual representation of the voids on a monthly basis for each of the two years allows us to immediately focus on the higher amount of voids in month 3 (March 2010)

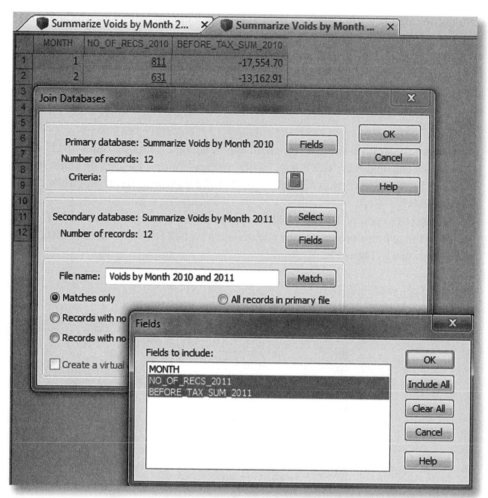

FIGURE 12.5 Preparing the Join of the Monthly Void Files for 2010 and 2011

as compared to the same month in 2011. Voids are negative sales amounts, so the points closer to the bottom of the chart represent more voids.

The month of March 2010 should be reviewed to determine the reason why there are almost double the number of void transactions and double the dollar values.

We can summarize the 2010 voids by MONTH and then by OP_ID with the results shown in Figure 12.8.

For almost every month, operator TM3 has many more voids in 2010 than operator DM1. We would seek explanations for this by examining the work schedule of the employees or analyzing the login data file from the POS system. At this stage we have some concerns with operator TM3.

The POS system is programmed so all voids require someone to authorize them. The organization's policy is to have a different person from the operator to authorize any voids. We can extract from our void data of 9,384 records where the transaction had the same person authorizing the void as the operator. In general, this would be a breach

MONTH	NO_OF_RECS_2010	BEFORE_TAX_SUM_2010	NO_OF_RECS_2011	BEFORE_TAX_SUM_2011
1	811	-17,554.70	865	-18,451.30
2	631	-13,162.91	665	-14,105.19
3	1410	-29,530.35	734	-15,726.33
4	844	-17,790.06	833	-17,615.17
5	758	-16,198.42	767	-15,985.66
6	792	-17,713.23	744	-16,188.92
7	548	-5,420.85	505	-5,143.95
8	537	-5,532.87	409	-4,241.08
9	880	-12,266.01	938	-13,851.20
10	771	-11,158.77	961	-13,898.47
11	645	-12,996.47	798	-16,278.71
12	757	-16,427.68	752	-17,539.82

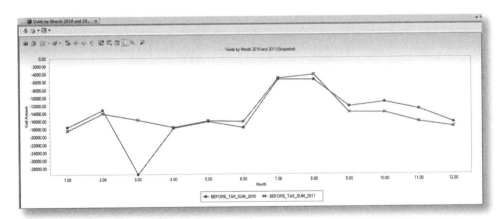

FIGURE 12.6 Joining the Voids Output and Preparing the Chart

FIGURE 12.7 Voids by Month for Years 2010 and 2011

of the organization's policy but we expect a few instances of this occurring when there are no others available to authorize the void of a sale entered by the operator. Extracting to a new file using the equation of OP_ID = = AUTH_ID, we found 4,452 matching transactions, as shown in Figure 12.9.

Summarize by month by ope... ×

	MONTH	OP_ID	NO_OF_RECS	BEFORE_TAX_SUM
1	1	DM1	343	-7,556.59
2	1	TM3	468	-9,998.11
3	2	DM1	249	-5,374.29
4	2	TM3	382	-7,788.62
5	3	DM1	583	-11,861.31
6	3	TM3	827	-17,669.04
7	4	DM1	364	-7,784.83
8	4	TM3	480	-10,005.23
9	5	DM1	338	-7,410.28
10	5	TM3	420	-8,788.14
11	6	DM1	327	-7,478.18
12	6	TM3	465	-10,235.05
13	7	DM1	345	-3,459.32
14	7	TM3	203	-1,961.53
15	8	DM1	359	-3,881.39
16	8	TM3	178	-1,651.48
17	9	DM1	387	-5,176.37
18	9	TM3	493	-7,089.64
19	10	DM1	294	-3,727.48
20	10	TM3	477	-7,431.29
21	11	DM1	289	-5,187.42
22	11	TM3	356	-7,809.05
23	12	DM1	376	-7,442.25
24	12	TM3	381	-8,985.43

FIGURE 12.8 Void Transactions for 2010 Summarized by Month and Then by Operator

Operator same as Authorizer... ×

	OP_ID	AUTH_ID	INV_NUM	INV_DATE	INV_TIME	PROD_CODE	QTY	UNIT_PRICE	BEFORE_TAX	SALES_TAX	AFTER_TAX	PAY_TYPE	DAY_NUM	MONTH	DAY
4426	DM1	DM1	2052600	30/12/2010	10:42:46	2	-2	5.490	-10.98	-0.66	-11.64	VOID	364	12	30
4427	DM1	DM1	2052645	30/12/2010	11:26:59	1	-1	5.990	-5.99	-0.36	-6.35	VOID	364	12	30
4428	DM1	DM1	2052651	30/12/2010	11:32:18	102	-4	5.990	-23.96	-1.44	-25.40	VOID	364	12	30
4429	DM1	DM1	2052696	30/12/2010	12:16:13	13	-7	0.990	-6.93	-0.42	-7.35	VOID	364	12	30
4430	DM1	DM1	2052717	30/12/2010	12:36:49	6	-1	8.990	-8.99	-0.54	-9.53	VOID	364	12	30
4431	DM1	DM1	2052739	30/12/2010	12:59:00	103	-3	5.990	-17.97	-1.08	-19.05	VOID	364	12	30
4432	DM1	DM1	2052753	30/12/2010	13:12:32	100	-3	8.990	-26.97	-1.62	-28.59	VOID	364	12	30
4433	DM1	DM1	2052763	30/12/2010	13:23:20	9	-6	1.990	-11.94	-0.72	-12.66	VOID	364	12	30
4434	DM1	DM1	2052767	30/12/2010	13:27:22	1	-5	5.990	-29.95	-1.80	-31.75	VOID	364	12	30
4435	DM1	DM1	2052773	30/12/2010	13:33:24	11	-7	1.990	-13.93	-0.84	-14.77	VOID	364	12	30
4436	DM1	DM1	2052792	30/12/2010	13:56:44	2	-6	5.490	-32.94	-1.98	-34.92	VOID	364	12	30
4437	DM1	DM1	2053268	31/12/2010	10:15:42	2	-6	5.490	-32.94	-1.98	-34.92	VOID	365	12	31
4438	DM1	DM1	2053300	31/12/2010	10:47:48	1	-6	5.990	-35.94	-2.16	-38.10	VOID	365	12	31
4439	DM1	DM1	2053311	31/12/2010	11:01:12	11	-2	1.990	-3.98	-0.24	-4.22	VOID	365	12	31
4440	DM1	DM1	2053336	31/12/2010	11:25:58	12	-1	1.990	-1.99	-0.12	-2.11	VOID	365	12	31
4441	DM1	DM1	2053383	31/12/2010	12:11:54	105	-4	9.990	-39.96	-2.40	-42.36	VOID	365	12	31
4442	DM1	DM1	2053396	31/12/2010	12:25:52	8	-1	1.490	-1.49	-0.09	-1.58	VOID	365	12	31
4443	DM1	DM1	2053414	31/12/2010	12:44:44	13	-7	0.990	-6.93	-0.42	-7.35	VOID	365	12	31
4444	DM1	DM1	2053417	31/12/2010	12:48:55	2	-3	5.490	-16.47	-0.99	-17.46	VOID	365	12	31
4445	DM1	DM1	2053420	31/12/2010	12:51:04	105	-4	9.990	-39.96	-2.40	-42.36	VOID	365	12	31
4446	DM1	DM1	2053437	31/12/2010	13:05:54	101	-7	7.990	-55.93	-3.36	-59.29	VOID	365	12	31
4447	DM1	DM1	2053438	31/12/2010	13:06:29	8	-1	1.490	-1.49	-0.09	-1.58	VOID	365	12	31
4448	DM1	DM1	2053451	31/12/2010	13:17:43	101	-4	7.990	-31.96	-1.92	-33.88	VOID	365	12	31
4449	DM1	DM1	2053453	31/12/2010	13:20:10	13	-3	0.990	-2.97	-0.18	-3.15	VOID	365	12	31
4450	DM1	DM1	2053466	31/12/2010	13:34:42	105	-1	9.990	-9.99	-0.60	-10.59	VOID	365	12	31
4451	DM1	DM1	2053476	31/12/2010	13:47:05	100	-7	8.990	-62.93	-3.78	-66.71	VOID	365	12	31
4452	DM1	DM1	2053481	31/12/2010	13:53:17	6	-1	8.990	-8.99	-0.54	-9.53	VOID	365	12	31

FIGURE 12.9 Void Transactions Where the Authorizer Is the Same as the Operator for 2010

Almost half of all the voids in 2010 were authorized by the same person who registered the sale in the first place. This is a significant violation of company policy. Using this new file, titled "Operator Same as Authorizer," we can again summarize by MONTH and AUTH_ID, totaling on the BEFORE_TAX field.

	MONTH	AUTH_ID	NO_OF_RECS	BEFORE_TAX_SUM
1	1	DM1	172	-3,633.57
2	1	TM3	221	-5,109.93
3	2	DM1	175	-3,773.71
4	2	TM3	121	-2,483.62
5	3	DM1	438	-9,057.70
6	3	TM3	189	-4,018.37
7	4	DM1	277	-5,933.65
8	4	TM3	88	-2,058.37
9	5	DM1	276	-6,114.65
10	5	TM3	94	-1,993.94
11	6	DM1	239	-5,560.96
12	6	TM3	117	-2,369.10
13	7	DM1	309	-3,117.50
14	7	TM3	19	-192.13
15	8	DM1	323	-3,314.19
16	8	TM3	18	-156.34
17	9	DM1	350	-4,477.03
18	9	TM3	52	-763.35
19	10	DM1	271	-3,431.97
20	10	TM3	45	-804.11
21	11	DM1	249	-4,372.12
22	11	TM3	42	-713.80
23	12	DM1	354	-7,063.48
24	12	TM3	13	-333.34

FIGURE 12.10 Result of Summarizing by Month and Authorization ID Where the Authorizer and Operator Is the Same Person

With the exception of the first month, it is actually DM1 who we should be focusing our review on; Figure 12.10 shows DM1 breached policy frequently. It seems that our initial targeting of TM3 was incorrect, as TM3 had most of their voids authorized by another party. Of course, collusion is a possibility but we should place that as a lower risk unless additional anomalies point us in that direction.

A test on voids that we can perform with this data file ensures that there is a corresponding sale to each void and that the timestamps of the transactions are relatively close together. Any departures from these are anomalies, as they would not meet the normal flow of the business process for voiding transactions. The anomalies may be indication of fraud.

Using our "Sales—2010" data set, ensuring that the file is not indexed in any way, we can extract to a new file all void transactions and the transactions immediately preceding the void transactions for matched pairs. The equation to accomplish this would be

$$PAY\_TYPE == \text{"VOID"}. OR. @GetNextValue(\text{"PAY\_TYPE"}) == VOID$$

The equation instructs IDEA to extract any record where the payment type field contains the word VOID. Also extract any records where the next record (that is, get the next value that matches) in the payment type field contains the word VOID.

The results are displayed in Figure 12.11.

	OP_ID	AUTH_ID	INV_NUM	INV_DATE	INV_TIME	PROD_CODE	QTY	UNIT_PRICE	BEFORE_TAX	SALES_TAX	AFTER_TAX	PAY_TYPE	
18743	DM1		2053476	31/12/2010	13:47:05	100	7	8.990	62.93	3.78	66.71	XXXX-XXXX-XXXX-XXXX	
18744	DM1	DM1	2053476	31/12/2010	13:47:05	100	-7	8.990	-62.93	-3.78	-66.71	VOID	
18745	DM1		2053481	31/12/2010	13:53:17	6	1	8.990	8.99	0.54	9.53	XXXX-XXXX-XXXX-XXXX	
18746	DM1	DM1	2053481	31/12/2010	13:53:17	6	-1	8.990	-8.99	-0.54	-9.53	VOID	
18747	TM3		2053506	31/12/2010	14:17:28	105	5	9.990	49.95	3.00	52.95	XXXX-XXXX-XXXX-XXXX	
18748	TM3	AH2	2053506	31/12/2010	14:17:28	105	-5	9.990	-49.95	-3.00	-52.95	VOID	
18749	TM3		2053508	31/12/2010	14:18:29	8	1	1.490	1.49	0.09	1.58	XXXX-XXXX-XXXX-XXXX	
18750	TM3	AH2	2053508	31/12/2010	14:18:29	8	-1	1.490	-1.49	-0.09	-1.58	VOID	
18751	TM3		2053528	31/12/2010	14:39:13	105	7	9.990	69.93	4.20	74.13	XXXX-XXXX-XXXX-XXXX	
18752	TM3	AH2	2053528	31/12/2010	14:39:13	105	-7	9.990	-69.93	-4.20	-74.13	VOID	
18753	TM3		2053579	31/12/2010	15:26:27	6	1	8.990	8.99	0.54	9.53	XXXX-XXXX-XXXX-XXXX	
18754	TM3	AH2	2053579	31/12/2010	15:26:27	6	-1	8.990	-8.99	-0.54	-9.53	VOID	
18755	TM3		2053582	31/12/2010	15:28:11	4	4	3.990	15.96	0.96	16.92	XXXX-XXXX-XXXX-XXXX	
18756	TM3	AH2	2053582	31/12/2010	15:28:11	4	-4	3.990	-15.96	-0.96	-16.92	VOID	
18757	TM3		2053592	31/12/2010	15:39:50	8	4	1.490	5.96	0.36	6.32	Cash	
18758	TM3	AH2	2053592	31/12/2010	15:39:50	8	-4	1.490	-5.96	-0.36	-6.32	VOID	
18759	TM3		2053593	31/12/2010	15:41:17	100	1	8.990	8.99	0.54	9.53	XXXX-XXXX-XXXX-XXXX	
18760	TM3	AH2	2053593	31/12/2010	15:41:17	100	-1	8.990	-8.99	-0.54	-9.53	VOID	
18761	TM3		2053601	31/12/2010	15:48:12	4	3	3.990	11.97	0.72	12.69	Cash	
18762	TM3	AH2	2053601	31/12/2010	15:48:12	4	-3	3.990	-11.97	-0.72	-12.69	VOID	
18763	TM3		2053661	31/12/2010	16:43:38	10	4	1.990	7.96	0.48	8.44	Cash	
18764	TM3	AH2	2053661	31/12/2010	16:43:38	10	-4	1.990	-7.96	-0.48	-8.44	VOID	
18765	TM3		2053689	31/12/2010	17:12:00	102	1	5.990	5.99	0.36	6.35	XXXX-XXXX-XXXX-XXXX	
18766	TM3	AH2	2053689	31/12/2010	17:12:00	102	-1	5.990	-5.99	-0.36	-6.35	VOID	
18767	TM3		2053721	31/12/2010	17:40:57	11	6	1.990	11.94	0.72	12.66	XXXX-XXXX-XXXX-XXXX	
18768	TM3	AH2	2053721	31/12/2010	17:40:57	11	-6	1.990	-11.94	-0.72	-12.66	VOID	

FIGURE 12.11   Results of Matching Sales to Voids 2010

Our Void file for 2010 had 9,384 records and our new matching file had exactly double the number of transactions—18,768. We can be assured that every void had a matching sale whether the sale was made in cash or by credit card. Matching sales and voids have the same amounts, with one being positive and the other negative. Performing a control total on either the BEFORE_TAX field or AFTER_TAX field results in a net of zero, giving us further confidence that the operator did not enter any arbitrary void amounts to pocket cash or transfer credit card amounts. The invoice numbers are also paired properly, as well as the invoice time sequencing.

We can obtain a breakdown between cash voids and credit card voids by summarizing this newly created file by PAY_TYPE and totaling on the BEFORE_TAX field. Cash voids were $72,474 in total and credit card voids totaled $103,277. This is the reverse of sales where cash sales were more than double that of credit card sales.

Coupon Tests

We will focus on "Ed's Football Game—Touchdown" coupon redemptions since we identified this as an area of concern from the results shown in Figure 12.3.

From the "Sales—2011" file we extract all transactions that contain "Ed's Football Game—Touchdown" in the payment type field. We note that there were 179 records extracted and each transaction amount was $50 redeemed before taxes or $53 including taxes.

We will match the coupon redemption to that of the sale as we did with the void transactions. Using the equation of PAY_TYPE = = "Ed's Football Game—Touchdown" .OR. @GetNextValue("PAY_TYPE") = = "Ed's Football Game—Touchdown," we obtained the results shown in Figure 12.12.

	LOC_ID	OP_ID	AUTH_ID	INV_NUM	INV_DATE	INV_TIME	PROD_CODE	QTY	UNIT_PRICE	BEFORE_TAX	SALES_TAX	AFTER_TAX	PAY_TYPE	DAY
330	4	TM3		1252182	26/12/2011	15:09:27	100	6	8.990	53.94	3.24	57.18	XXXX-XXXX-XXXX-XXXX	
331	4	TM3		1252182	26/12/2011	15:09:27	91001	1	-50.000	-50.00	-3.00	-53.00	Ed's Football Game - Touchdown	
332	4	TM3		1252246	26/12/2011	16:10:13	105	5	9.990	49.95	3.00	52.95	Cash	
333	4	TM3		1252246	26/12/2011	16:10:13	91001	1	-50.000	-50.00	-3.00	-53.00	Ed's Football Game - Touchdown	
334	4	TM3		1252266	27/12/2011	16:40:02	100	4	8.990	35.96	2.16	38.12	XXXX-XXXX-XXXX-XXXX	
335	4	TM3		1252266	27/12/2011	16:40:02	91001	1	-50.000	-50.00	-3.00	-53.00	Ed's Football Game - Touchdown	
336	4	TM3		1252135	28/12/2011	14:34:02	10	2	1.990	3.98	0.24	4.22	XXXX-XXXX-XXXX-XXXX	
337	4	TM3		1252136	28/12/2011	14:34:28	91001	1	-50.000	-50.00	-3.00	-53.00	Ed's Football Game - Touchdown	
338	4	TM3		1252155	28/12/2011	14:55:12	1001	1	1.290	1.29	0.08	1.37	XXXX-XXXX-XXXX-XXXX	
339	4	TM3		1252156	28/12/2011	14:56:38	91001	1	-50.000	-50.00	-3.00	-53.00	Ed's Football Game - Touchdown	
340	4	TM3		1252210	28/12/2011	15:44:44	103	1	5.090	5.99	0.36	6.35	Cash	
341	4	TM3		1252211	28/12/2011	19:45:27	91001	1	-50.000	-50.00	-3.00	-53.00	Ed's Football Game - Touchdown	
342	4	TM3		1252332	28/12/2011	17:42:49	105	1	9.990	9.99	0.60	10.59	Cash	
343	4	TM3		1252173	28/12/2011	17:44:15	91001	1	-50.000	-50.00	-3.00	-53.00	Ed's Football Game - Touchdown	
344	4	TM3		1252173	29/12/2011	15:01:06	102	7	5.990	41.93	2.52	44.45	Cash	
345	4	TM3		1252173	29/12/2011	15:01:06	91001	1	-50.000	-50.00	-3.00	-53.00	Ed's Football Game - Touchdown	
346	4	TM3		1252174	29/12/2011	15:01:41	91001	1	-50.000	-50.00	-3.00	-53.00	Ed's Football Game - Touchdown	
347	4	TM3		1252184	30/12/2011	15:26:10	105	2	9.990	19.98	1.20	21.18	Cash	
348	4	TM3		1252184	30/12/2011	15:26:10	91001	1	-50.000	-50.00	-3.00	-53.00	Ed's Football Game - Touchdown	
349	4	TM3		1252282	30/12/2011	17:05:57	4	2	3.990	7.98	0.48	8.46	XXXX-XXXX-XXXX-XXXX	
350	4	TM3		1252283	30/12/2011	17:06:32	91001	1	-50.000	-50.00	-3.00	-53.00	Ed's Football Game - Touchdown	
351	4	TM3		1252291	30/12/2011	17:14:36	11	3	1.990	5.97	0.36	6.33	Cash	
352	4	TM3		1252292	30/12/2011	17:14:53	91001	1	-50.000	-50.00	-3.00	-53.00	Ed's Football Game - Touchdown	
353	4	TM3		1252133	31/12/2011	14:27:33	4	1	3.990	3.99	0.24	4.23	Cash	
354	4	TM3		1252134	31/12/2011	14:28:16	91001	1	-50.000	-50.00	-3.00	-53.00	Ed's Football Game - Touchdown	
355	4	TM3		1252340	31/12/2011	17:50:44	100	7	8.990	62.93	3.78	66.71	XXXX-XXXX-XXXX-XXXX	
356	4	TM3		1252342	31/12/2011	17:52:28	91001	1	-50.000	-50.00	-3.00	-53.00	Ed's Football Game - Touchdown	

FIGURE 12.12 Results of Matching the Coupon Redemption to the Preceding Sale

There were 356 records extracted, so we know there are no matching pairs such as we found in the voids analysis. The result also shows that invoice numbers of the sale to the coupon redemption do not always match. In most cases, the coupon redemption exceeds the sales amount. Either the customer was entitled to a cash refund if the value $50 was not totally spent or the employee was pocketing the difference. No authorization is needed to redeem coupons as the AUTH_ID field was always not populated.

By summarizing the extracted file where the payment type was "Ed's Football Game—Touchdown" by the MONTH field, we can see, in the left side of Figure 12.13, that for 2011 redemptions only took place in November and December. By summarizing on the operator shown on the right side of Figure 12.13, it is only TM3 who redeems these coupons.

The year 2010 had similar results. That is, redemptions were only done by TM3 and in November and December only. Possibly the coupons are only valid during the last two months of the year, but why are redemptions only done by TM3?

FIGURE 12.13 Coupon Redemption File Summarized by Month on the Left and Summarized by Operator on the Right

Clearly, further review of these redemptions is necessary.

Other Data Analytical Tests

Where there are additional data fields that provide relevant information or additional data sets are available, there is the potential of performing other analytical tests such as:

- Summarize by month for each business location the sales adjustments such as refunds, voids, and discounts. Review results for exceptionally high adjustments.
- Perform trend analysis or time series analysis separately, using each of the sales adjustments as a trend field and the total or global adjustments for the entire business as the reference field to determine unusual trends. The audit unit should be each of the locations.
- Similar to trend analysis, correlate each of the sales adjustments with the global adjustments using the location as the audit units. Review locations with low-correlation results.
- Extract duplicate credit card numbers used to refund goods or matched to voids.
- Extract where sales were made to one credit card number but refunded to another credit card number.
- Identify sales paid by credit cards but refunded in cash.
- Summarize to determine the percentage of refunds made to credit cards versus those to cash.
- Extract and review sales and the related refunds of merchandise that were transacted on the same day. It is less likely that a customer would purchase an item and return it within the same day.
- Perform duplicate key extraction to identify duplicate returns.
- Extract sales and sales adjustments for employees who have approval authorities for the adjustments.
- Join the inventory file to the sales file and calculate any differences on a day-by-day analysis basis.
- Summarize adjustments by inventory number, such as SKU or SKN, to compare to voids and refunds by inventory number. Large or unusual adjustments to reduce inventory may be a method to conceal register disbursement fraud.
- Extract and review book adjustments that can change inventory totals, such as writing off shortages and obsolescence. Ensure credits to the perpetual inventory system and accounts receivable are valid.

- Extract and review the markdown of merchandise for clearance sale and those sold on the same day to ensure that those were not actually unauthorized discounts.
- On a global basis, use Benford's Law to determine whether there are excessive numbers of voids and returns just under the review or approval limits.
- Perform statistical sampling on returns and voids and verify with customers on a test basis if anomalies were ascertained by previous tests.

 ## CONCLUSION

With the exception of an acceptable level of shrinkage, these types of fraud schemes can be easily combated. Strict adherence to internal controls and policies will deter the frauds. There must be separation of duties of the employees. Sales personnel should not be permitted to reverse or adjust their own sales. All voided sales must have the original sales receipts attached. The register should be programed so each employee has his or her own unique login code. Managers need to login to reverse or void any sales. Physical inventory needs to be validated on a regular basis.

Register disbursement fraud leaves audit trails. Sales are recorded and entered into the business system. To remove funds and yet have the daily register or cash-out sheets reconcile, the fraudster must create a false transaction or entry before they can take any funds. Without the fraudulent entries, there would be significant and obvious cash shortages. It is these entries that allow the opportunity for data analytics to detect anomalies for additional review.

CHAPTER THIRTEEN

Noncash Misappropriations

FRAUDSTERS PREFER CASH SCHEMES because they do not involve the added steps of conversion that are required for noncash-misappropriation schemes. However, organizations are more aware of the risk of losing cash and normally have stricter controls over cash than noncash assets. Noncash assets that are commonly misappropriated include inventory, supplies, equipment, and proprietary information.

Misappropriation of these types of assets is simple to do as employees in the normal course of their duties must have access to these items. The theft is easy but the concealment of the theft is difficult where there are good internal controls. Even with the best of internal controls, infrequent misappropriations may not be noticed or are accepted as normal business losses or shrinkage.

Inventory comprises large-dollar amounts in retail business and also in manufacturing concerns. Retail sales staffs require access to the merchandise inventory and employees in the manufacturing sector need access to material inventory as part of their jobs. Though not as common as cash schemes, inventory is very susceptible to theft.

 ## TYPES OF NONCASH MISAPPROPRIATIONS

There are various forms of noncash misappropriation that include misuse, abuse, unconcealed misappropriations, transfer of assets, and proprietary information. There is no direct involvement of cash at the point of misappropriation from the organization.

Misuse and Abuse

Misuse of the organization's assets does not usually involve theft but rather the use of the asset without proper authorization. The asset may be borrowed and then returned.

235

Typically, the direct cost to the organization is relatively minor if the asset is returned in good condition. There would be only regular wear and tear from the short-term use.

Most people do not view borrowing assets as a serious fraud and certainly not a criminal action. However, they do not see the potential downside, as people never anticipate bad things happening.

The risk and expense to the organization are potential legal liability and loss of reputation. At times the organization's borrowed asset or equipment may be used to compete with the organization. An employee may borrow equipment to perform side jobs for himself rather than for his employer.

Suppose a company van was borrowed by an employee to use for a weekend side project. The signage on the van would have the company's logo and name. If something goes wrong with the job, the customer would seek corrective actions from the company, as they believe it was authorized. In the event of an accident involving the company vehicle, the company's insurance would get involved. Coverage may be an issue depending on the insurance policy.

Unconcealed Misappropriations

This type of theft of assets is the easiest to perform. Just take the goods and walk away. There is no attempt to adjust the books and records to conceal the action. A variation of this is to short-ship goods to customers. A short shipment is when items are listed in the shipping document but not included in the shipment and not received by the recipient.

When an accomplice is involved, there could be false sales made. The employee does not enter the sale in the register and just gives the goods to the accomplice. There may be a nominal amount of money paid or appeared to be paid with a credit card so that the sale transaction looks normal to observers or security cameras. Another use of an accomplice is to return merchandise for refunds of good stolen by the employee.

Unconcealed misappropriations can occur during regular business hours in plain sight of other employees. Most people would assume that their coworker is removing the asset or merchandise as part of their duties, especially if perpetrated by long-time, trusted employees. Even if some suspect that the action is not legitimate, they might not interfere for a number of reasons.

- It is merely a suspicion.
- Poor employee–management relationship.
- Lack of a whistleblowing process.
- The perpetrator holds a senior position.
- Employees do not want to get involved as they feel it is not their responsibility.

Transfer of Assets

The employee requests material to be used in a project. The project may be a fabrication where the employee can then keep all the requested material. If it is for a legitimate project, an excess amount may be requisitioned and the difference needed for the job is retained by the employee. This type of scheme requires no inventory record concealment as the requisition authorizes the reduction of inventory on hand.

Falsified transfer authorizations forms would allow for the removal of goods from the stockroom or warehouse area. The physical removal process can be done in plain sight as this is part of the normal work flow.

Proprietary Information

Intangible assets such as proprietary information are subject to misappropriations also. This type of asset is difficult to protect because restricting access prevents employees from doing their jobs. Unlike tangible assets where people have an idea of the value of the assets, people do not normally see any dollar value attached to information and may not handle it with care like cash. Likely, the information is only valuable to competitors. Sensitive information includes customer information, formulas, trade secrets, marketing strategies, products, and expansion developments.

Even if this type of information may not be of any direct benefit to the employee involved in misappropriation or loss, the damage to the organization may include embarrassment, loss of reputation, and exposure to legal liabilities.

 ## CONCEALMENT OF NONCASH MISAPPROPRIATIONS

Concealment can take place by the falsification of either sales or purchase records. Inventory records can also be falsified to hide shortages.

Falsifying Sales or Purchase Records

Where inventory or other assets are purchased by the organization and then misappropriated by employees, the misappropriation is considered as part of a noncash scheme. Where employees initiate and cause the organization to purchase goods or services that were not provided or inadequately delivered, then the fraud forms part of billing schemes. Billing schemes are discussed in Chapter 8. Noncash misappropriation occurs due to the opportunity to steal available goods.

False shipping documents can be created along with false sales documents. This would generate a sale that would reduce the inventory to that of the after-theft level. The billing to the customer may sit in accounts receivable, be aged, and then written off. Variations of this concealment scheme include:

- Removing the sales documentation from the file before it is sent to accounting for billing.
- Understating the amount of goods actually sold and shipped to an accomplice for billing purposes. Shipping documents may also be adjusted afterward to match the lower quantity in the billing documents.
- Charging the sale to a customer with a large accounts receivable balance where it may not be as noticeable and may subsequently be written off.
- Access to accounts receivable records or, through an employee accomplice, to discount or write off the false sale to bad debts.

If goods are shipped to the fraudster or to the accomplice, there is no need for the fraudster to remove the goods himself. The transaction would appear to be a normal one as it falls under the regular business sales process.

When the receiving department accepts delivered goods, the employee provides accounting with a copy of the actual quantities received so the vendor will be paid in full. However, for inventory records, the shipment is recorded as short shipped with the fraudster misappropriating the difference. A variation of this scheme is for the fraudster to record the rejection of some of the quantity as substandard or damaged and keep the rejected pieces for herself. Recording fewer goods than actually received could be in preparation for a later theft or to cover earlier misappropriations.

Falsifying Inventory Records

While losses may not be detected until the next inventory-taking process, the fraudster may make efforts to conceal the misappropriations by falsifying inventory records so the fraud scheme can continue. Perpetual inventory is a method of accounting for inventory. It allows for real-time or near-real-time updating when goods are purchased or sold so that a balance of goods on hand is maintained. Perpetual inventory need not be updated manually except when physical inventory counts differ from the perpetual inventory balance.

The normal recording process in perpetual inventory for a sale is to reduce the inventory by the amounts sold. When goods are received from purchase, inventory is updated to increase by the amount received. Periodically, a physical count of the actual inventory on hand is done and the numbers reconciled to the perpetual inventory balances.

The fraudster requires access to inventory records to accomplish this. The goods can be written off as obsolete, damaged, or scrapped. Alternatively, the fraudster may convince a coworker with the authority to do so. Items recorded as written off, returned to the vendor, or as sales become permanently concealed. Additional methods of falsifying inventory records include:

- Forcing the change in the perpetual inventory balance by methods such as debiting the perpetual inventory account and crediting cost of goods sold.
- Altering physical inventory count sheets before they go for reconciliation with the booked inventory amounts.
- Padding the inventory during the physical inventory count process by including empty boxes into the count.

Falsified stocktaking is a temporary concealment process—the discrepancy between the count and the perpetual inventory figures will arise again when the next physical inventory is taken. However, by then the fraudster may have left the organization or, with such long passage of time, the audit trail to identify the culprit may be lost.

 ## DATA ANALYTICS

The need of relevant data files is paramount for the detection of noncash misappropriations. Since noncash assets are physical items that have been recorded in the organization's business system, there tend to be audit trails whether the misappropriations were concealed or not.

Data Files

Data files that can be used to apply analytical tests include:

- Shipment register
- Receiving logs
- Sale register
- Inventory
- Employee master
- Accounts receivable
- Purchase
- Access logs to the inventory module

Data Analytical Tests

Computerized testing can identify anomalies that are red flags for potential noncash-misappropriation schemes. Sales and purchase transactions that impact inventory form the most significant volumes in many organizations. Data analytics can reduce the number of transactions to review. These tests include:

- Join the shipment register file to the sales register data file and extract no matches of corresponding sales.
- Join the employee master file on the address field to the shipment register file and extract matches to addresses.
- Extracts posting to those accounts receivable that have had no transactions for a specific period of time. These dormant accounts may have been used to post fraudulent sales for the purpose of concealment.
- Perform the relative size factor test on sales by customer to identify large jumps. The unusually large sale transaction may have been used for concealment.
- Extract items that have falling gross margins. These could be the result of cost of goods sold amounts increasing without a corresponding increase in sale prices due to falsifying inventory.
- Calculate the inventory turnover rates and review those items with both very high and very low turnovers.
- Analyze shrinkage. The focus should be on both properly recorded items and those not properly recorded or authorized.
- Join the purchase file with the inventory file to ensure matches.
- Analyze purchases that are higher than normal over periods. Trend analysis can be used.
- Join the receiving log to the payment file to match amounts. The receiving log may have recorded lower than the actual receipts to conceal inventory shortages.
- Duplicate key detections for inventory records with the same amount, quantity, and item. Inventory may have been increased by using the same documentation.
- Extract where inventory unit prices are greater than sales prices. The unit price may have been increased to increase the inventory balance amount to conceal missing goods.

- Extract all inventory items coded as obsolete but that have minimum order quantities in the inventory master file. The write-off is a red flag of concealment.
- Extract inventory receipts of items that are excessive as compared to prior years. The overordered items could be available for misappropriation.
- Extract and review all inventory items with negative balances. Fraudulent shipments recording may have exceeded the actual units on hand.
- Perform trend analysis on inventory written off as scrap.
- Extract and review all entries to perpetual inventories other than sales and purchases updates.
- Extract inventory adjustments, accounts receivable write-downs, and asset transfers. Summarize the extracted files individually by employee to analyze. High amounts may indicate concealment. Standard deviation calculations or Z-score can aid in determining which employees to focus additional attention on.
- Analyze increases in bad debts to isolate the write-off of false sales.
- Match material requisitioned to that used in the projects.
- Extract from the inventory module access log for adjustments made. Summarize by employee and review those with excessive log-ins to make adjustments. The log information may also reveal a lack of segregation of duties.

CONCLUSION

Even with the best of internal controls in place and with strict adherence to them, noncash misappropriation will still take place. Internal controls may help to make concealment of the theft more difficult, but unconcealed five-finger discounts and the shrinkage of goods cannot be eliminated. Employees need access to the goods to perform their jobs. Oversight cannot be implemented every moment, not even with security cameras.

Organizations need to be proactive in noncash fraud prevention regardless of how honest they believe their employees are.

Segregation of duties is the best starting point. The processes of ordering goods, receiving goods, making payments, updating inventory records, authorizing requisitions of material or of assets need to be performed by different people. Assets may be stolen just like inventory. New furniture or equipment ordered and received by the same person may be misappropriated and the old assets continued to be used. Accounts payable would make payment to the vendor assuming that the new assets are being used. The person responsible for any dispositions such as assets should not be the same person responsible for receipt of the proceeds. It should go through the normal accounts receivable channels.

Additional safeguards include:

- Allow physical access to assets only to those whose job requires access.
- Secure access after business hours to reduce the opportunity of theft and manipulation of records to conceal the loss.
- Asset removal must be properly authorized along with the proper documentation support.

- Write-offs of assets or scrapping of assets should be done only with independent authorization.
- Install security cameras to safeguard assets and for the security of employees.
- Invoices should be matched to receiving logs and reports before issuing payments to vendors.
- Take physical inventory on a regular basis by someone not associated with the purchasing or warehousing area.
- Occasionally perform inventory counts with unannounced visits.
- Physical inventory counts should be diligent, comprehensive, and include test checking of box contents.
- Test check count sheets by independent personnel.
- Any significant discrepancies between book inventory amounts and the physical count should be reviewed and cleared before permanently making the adjustments to inventory records.
- Restrict confidential information to those who require the knowledge and access to perform their duties.
- Educate employees that proprietary information is every bit as valuable as expensive assets.

Any amount of significant shrinkage is a red flag of fraud. Investigation of where and why it occurred needs to be followed up immediately. Delays would increase the losses and signal to the fraudster that the scheme is working well and can be expanded upon. Success in this simple area of fraud may provide encouragement to deploy more complex and more lucrative fraud schemes.

CHAPTER FOURTEEN

Corruption

WHEN MOST PEOPLE THINK OF CORRUPTION, bribery usually comes to mind. While bribery is the most common of corruption schemes, corruption also includes extortion, illegal gratuities, and conflict of interest.

Corruption is where someone using the role of an employee colludes with a third party where the employee obtains a benefit. The major difference between corruption and other fraud schemes from a data analytical perspective is that the benefit is not recorded in the business system records. It is completely off the books of the organization that the employee works for.

 BRIBERY

The most common corruption scheme is bribery. It is given to influence a decision or act to occur. It may be given ahead or after the act has occurred. The technical definition of bribery is restricted to that of influencing public officials. We will use the term *bribery* to include situations where employees of commercial enterprises influence business decisions. Bribes are given to the employees to obtain an advantage over others. Therefore not only will the organization suffer losses that may include excessive pricing and lower quality products, but competitors of the briber also suffer from their loss of business opportunities. Losses for the employee's organization are usually not immediate. There is no theft of assets or anything tangible from the organization so there is no apparent loss. Eventually there must be a cost to the organization. A bribe is given based on a business decision for business purposes. There must be a benefit to the briber of at least the value of the bribe, but usually significantly higher. A commercial return is expected for the bribe or else the bribe would not have been given in the first place. Bribes can take the form of cash, gifts, trips, and promises of future employment or contracts. These under-the-table payments do not directly have to benefit the corrupt employee as they can be directed to accomplices or relatives to conceal the gain.

Overbilling Schemes

Overbilling schemes are associated with purchase contracts. A bribe is given to the employee of the organization in order for the vendor to be selected over others. Benefits to the vendor include providing the goods or services at higher prices than competitors or providing lower-valued or poor-quality goods. Alternatively, or in addition, there could be unfavorable costs included in the contract, such as excessively high costs for additions or any other variations over the basic contract. The bottom line is that the organization eventually pays far more for the goods or services than they otherwise would have.

In order for the bribe to be of value, it must be given to someone with the ability to authorize or to arrange authorization of purchases. If the corrupt employee cannot authorize the purchase, then he or she must use techniques, such as forging the purchasing documents, to convince an authorizing officer that there is a need for the product, or include the fraudulent purchasing documents among legitimate ones for signature. The vendor has an employee working on the inside of the organization to vouch for any false documents or information provided by the vendor. The false documentation may include fraudulent invoices submitted to the organization and the corrupt employee ensures that they are paid.

Underbilling Schemes

In underbilling schemes, the organization sells their goods at less than regular amounts charged to other customers. The purchaser that paid a bribe obtains a better deal than otherwise entitled to. The selling organization receives a less than favorable price. The cost savings to the purchaser would normally exceed the amount of the bribe.

TENDER SCHEMES

Tender schemes are also known as *bid rigging*. Here, the bribe is given to influence the awarding of a contract, whether it is for sales, purchasing, or construction contracts. The reason for the bribe may be because the bidder's cost is not competitive, the bidder does not have a quality product, or a combination of both. The bribe may be offered just to be able to get an edge over the competition to obtain the business. Having an insider provides a significant advantage over competitors. One such method is to pay a bribe to be able to see the specifications of the tender requirements earlier than when they are officially made available. This allows a longer lead time for the bidder to prepare their tender documents.

Tender schemes can be invoked at any stage of the bidding process. Prior to offering to accept bids, the procurement requirements can be written to favor a specific supplier. It could also be decided that the organization would have no choice other than to proceed with the sole-source supplier route given that only one supplier can meet the organization's requirements. Alternatively, the job can be split so that each component falls below the threshold amount of requiring tenders. The sole-source jobs can then be allocated to preferred suppliers.

When the tender is advertised, techniques to restrict the pool of qualified vendors may be utilized. For example, a minimal amount of time can be allowed for the submission of bids, making it difficult for those vendors without prior knowledge to submit their complete tender documents on time. Vendors may also bribe employees for information on how to best prepare their tender documents.

As an aside, no bribes need to be paid if the vendors are in collusion. The vendors may agree among themselves to designate the successful bidder on a rotational basis. This way, the vendors can consistently maintain high prices with the successful bidder having prices below the other vendors yet still above the market rates. If there are a number of jobs available for tender, another collusion method would be bid pooling. This is where the vendors split up the contract so each gets a piece of the work. There is a designated winner for each of the jobs so everyone's successful bid is at the prices they wanted.

When the tenders have been submitted, certain bid documents can be lost or deemed incomplete to reduce competition. The person with access to the sealed bids can open them to extract the bid information and provide the details to the preferred vendor. With the information, the vendor who paid the bribe for the information can just underbid the lowest amount. If the bid is at market rates, the successful vendor may still be able to make an additional profit when the organization requires modifications above the basic contract.

 ## KICKBACKS, ILLEGAL GRATUITIES, AND EXTORTION

Kickbacks are usually associated with the purchasing function. It is those employees who have regular dealings with vendors that may develop special and close relationships that can lead to kickbacks. The employee would receive consideration, usually in money, to divert business to the vendor. The employee receives the kickback from the vendor with no record of such payments recorded in the employee's organization. Kickbacks sometimes are calculated as a percentage of the special transactions to ensure a steady and continued relationship. Even if there is no direct and immediate loss to the organization because of kickbacks, eventually, the organization would be subjected to either higher prices or lower quality or both by the vendor. Because of the secure business arrangement, the vendor would feel secure enough to raise prices to more than cover the cost of the kickbacks. Due to the payments to the corrupt employee, continued business with the organization is assured. The vendor may then graduate to overbilling schemes or even totally falsified invoices with the aid of the employee.

The employee may not have solicited gratuities and the gratuities may not have been an influencing factor for the business decision that favored the payer. The vendor shows appreciation after the fact for the approval of the business decision. It is illegal because the gratuity was not disclosed or approved by the organization. Most organizations prohibit the acceptance of gratuities and limit the dollar value of any gifts openly received to a nominal amount that is within acceptable business norms. There is the assumption that receipt of any illegal gratuities may influence future business transactions with the vendor.

Extortion is where the corrupt employee initiates a demand of payment to provide a decision favorable to the vendor. The demand itself, regardless of the receipt of any benefits, is a criminal offense. It is the opposite of a bribe where the vendor pays to obtain a favorable position. In commercial extortion, the employee may demand payment in order to allow the vendor to continue doing business with the organization. Failure to meet the demand would mean being cut out of any future business dealings. Other extortion threats include harm of reputation or physical harm, intimidation, and coercion.

Bribery, illegal gratuities, and commercial extortion all have the same results of an employee of an organization receiving an illicit payment from another party such as a vendor.

 ## CONFLICT OF INTEREST

Conflict of interest occurs when the employee has an undeclared personal interest in transactions with the organization. It is not having the personal interest in a business that deals with the employee's organization that is the main issue, but rather the undeclared or undisclosed interest that is the problem. Even if the organization suffered no losses and may have profited by the business relationship, the mere fact that it is undisclosed creates a conflict of interest. It is not a conflict if all the parties have full knowledge of the relationship and transact under normal commercial interests. If the transactions are normal and reasonable, the employee need not conceal the interest with the employer. However, some organizations prohibit any dealing with companies that employees have material interests in.

Conflict of interest is fraud because the employee takes advantage of the organization's trust in expecting that the employee will act in the best interests of the organization. It is not expected that the employee would have ulterior motives and act according to self-interest rather than that of the organization. Self-interest actions include steering the organization into transacting with a supplier or customer that they may not have otherwise used. Conflict occurs when the employee can influence a decision of the organization to benefit a party that the employee has an undisclosed interest in. Conflict-of-interest schemes include:

- Sales schemes where the organization may sell to the employee-related party at a lower price or a higher discount that otherwise would not be warranted. An example may be the granting of high-volume discount prices even though the purchaser had not met the required volume. There would be a loss of revenue to the organization. The scheme may include delayed billings for the sales or unwarranted write-offs that are authorized.
- Purchasing schemes favor a supplier that the employee has an economic interest in. While there may not be any immediate monetary loss if prices are at market rates, there is always the potential of future overpricing. Property flips are high-profit

purchasing schemes. If an employee is aware that an organization is interested in a particular building, piece of land, or another business and wishes to make a purchase, the employee can make the purchase first and then resell it to the organization at a higher price.

- Business diversion schemes are where business that normally goes to the organization where the employee works is diverted to a business that the employee has an interest in. Unless there is a noncompetition clause in the employee's contract, an employee leaving the organization to go into business is not fraud even if the business directly competes against the organization. It is what the employee takes before leaving that may fall under conflict of interest. One such action may be to divert resources to a business that the employee has an interest in or will have an interest in after leaving the organization. Another resource diversion is where the employee still works for the organization and uses some of the time or equipment for activities of his other business. There is then a conflict even if the direct cost to the organization is low. The organization is in fact subsidizing the other employee's business. At the minimum, the loss would be in time and in productivity.

Conflict-of-interest schemes do not always have to directly benefit the employee of the organization. The benefit may be granted to a friend or relative.

DATA ANALYTICAL TESTS

Payments to the corrupt employee do not exist in the organization's books and records. They cannot be extracted out from any available data sets. What data analytics can do is to detect transactions that raise red flags that may be associated with corruption. Many of the tests to detect corrupt purchasing schemes are the same as those outlined in Chapter 8 for billing schemes. Similarly, a number of the tests outlined in Chapter 13 for noncash misappropriations in the area of falsifying sales records and inventory records can be used to detect corrupt sales schemes.

There must be some sort of relationship between the corrupt employee and the other party such as a vendor or purchaser. If we have access to the other party's data, we can cross-reference payment information to those in our organization by using IDEA's join feature, looking for matches of names, addresses, phone numbers, and other identifying information. Since it is unlikely that we have access to the other party's records to perform general tests, we turn to our own records to detect anomalies where it may signify a high relationship between the employee and the other parties.

The GEL-1 general test and the GEL-2 targeted test provide links between one field with another field in data sets. The GEL tests are explained in detail in Chapter 6. These tests are very powerful in providing potential links between employees and outside parties. An example of the two tests is worth summarizing and repeating here.

Figure 14.1 displays the results of the GEL-1 test where we are testing to see if there is any relationship between sales representatives and clients from a sales transaction file.

	SALESREP	CLIENT_NO	TRAN_PER_FREQ_CLIENT_NO	TOTAL_FOR_SALESREP	GEL_1 ▼
1	119	92241	93	96	0.9688
2	117	92326	93	99	0.9394
3	110	92431	143	167	0.8563
4	108	40730	132	164	0.8049
5	105	30608	120	160	0.7500
6	115	92323	57	96	0.5938
7	113	60300	54	105	0.5143
8	118	60300	48	111	0.4324
9	122	40712	30	84	0.3571
10	120	92100	39	114	0.3421
11	107	40312	36	120	0.3000
12	128	20914	15	51	0.2941
13	127	20954	27	105	0.2571
14	121	61503	21	93	0.2258
15	125	11600	27	138	0.1957
16	104	10201	28	164	0.1707
17	124	12203	12	72	0.1667
18	126	21139	21	153	0.1373
19	123	20005	12	93	0.1290

Tabs: Join G1-7.IMD × | Summarization G1-6.IMD × | Join G1-9.IMD ×

FIGURE 14.1　Result of Using the GEL-1 Test

The GEL-1 ratio shows an overview of the link between the sales representatives and the clients. Sale representative 119 has the highest relationship. Sales representative 105 also has a high relationship. We will perform the GEL-2 test specifically on sales representative 105 as 75 percent of all sales transactions were with one customer. There were only 40 transactions with other customers.

	CLIENT_NO	NO_OF_RECS	GROSS_SALE_SUM	TOTAL_NO_OF_RECS	GEL2	CRITERIA
1	30501	40	189,638.76	54	0.7407	105
2	30608	120	824,092.78	131	0.9160	105

Tabs: Sales transactions-Database.IMD | Sales transactions-Database - step 1... | GEL2 - Sales transactions-Datab...

FIGURE 14.2　Results of Using the GEL-2 Test

The resulting file in Figure 14.2 shows that sales representative 105 dealt 120 times out of 131 with client number 30608, while the client purchased from all other sales representatives only 11 times. In addition, this sales representative sold 40 times to client number 30501, while the same client purchased from all other sales representatives only 14 times. Transactions with client number 30608 totaled $824,092; client number 30501 totaled $189,638.

Clearly, there is a strong business relationship between this sales representative and clients 30608 and 30501. Of course, further investigations are needed but these tests provide a starting point for review.

Other potential relationships that can be highlighted with GEL test examples include comparing the fields of the contracting officer with winning bids or purchasing officers with purchase transactions. The employee who authorized the payment field can be linked with the vendor field.

Other Data Analytical Tests

Additional tests that can be applied to detect red flags of corruption include:

- Summarize by supplier and review those winning the most bids and review related contracts for potentially unfavorable terms.
- Using the @Age function, calculate the number of days between bid submission date and bid close date. Compare those with the shortest day difference to winning tenders. This could be an indication of waiting to be provided information from other tenders by a corrupt employee. An example of the equation is @ Age(BID_CLOSE_DATE, BID_REC_DATE) that would result in the difference in number of days between the bid closing date and the date that each bid was received.
- Employ Z-scores or standard deviation tests to determine how far from the norm the lowest bidder is. If the lowest bid is just under the next lowest bid, documentation of the winning bid should be given additional attention to determine if additional investigation is needed.
- Summarize by successful bidders by each year and chart for significant increases in contract values over the years.
- Use the Z-scores test to isolate very large differences in bid amounts and review.
- Extract payments coded as extras or adjustments from winning tenders to determine if they are excessively charging for variations.
- Run the duplicate key detection test against various information fields, such as phone number, fax number, address, contact name, and so on, to see if there are multiple bids by the same vendor under different corporate identities.
- Join several years of winning-bid names for matches to detect those that consistently are awarded the contacts and review in detail.
- Summarize by purchase type and then by vendor and review those areas with a limited amount of vendors. These could be sole-source contracts for favored vendors.
- Summarize by purchase type, totaling on the sum and average for each year for several years, and join the files. For selected purchase types, chart the average prices over the years to easily visually identify any rapid price increases that may be fraudulently inflated.
- Extract damaged or rejected items from the receiving log file and summarize by vendor. Large numbers of rejected items for a particular vendor may indicate that substandard quality goods are being purchased due to a bribery scheme.
- Using the aging function of @Age, review accounts receivable with lengthy past-due dates. These may be associated with favorable-credit-terms sale schemes.
- Using the aging function of @Age, review accounts payable that are paid unusually early, which could indicate preferred vendor or underpurchase schemes.

CONCEALMENT

There are no records of corruptions in the victim organization's business records so there are no entries that need to be concealed. However, for the business paying the bribe, there may be a need to conceal the bribe payment. Typically, bribes are charged to accounts such as "Consulting Fees" or "Referral Commissions" and the check is paid to the corrupt employee as if he or she was a service provider. Payment for services avoids any inventory discrepancies that would be caused if the payment were booked as a purchase of goods. A slush fund created mainly for the purpose of bribes may be set up by the business by creating false invoices and making payments to the false entity with the slush fund bank account.

Other methods of concealment include promises of future employment or consulting contracts, loans at very favorable terms that may be eventually forgiven, or the transfer of assets or property at below fair market value to the corrupt employee.

 CONCLUSION

Losses in an organization are not restricted to theft of assets or resources. Significant losses can be suffered by insidious actions taken by even a single corrupt employee who is in collusion with outside parties. These fraudulent transactions may not be discovered for many years given the trust of the employee and that concealment is not required. The frauds are not recorded in the business system's records and are difficult to uncover by routine audits or examination of the accounting records. Data analytics can help to red-flag transactions that are unusual and have the possibility of being associated with corruption schemes. In many cases, the red flags are normal anomalies. When a number of these anomalies arise, there is a need to perform further investigation to confirm or eliminate the possibility of corruption.

In addition to strong internal controls (mentioned many times over), combating corruption schemes requires additional safeguards. When possible, any major contracts with suppliers should have a right-to-audit clause in regard to the supplier's books and records. Not only would there be assurances that the supplier is making a fair profit from the organization, but the records may reveal any links between employees of the organization and the supplier. The organization should have a whistleblowing process in place. The process should facilitate the reporting of improper conduct, illegal activities, or unethical behaviors. Many times, internal direct reporting of wrongful activities has proven very difficult or ineffective. The process can be operated internally or contracted with a third party that can be reported anonymously while giving the option to the whistleblower to leave contact information. The contact process may be a telephone hotline, website form completion, email contact, or a combination of these. The whistleblowing process should be easily accessible to all employees, clients, contractors, suppliers, and the public. Company policies, especially ethics policies, should be made clear to all employees. Education of employees as to the definition of conflict of interest and what is considered as proper hospitality to accept is extremely important. After all, there is a line between bribery and normal promotions provided by vendors and suppliers that is sometimes unclear. However, the line differs in different organizations. If a vendor gives an employee a bottle of wine during Christmas, it is probably acceptable. If it was a paid holiday trip, then it would probably not be acceptable. What about those gifts in between? Defined, clear, and reasonable policies need to be in place.

CHAPTER FIFTEEN

Money Laundering

ONEY LAUNDERING IS A FINANCIAL TRANSACTION SCHEME to conceal or attempt to conceal the identity of proceeds illegally obtained so that the proceeds appear to come from legitimate sources.

Money laundering is a global problem that is being tackled by governments. There are many government organizations, or those sponsored by governments, involved in various roles to combat money laundering. Some of these anti-money laundering (AML) organizations collect financial information for detection purposes while others foster cooperation and implementation of standards among member countries. These organizations provide a wealth of informational resources.

- The Financial Action Task Force (FATF) (www.fatf-gafi.org/pages/aboutus/ whoweare) is an intergovernmental policy-making body that sets standards to combat money laundering and terrorist financing.
- The Organisation for Economic Co-operation and Development (OECD) (www.oecd .org/about) membership consists of 34 countries that work together to promote policies for better economic and social well-being. Policies include those relating to AML.
- The Egmont Group of Financial Intelligence Units (www.egmontgroup.org/about) provides a forum for members around the world to combat money laundering and terrorist financing.
- The Financial Transactions and Reports Analysis Centre of Canada (FINTRAC) (www.fintrac-canafe.gc.ca/fintrac-canafe/1-eng.asp) receive financial transaction reports and analyze the data to detect trends and patterns of money laundering and terrorist financing.
- The Financial Crimes Enforcement Network (FinCEN) (www.fincen.gov/about_ fincen/wwd) is a part of the United States Department of Treasury that collects financial transactions data and analyzes the data for law enforcement purposes to combat money laundering.

Our concern is whether our organization is unwittingly or otherwise involved in the money-laundering process. We should understand the stages of money laundering and the red flags of potential money laundering.

THE MONEY-LAUNDERING PROCESS

When money is obtained from various illegal activities—such as corruption, bribery, tax evasion, drugs—where the criminal does not want the authorities to know the source of the income, they engage in money laundering. Money laundering disguises the illegal origin and legitimizes the funds so they can be openly used.

There are three main stages in the money-laundering process, each with its own complexity and risk.

The Placement Stage

This is the riskiest stage of the money-laundering process. Large cash deposits and frequent suspicious deposits are required to be reported to government entities such as FINTRAC and FinCEN. The objective is to place the cash into foreign or domestic bank accounts without raising red flags. To make the dirty money appear to be clean, deposits are made into domestic banks by splitting the large amount into smaller amounts and making multiple deposits below reporting limits to avoid detection. This is known as *smurfing* or structuring. Often, currency exchange businesses are used for these smaller amounts and to obtain alternative currencies for deposit.

For deposit to foreign entities, the cash needs to be smuggled out of the country. Funds are converted to large denominations to reduce the bulk. Purchasing diamonds and other jewels or precious metals by converting the cash can also facilitate the smuggling. Electronic transfers and other payment methods, such as gift cards, are tools that can be used in the placement stage. Additional placement methods include:

- Use of insurance products such as immediate or deferred annuities.
- Use of investment-related transactions such as purchases of securities.
- Use of nonbank financial services such as wire transfer companies and currency exchange entities.

The Layering Stage

The layering stage is the most complex of all the stages; this is where the origin of the money is being made difficult to trace. A number of transactions or layers need to be put between the original sources of the funds before they are brought back into the legal economy. Funds might be moved to foreign countries that usually have strong bank secrecy laws, moved into accounts in the name of others who are nominees, or moved to accounts held by offshore corporations where the beneficial ownership is hidden and the funds can be withdrawn and redeposited to a number of other accounts.

Other layering tools and techniques include:

- Bank secrecy laws
- Offshore banks
- Tax havens
- Shell corporations
- Trusts
- Intermediaries
- Walking accounts

Walking accounts are frequently used as they are very effective as a layering tool. An account is opened in one foreign jurisdiction where funds are deposited. The account is arranged so that all deposited funds are immediately transferred to another account, usually in another jurisdiction. The first bank is instructed to notify the second bank if any inquiries to the account are made. The second bank then has instructions to transfer the funds to a third bank. This provides the criminal with additional protection from investigation and seizure by law-enforcement agencies.

The Integration Stage

In the integration stage, the money enters back into the legitimate economy where it appears to have come from legal and normal transactions. Depending on the layering stage, the return may appear to come from a sale of assets such as real estate. Funds may be integrated back and appear to be from legal sources such as:

- False loans from self-owned offshore companies. Loans come back into the country tax free and, if the loan is for business purposes, interest is deductible from the domestic business when the interest is paid to the self-owned offshore company. A variation of this is to legitimately borrow funds from an offshore bank where illicit funds are deposited. The loan is guaranteed by the deposited amounts.
- False inheritances.
- False gambling winnings such as from casinos. In casinos, chips can be purchased and then cashed back to be settled by a check or wire transfer that provides evidence of the source of the money.
- Credit cards issued by an offshore bank. Cash can be withdrawn or bills can be paid via the offshore bank.
- Salary from false businesses. Self-owned offshore companies can pay consulting or director's fees.
- Importing and exporting. Selling to self-owned offshore companies and overbilling explains the incoming revenue. Purchasing at lower-than-market prices from a self-owned offshore company and then reselling at market value produces a high-gross margin that justifies the profit and funds. False-services income explains the source of funds while avoiding having to physically deal with actual goods.
- Real estate transactions. By selling property to a self-owned foreign company at an inflated price, the difference between the selling price and cost is placed on

the books as legitimate capital gains. A variation of this can be done locally by paying the independent third-party owner a below-market price and giving them the difference from the market price secretly in cash. The property then can be sold at fair market value, thereby legitimizing the capital gain. Deposit returns from failed real estate purchase transactions from lawyers can also justify the source of funds.

■ Commingling the funds with legitimate income. High cash-based businesses, such as bars, restaurants, vending machines, ATMs, casinos, and nightclubs, can have illicit funds mixed with legitimate revenues to explain the source of money.

Once the money appears to have come from legal sources, the fraudster or criminal can use the money for personal enjoyment without fear of the funds being tied to illegal activities. Excess funds can be used to make legitimate investments such as real estate, securities, or for financing other businesses.

OTHER MONEY TRANSFER SYSTEMS AND NEW OPPORTUNITIES

There are alternative and parallel remittance systems that have existed for hundreds of years that are outside of the traditional banking and financial channels. *Fei chien* started in China and *hawala* comes from Pakistan and India. Both *hawala* and *hundi chitti* can be used interchangeably. More recently, from Somalia, *al-barakat* joined the informal-remittance systems. These alternative systems are similar but with small differences in operation. These systems are not necessarily underground banking systems, as they are not illegal in most countries and are operated in the open.

We will discuss hawala as it makes the most use of trust between the hawala dealers. Typically, there is a family relationship or regional affiliation between the dealers. Money transfers between the dealers are not actually transferred from one country to another. Suppose an individual in Canada wishes to transfer some funds to a relative in India. The individual in Canada would go to a local hawala dealer, pay them, and then the dealer delivers instructions by phone, fax, or e-mail to the hawala dealer in India. The hawala dealer in Canada has an established business or trusted relationship with the hawala dealer in India. The hawala dealer in India then pays the agreed amount to the intended recipient. If no funds are wired between countries, how does the dealer in India get paid? There are a number of scenarios.

■ The two hawala dealers are business partners and transferring money is only a part of their normal business activities. If the business is an importing and exporting business, the funds can be covered in the next shipment from Canada to India and underbilled by the delivered amount. If goods are moving from India to Canada, then overbilling by the delivered amount can be done.
■ The hawala dealer in India may owe money to the dealer in Canada.
■ The Canadian hawala dealer may already have funds with the dealer in India.

People may use the hawala system over traditional banking transfers due to:

- **Cost efficiency**. Banks charge more for the transfer and provide poorer exchange rates.
- **Efficiency**. The funds are delivered to the recipient more quickly than banks can do in most cases.
- **Lack of bureaucracy**. Banks require identification or a bank account with the transferring bank.
- **Lack of paper trail**. This could be due to legitimate reasons, tax evasion, or money laundering.

Since hawala is a remittance system, it can be used at any of the placement, layering, or integration stages. A red flag of a hawala bank account is that it always has significant deposit activities along with outgoing transfers. Typically, the wire transfers are to Great Britain, Switzerland, and Dubai—the major financial centers involved with hawala. Given the nature of hawala, the deposits and transfer amounts will not normally balance or even match.

New technology allows for new, more convenient payment methods for consumers and also provides new opportunities for money laundering. These include:

- Mobile payments from smartphone
- Stored-value cards such as prepaid credit cards
- Digital currencies
- Online auctions
- Online casinos
- Opening bank accounts online and in different countries
- Use of identity theft to facilitate online illicit activities

Criminals can mix the old with the new to move money to further reduce the risks of detection. While new technology adds complexity for law enforcement, unlike cash, technology leaves electronic trails such as IP addresses that might be traced. Auditors need to be aware of these fraud schemes when analyzing data sets and performing audit tests.

 ## AUDIT AREAS AND DATA FILES

When analyzing electronic data, it must be done over longer time frames to be able to detect any patterns. Occasional anomalies might be false positives. Money laundering may either be off-book transactions or on-book transactions. There would be no record of the off-book transactions in the business system's data sets. On-book transactions involve either income statement laundering or balance sheet laundering. Income statement laundering is done by overstating income, where more revenue is recorded in the books of a business than was actually earned. Overstating revenue creates a tax liability. To offset the taxes, the business overstates expenses to compensate. In balance sheet laundering, cash is deposited in the bank and checks are written against the cash in the bank. The deposits and check payments do not enter into the income statement to produce a potential tax liability.

Useful data files of the organization for analysis include:

- Payment register
- Downloaded bank statements
- Sales
- Expenses
- Fixed asset register
- Investment register
- Loan accounts
- Customer master
- Vendor master

Data Analytical Tests

We can use general tests to detect anomalies that can be associated with red flags for money laundering. Several Benford's Law tests can be used to highlight abnormal duplications. These duplications may be the result of making up expense numbers to offset illicit funds recorded in revenue to avoid paying tax on the excess revenues. The duplications may also be in the made-up revenue recorded in the sales register. The first two digits test, the last two digits test, and the numbers duplication test of Benford's Law (discussed in Chapter 5) can be utilized. The relative size factor test can flag transactions in sales or expenses that are out of line for each customer or vendor. The same-same-same test and the same-same-different test can output specific duplications within selected fields, and those duplications with a selected difference field. The even amounts test can provide us with payments paid in exactly even thousands or hundreds of thousands.

Overbilling and underbilling scheme tests (outlined in Chapter 14) used in corruption schemes can be tested for money laundering, too. Other possible tests include:

- Extract and review cash transactions from the payment register.
- Extract from sales or accounts receivable files high amounts paid with cash as the tender.
- Compare bank deposits with sales by joining electronic bank statement records with accounts receivable credits.
- Summarize sales from source categories for each year, join, and chart to determine unusual increases in revenue.
- Extract from the asset register significant additions and disposals and review. Test if transactions were at fair market value.
- Extract from the asset register items that are not normally associated with the nature of the business, such as works of art, precious metals, and so on.
- Extract from the liabilities loan accounts and review for unusual arrangements.
- Extract high-interest payments made and review.
- Extract related-party transactions from purchase and sales.

- Extract from the customer master file new additions and join to sales. Summarize sales by the new customers and review the customer master file for significant transactions to ensure that the identity information of the new customers is clear. Ensure that there is an economic relevance for the transactions.
- Extract from the vendor master file new additions and join to purchases. Summarize purchases by the new vendors and review the vendor master file for significant transactions to ensure that the identity information of the new vendors is clear. Ensure that there is an economic relevance for the transactions.
- Summarize sales by unit item. Summarize costs of goods sold by unit item and join to the summarized sales file. Calculate the gross margin and extract those with unusually high margins.
- Summarize sales by unit item and by customer and extract those customers who were charged significantly more than normal. The Z-score test would be appropriate here.
- Extract transactions with offshore entities.
- Create a list or file containing countries that are considered high risk for money laundering and extract transactions with those countries. At the time of writing, the Financial Action Task Force recommends applying countermeasures to protect the financial system when dealing with Iran and the Democratic People's Republic of Korea (North Korea). They also indicate that Algeria, Ecuador, Ethiopia, Indonesia, Myanmar, Pakistan, Syria, Turkey, and Yemen have not made sufficient progress to correct identified deficiencies.

CONCLUSION

Money laundering is a business! Like all other businesses, it is repetitive and uses methods that are tried and true. When necessity requires innovation, then the business moves to new methods to avoid detection.

As auditors or investigators for the organization, we need to ensure that vendors, customers, or corrupt employees are not using the organization to facilitate money laundering. By reviewing suspicious transactions, assisted by data analytics, we are taking responsible steps to mitigate the risk of unwittingly being associated with money-laundering schemes.

CHAPTER SIXTEEN

Zapper Fraud

THE BASIC CASH REGISTER has evolved into electronic cash registers and now to computerized point-of-sale (POS) systems. Point-of-sale systems are typically attached to a computer that may include a cash drawer, receipt printer, and a credit or debit card terminal. Many systems have touch screens to simplify information entry and may have a barcode scanner or even be complemented with a radio frequency identification (RFID) reader. Weighing scales may also be attached for use in certain types of stores, such as grocery stores. POS systems can integrate with accounting modules and inventory systems. If the inventory module is utilized, the business' inventory control is the POS system. Since sales are recorded in real time, inventory records are immediately updated.

POS systems provide a wealth of information relevant to operating the business efficiently. Sales data can be analyzed so that inventory replacement and levels can be adjusted accordingly. Sales histories can provide trends to influence purchasing decisions. Accuracy is significantly improved with the POS system, in terms of charging correct sale prices and related payments by customers. Cash received from customers is better controlled to prevent theft as POS systems provide information and audit trails to trace or isolate any problems.

Traditionally, retailers and those in the hospitality industry predominantly used POS systems. Today, you will find many industry-specific POS packages, including automotive maintenance shops, municipal community recreations, dry cleaners, spas, hairdressers, and more.

POS systems provide many types of reports to the business. This is possible because the system captures and retains transaction-level, detailed records. As such, much data is available to the auditor for review.

Not only do auditors need to be aware of the employee register-disbursement schemes discussed earlier, but they must also know about electronic suppression of sales techniques.

Electronic suppression of sales is popularly known as *zapper fraud*, and those with high-level access to the POS system perpetrate it. They are normally the owner/shareholder of the business or a manager who runs the business on behalf of the owner. Zapper software is separate from the POS system created by the POS system-software developers or by third parties. These are external programs that can be executed from a DVD/CD or other removable media such as a USB key. Phantomware is software that is included with the POS system and built in. Normally, phantomware is not well documented in the POS user's manual if it is documented at all. While zapper software's main purpose is to delete sales, phantomware sometimes has the capability to perform maintenance functions on the POS data.

What is the advantage of using a zapper? The POS system provides controls that make it difficult for staff to skim money from the business. The employees' cash-out sheets reconcile with the till and POS-system information. The owner wishes to retain these controls and uses zapper software after the employees cash out. The zapper software is executed after the close of business either on a daily, weekly, monthly, or other periodic basis. Employees are never aware that the owner is skimming.

Why would the owner skim from the business that he owns? The owner has many partners that have an interest in the business receipts. The government is a partner in terms of goods and services tax or value-added tax collected by the business on its behalf (GST/HST, VAT) and profits subject to income taxes. Another partner may be the landlord that bases rent partially on a percentage of sales. The business may be a franchisee that has to pay royalties to the franchisor. Finally, the business may have silent partners or investors that the managing partner is cheating on. It may be a combination of some or all of the mentioned situations. In that event, it would be extremely lucrative for the managing partner to delete sales and pocket the proceeds.

Our discussion will focus on the hospitality sector, as restaurant POS systems are not normally linked to the inventory module, which makes the deletion of sales much harder to detect. The retail sector tends to have their products programmed into the POS system for ease of completing the sale at checkout. The inventory module is usually linked to the POS sales system. Even if the inventory module is not activated, the fact that the business has goods or inventory means these can be traced to sales. One possible exception may be grocery stores where there is much spoilage and the cost of goods is difficult to correlate to sales.

There are hundreds of different types of POS systems available for the hospitality industry. They are normally networked and may have many stations. POS systems are effective for restaurants. As soon as the server makes an entry into the POS system, it immediately starts a process. The order could be sent to the terminal at the bar for drinks while food orders are sent to the kitchen for preparation. The POS has table-management capabilities in table assignments and tracks any table changes. Table changes may be in combining two tables or moving customers from a less desirable table to a better table. Food orders must be brought to the right table. Payments can be processed since debit and credit card terminals are linked wirelessly to the POS. Loyalty or VIP cards can be tracked and the applicable discounts be applied. The POS also acts as a time clock for hourly wages for servers when they log in and out of the system. The system can provide management with a host of reports to enable better decision making and restaurant management, as seen in Figure 16.1.

The POS retains much detail data in order to be able to produce these reports. Therefore, data sets are available to the auditor for examination. The data sets are rich with information. Unless maintenance was done for the data, each transaction is appended to the database. Some data sets contain data from the first day the POS system was in operation. Typical database maintenance available in many systems would be to back up and archive the database and start a new database from a certain date on. This procedure reduces the size of a working or production database to make it more efficient by having less to process and save.

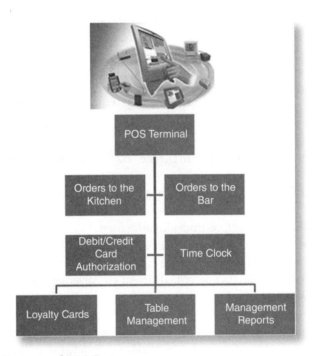

FIGURE 16.1 Features of POS Systems

Taxation authorities around the world are very concerned about the use of zappers to delete sales. They are the partners with the most to lose as sales tax, goods and service tax, or value-added tax are involved and the taxation of profits is in effect zapped.

The Organisation for Economic Co-operation and Development (OECD) published a report titled "Electronic Sales Suppression: A Threat to Tax Revenues"[1] in 2013. It can be obtained at www.oecd.org/ctp/crime/ElectronicSalesSuppression.pdf.

The report states, "Tax administrations are losing billions of dollars/euros through unreported sales and income hidden by the use of these techniques. A Canadian restaurant association estimates sales suppression in Canadian restaurants at some CAD 2.4 billion in one year."

The report provided these international examples.

- In one case investigated in Norway there was a sum equivalent to EUR 7 million underreported.

- In a South African case the wholesalers had expatriated a sum equivalent to EUR 22 million out of South Africa.
- In an investigation by Slovenia inspections carried out in retail stores at the end of the trading day, they found sales in the systems at that time were three times the volume on other days.

The OECD report discusses undercover operations to target POS manufacturers. "Canada has used an undercover operation targeting a software developer where the officers posed as wealthy restaurant owners from abroad seeking to open restaurants in Vancouver. In the operation the undercover officers negotiated with a software developer for the purchase of a zapper and the evidence gained provided sufficient grounds for search warrants of the developers' premises."[2]

Printed news reporting of this undercover operation stated, "Zapper software manipulates and conceals the trail of sales transactions and renumbers the sales record, removing any gaps so that the tax crime is not detected by routine tax audits."[3]

The news report suggests that zapper software is sophisticated and difficult to detect by routine audits.

Court documents reveal, "Between October 2000 and August 2008, Mr. Au sold the Profitek system, along with the zapper program, to 23 known restaurant owners who have deleted cash sales for the purpose of evading income and sales taxes owing to the federal and provincial governments. The Canada Revenue Agency ('CRA') has completed audits for 14 of the 23 restaurants under investigation. The 14 audited restaurants suppressed a total of $14,000,000 in sales, which resulted in a loss of $2,400,000 in federal income tax and $1,000,000 in GST remittances."

The court document further described Mr. Au's involvement in selling and supporting the zapper software.

"Between May and August 2008, two RCMP officers, posing as new restaurant owners, negotiated the purchase of a Profitek system from Mr. Au. On June 16, 2008, one of the officers asked Mr. Au whether he could manipulate taxes with the POS system. Mr. Au replied that he had many satisfied Chinese customers and that cash transactions could be deleted using an additional program that cost $1,500. It was quick and easy to use and Mr. Au said he could install this program once the Profitek system was set up. Mr. Au assured the officers that they should not fear a government audit. Mr. Au said there was no danger of the government detecting the software on their computer; however, they had to keep the disc containing the software in a safe location.

"Lastly, Mr. Au assured the officers that troubleshooting was part of the zapper service offered to customers."[4]

So how does the Canada Revenue Agency detect the use of zappers? An internal report entitled "Electronic Suppression of Sales (ESS) Report on Phase One of CRA's Strategy to Address ESS," obtained under the Access to Information Act and Privacy Act, states the following.

> The best success in identifying zapper activity has come from in-depth analysis of the data produced by the POS systems. This has been accomplished by importing the raw databases into IDEA. IDEA allows flexibility to users with analyzing data. Unusual trends such as low cash sales and low average cash

bills can be quickly identified using IDEA. In addition, by analyzing the raw databases, unusual and inconsistent information can sometimes be identified.

With the assistance of data analytical software, the report estimated the amount of unreported sales to be over $71 million for the 76 cases involving potential ESS. At approximately $1 million per case, the stakes are very high.

Using IDEA, we can analyze various anomalies in POS system data sets and also perform the trends as outlined in the report.

Most POS systems are designed in the same general way somewhat to how many accounting systems are designed. All accounting software has a general ledger, a sales journal, and a disbursement journal. These are integrated internally when transactions are entered and processed. Similarly, POS Systems' main data sets are the Header (Sales) file, the Detail Sales file, and the Tender (payment) file. They may have different file names in different POS systems. Basic analyses are done on the data from these three files. The three files can be analyzed separately, but better analysis can be done if the three files are combined as a master file. There are also many other files in the POS system that can be analyzed and compared to the master file to detect anomalies.

To internally integrate the separate files in the POS, a unique transaction or reference number is necessary for the software to operate. Some systems use this unique transaction identification number as the bill number printed on the check or bill given to the customer. Most systems do not use a unique internal number as the bill number because the internal numbers may be sequential. Printing out that number on the bills would give competitors knowledge of the volume of business that the restaurant has. Other methods are used on the printed bills, including an automatic daily reset of bill numbers. In other words, the first bill of the day would always start at the number one.

However, for the internal number, there is little reason for the POS system not to be in sequential order and to continue each day. This unique internal number is important in our analysis, as it is the match key or common key to join files together.

 ## POINT-OF-SALES SYSTEM CASE STUDY

For our case study, we will use data from a quick-service restaurant. A quick-service restaurant is also known as a fast-food restaurant. You have seen some of the data set as it was used in the Data Familiarization, Arranging and Organizing Data, Nonstatistical Sampling Methods, and the Z-score sections of the book.

The steps outlined will not be identical for data sets from other POS systems, but the basic concepts can be used with any system. For example, you can use the two dBase files from the IDEA training course to perform some of the tests. The available fields are shown in Figure 12.1 in Chapter 12. Those files represent one location of a quick-service or fast-food hamburger chain and are named "ED-Sales-2010-L4.DBF" and "ED-Sales-2011-L4.DBF."

First, we need to create the master file and other files so that we can perform our analysis. We do this by using the "Header Sales," "Detail Sales," and the "Tender" files.

The "Header Sales" file contains a single record for each sale or bill in the POS system. Some of the fields typically include a unique identifier (TXNID in this case), various data and time fields (order date/time, close of bill data/time, etc.), bill number, bill amounts, taxes, transaction status codes, and employee identification.

The "Detail Sales" file contains multiple records or line items associated with each bill controlled by the unique identifier number. The date and time of the order, items ordered, quantity, price, and amount are included. Other fields that the "Detail Sales" file may have are bill reference number (references that are printed out on the hardcopy bills) and item-ordered categories.

The "Tender" file is the payment file and is populated by the payment or tender method used by the customer to pay the bill. Tender methods include cash, various types of credit cards, debit cards, and gift cards. Also included are the unique transaction identifier number, payment date and time, tender type code, and payment amounts. Other fields that may be included are credit/debit card information, transaction status code, and employee identification.

There are differences in the various POS systems but all POS systems have a relationship between the "Header Sales" file, the "Detail Sales" file, and the "Tender" file. Typically, as in our case, the total field in the Header file is equal to the summary or total of the payments in the tender file. The reason why we have to total the payments is that a single bill can be paid by more than one type of tender. For instance, a bill of $100.00 is paid by $20.00 cash and the balance of $80.00 by debit card. Sometimes when a number of customers split a bill, there may be a number of different types of tender payments to settle the bill that could include any combination of cash, Visa, American Express, gift certificates, debit cards, MasterCard, promotional coupons, and so on.

The header subtotal field is equal to the total of the amounts by the unique transaction identifier from the detail file.

Within the header file itself, the subtotal less discounts plus taxes is equal to the total.

In our case, the tender file contains a field for gratuities or tips. Some POS systems or setups will use one of the multiple tax fields available to account for tips. Some systems cash out tips on credit or debit cards by applying the tip portion to the cash-tender field as a negative amount. For instance, a credit card payment of $40.00 contains a $5.00 gratuity. The full amount of $40.00 would be in the credit card tender field and −$5.00 is recorded in the cash-tender field. Gratuities have to be accounted for to ensure that they do not end up as sales in our analysis.

When we are analyzing sales, we use the "Header" file, as the information is before taxes or taxes can be excluded. When we are analyzing the payments or tenders, we include taxes, as that is what was actually received by the restaurant.

In our analysis to reconcile the sales data to the sales reports generated by the POS system, we should exclude all transactions other than those that were closed or completed. Typically, as in our case, the closed transactions are coded with the letter *C* in the STATUS field. Other status items, such as the letter *V* representing voids, should not be included as sales.

File Preparation

Preparing the data files for analysis involves many steps that seem complex at times. This is especially true when you are performing the steps for the first time for POS systems you have not encountered before. By understanding the file-preparation steps in this case study, you can apply similar steps to other POS system data files. The objective is to end up with a good master file that you can use as the basis for your analysis.

Step 1. Using the "Header Sales" file, we append a new field called HD_NETA-MOUNT (short for *header net amount*), as shown in Figure 16.2. This field excludes discounts and taxes so the equation is:

$$SUBTOTAL - DETAILDISCTOTAL - DISCTOTAL$$

	SUBTOTAL	DISCTOTAL	DETAILDISCTOTAL	HD_NETAMOUNT	TAX1	TAX2	TAX3	TAX4
89583	5.7500	0.00	0.00	5.75	0.2900	0.4600	0.00	0.00
89584	6.2500	0.00	0.00	6.25	0.3100	0.5000	0.00	0.00
89585	5.7500	0.00	0.00	5.75	0.2900	0.4600	0.00	0.00
89586	5.7500	0.8800	0.00	4.87	0.2500	0.3900	0.00	0.00
89587	7.9500	0.00	0.00	7.95	0.4000	0.6400	0.00	0.00
89588	14.7000	0.00	0.00	14.70	0.7400	1.1800	0.00	0.00
89589	12.5000	0.00	0.00	12.50	0.6300	1.0000	0.00	0.00
89590	5.7500	0.00	0.00	5.75	0.2900	0.4600	0.00	0.00
89591	5.7500	0.8800	0.00	4.87	0.2500	0.3900	0.00	0.00
89592	6.2500	0.00	0.00	6.25	0.3100	0.5000	0.00	0.00
89593	5.7500	0.8800	0.00	4.87	0.2500	0.3900	0.00	0.00
89594	46.9000	0.00	0.00	46.90	2.3500	3.7500	0.00	0.00
89595	8.2500	0.00	0.00	8.25	0.4100	0.6600	0.00	0.00
89596	27.1500	0.00	0.00	27.15	1.3600	2.1700	0.00	0.00
89597	8.9500	0.00	0.00	8.95	0.4500	0.7200	0.00	0.00
89598	12.0000	1.8400	0.00	10.16	0.5100	0.8100	0.00	0.00
89599	8.2500	0.00	0.00	8.25	0.4100	0.6600	0.00	0.00
89600	6.7500	1.0400	0.00	5.71	0.2900	0.4600	0.00	0.00
89601	29.9500	0.00	0.00	29.95	1.5000	2.4000	0.00	0.00
89602	8.9500	0.00	0.00	8.95	0.4500	0.7200	0.00	0.00
89603	16.5000	0.00	0.00	16.50	0.8300	1.3200	0.00	0.00
89604	6.7500	0.00	0.00	6.75	0.3400	0.5400	0.00	0.00
89605	6.7500	0.00	0.00	6.75	0.3400	0.5400	0.00	0.00
89606	6.7500	0.00	0.00	6.75	0.3400	0.5400	0.00	0.00

Header Sales.IMD ×

FIGURE 16.2 Creating a Net Amount Field

Step 2. We summarize the "Detail Sales" file by the unique transaction identifier of TXNID and total the fields of PRICE, AMOUNT, and NETAMOUNT. Fields to include in the output file are ORDERTIME_DATE and ORDERTIME_TIME.

Name this new file "1 Detail Summary."

This provides one TXNID from the details with a total for each of the PRICE, AMOUNT, and NETAMOUNT fields. All the separate line items have been rolled up and associated with the unique transaction identifier and we are working with totals per TXNID now.

Step 3. Within the "1 Detail Summary" file, rename NO_OF_RECS to DETAIL_NO_OF_RECS as shown in Figure 16.3. This identifies that the number of records came from the "Detail Sales" file. The original line details can be displayed by clicking on any data content in the DETAIL_NO_OF_RECS field. For instance, there are 10 line items (menu items ordered) that are associated with TXNID number 3. By clicking on the number 10, which has an underscore, the 10 records will display.

	TXNID	DETAIL_NO_OF_RECS	PRICE_SUM	AMOUNT_SUM	NETAMOUNT_SUM	ORDERTIME_DATE	ORDERTIME_TIME
1	1	6	18.6500	18.6500	18.6500	09/07/2007	01:00:13
2	3	10	52.3000	52.3000	52.3000	09/07/2007	15:01:25
3	6	7	44.8500	47.3500	47.3500	09/07/2007	15:12:13
4	7	4	24.2000	24.2000	24.2000	09/07/2007	15:13:42
5	8	6	27.5500	27.5500	27.5500	09/07/2007	15:18:32
6	9	1	9.9500	9.9500	9.9500	09/07/2007	15:22:01
7	10	3	19.1500	19.1500	19.1500	09/07/2007	15:45:29
8	11	3	14.8500	14.8500	14.8500	09/07/2007	15:55:20
9	13	3	11.1500	11.1500	11.1500	09/07/2007	15:59:17
10	14	3	16.8500	16.8500	16.8500	09/07/2007	16:04:54
11	15	1	8.9500	8.9500	8.9500	09/07/2007	16:11:02
12	16	6	25.9500	27.4500	27.4500	09/07/2007	16:19:01
13	20	2	55.9500	59.9500	59.9500	09/07/2007	16:57:15
14	21	3	24.1500	24.1500	24.1500	09/07/2007	16:58:45
15	22	3	0.00	0.00	0.00	18/07/2007	21:24:23
16	26	10	68.1000	68.1000	68.1000	19/07/2007	14:35:42
17	27	3	14.5000	14.5000	14.5000	19/07/2007	15:40:44
18	28	3	21.7500	21.7500	21.7500	19/07/2007	15:45:51
19	30	4	30.1500	30.1500	30.1500	19/07/2007	15:52:03
20	32	4	0.00	0.00	0.00	19/07/2007	15:59:49
21	33	1	1.1000	1.1000	1.1000	19/07/2007	16:01:13
22	34	1	7.7500	7.7500	7.7500	19/07/2007	16:02:20
23	35	1	7.7500	7.7500	7.7500	19/07/2007	16:03:09
24	36	1	5.2500	5.2500	5.2500	19/07/2007	16:04:56
25	37	4	8.2500	8.2500	8.2500	19/07/2007	16:05:29
26	38	3	3.3000	3.3000	3.3000	19/07/2007	16:05:38
27	39	3	21.7500	21.7500	21.7500	19/07/2007	16:07:34
28	41	8	38.2500	38.2500	38.2500	19/07/2007	16:12:12

FIGURE 16.3 Summarized File with Renamed Field

Step 4. Join the "Header Sales" file to "1 Detail Summary." Designate the "Header Sales" file as the primary file and the "1 Detail Summary" file as the secondary file. Use TXNID as the Match Key Fields and select the "All records" in both files join option. Name this file "1 Header Detail Join." We now have all the fields and information from both files together.

Step 5. There are duplicate (25,162 records in this particular file) TXNIDs in the "Tender" file due to a payment and then a reduction due to discount, refund, and so on in the PAYAMOUNT field. Perform a summarization by TNXNID and TENDERTYPEID, and total on the PAYAMOUNT and GRATUITY fields using the "Tender" file. Fields to include in the output file are the TENDERDESC1, PAYTIME_DATE, and PAYTIME_TIME fields.

Name the file "1 Tender Summary."

This will net out the negative amounts by totaling the PAYAMOUNT field. In addition, we total the GRATUITY field in case this amount is also adjusted. We output the TENDERDESC1, PAYTIME_DATE, and PAYTIME_TIME fields so these fields are available for future analysis.

Step 6. Using the "1 Tender Summary" file, we need to extract all noncash gratuities if we are to perform various cash versus noncash types of analysis later.

We perform a direct extraction using the equation of:

@Upper(@AllTrim(TENDERDESC1)) < > "Cash" .AND. GRATUITY_SUM < > 0

Call this new file "1 Non Cash Gratuity."

@AllTrim function removes leading and trailing spaces from the TENDERDESC1 character field before comparing the field for < > (not equal) Cash. While the @Upper function converts the TENDERDESC1 field internally to uppercase, it is not necessary for this file. Both the @AllTrim and the @Upper functions were used here as safety measures in case of inconsistent entries.

Step 7. In the "1 Non Cash Gratuity" file, change the field name from GRATU-ITY_SUM to NON_CASH_GRATUITY for us to identify that the field contains noncash gratuities. The results are shown in Figure 16.4.

	TXNID	TENDERTYPEID	NO_OF_RECS	PAYAMOUNT_SUM	NON_CASH_GRATUITY	TENDERDESC1	PAYTIME_DATE	PAYTIME_TIME
386	116000	4	1	10.5000	0.1600	Debit	02/04/2010	18:59:16
387	117985	4	1	10.0000	0.1100	Debit	20/04/2010	19:13:03
388	118094	2	1	25.0000	3.8600	MasterCard	21/04/2010	20:23:11
389	118308	4	1	30.0200	3.3000	Debit	23/04/2010	16:56:32
390	118333	4	1	11.0000	0.8800	Debit	23/04/2010	18:05:14
391	118335	2	1	9.0000	0.0100	MasterCard	23/04/2010	18:26:46
392	118377	2	1	3.0000	0.6800	MasterCard	23/04/2010	19:48:11
393	118694	2	1	5.0000	1.2200	MasterCard	26/04/2010	19:21:59
394	118948	2	1	6.2500	0.0300	MasterCard	29/04/2010	12:28:27
395	119002	2	1	50.0000	7.1700	MasterCard	29/04/2010	19:16:00
396	119179	2	1	20.0000	5.3100	MasterCard	30/04/2010	21:04:07
397	119237	4	1	10.0000	1.2400	Debit	01/05/2010	16:51:47
398	119354	2	1	40.0000	7.0600	MasterCard	02/05/2010	16:23:01
399	120059	2	1	22.0400	0.6200	MasterCard	08/05/2010	17:40:15
400	120086	2	1	25.0000	3.5800	MasterCard	08/05/2010	18:18:13
401	120519	4	1	21.0000	2.3500	Debit	11/05/2010	19:11:27
402	120727	4	1	10.2000	2.0100	Debit	13/05/2010	18:22:28
403	120869	5	1	10.0600	1.3000	AME	14/05/2010	19:14:48
404	121415	2	1	20.0000	2.1500	MasterCard	19/05/2010	19:21:24
405	121501	4	1	10.2500	0.1300	Debit	20/05/2010	18:35:53
406	121733	2	1	65.0000	2.8500	MasterCard	22/05/2010	16:59:19
407	121805	2	1	6.7000	0.0300	MasterCard	22/05/2010	20:52:05
408	122534	2	1	25.0000	3.3000	MasterCard	29/05/2010	20:21:38
409	122820	4	1	40.0000	13.2100	Debit	01/06/2010	17:22:20
410	122827	4	1	30.0000	4.9700	Debit	01/06/2010	17:44:49
411	123048	2	1	20.2600	0.1500	MasterCard	03/06/2010	16:36:38

FIGURE 16.4 Noncash Gratuities Isolated

Step 8. Using the "1 Non Cash Gratuity" file, summarize by the TXNID field and total on the PAYAMOUNT_SUM and the NON_CASH_GRATUITY fields.

Call this file "1 Non Cash Grat Summary." This is the continuation of the process to isolate and distinguish cash and noncash items.

Step 9. Perform a summarization on the "1 Tender Summary" file by using TENDERDESC1 as the field to summarize and use the Numeric fields to total option on the fields NO_OF_RECS, PAYAMOUNT_SUM, and GRATUITY_SUM.

Call this new file "1 Tender Types." This provides us with a total of the number of transactions, amounts paid, and gratuities for each tender type as displayed n Figure 16.5.

Step 10. Using the "1 Tender Summary" file, extract from the TENDERDESC1 field each of the seven tender types—AME (American Express), cash, debit, gift certificate, MasterCard, no change, and Visa. This is done by using the Key Value Extraction option or by Direct Extraction using multiple extractions. An example of both methods is displayed in Figures 16.6 and 16.7 for comparison purposes.

	TENDERDESC1	NO_OF_RECS1	NO_OF_RECS_SUM	PAYAMOUNT_SUM_SUM	GRATUITY_SUM_SUM
1	AME	735	735	13,655.7500	1.3000
2	Cash	20524	32092	288,592.7600	0.00
3	Debit	52519	52540	1,006,967.4600	139.9500
4	Gift Certificate	43	44	852.9800	0.00
5	MasterCard	5318	5319	140,576.5600	2,008.2800
6	No Change	4	4	-37.6200	0.00
7	Visa	6712	6712	199,755.9600	0.1100

FIGURE 16.5 Payment Tender Types

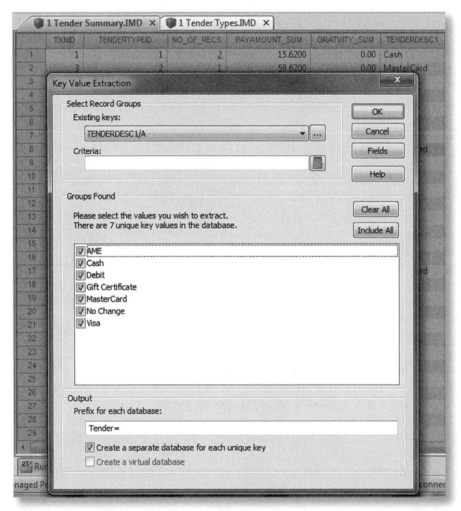

FIGURE 16.6 Key Value Extraction of Tender Types

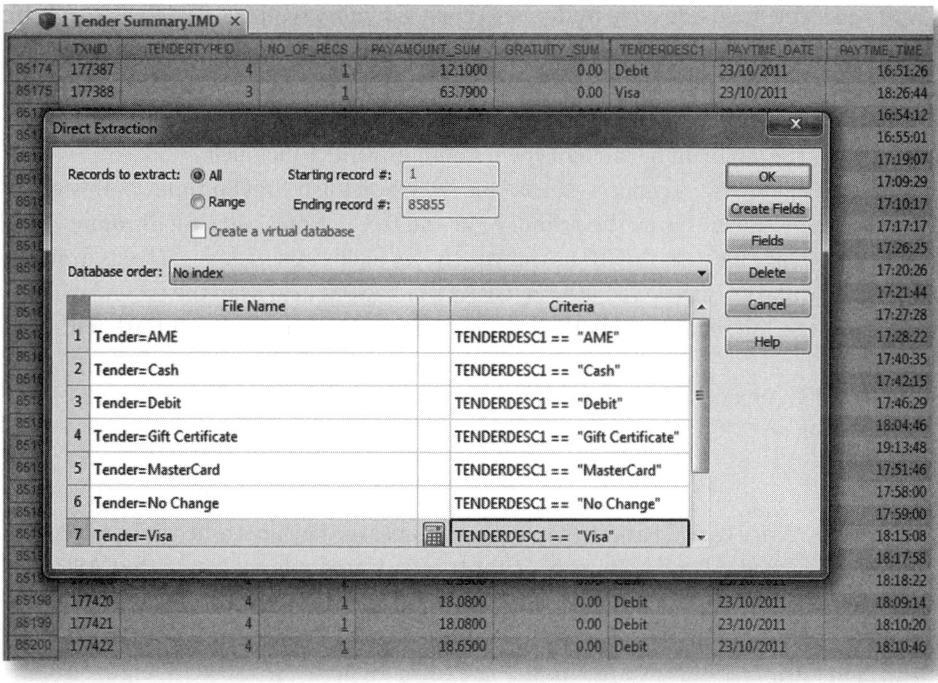

FIGURE 16.7 Direct Extractions of Each Tender Type

A Key Value Extraction is simpler to perform since much less typing is involved. You merely have to select the record groups in the existing keys menu. If the keys do not exist, click on the ". . ." button and then select the field to define the key. In the Groups Found box, all the unique keys are presented to you. They are checked by default and you can uncheck any of those that you do not need to extract into a separate database. In our case, we will leave them all selected as each tender type is needed. In the Output box, the Prefix for each database field is entered as "Tender=." Each file created will commence with that file name. For example, the cash database will be named by IDEA as "Tender= =Cash." If in the prefix, you merely enter Tender, the output file name would be "Tender = Cash." Note that IDEA's = = (or double equal) means an exact match of the whole word(s). The single equal = returns the text entered and any words beginning with that text. An equation of fieldname = "Cash" will return the contents of *cash, cashier, cashiers, cashmere,* and so on in that field. The single versus double equal is only relevant for character fields and not numeric fields. It is also not relevant in file names in our example here, but the author prefers the selected format so that the file name describes the type of equation match and is available at a glance.

Using the direct-extraction method and multiple extractions, note that the entire file name must be typed (a single = is used this time to highlight the difference from the key value extraction file names. The double equal or single equal would be relevant in the equations under the Criteria heading if the TENDERDESC1 field contained longer similar words.

Even if you are using copy-and-paste shortcuts, more typing is obviously required.

Step 11. For each of the output files, append a field name that is the same as the file name used (e.g., for "Tender = =Visa," append the field name "Visa") except for the "Tender= =Cash" file. Use the equation of PAYAMOUNT_SUM – GRATUITY_SUM. This will give us the payment by tender type without gratuities included.

Step 12. Join the "Tender = =Cash" file to "1 Non Cash Grat Summary." Designate the "Tender= =Cash" file as the primary file and the "1 Non Cash Grat Summary" file as the secondary file. Use TXNID as the Match Key Fields and include all fields from the primary file and only the NON_CASH_GRATUITY_SUM field from the secondary file.

Select the "All records" in both files join option and name the file "1 Cash with Non Cash Grat."

Step 13. Append a field named CASH in the "1 Cash with Non Cash Grat file." Use the equation of:

$$\text{PAYAMOUNT\_SUM} + \text{NON\_CASH\_GRATUITY\_SUM}$$

It is necessary to add back the noncash gratuities as they are cashed out or deducted from cash received. After the adjustment, the true cash amounts are now in the CASH field.

Step 14. Append all noncash files (AMX, debit, gift certificate, MasterCard, no change, and Visa) from the key value extraction procedure from step 10 to the "1 Cash with Non Cash Grat" file. Name this file "1 Tender Append" as shown in Figure 16.8.

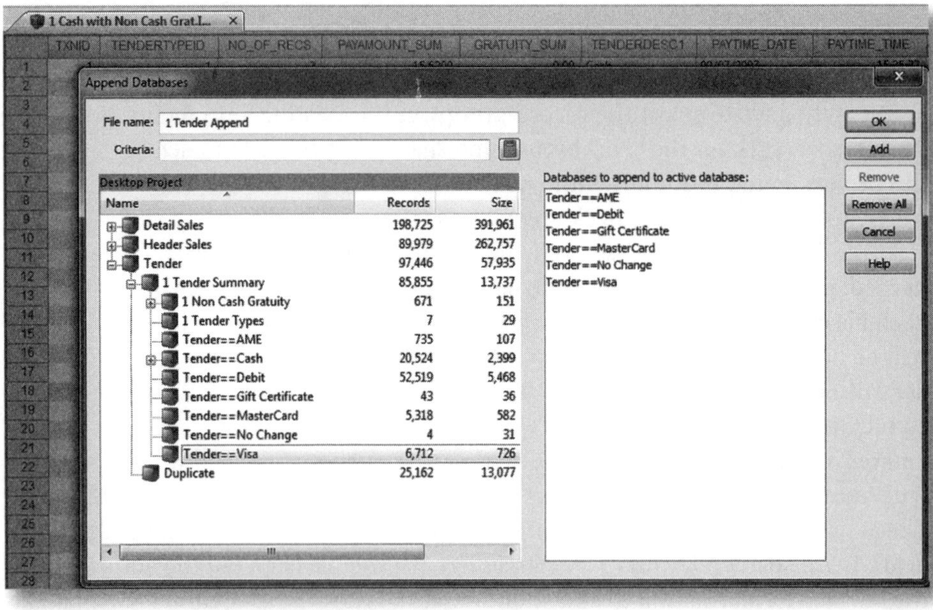

FIGURE 16.8 Combining All Tender Types

Step 15. Summarize on TXNID using the "1 Tender Append" file and total on the numeric fields of PAYAMOUNT_SUM, CASH, AME, DEBIT, GIFT_CERTIFICATE, MASTERCARD, NO_CHANGE, and VISA. Add in the fields to include option PAYTIME_ DATE and PAYTIME_TIME. These two fields may be of potential use for future analysis.

Call this file "1 Tender Summary Analysis."

Step 16. Append the T_CHECK field in the "1 Tender Summary Analysis" file using the equation of:

PAYAMOUNT_SUM_SUM – AME_SUM – CASH_SUM – DEBIT_SUM – GIFT_
CERTIFICATE_SUM – MASTERCARD_SUM – NO_CHANGE_SUM – VISA_SUM

This field checks the integrity of all the previous tender-file calculations we performed. All the resulting records in the T_CHECK (total check) field should be zero to be valid.

Step 17. Using the "1 Header Detail Join" file created in step 4 as the primary file, join it to the "1 Tender Summary Analysis" file created in steps 15 and 16 as the secondary file. Use the join option of "All records" in both files and the match key of TXNID as in Figure 16.9.

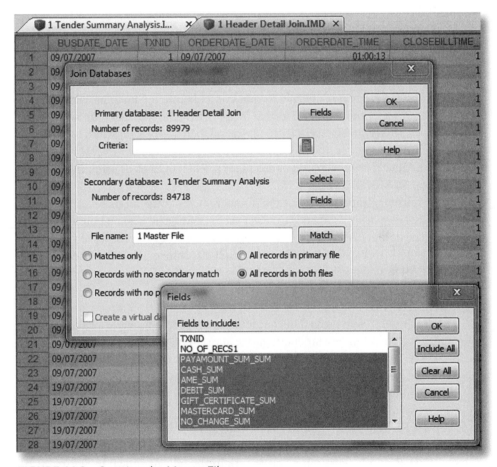

FIGURE 16.9 Creating the Master File

Include all fields from the primary file and, in the secondary file, include the fields of PAYAMOUNT_SUM_SUM, AME_SUM, CASH_SUM, DEBIT_SUM, GIFT_CERTIFICATE_

SUM, MASTERCARD_SUM, NO_CHANGE_SUM, VISA_SUM, PAYTIME_DATE, PAY-
TIME_TIME, and T_CHECK (all fields except TXNID and NO_OF_RECS1).

Name this file "1 Master File."

Step 18. In the "1 Master File," append the following fields along with their related equations.

C_CHECK as a virtual number field with two decimal places using the equation of: TOTAL – PAYAMOUNT_SUM_SUM.

This control-check field ensures that the total bill amount was paid. If the field content is zero, then payment has been received for the order. Where the C_CHECK field is not zero, payment is still outstanding. Explanations are needed for the discrepancies. These are likely phone orders that were never picked up, canceled orders, or given to a patron as promotion, or for incorrectly cooked orders. There were 1,817 records totaling $52,104.18 in data where the field is not zero.

YEAR as a virtual numeric field with 0 decimal places using the equation of: @Year(BUSDATE_DATE).

The @Year function returns the year in numeric format from a date. In this case, the function is applied to the BUSDATE_DATE field.

YEAR_MONTH as a virtual character field with a field length of 8 using the equation of: @Dtoc(BUSDATE_DATE, "YYYY-MM").

This function converts date field format contents into a character field. You can control the output for the converted format by specifying the date mask. In our case, the output displays as a four-digit year with a dash and then a two-digit month in character format (e.g., 2010-01).

FIN_YEAR as a virtual character field with a field length of 10 using the equation of: @FinYear(BUSDATE_DATE, "0331").

The @FinYear function returns a character string of the financial or fiscal year that the date falls within. You need to select the relevant date field and input the fiscal year-end. The output display is in YYYY–YYYY format. We enter the fiscal year-end of March 31; where the BUSDATE_DATE is 21/10/2010 (October 21, 2010), the content of the FIN_YEAR field would be "2010–2011."

QUARTER as a virtual numeric field with zero decimal places uses the equation of: @Qtr(BUSDATE_DATE, "0331").

This function, from a given date, outputs the quarter in numeric format of one to four. Similar to the @FinYear function, the fiscal year-end date must be entered. Where the BUSDATE_DATE is 21/10/2010, the QUARTER field would display 3 as the third quarter based on a March 31 year-end.

These additional fields allow us to perform analysis based on various date milestones such as annually, quarterly, or monthly.

Step 19. Perform a Key Value Extraction using the "1 Master File." Choose STATUS from the existing keys menu in Select Record Groups. Ensure that all four unique key values—C, D, P, and V—contain a checkmark in the box, as shown in Figure 16.10. Select the fields to output by clicking the Fields button. These fields are the ones you will be using for analysis depending on the analysis that is planned; it is at the user's discretion to select fields. We include the following field to ensure that we have all the necessary fields for any potential tests that can be done.

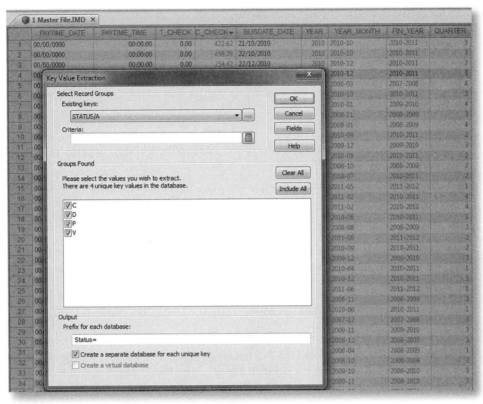

FIGURE 16.10 Key Value Extractions of Status Codes

BUSDATE_DATE, TXNID, STATUS, ORDERDATE_DATE, ORDERDATE_
TIME, CLOSEBILLTIME_DATE, CLOSEBILLTIME_TIME, TOTAL, TAX1,
TAX2, TAX3, BILLNUM, CUSTOMERID, REVENUECENTRE, SECTIONID,
HD_NETAMOUNT, DETAIL_NO_OF_RECS, PRICE_SUM, AMOUNT_SUM,
NETAMOUNT_SUM, ORDERTIME_DATE, ORDERTIME_TIME, AME_SUM,
CASH_SUM, DEBIT_SUM, GIFT_CERTIFICATE_SUM, MASTERCARD_SUM,
NO_CHANGE_SUM, VISA_SUM, PAYAMOUNT_SUM_SUM, C_CHECK, T_
CHECK, PAYTIME_DATE, PAYTIME_TIME, YEAR, YEAR_MONTH, FIN_
YEAR, and QUARTER.

We left out fields that we know for certain are not necessary for our review. For
example, we excluded TAX4 as it was never populated in our file.

The file extracted is automatically named as follows, based on the unique key values
selected and the prefix for each database entered:

- *Status= = C*
- *Status= = D*
- *Status= = P*
- *Status= = V*

The status codes represent the following:

- C = Closed bill
- D = Deleted bill
- P = Parked bill (some files and systems use the letter *P* to designate promotional items)
- V = Void bill

Step 20. For only the "Status = = C" file created in the last step, append the following fields and equations.

$$\text{S\_CHECK: PAYAMOUNT\_SUM\_SUM} - \text{AME\_SUM}$$
$$- \text{CASH\_SUM} - \text{DEBIT\_SUM} - \text{GIFT\_CERTIFICATE\_SUM}$$
$$- \text{MASTERCARD\_SUM} - \text{NO\_CHANGE\_SUM} - \text{VISA\_SUM}$$

Check to ensure that all tender types for each bill (TXNID) total to the amount paid. All amounts in the field should net to zero. There are no records with nonzero amounts.

$$\text{CASH\_ONLY: @If(TOTAL = CASH\_SUM, HD\_NETAMOUNT, 0)}$$

This field populates the CASH_ONLY field with the amount from the "Header Sales" file before taxes (HD_NETAMOUNT). The formula populates the field if the total amount is equal to the debit total and the debit summary from the "Tender" file. If not, a zero amount is entered.

$$\text{DEBIT\_ONLY: @If(TOTAL = DEBIT\_SUM, HD\_NETAMOUNT, 0)}$$

This field populates the DEBIT_ONLY field with the amount from the "Header Sales" file before taxes (HD_NETAMOUNT). The formula populates the field if the total amount is equal to the debit total and the debit summary from the "Tender" file. If not, a zero amount is entered.

$$\text{CREDIT\_ONLY: @If(TOTAL = AME\_SUM .OR. TOTAL}$$
$$= \text{MASTERCARD\_SUM .OR. TOTAL = VISA\_SUM, HD\_NETAMOUNT, 0)}$$

This field populates the CREDIT_ONLY field with the amount from the "Header Sales" file before taxes (HD_NETAMOUNT). The formula populates the field if the total of any credit card amount is equal to the credit total and the credit summary from the "Tender" file. If not, a zero amount is entered.

$$\text{BLEND\_OTHER\_ONLY: @If(CASH\_ONLY = 0 .AND. CREDIT\_ONLY}$$
$$= 0 \text{ .AND. DEBIT\_ONLY = 0, HD\_NETAMOUNT, 0)}$$

If there are no amounts in the cash, credit, or debit columns, then the amount must be a blended payment and the amount before taxes is returned or a zero is populated.

$$\text{CASH\_COUNT: @If(CASH\_ONLY < > 0, 1, 0)}$$

This field enters a count of 1 if the CASH_ONLY field contains an amount. If there is no amount, a zero is entered into this field. This field will provide us the number of cash transactions in a future analysis.

DEBIT_COUNT: @If(DEBIT_ONLY < > 0, 1, 0)

This field enters a count of 1 if the DEBIT_ONLY field contains an amount. If there is no amount, a zero is entered into this field. This field will provide us the number of debit card transactions in a future analysis.

CREDIT_COUNT: @If(CREDIT_ONLY < > 0, 1, 0)

This field enters a count of 1 if the CREDIT_ONLY field contains an amount. If there is no amount, a zero is entered into this field. This field will provide us the number of credit card transactions in a future analysis.

BLEND_COUNT: @If(BLEND_OTHER_ONLY < > 0, 1, 0)

This field enters a count of 1 if the BLEND_OTHER_ONLY field contains an amount. If there is no amount, a zero is entered into this field. This field will provide us the number of blended payment transactions in a future analysis.

Gap Detection

In testing for completeness, we can use the gap detection feature of IDEA to determine if there are any missing items in the unique transaction identification numbers in the TXNID field. Gap detection works in numeric fields, character fields, and date fields. In our case, we will be applying it on our numeric TXNID field.

IDEA has a maximum limit of 10,000 gaps. If there are more than 10,000 gaps, only the first 10,000 are displayed. It is not expected that an auditor would be interested in examining gaps of more than 10,000. However, for a large POS-system database there may be more than 10,000 gaps if zapper software is used to delete many sale transactions.

From the final results shown in Figure 16.14 you can see there are 88,487 gaps.

Step 1. Using the "1 Master File," summarize by the TXNID field to eliminate any potential duplicate transaction identification numbers. In addition, summarization indexes and sequences the TXNID field so gaps may be determined. Name the new file "Gap Summary."

Step 2. If we use the Gap Detection feature built into IDEA, we merely have to select the feature and then select TXNID as the field to use, as in Figure 16.11.

Instead of using the built-in Gap-Detection feature, for the second step we will add three fields to manually calculate any missing items.

Append these fields with their related equations.

TXNID_FROM: @If(@GetNextValue("TXNID") < >0, @If(TXNID = @GetNextValue("TXNID") − 1, 0, TXNID + 1), 0)

The @GetNextValue function obtains the next value in the selected field. This formula uses the next value in the TXNID field to check if the next value minus one is equal to the current value. If it is equal, then it inputs a zero. If it does not equal, then the TXNID plus one is input in the new field. This formula is applied only if it passes the first test of the next value not being zero. If the next value is zero, it would input a zero in the TXNID_FROM field.

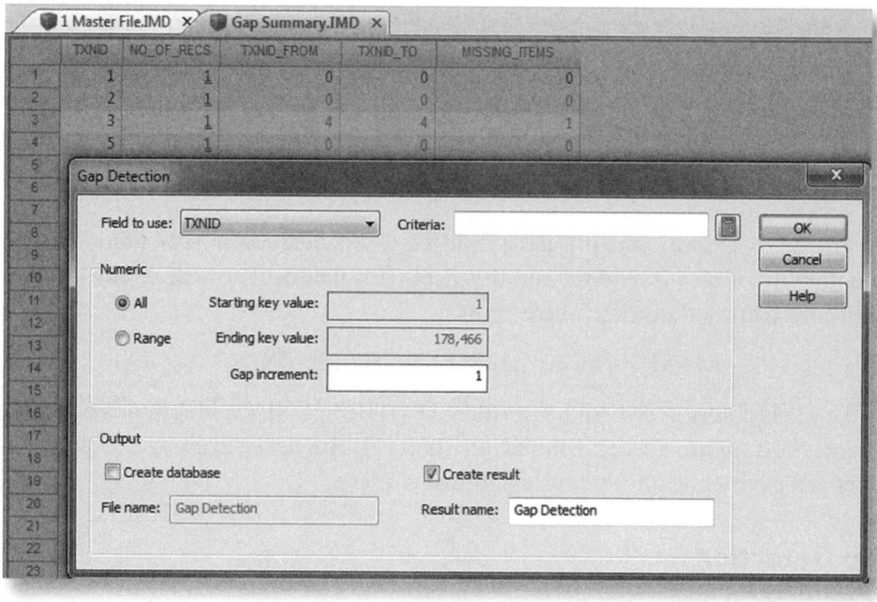

FIGURE 16.11 IDEA Gap Detection

TXNID_TO: @If(TXNID = @GetNextValue("TXNID") – 1, 0, @If(@ GetNextValue("TXNID") – 1 = –1, 0, @GetNextValue("TXNID") – 1))

This formula tests if the current value is equal to the next value less one, then a zero is input in the TXNID_TO field. If it does not meet this criterion, then test to see if the next value less one is equal to minus one. If it is equal to minus one, then a zero is input. If it does not equal minus 1, then it applies the next value less 1 in the TXNID_TO field.

MISSING_ITEMS: TXNID_TO – TXNID_FROM + @If(TXNID_FROM = 0, 0, 1)

Once we have the contents of both the TXNID_FROM and the TXNID_TO fields, we can calculate the number of missing items. If the TXNID_FROM field contains a zero, then zero is added to the difference of the TXNID_TO and the TXNID_FROM fields. If the TXNID_FROM field is not equal to zero, then one is added to the difference of the TXNID_TO and the TXNID_FROM fields. Refer to the results in Figure 16.12.

Step 3. From the "Gap Summary" file, create a new temporary file by direct extraction using the equation of @Recno( ) > 0 .AND. TXNID_FROM < > 0. Call this new file "Temp Summary Gap." This step extracts all records where the TXNID_FROM field is not zero and the record number is greater than zero, as shown in the results in Figure 16.13.

Step 4. Perform an extraction from the "Temp Summary Gap" file by using the equation TXNID_TO > 0. Select as fields to include: TXNID_FROM, TXNID_TO, and MISSING_ITEMS. Name this file "1Master File—Gap." Perform a Control Total on the MISSING_ITEMS field to total the numbers in that field, as displayed in Figure 16.14.

	TXNID	NO_OF_RECS	TXNID_FROM	TXNID_TO	MISSING_ITEMS
53	61	1	0	0	0
54	62	1	63	65	3
55	66	1	67	67	1
56	68	1	0	0	0
57	69	1	0	0	0
58	70	1	71	71	1
59	72	1	0	0	0
60	73	1	0	0	0
61	74	1	75	77	3
62	78	1	79	79	1
63	80	1	0	0	0
64	81	1	0	0	0
65	82	1	0	0	0
66	83	1	0	0	0
67	84	1	85	85	1
68	86	1	0	0	0

(Gap Summary.IMD ✕)

FIGURE 16.12 Fields Appended for Manual Gap Calculation

	TXNID	NO_OF_RECS	TXNID_FROM	TXNID_TO	MISSING_ITEMS
1	3	1	4	4	1
2	11	1	12	12	1
3	28	1	29	29	1
4	39	1	40	40	1
5	50	1	51	51	1
6	52	1	53	53	1
7	57	1	58	58	1
8	59	1	60	60	1
9	62	1	63	65	3
10	66	1	67	67	1
11	70	1	71	71	1
12	74	1	75	77	3
13	78	1	79	79	1

(Temp Summary Gap.IMD ✕)

FIGURE 16.13 Intermediate Step for Gap Calculation

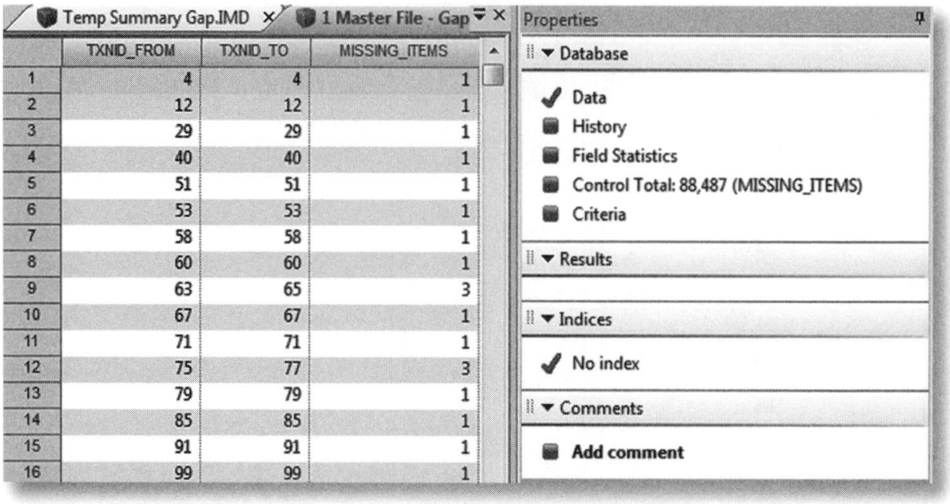

	TXNID_FROM	TXNID_TO	MISSING_ITEMS	
1	4	4	1	
2	12	12	1	
3	29	29	1	
4	40	40	1	
5	51	51	1	
6	53	53	1	
7	58	58	1	
8	60	60	1	
9	63	65	3	
10	67	67	1	
11	71	71	1	
12	75	77	3	
13	79	79	1	
14	85	85	1	
15	91	91	1	
16	99	99	1	

Properties ▼

▼ Database
- ✓ Data
- ■ History
- ■ Field Statistics
- ■ Control Total: 88,487 (MISSING_ITEMS)
- ■ Criteria

▼ Results

▼ Indices
- ✓ No index

▼ Comments
- ■ Add comment

FIGURE 16.14 Results of the Manual Gap Calculation

While we have conclusive evidence that there are 88,487 transaction identification numbers missing and that suggests sales may have been deleted, there is not enough evidence to arrive at that conclusion. Maybe there is some legitimate reason why the numbering system had so many gaps. We need to perform additional analysis.

Analysis of POS Data

Now we are ready to start analyzing the data sets we created and modified by appending necessary fields.

We will produce sales analysis files by fiscal year, quarterly, and monthly for the "Status == C" file. This file contains all the closed bills, meaning that the transactions were completed.

Financial (Fiscal) Year Reconciliation

We specified earlier, in the @function, that the fiscal year-end is March 31. The data starts on July 9, 2007 and ends on November 1, 2011. For financial year 2007 to 2008 we have only nine months of data, and for the 2011 to 2012 financial year we have only seven months. For 2008 to 2009, 2009 to 2010, and 2010 to 2011, we have complete years and can reconcile sales to the trial balance for the year.

Summarize on the FIN_YEAR field and total on the following fields of TOTAL, TAX1, TAX2, TAX3, HD_NETAMOUNT, PAYAMOUNT_SUM_SUM, CASH_ONLY, CREDIT_ONLY, DEBIT_ONLY, BLEND_OTHER_ONLY, CASH_COUNT, DEBIT_COUNT, and BLEND_COUNT. Name the new file "Fiscal Year Sales Summary," as displayed in Figure 16.15.

The HD_NETAMOUNT_SUM field contains the sales totals for income-statement purposes, as these amounts are net sales that exclude taxes.

	FIN_YEAR	NO_OF_RECS	TOTAL_SUM	TAX1_SUM	TAX2_SUM	TAX3_SUM	HD_NETAMOUNT_SUM	PAYAMOUNT_SUM_SUM_SUM
1	2007-2008	15240	317,395.0600	15,839.1800	22,287.0000	0.00	279,268.08	317,395.0600
2	2008-2009	18898	373,451.0300	16,554.4700	26,395.0100	0.00	330,501.55	373,451.0300
3	2009-2010	17720	338,546.6000	15,017.9700	23,924.7100	0.00	299,603.92	338,546.6000
4	2010-2011	18310	362,693.3400	16,084.2300	25,627.1400	0.00	320,981.97	362,693.3400
5	2011-2012	14599	258,277.8200	11,455.7600	18,236.3200	0.00	228,585.74	258,277.8200

FIGURE 16.15   Fiscal Year Sales Summary

Quarterly Reconciliation

Summarize on the FIN_YEAR and QUARTER fields and total on the following fields: TOTAL, TAX1, TAX2, TAX3, HD_NETAMOUNT, PAYAMOUNT_SUM_SUM, CASH_ONLY, CREDIT_ONLY, DEBIT_ONLY, BLEND_OTHER_ONLY, CASH_COUNT, DEBIT_COUNT, and BLEND_COUNT. Name the new file "Quarterly Sales Summary." The financial year and quarterly amounts are based on our specifying the year-end as March 31 in step 18.

The HD_NETAMOUNT_SUM field contents may be used to reconcile sales by quarter.

Monthly Reconciliation

Summarize on the YEAR_MONTH field and total on the following fields of TOTAL, TAX1, TAX2, TAX3, HD_NETAMOUNT, PAYAMOUNT_SUM_SUM, CASH_ONLY, CREDIT_ONLY, DEBIT_ONLY, BLEND_OTHER_ONLY, CASH_COUNT, DEBIT_COUNT, and BLEND_COUNT. Name the new file "Monthly Sales Summary."

The HD_NETAMOUNT_SUM field contents may be used to reconcile sales by month.

Reconciliation—whether by month, quarter, or year—assures us that the raw POS data we obtained matches the reports that the POS system generates for financial-statement purposes. Any anomalies detected in the data may lead us to conclude that the financial-statement information contains errors or is incomplete.

Tender Analysis

Analyzing the tender type of payments tells us how customers settle their bills and in what volume for each tender type. As cash is always the most difficult to implement tight controls over, we would like to know how much cash is collected in relation to noncash collected. Our initial assumption is that there are no issues with noncash tenders. We will also create a file for credit card payments in case we later perform such analyses as credit card payments versus cash payments or credit card payments versus debit card payments.

Step 1. Open up the "Status = = C" file created in step 19 from the file preparation section. Summarize on PAYTIME_DATE and total fields CASH_SUM, AME_SUM, DEBIT_SUM, GIFT_CERTIFICATE_SUM, MASTERCARD_SUM, NO_CHANGE_SUM, and VISA_SUM. This gives us all completed transactions that are then totaled by date on each of the different types of tenders. Name this file "Summarize by Pay Date of Tenders."

Step 2. Append the following fields with the related equations as shown in Figure 16.16.

CREDIT_CARDS: AME_SUM_SUM
+ MASTERCARD_SUM_SUM + VISA_SUM_SUM

This creates a field with the three types of credit cards accepted by the business.

NON_CASH: AME_SUM_SUM + DEBIT_SUM_SUM
+ GIFT_CERTIFICATE_SUM_SUM + MASTERCARD_SUM_SUM
+ NO_CHANGE_SUM_SUM + VISA_SUM_SUM

In addition to credit cards, debit card amounts, amounts from gift certificates, and no-change tenders are accounted as noncash.

PAYTIME_DATE_YEAR: @Year(PAYTIME_DATE)

We extract just the year from the date field into a new field.

PAYTIME_DATE_MONTH: @Month(PAYTIME_DATE)

We extract from the date field just the month into a new field.

YEAR_MONTH: Virtual Character field with a length of 10 for @Str(PAYTIME_DATE_YEAR, 4, 0) + "-" + @Str(PAYTIME_DATE_MONTH, 2, 0)

The @Str function converts a numeric field to a character field. For the PAYTIME_DATE_YEAR field, we defined the number of characters to output as four and the number of decimal places as zero. We need four characters as the year has four positions. Similarly, in the PAYTIME_DATE_MONTH field, the month requires two positions and zero decimals.

We create—for ease of indexing and summarization—in a single field, the year and the month, which in this example is in the format 2011-10 that we will use in a subsequent step.

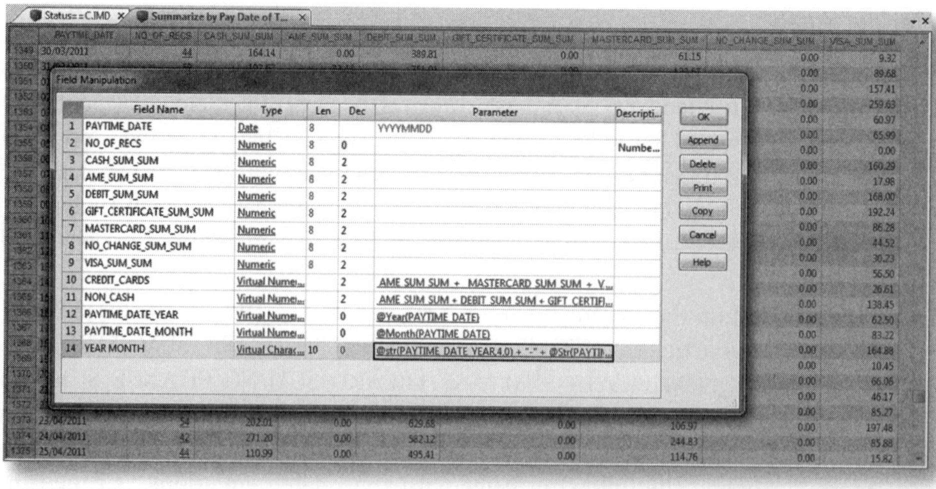

FIGURE 16.16 Summarized by Pay Date of Tender with Appended Fields

Step 3. Perform a summarization by YEAR_MONTH as shown in Figure 16.17. Total on the fields: CASH_SUM_SUM, AME_SUM_SUM, DEBIT_SUM_SUM, GIFT_CERTIFICATE_SUM_SUM, MASTERCARD_SUM_SUM, NO_CHANGE_SUM_SUM, VISA_SUM_SUM, CREDIT_CARDS, and NON_CASH.

Fields to include are PAYTIME_DATE_YEAR and PAYTIME_DATE_MONTH. Name the file "Summarize Tenders by Month." We now have a file that totals by month all the tenders.

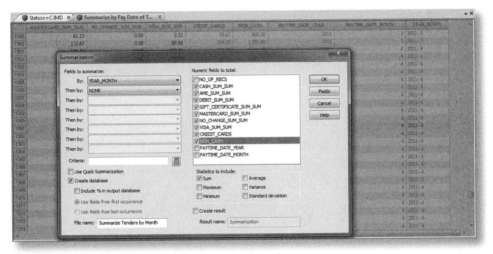

FIGURE 16.17 Summarize Tender Types by Month

Our data commenced in July 2007 and ended in November 2011. November was only a partial month. We can use a starting point of October 2007 and an ending point of October 2011 to capture complete months.

Step 4. Produce a chart within IDEA to compare between cash tenders and non-cash tenders. Using YEAR_MONTH >= "2007-10" .AND. YEAR_MONTH <= "2011-10" as the criteria, we can compare full months with the latest full months available. In the Chart box, select YEAR_MONTH as the X field. In the Y field(s) area, click to insert a checkmark for the CASH_SUM_SUM_SUM and NON_CASH_SUM fields. Select line as the graph type, with a legend on the bottom of the chart. Give "Cash vs Non Cash" as the chart title. Type "Month" as the X-axis title and "Amount" as the Y-axis title, as in Figure 16.18.

In Figure 16.19, the top line represents monthly noncash tender amounts and the bottom line represents monthly cash tenders. Noncash tenders significantly exceed cash tenders on a monthly basis. From the beginning, cash tenders declined monthly until about October 2008, and then cash tenders seem to be holding steady.

The spread between the two is less for the months starting in April 2011, with the exception of May 2011.

A similar type of chart can be produced to compare cash, debit cards, and credit cards, as they are the main tenders used. Debit is the most-used form of payment and cash seems to be the least used. Starting in April 2011 there was a surge of cash payments that surpassed credit card payments, as shown in Figure 16.20.

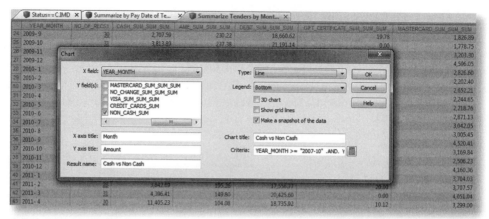

FIGURE 16.18 Preparing the Chart

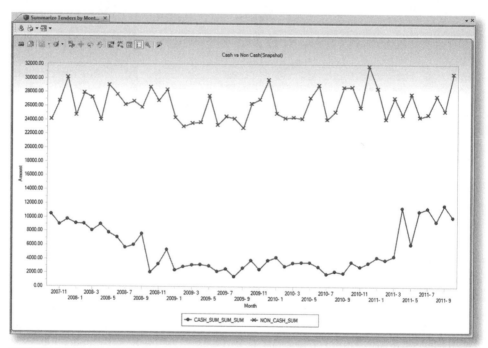

FIGURE 16.19 Cash versus Noncash Analysis Chart

Since debit cards are the favored tender type, we will analyze the monthly debit card payment trend and compare it to other years for the same months. We will also compare noncash payments.

Step 5. Open the "Summarize Tender by Month" file created in Step 3. Extract the following 4 files using their respective equations to get 12 months, from October of the current year to September of the next year. Since we had specified 2-character positions for the month in step 2 in the @Str(PAYTIME_DATE_MONTH, 2, 0) function, where the month is a single digit, a space needed to be placed in front. In our case for the equations below, a space should precede the 9 immediately following the dash.

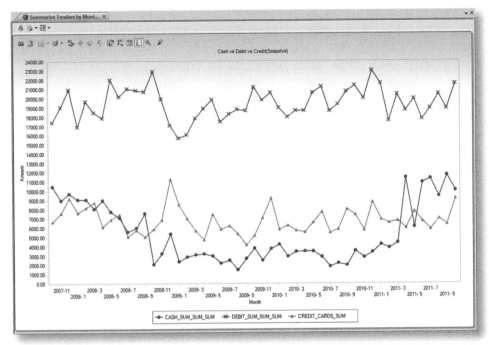

FIGURE 16.20 Cash versus Debit Card versus Credit Card Analysis

"2007-10 to 2008-9": YEAR_MONTH >= "2007-10" .AND.
YEAR_MONTH <= "2008- 9"

When the "2007-10 to 2008-9" file is created, change the names of the fields from CASH_SUM_SUM_SUM to CASH_2007_2008, DEBIT_SUM_SUM_SUM to DEBIT_2007_2008; CREDIT_CARDS_SUM to CREDIT_CARDS_2007_2008; and NON_CASH_SUM to NON_CASH_2007_2008.

"2008-10 to 2009-9": YEAR_MONTH >= "2008-10" .AND.
YEAR_MONTH <= "2009- 9"

When the "2008-10 to 2009-9" file is created, change the name of the fields from CASH_SUM_SUM_SUM to CASH_2008_2009; DEBIT_SUM_SUM_SUM to DEBIT_2008_2009; CREDIT_CARDS_SUM to CREDIT_CARDS_2008_2009; and NON_CASH_SUM to NON_CASH_2008_2009.

"2009-10 to 2010-9": YEAR_MONTH >= "2009-10" .AND.
YEAR_MONTH <= "2010- 9"

When the "2009-10 to 2010-9" file is created, change the name of the fields from CASH_SUM_SUM_SUM to CASH_2009_2010; DEBIT_SUM_SUM_SUM to DEBIT_2009_2010; CREDIT_CARDS_SUM to CREDIT_CARDS_2009_2010; and NON_CASH_SUM to NON_CASH_2009_2010.

"2010-10 to 2011-9": YEAR_MONTH >= "2010-10".AND.
YEAR_MONTH <= "2011- 9"

When the "2010-10 to 2011-9" file is created, change the name of the fields from CASH_SUM_SUM_SUM to CASH_2010_2011; DEBIT_SUM_SUM_SUM to DEBIT_2010_2011; CREDIT_CARDS_SUM to CREDIT_CARDS_2010_2011; and NON_CASH_SUM to NON_CASH_2010_2011.

We now have four separate files broken down to 12-month periods starting from October. We also renamed the tender fields to associate the proper year to each of the files.

Step 6. We now need to join the four files that contain 12 months of information together. For this, we have to join two files together and then use the resulting file to join the third file, and, finally, that resulting file will join with the fourth file.

For the first join, we use the "2007-10 to 2008-9" file as the primary file and the "2008-10 to 2009-9" file as the secondary file. For the primary file, the fields to include are YEAR_MONTH, CASH_2007_2008, DEBIT_2007_2008, CREDIT_CARDS_2007_2008, NON_CASH_2007_2008, PAYTIME_DATE_YEAR, and PAYTIME_DATE_MONTH. While a number of join options would provide the same results, we will use the Join using the "Matches only" option. Fields to include from the secondary file are: CASH_2008_2009, DEBIT_2008_2009, CREDIT_CARDS_2008_2009 and NON_CASH_2008_2009. Make the match keys as PAYTIME_DATE_MONTH for both primary and secondary files. Name the file "2007-2009."

Using the "2007-2009" file as the primary, join the "2009-10 to 2010-9" file as the secondary file to it. This time, accept the default selection of all for the fields to include from the primary file, and only include the CASH_2009_2010, DEBIT_2009_2010, CREDIT_CARDS_2009_2010, and NON_CASH_2009_2010 fields from the secondary file. Use PAYTIME_DATE_MONTH as the match keys for both primary and secondary files. Join using the "Matches only" option. Name the file "2007-2010."

Finally, using the "2007-2010" file as the primary file, join the secondary file of "2010-10 to 2011-9." Again, use all the fields to include from the primary file and only include the CASH_2010_2011, DEBIT_2010_2011, CREDIT_CARDS_2010_2011, and NON_CASH_2010_2011 fields from the secondary file. Use PAYTIME_DATE_MONTH as the match key for both primary and secondary files. Join using the "Matches only" option. Call this new file "2007-2011."

We now have a file where for each month, all the tender amounts for each year are in one record.

Step 7. Using the newly created file "2007-2011" that contains four full years of data, index the YEAR_MONTH field by ascending order even if it is already in the correct order. We want October to be the starting point in record number 1 and to end up with September as the ending point in record number 12.

This will make the index available in the database order pull-down menu for the next step—exporting the IDEA database into Excel, as shown in Figure 16.21. Exporting with an index will fix that particular order in Excel. Import the Excel file back into IDEA. This fixes the physical order of the records in the file. If all the default filenames were accepted in both the export and import, the newly created file should be automatically named "2007-2011-Database."

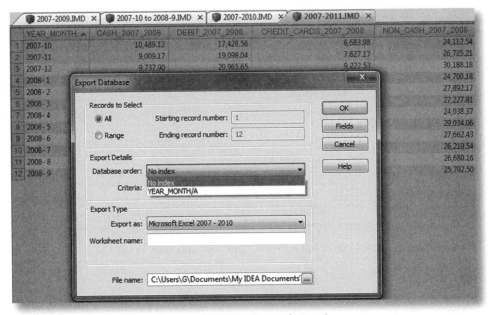

FIGURE 16.21 Exporting the Database to Microsoft Excel

Step 8. Access the Chart option in IDEA. Complete the following information in the Chart box as in Figure 16.22:

- *X* field: PAYTIME_DATE_MONTH
- *Y* field(s):   Check off all four cash fields, such as CASH_2009_2010
- *X* axis title: Month
- *Y* axis title: Amount
- Result name: Cash for same months
- Type: Line
- Legend: Bottom
- 3D chart: Uncheck this box
- Chart title: Cash for same months.

The type, legend, and 3D-chart selections can be adjusted to personal preferences.

You can see from Figure 16.23 that cash for the 2007 to 2008 periods slowly declined. For the two 12-month periods—2008 to 2009 and 2009 to 2010—cash amounts for most of the months were very close together. In fact, for October 2010 to March 2011, the cash tender trend followed the last 2 years' trend and then jumped in April 2011, declined somewhat in May 2011, and then increased for the rest of the year. Did this strange occurrence also take place with noncash tenders? Did it happen with debit cards, too? Let us continue with the analysis.

You can chart different types of analyses similar to comparing cash amounts for the same months in different years from the same "2007-2011-Database," as in Figure 16.24. The chart for the noncash comparison and another chart for the debit card comparison

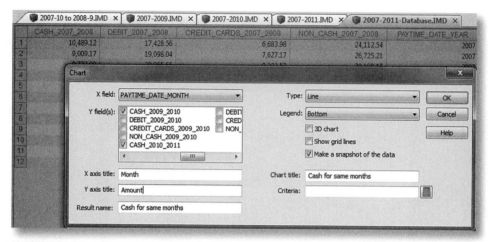

FIGURE 16.22   Chart Preparation for Monthly Cash Analysis

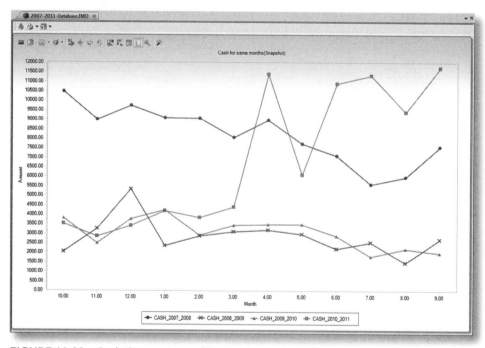

FIGURE 16.23   Cash Comparison of Same Months in Different Years

are shown in Figures 16.25 and 16.26. Debit card transactions should be one of the selections to review, as it is the tender used most frequently.

For all four years' 12-month periods, we can see noncash tenders moving very tightly together each month. For the month of November 2007, 2008, 2009, and 2010, there was virtually the same total amount of noncash tenders. Clearly, noncash tenders were consistently steady and did not vary wildly like the cash tenders.

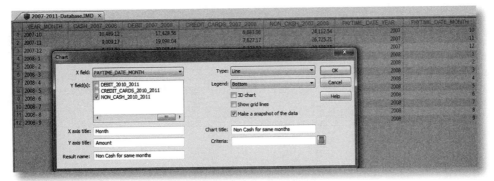

FIGURE 16.24 Chart Preparation for Monthly Noncash Analysis

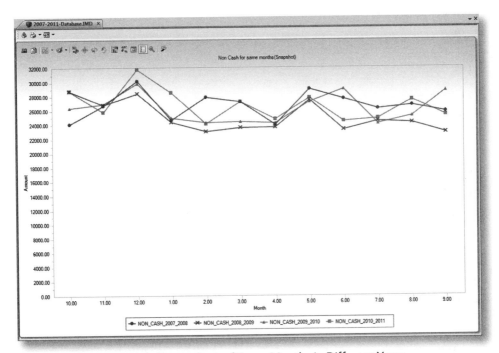

FIGURE 16.25 Noncash Comparison of Same Months in Different Years

Debit card tenders also follow a similarly tight trend for each month in different years, as seen in Figure 16.26. It seems that cash payments are an anomaly.

The anomalies did not happen in isolation, but were caused by intervention—or maybe it is more correct to say, prevented intervention. Data was obtained from the POS system during an unannounced visit by the taxation authorities on April 4, 2011. It appears that the surprise visit allowed that taxation authorities to obtain the data before there was an opportunity to delete cash sales for three days prior to the visit.

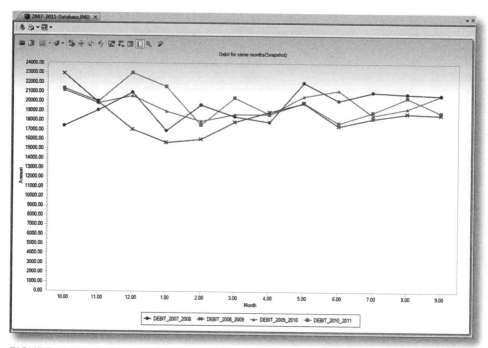

FIGURE 16.26 Debit Card Comparison of Same Months in Different Years

The chart in Figure 16.27 shows the cash sales and noncash sales (debit cards and credit cards) of one week prior to the visit and one week subsequent to the visit. The data is displayed in Figure 16.28.

Sales paid by a multiple of tender types (blended sales) are ignored on the chart due to immateriality. The chart in Figure 16.19 showed that on a monthly basis, noncash tenders always exceeded cash tenders significantly. When we started to compare each of the tenders on their own by the same months for different years, we saw how cash tender differed. Noncash tender and debit card tender were very similar for the same months in different years. It was only cash tender that had wild swings.

With the exception of a few days before the unannounced visit, the noncash sales were always higher than the cash sales. It can be concluded that zapping had not yet taken place for those few days before the taxation authorities had obtained a copy of the POS data. Cash sales declined immediately after the visit, suggesting that the deletion of cash sales had resumed. As can be seen in Figure 16.23, cash sales dropped for May 2011. The taxation authorities, after obtaining the data on April 4, 2011, left and did not have much contact with the restaurant. As such, they went back to deleting cash sales for the month of May. Cash sales increased in June 2011 as the taxation authorities returned that month to continue their audit.

The tax authorities were onsite observing the restaurant's operations and noting the number of customers patronizing the business. Invigilation took place on June 11

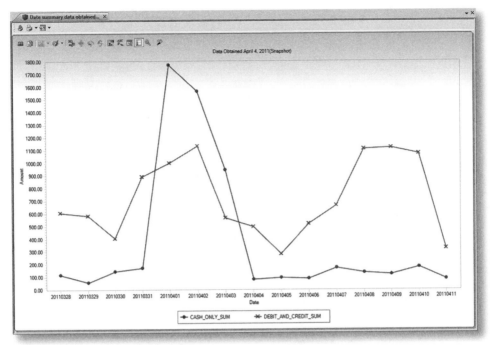

FIGURE 16.27   Chart of Data Obtained on April 4, 2011

	PAYTIME_DATE	NO_OF_RECS	CASH_ONLY_SUM	DEBIT_AND_CREDIT_SUM	BLEND_OTHER_ONLY_SUM	CASH_COUNT_SUM	DEBIT_CREDIT_COUNT_SUM	BLEND_COUNT_SUM
1	28/03/2011	39	115.89	606.42	0.00	10	29	0
2	29/03/2011	42	57.79	583.75	0.00	4	38	0
3	30/03/2011	44	145.22	407.25	0.00	11	33	0
4	31/03/2011	59	171.36	889.95	0.00	11	48	0
5	01/04/2011	145	1,771.99	1,000.40	7.95	91	53	1
6	02/04/2011	141	1,564.30	1,134.05	43.60	76	64	1
7	03/04/2011	75	945.05	567.90	0.00	43	32	0
8	04/04/2011	39	80.73	494.77	0.00	9	30	0
9	05/04/2011	27	94.83	281.23	0.00	9	18	0
10	06/04/2011	42	85.77	518.00	0.00	10	32	0
11	07/04/2011	57	170.35	664.75	0.00	15	42	0
12	08/04/2011	75	134.10	1,108.45	0.00	10	65	0
13	09/04/2011	70	120.50	1,118.45	8.95	9	60	1
14	10/04/2011	66	176.30	1,073.05	0.00	13	53	0
15	11/04/2011	28	83.65	324.60	0.00	8	20	0

FIGURE 16.28   Daily Data Prior to and after April 4, 2011

to 15, 2011 and on June 21 to 24, 2011. The data showed no gaps in the TXNID field during the period of June 21 to 24, 2011. For the period of June 11 to 15, 2011, there were also no gaps for those dates with the exception of June 15, 2011. The data showed 38 TXNID numbers missing for June 15, 2011.

While performing the observations, the auditors had obtained a closing report after the lunchtime rush. The closing report was printed at 13:41 and contained the information in Table 16.1.

TABLE 16.1   Closing Report June 15, 2011 at 13:41

Tender	Quantity	Amount
Cash	6	$36.94
Visa	1	10.12
Debit	4	34.99
Total	11	$82.05

An examination of the data for transactions before 13:41 for June 15, 2011, shows the details presented in Table 16.2 and Figure 16.29.

TABLE 16.2   Payment Data for June 15, 2011

Tender	Quantity	Amount
Cash	2	$27.29
Visa	1	10.12
Debit	4	34.99
Total	7	$72.40

	TXNID	PAYTIME_DATE	PAYTIME_TIME	PAYAMOUNT_SUM_SUM	CASH_SUM	VISA_SUM	DEBIT_SUM	AME_SUM	MASTERCARD_SUM
1	164258	15/06/2011	11:56:40	15.4900	0.00	0.00	15.49	0.00	0.00
2	164260	15/06/2011	12:34:10	17.9700	17.97	0.00	0.00	0.00	0.00
3	164261	15/06/2011	12:35:12	6.5000	0.00	0.00	6.50	0.00	0.00
4	164262	15/06/2011	12:44:46	10.1200	0.00	10.12	0.00	0.00	0.00
5	164263	15/06/2011	12:47:19	6.5000	0.00	0.00	6.50	0.00	0.00
6	164264	15/06/2011	12:47:26	6.5000	0.00	0.00	6.50	0.00	0.00
7	164268	15/06/2011	13:40:00	9.3200	9.32	0.00	0.00	0.00	0.00
8	164270	15/06/2011	14:35:50	2.5200	0.00	0.00	2.52	0.00	0.00
9	164271	15/06/2011	15:23:06	21.6400	0.00	0.00	21.64	0.00	0.00
10	164273	15/06/2011	15:40:12	21.5900	0.00	21.59	0.00	0.00	0.00
11	164274	15/06/2011	16:02:05	8.1900	0.00	0.00	8.19	0.00	0.00
12	164275	15/06/2011	15:52:54	35.2000	0.00	0.00	35.20	0.00	0.00

FIGURE 16.29   Tender Payment Data for June 15, 2011

Subsequent to the auditors leaving the premises, 38 sales were zapped, including 4 sales that were made before 13:41 and for which a closing report was generated and retained by the auditors. The person doing the zapping either had forgotten that the auditors had a copy of the closing report or was not given this information!

During the observation period, it was noted that cash as a percentage of total sales was almost 60 percent; the reported average was 10 percent and increased to 30 percent after the audit started.

Backup Data Analysis

A backup data folder was found with data tables that contained information from July 2007 to October 2007, as shown in Table 16.3. The month of July contained 14 days of data while the month of October had 1 day of data. The backup data (BU) was compared to the live or production data (Prod) in the table that follows. All tenders from both the backup and production files were identical with the exception of the cash tender. For the 76-day period, there was a cash variance of $68,036 between the backup data and the production data files. The backup file had the true sales information and confirmed that the zapper program only deletes cash sales and no other types of tender sales.

TABLE 16.3 Backup Data: July 2007 to October 1, 2007

Month	Cash BU	Cash Prod	Credit BU	Credit Prod	Debit BU	Debit Pro	Blended BU	Blended Prod
July	19,153	5,344	2,673	2,673	8,465	8,465	3	3
August	36,808	10,293	6,434	6,434	19,222	19,222	35	35
September	35,985	8,888	6,160	6,160	17,056	17,056	121	121
October	938	323	134	134	379	379	0	0

The training data tables were examined and additional evidence of zapping was found. These tables were not actually pseudo-transactions used for training purpose for new users of the POS system. These particular tables stored prezapped data.

The taxation authorities made no mention of the training data tables in their very detailed working papers provided to the taxpayer. They had disclosed all the other anomalies previously mentioned. It was likely that the taxation authorities already had such an overwhelming case that they did not need to perform additional analysis. Normally, training data tables do not reveal any information of interest. The point to be made here is that low-risk files should not always be overlooked in the interest of time savings depending on your audit objectives.

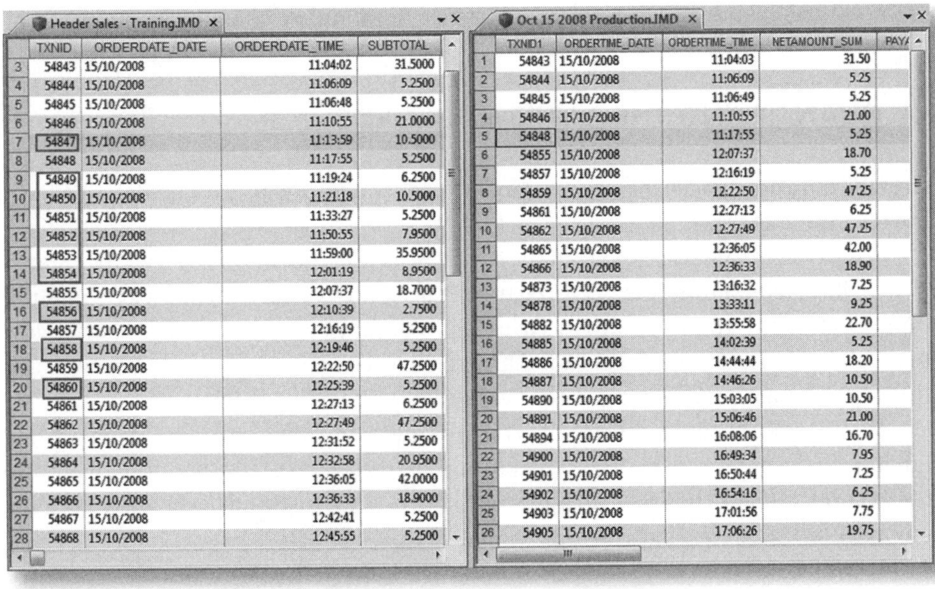
Header Sales - Training.IMD

	TXNID	ORDERDATE_DATE	ORDERDATE_TIME	SUBTOTAL
3	54843	15/10/2008	11:04:02	31.5000
4	54844	15/10/2008	11:06:09	5.2500
5	54845	15/10/2008	11:06:48	5.2500
6	54846	15/10/2008	11:10:55	21.0000
7	54847	15/10/2008	11:13:59	10.5000
8	54848	15/10/2008	11:17:55	5.2500
9	54849	15/10/2008	11:19:24	6.2500
10	54850	15/10/2008	11:21:18	10.5000
11	54851	15/10/2008	11:33:27	5.2500
12	54852	15/10/2008	11:50:55	7.9500
13	54853	15/10/2008	11:59:00	35.9500
14	54854	15/10/2008	12:01:19	8.9500
15	54855	15/10/2008	12:07:37	18.7000
16	54856	15/10/2008	12:10:39	2.7500
17	54857	15/10/2008	12:16:19	5.2500
18	54858	15/10/2008	12:19:46	5.2500
19	54859	15/10/2008	12:22:50	47.2500
20	54860	15/10/2008	12:25:39	5.2500
21	54861	15/10/2008	12:27:13	6.2500
22	54862	15/10/2008	12:27:49	47.2500
23	54863	15/10/2008	12:31:52	5.2500
24	54864	15/10/2008	12:32:58	20.9500
25	54865	15/10/2008	12:36:05	42.0000
26	54866	15/10/2008	12:36:33	18.9000
27	54867	15/10/2008	12:42:41	5.2500
28	54868	15/10/2008	12:45:55	5.2500

Oct 15 2008 Production.IMD

	TXNID1	ORDERTIME_DATE	ORDERTIME_TIME	NETAMOUNT_SUM	PAY/
1	54843	15/10/2008	11:04:03	31.50	
2	54844	15/10/2008	11:06:09	5.25	
3	54845	15/10/2008	11:06:49	5.25	
4	54846	15/10/2008	11:10:55	21.00	
5	54848	15/10/2008	11:17:55	5.25	
6	54855	15/10/2008	12:07:37	18.70	
7	54857	15/10/2008	12:16:19	5.25	
8	54859	15/10/2008	12:22:50	47.25	
9	54861	15/10/2008	12:27:13	6.25	
10	54862	15/10/2008	12:27:49	47.25	
11	54865	15/10/2008	12:36:05	42.00	
12	54866	15/10/2008	12:36:33	18.90	
13	54873	15/10/2008	13:16:32	7.25	
14	54878	15/10/2008	13:33:11	9.25	
15	54882	15/10/2008	13:55:58	22.70	
16	54885	15/10/2008	14:02:39	5.25	
17	54886	15/10/2008	14:44:44	18.20	
18	54887	15/10/2008	14:46:26	10.50	
19	54890	15/10/2008	15:03:05	10.50	
20	54891	15/10/2008	15:06:46	21.00	
21	54894	15/10/2008	16:08:06	16.70	
22	54900	15/10/2008	16:49:34	7.95	
23	54901	15/10/2008	16:50:44	7.25	
24	54902	15/10/2008	16:54:16	6.25	
25	54903	15/10/2008	17:01:56	7.75	
26	54905	15/10/2008	17:06:26	19.75	

FIGURE 16.30 Comparison of Backup Sales File and Sales File

In Figure 16.30, a side-by-side comparison of the *Header Sales* file from the training data tables on the left side with the *Header Sales* production file on the right shows the differences for the start of the day sales. Gaps in the TXNID field in the production file can be found in the training file highlighted in the box around the specific transaction identification numbers.

The training sales file for October 15, 2008, showed the starting TXNID of 54841 with a time of 10:54 and the ending TXNID of 54897 with a time of 16:22. There were no transactions recorded after 16:22. The training sales file up to TXNID of 54897 had 57 transactions with no gaps. It contained sales paid by various tender types.

The production file starting TXNID was 54843 with a time of 11:04. The ending transaction number was 54943 ending at 21:09. There were 55 missing TXNID numbers. Since there was an earlier cut-off of the training file data, only 35 of these 55 production file gaps were found in the training file. It was curious that there were no sales paid wholly in cash. Some sales had blended payment of cash and some other tender. For the entire day, the production file showed only 46 sales.

The author speculates that POS-system maintenance takes place at this particular location every October. The backup file data was cut off in October 2007 and the training sales file contained data only for October 15, 2008. When system maintenance is performed, backup files or traces of prezapped data may be left behind.

This theory is strengthened by the fact that in another case, a restaurant using the same POS system that was sold, installed, and maintained by the same technician had a software upgrade done in November 2009. This was clearly seen in the data as the TXNID number that was sequentially generated was changed in the afternoon of that particular date to a TXNID generated based on a time factor.

The taxation authorities found a backup file that contained prezapped data for seven days in November 2010. After matching the backup file to the production file, 310 transactions were found in the backup file that were not in the production file. All of the deleted transactions were paid for in cash, totaling over $6,500.

QUANTIFYING THE ZAPPED RECORDS

Average bill amounts for the various tender types should always be calculated to see if the results make sense.

A good place to start is to look at the field statistics feature in IDEA. From the "Status == C" file (step 20 from the File Preparation section), we have the net value and the number of records totals. There is an average value figure also, but we have to discount that calculation as our fields contain many records with zero items due to how we built the original master file, as seen in the field statistics of Figure 16.31.

We can use the number of positive records and a calculator to divide the net value amount by the number of positive records to derive the average bill amount. To illustrate the export feature of the field statistics, we will export to Excel and use Excel to perform our calculations, as in Figure 16.32.

In cell O1029, we divide the net value of 250,617 by the number of positive records of 19,394 to obtain the average cash bill amount. We copy and paste the

Numeric Statistics	CASH_ONLY	DEBIT_ONLY	CREDIT_ONLY	BLEND_OTHE...	CASH_COUNT	DEBIT_COUNT	CREDIT_COL
Net Value	250,617.00	886,439.44	310,606.36	11,278.46	19,394	52,107	12
Absolute Value	250,617.00	886,439.44	310,606.36	11,278.46	19,394	52,107	12
# of Records	84,767	84,767	84,767	84,767	84,767	84,767	84
# of Zero Items	65,373	32,660	72,048	84,280	65,373	32,660	72,
Positive Value	250,617.00	886,439.44	310,606.36	11,278.46	19,394	52,107	12,
Negative Value	0.00	0.00	0.00	0.00	0	0	
# of Positive Records	19,394	52,107	12,719	487	19,394	52,107	12,
# of Negative Records	0	0	0	0	0	0	
# of Data Errors	0	0	0	0	0	0	
# of Valid Values	84,767	84,767	84,767	84,767	84,767	84,767	84
Average Value	2.96	10.46	3.66	0.13	0.23	0.61	
Minimum Value	0.00	0.00	0.00	0.00	0	0	
Maximum Value	309.76	290.85	336.40	122.20	1	1	
Record # of Min	2	1	1	1	2	1	
Record # of Max	28,127	50,219	65,690	62,405	1	16	
Sample Std Dev	7.86	12.29	11.27	2.15	0.42	0.49	
Sample Variance	61.72	151.14	126.98	4.60	0.18	0.24	
Pop Std Dev	7.86	12.29	11.27	2.15	0.42	0.49	
Pop Variance	61.72	151.14	126.98	4.60	0.18	0.24	
Pop Skewness	5.446091	1.993772	5.004321	22.597267	1.291298	-0.471408	1.955

FIGURE 16.31 Field Statistics of Closed Sales Transactions File

formulas and text to the DEBIT_ONLY and CREDIT_ONLY area of the spreadsheet to obtain those results for average debit card and average credit card amount respectively.

By extracting the data for April 1, 2011, April 2, 2011, and April 3, 2011, into separate files, we can compare the average bill amount for each tender type from the entire database with those days immediately before the data was obtained from the unannounced visit, as shown in Table 16.4.

TABLE 16.4 Average Bill Amounts

Date	Cash	Debit	Credit
July 9/2007–Nov 1/2011	$12.92	$17.01	$24.42
Apr 1/2011	19.26	17.10	23.01
Apr 2/2011	20.58	16.48	24.43
Apr 3/2011	21.98	13.85	34.65

It would seem that the average cash bill should approximate $20.00 as in all likelihood, larger cash sales amounts were deleted to have the average low spread over the entire data set. Applied to the 88,487 missing transactions, the amount projected as zapped would total $1,769,740 (88,487 * $20). Even if the low-cash average of $12.92 that remained in the database was conservatively used for the estimate, the zapped amount would still exceed $1 million.

Other average bill analyses that can be considered would be on the backup data file that contained data from July to October 2007 and the invigilation date data. The training data file for part of the day for October 15, 2008, may contain too few records

CASH_ONLY

Net Value	250,617.00	Absolute Value	250,617.00	Average Bill 12.92
# of Records	84,767	# of Zero Items	65,373
Positive Value	250,617.00	Negative Value	0.00
# of Positive Records	19,394	# of Negative Records	0
# of Data Errors	0	# of Valid Values	84,767
Average Value	2.96	Minimum Value	0.00
Maximum Value	309.76	Record # of Min	2
Record # of Max	28,127	Sample Std Dev	7.86
Sample Variance	61.72	Pop Std Dev	7.86
Pop Variance	61.72	Pop Skewness	5.446091
Pop Kurtosis	69.032934		

DEBIT_ONLY

Net Value	886,439.44	Absolute Value	886,439.44	Average Bill 17.01
# of Records	84,767	# of Zero Items	32,660
Positive Value	886,439.44	Negative Value	0.00
# of Positive Records	52,107	# of Negative Records	0
# of Data Errors	0	# of Valid Values	84,767
Average Value	10.46	Minimum Value	0.00
Maximum Value	290.85	Record # of Min	1
Record # of Max	50,219	Sample Std Dev	12.29
Sample Variance	151.14	Pop Std Dev	12.29
Pop Variance	151.14	Pop Skewness	1.993772
Pop Kurtosis	10.718131		

CREDIT_ONLY

Net Value	310,606.36	Absolute Value	310,606.36	Average Bill 24.42
# of Records	84,767	# of Zero Items	72,048
Positive Value	310,606.36	Negative Value	0.00
# of Positive Records	12,719	# of Negative Records	0
# of Data Errors	0	# of Valid Values	84,767
Average Value	3.66	Minimum Value	0.00
Maximum Value	336.40	Record # of Min	1
Record # of Max	65,690	Sample Std Dev	11.27
Sample Variance	126.98	Pop Std Dev	11.27
Pop Variance	126.98	Pop Skewness	5.004321
Pop Kurtosis	44.248428		

FIGURE 16.32 Field Statistics Export to Microsoft Excel

to determine a valid average but can be reviewed for completeness. It may be most appropriate to take the average of all these analyses.

ADDITIONAL POS DATA FILES TO ANALYZE

We have seen the effectiveness of comparing backup files to the production files. The backup may contain prezapped transactions that are not in the production files. We created a master file to test other files against. In addition to backup files there are numerous other files that may be tested against the master file. The log file of orders sent to the kitchen or bar may contain information referencing a bill or transaction identification number that was deleted in the production file. Table management data may also contain transaction information no longer in the master file. Potentially, the log file of servers or wait staff logging in and out of the system may reference the transaction IDs of bills assigned to their tables. Some restaurants issue or sell VIP cards that entitle the holder to discounts or extras. Analysis of the VIP transactions in the data set may reveal anomalies in either the *Detail Sales* or *Header Sales* files if any of those sales records were deleted. Split or combined bills that were deleted may also leave traces of zapping. When the patrons of a table subsequently ask for separate bills, the initial bill and orders must be split. Many POS systems have the capabilities of even splitting jugs of draft beer between any numbers of patrons at the table. Conversely, when two bills are opened for separate tables and then subsequently combined it may leave a trail if the combined bill was later zapped. Combined bills may occur when patrons meeting at the restaurant did not realize until later that the other party had arrived. Another bill was then opened for the late-arriving patron and must be combined later.

Many POS systems have a data file that has the daily sales recorded similar to a Z total in cash registers. In cash registers, a Z total tape is run at the end of the business day. The tape prints out the daily information, such as the total collected for each tender type, voids, refunds, and so on. The Z report prints the total sales and then resets the total sales amount back to zero for the start of the next business day. It also has a cumulative life to date total. The Z report differs from a cash register's X report, which provides the sales total up to the time it is initiated. It basically reads the information and does not reset any amounts. You can run the X report periodically throughout the day to see the sales totals at any time.

Some POS systems have a nonresettable total file that contains the daily totals, like the Z totals, and also cumulative totals. When this file is available, it is a simple matter to compare the nonresettable total file daily amounts to the daily total in the production file or daily reports. These amounts should be identical unless sales in the production file were deleted. Even if the amounts are identical, it may be that the zapper adjusts not only the production file data, but also the corresponding amounts in the nonresettable total file.

A typical POS system Z file contains fields such as the date and time when the closing reports are run. There may be duplicate dates if the closing report is processed after midnight and the next day processed before midnight. The number of bills for the day and total amount for the day, along with the user ID of the person accessing the closing report option, populates the file. There may also be cumulative number of bills and cumulative daily amounts recorded since the start of the POS system's Z file.

This type of POS system log file is very effective in detecting and quantifying deleted amounts.

 ## MISSING AND MODIFIED BILLS

Indicators and the detection of zapper usage are not restricted solely to analyzing the POS system data directly. One method of positively identifying zapper fraud is the use of bills. This method is used by a number of taxation authorities and is outlined in the

2007 Superior Court case decided in Montreal, Quebec, Canada of "Weinstein & Gavino Fabrique et bar à pâtes compagnie ltée c. Québec (Sous-ministre du Revenu)."[5]

The Quebec Ministry of Revenue was performing a province-wide program where 234 restaurants were randomly selected for inspection. They were doing a study of how restaurants were collecting and remitting sales taxes and how they were accounting for their sales. At issue was that three separate restaurants, "in individual legal proceedings, each claims to have been the victim of an unreasonable search and seizure of computerized accounting records—without warrant—by inspectors from the Quebec Ministry of Revenue (the 'Ministry') at their restaurants."[6]

The case outlines the process and some of the methodologies utilized by the Quebec Ministry of Revenue. At various times of the day and over a period of several months, inspectors from the Ministry working undercover would order at least 10 separate meals at each of the restaurants. They would pay for the meal in cash and obtained a receipt. Where it was not possible to retain the receipt, the inspector would take a picture of the receipt. The inspector along with a computer technician would later go back to the restaurant and perform an inspection. The computer technician would make a copy of the POS system's databases first. Then the Ministry employees, along with a representative of the restaurant, would look in the POS system for the 10 bills that were obtained previously by Ministry staff.

Any bills that could not be found recorded in the POS system provided evidence that the sales were deleted with the aid of zapper software.

The appeal of the three restaurants in this case was unsuccessful. The Ministry continues to use missing bills as hard evidence of sales suppression and a number of other taxation authorities either formally or informally follow this simple procedure. An informal approach includes obtaining receipts from other sources. Other sources may be receipts copied from the audit of other taxpayers claiming the restaurant meal as an expense. Receipts may also appear on personal reviews of restaurants or on blogs on Internet websites. People post pictures of the food they ordered and also the bill to show the name of the dishes. In some jurisdictions, politicians post their expenses on publicly accessible websites in the interest of governmental openness and transparency.

This approach not only is effective to provide evidence of zapping when bills are not in the POS system, but can also combat different methods of zapping. While many zappers delete the entire bill, some zappers leave the bill in the system but delete line items. For instance, if a bill at a table of four patrons had four main courses on it, two of the main courses can be deleted using this type of zapper. This is not the favored method as it is more labor intensive. However, if this type of zapping is automated, then it would not be difficult to analyze average sales per patron. The POS system retains the information of the number of patrons or guests at each table. Many bills have the number of guests printed right on it. Zappers normally would not reduce the number of guests on the bills where line items were deleted. Average per guest would drop significantly once zapping is started. Anomalies such as the bill showing some of the guests at the table did not order anything may also be a result of zapping.

Another method of zapping is to substitute a high-cost meal item with a low-cost item, such as a soup substituted for a high-priced steak. This leaves the bill in the system where there would be no issues with transaction identification number sequencing.

Even if the bill is unaltered as to the amount total in the POS system, it may be possible that the only item changed is the bill number. This would suggest that while this particular bill was not modified or deleted, other bills were zapped and renumbered, thereby changing the bill number on the bill that was being examined.

THE MARKUP RATIOS

Many auditors rely on a markup approach of purchases to project sales revenue. While the markup approach may be effective, if calculated properly, for alcohol purchases, it is nearly impossible to use this method for food. After all, how does one calculate the markup of a plate or bowl of stew that contains potatoes, meat, vegetables, and other ingredients? In addition, for this method to work, there has to be an assumption that all purchases have been recorded in the cost of goods sold.

When businesses zap cash sales, they have much cash on hand. Some of this cash is normally shared with suppliers and restaurant staff. They are paid in cash and most of the amounts are not recorded as expenses in the books of the restaurant. Experienced business owners know to keep the various costs-to-sales ratios in line by balancing the amount of costs recorded to the amount of sales deleted.

Gross margins for restaurants vary so much due to a host of factors, including the type of restaurant, the location, popularity, prices charged, and so on. It has been suggested that the cost for food and beverages forms 32 percent of the sales price. This can vary much depending on the circumstances. If a restaurant does their own preparations from scratch, then their wages will be higher but food costs lower. An example of this would be the chopping and slicing of vegetables done in the restaurant as opposed to purchasing the vegetables prechopped and sliced. The less preparation required, the higher the food cost but there will be some saving of salary costs.

Consider a scenario where a popular, fair-size restaurant records in their books all food and beverage costs. Actual gross revenue is $3.5 million and $500,000 was zapped, as seen in Table 16.5. Would a difference in 5 percent gross margin raise any red flags when comparing it to other similar restaurants in the area?

TABLE 16.5 Hypothetical Deletion of 5 Percent of Sales

	Actual	Percentage	Post-Zapped	Percentage
Sales	$3,500,000	100%	$3,000,000	100%
Cost of Goods	1,120,000	32	1,120,000	37
Gross Margin	2,380,000	68	1,880,000	63

Some businesses would record as expenses supplies purchased from one source but not similar supplies from another source where they paid in cash. Analyzing the usage of supplies may provide an indicator that this is occurring. For instance, analyzing the number of items—such as place mats or napkins—purchased against the estimated number of patrons may indicate that there were not enough of these supplies purchased. How was the business able to continue operating without napkins?

Traditional analysis of purchases, aided by data analytics, should also be considered. In the "Detail Sales" file, the type of sales are logged and printed out on the bill to the customer. Typically, the POS system would have fields such as CATNUM, SUBCATNUM, and ITEMNUM to represent food categories, subcategories, and specific menu items, as displayed in Figure 16.33.

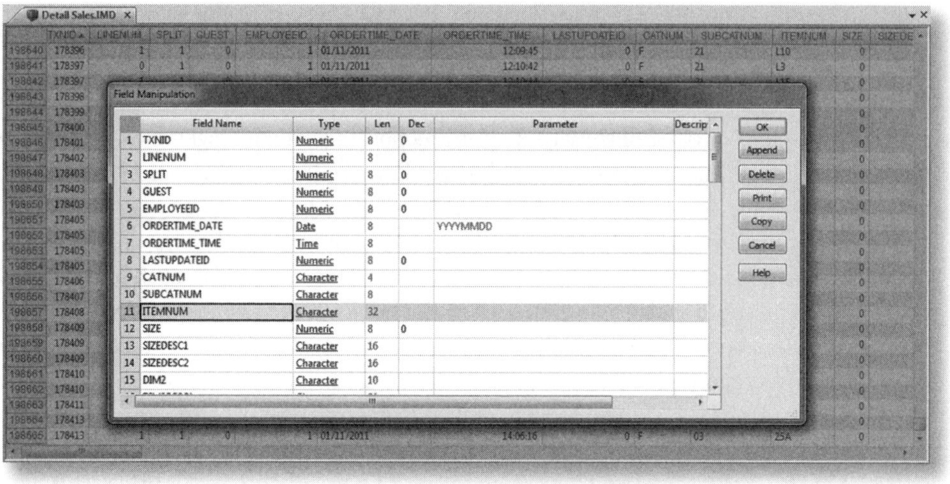

FIGURE 16.33   Menu Food Items, Categories, and Subcategories

While it may not be possible to compare purchases of food items to food sales, beverage purchases can easily be related to sales, especially canned or bottled drinks. By organizing the data by beverage CATNUM, SUBCATNUM, and ITEMNUM fields, comparisons can be made against purchases of those items. Some zapper software, in automated mode, will delete alcohol sales while some will not. This type of analysis can be done from reports directly printed or exported from the POS system without going into the native databases. Owners can use these types of reports and analysis to monitor cost and sales.

Analysis of recorded wages may also provide another indicator for zapping. If the business is paying wages in cash, estimating the number of employees and their hours against the amount of wages booked may provide some incredible results, such as employees working for much less than legal per-hourly rates. It is not unusual to see that the booked calculations have staff working for less than a dollar an hour.

CONCLUSIONS AND SOLUTIONS

Zappers, unless absolutely perfectly designed to interface with every related table or file in the system to execute the changes made to the sales data, leave traces of zapping. Data analytics can be employed on POS system databases to identify the anomalies. Once a single instance of zapping is detected, additional resources can be budgeted to expand the investigation to find additional evidence and to quantify the fraud amounts.

An article with the interesting title of "How to Get Caught Using Zappers"[7] concludes, "While you may get away with the use of a zapper for a while, there are too many ways you could be tripped up. When it does happen, the penalties will be severe. It is not worth taking the risk." What is unique is that the author of the article is an accountant who owned and operated a restaurant for over 10 years and is experienced with POS systems. He has firsthand knowledge of both the operational and the financial side of the restaurant business. Since he was one of the first to write in detail about zappers and the restaurant business, I had frequently pointed to the article when training auditors or presenting to various taxation authorities.

In discussions with tax lawyers and tax accountants, it is not unknown that in some cases, over $100,000 a month was zapped. This is not inconsistent with the report from the Canadian taxation authorities that their average cases had evidence of deleted sales of $1 million. In some cases, it would appear that managing shareholders were zapping without the knowledge of the silent shareholders. Given the significance of the issue, taxation authorities are combating zappers in various ways to reduce revenue losses.

The OECD paper outlines a number of solutions including, "The range of solutions has increased and evolved from the original Italian 'fiscal till' (where the sales data is saved to a recording device at the end of the working day) to the Portuguese 'certified POS software' (where the system is required to produce encrypted sales data with digital signatures that validate a genuine transaction). One of the key evolutions in these technical solutions is that the POS data is now secured upon creation of the data rather than in early systems at the end of the day's business."[8]

Countries with fiscal-till solutions include Argentina, Brazil, Bulgaria, Greece, Hungary, Latvia, Lithuania, Malta, Poland, Russia, Turkey, and Venezuela. The province of Quebec in Canada implemented a measure since 2011 whereby restaurants must have a sales recording module (SRM). The SRM is a secured device that is connected between the POS system and the printer. The measure made it mandatory for bills to be issued to customers. Quebec is contemplating requiring bars to have SRM devices in 2015. The Canadian government passed legislation making it illegal to use, purchase, possess, design, develop, or manufacture zappers or electronic suppression of sales devices starting in 2014. Many states in the United States had already passed similar types of legislation.

POS-system owners must be even more vigilant and take prudent measures to ensure that there are no zapper devices present in their POS systems, including those that may have been left behind by current or former employees.

There is a large market for this electronic suppression of sales software and technology and there will always be a need for counter-zapping. Hardware, software, and data analytics need to be included in the arsenals of tax authorities. A paper by Richard T. Ainsworth titled "Zappers & Phantom-Ware: A Global Demand for Tax Fraud Technology"[9] provides background and examples of zappers.

A number of POS systems have built-in maintenance utility programs that can be used to delete sales. This can loosely be called *phantomware*. In one particular POS system, the maintenance utility program performs automated repair functions, such as removing invalid table links and moving all opened transactions from previous days to the current day's sales. Included in the utility is a database editor. The database editor is not well documented in the user's manual. The editor allows for deletion of sales in the database. Even though the reports generated will show results after the deletion of sales, internally it makes little effort to disguise the deletions. The nonresettable total file retains information about deleted transactions. Another file contains a date field of the transactions, where the date changes from when the transaction took place to the date that the transaction was deleted. This file's transaction number also changes to a special flag. There are other electronic trails that identify that deletions of sales records had taken place.

Regardless what methods are used by taxation authorities to safeguard tax revenues, POS-system owners should from time to time have data analytics performed to ensure that they are safeguarding their sales revenues from zapper fraud. In a robust POS system, there will always be some trace evidence of zapping when analyzing its data. Consider this: Suppose there was a power outage or some other sort of malfunction while the database was being written to or updated. A good POS system must be able to automatically, or with the assistance of the POS system manufacturer, rebuild or repair any corrupted database. As such, the system must retain redundant data. Zappers are unlikely to be so sophisticated that all traces of deletions are totally eliminated.

 NOTES

1. Organisation for Economic Co-operation and Development (OECD), *Electronic Sales Suppression: A Threat to Tax Revenues*, accessed January 30, 2014, www.oecd.org/ctp/crime/electronicsalessuppressionathreattotaxrevenues.htm.
2. Ibid.
3. *Vancouver Sun*, "Richmond Company, Workers Charged with Selling 'Zapper' Software Designed to Steal from Taxman," October 10, 2009, www.canada.com/story_print .html?id=79420a47-1a9d-415d-8b85-a1eb1217f524&sponsor=.
4. "*Regina v. David Au, Cara Tang, and InfoSpec Systems Inc*," accessed January 30, 2014, www.canlii.org/en/bc/bcsc/doc/2011/2011bcsc75/2011bcsc75.html?searchUrlHash =AAAAAQAMMjAxMSBiY3NjIDc1AAAAAAE.
5. *Weinstein & Gavino Fabrique et Bar a Pates Compangnie Ltee and Roger Costa and Tom Nacos v. Le Sous-Ministre du Revenu du Quebec, et al.*, accessed February 9, 2014, www .canlii.org/en/qc/qccs/doc/2007/2007qccs6339/2007qccs6339.html?searchUrlHash= AAAAAQAQd2VpbnN0ZWluIHphcHBlcgAAAAB.
6. Ibid.
7. Paul S. Hewitt, "How to Get Caught Using Zappers," *Canadian Restaurant Tax Advisor*, accessed February 11, 2014, http://cdnbartaxadvisor.wordpress.com/2009/11/14/how-to-get-caught-using-zappers.
8. OECD, *Electronic Sales Suppression*.
9. Richard T. Ainsworth, "Zappers & Phantomware: A Global Demand for Tax Fraud Technology," www.bu.edu/law/faculty/scholarship/workingpapers/documents/AinsworthR060208.pdf.

17

Automation and IDEAScript

DEASCRIPT IS A PROGRAMMING tool in IDEA that allows for combining numerous steps into a single procedure. The programming language is similar to that of Microsoft's Visual Basic for Applications. IDEAScript files are also known as macro files. It is a file that performs a series of actions when executed. IDEAScript can record actions for editing and modification to make the macro good for general use—any user can apply the script to any suitable data files. IDEAScript is a powerful tool that speeds up repetitive procedures.

IDEAScript can be used for:

- **Automating repetitive tasks.** Regular tasks, such as monthly data that needs to be analyzed, can use IDEAScript to run and repeat the required procedures automatically. IDEAScript can be efficiently used when certain procedures are required to be applied in multiple locations such as departments, divisions, and branches. Another frequent repetitive task is to import files. This can be automated to select the input files, specify the output names, perform the imports, and perform required data cleanup or scrubbing.
- **Creating an automated-analysis system.** A set of tests or procedures can be integrated into an IDEAScript where the user may select particular tests to apply.
- **Controlling other software packages.** Using Microsoft's object linking and embedding (OLE) technology, other OLE-enabled software can be controlled from within IDEA. One example is that of sending IDEA data into an Excel spreadsheet. IDEAScript performs analysis tasks such as summarization, sends the summarized data into an Excel spreadsheet, and then the IDEAScript instructs Excel to chart the summarized data into bar graphs.
- **Creating custom tests.** IDEAScript can be used to create specific tests based on the user's or the organization's needs. Typically, these would be performing calculations that involve comparisons and equations.

In using IDEAScript, work will be performed faster and the results will contain fewer errors. The analyses are done more consistently and can be undertaken by other staff members. Standards are adhered to by all users.

 ## CONSIDERATIONS FOR AUTOMATION

The following steps should be considered when planning to create an IDEAScript.

- Identify those tasks that are frequently repeated. The more often the procedures need to be repeated, the better suited they are to invest the time to create the IDEAScript.
- Select those procedures that are well defined and well understood. It is likely that the user understands the task well, as he or she has performed the procedures often.
- Plan the macros carefully to ensure the results are those expected.
- Include user-input dialog boxes so that others can use the IDEAScript. Investing some additional work to make the script as flexible as possible so it is useful to others increases the value of the script.
- Plan to test the IDEAScript on other computers with different versions of IDEA for compatibility and to ensure that the script works as expected.

Visual Script versus IDEAScript

Visual Script can create and edit macros in IDEA. Visual Script is a visual representation of batch processing that allows for simple dragging (or double clicks) of desired action choices from the left side of the window to the right side for project steps of the Visual Script screen, as shown in Figure 17.1.

Visual Script, like IDEAScript, allows for automation of repetitive tasks. However, the automation can be performed without the complexity of knowing any programming and writing code. While easier to use, there are limitations, such as not being able to create message boxes, nor will Visual Script run in the IDEA Server environment. Visual Scripts have the .vscript filename extension and are saved to the default Macros .ILB folder under the active project folder.

Visual Scripts can be later converted to IDEAScripts, if desired, through an option in the Visual Script Editor. Because of the easy conversion to IDEAScript, you can start the steps for your macro in Visual Script, convert it to IDEAScript, and then code additional functionalities within the IDEAScript editor. Visual Script has the ability to include IDEAScripts into it. This makes it simple to group together a number of IDEAScripts and have Visual Script run them all. Visual Script is an excellent personal tool.

IDEAScript is much more powerful than Visual Script. Because of its power, it is rich in abilities that allow flexibility in creating macros. IDEAScript can use dialog boxes, control other software applications, and interact with the operating system. An example of the IDEAScript editor window with a sample script is shown in Figure 17.2.

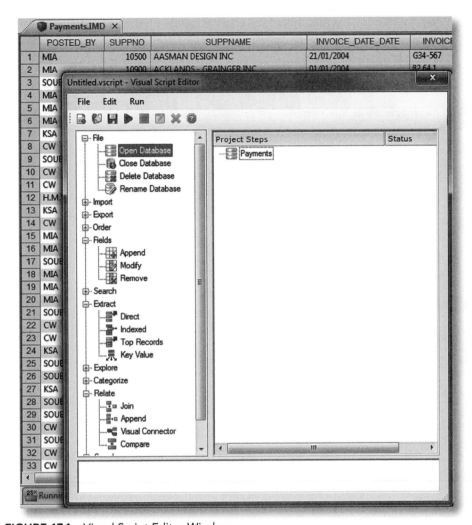

FIGURE 17.1 Visual Script Editor Window

IDEAScripts can be saved in three different formats designated by the filename extension. Each format has its own unique advantage.

- **iss:** This is the default format. The coding is open and allows any user to view it and to modify the script as they wish. The script can only be executed from within IDEA or from the IDEAScript Editor.
- **ise:** This is the compiled version of the script. As it is compiled, the coding cannot be seen nor can any changes be made to the script. Changes can only be made in the iss file, which then has to be compiled again. This format is good for distribution to ensure that nothing is inadvertently changed or if you wish to protect your code. The ise file can only be executed from within IDEA.

- **exe:** This format is similar in properties to that of the ise format with the exception that it is compiled as a Windows executable file. IDEA does not have to be opened to run the file. However, IDEA must be installed for the script to work.

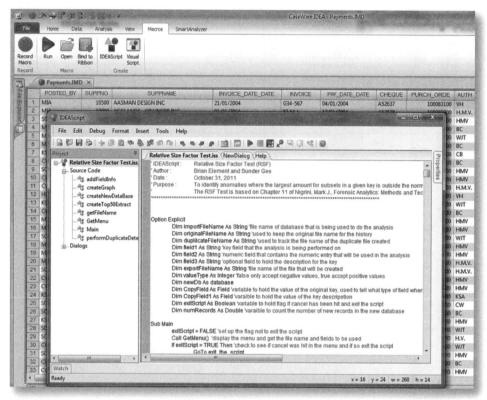

FIGURE 17.2   IDEAScript Editor Window

 CREATING IDEASCRIPTS

This book does not go into the details of programming IDEAScripts. The purpose is to provide an overview of both the simplicities of creating basic scripts and the complexities of creating scripts with user interface dialog boxes and performing intricate procedures. Complex scripts are included in this book's companion website. While complex scripts may have thousands of lines of code, the one in Figure 17.3 has merely 11 lines.

The script in Figure 17.3 is an example of interacting with the Windows operating system function of renaming a file in a folder. This script does not include dialog windows to allow a user to select the folder and file to be renamed. It is hard-coded into the script that the "text.txt" file must be in the C:\data folder. It can only be renamed to "text_renamed.txt." The "CreateObject" function allows IDEAScript in IDEA to access Windows file-system functions and other application functions, such as in Microsoft Excel.

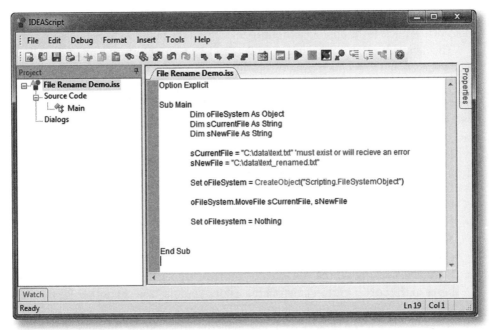

FIGURE 17.3 IDEAScript to Rename a File

An example of a dialog box is shown in Figure 17.4. The IDEAScript extracts transactions with even thousand amounts from the active file in IDEA. The script takes all numeric

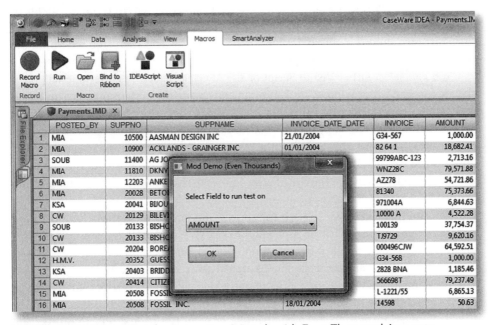

FIGURE 17.4 Dialog Box for Extracting Records with Even Thousand Amounts

fields within the file and allows the user to select the field to apply the test on. In this case, the AMOUNT field is the appropriate one to select from the pull-down selection box.

The detailed script is reproduced in Figure 17.5 to highlight the additional lines of code necessary to produce a dialog box along with the user being able to select the numeric field to apply the test on. The script was opened in a text editor that displays more coding than if opened in the IDEAScript editor. The IDEAScript editor hides the code for the creation of dialogs and their supporting variables. Unless you are a power user, you normally need not be concern with this.

In contrast, when using Visual Script, as shown in Figure 17.6, the procedure is:

- Under File, select Open Database. All databases in the current project are offered for selection. Choose "Payments" as the file to open.
- Under Extract, select Direct. The direct extraction option opens up. Enter in the File Name area MOD Thousand. Enter the equation of (AMOUNT % 1000) = 0 in the Criteria area or Equation editor.
- By double clicking on the "Payments" filename under the Project Steps, all databases in the current project are offered again. You may select another file to apply the even thousands Visual Script to.
- By double clicking on Direct Extraction under the Project Steps, the Direct Extraction option opens up where you can modify the output filename and change the equation.

Clearly, Visual Scripts are simpler to create but the user needs some knowledge to apply, such as being able to understand the equation and modify it. IDEAScripts are more complex for the programmer but easier for the user. They are also more accurate if error checking is built in. These statements are only true if user input or dialog boxes are involved. Creating simple IDEAScripts can be as easy as recording the steps that you are taking to accomplish a task. Figure 17.7 shows how you can start and stop recording a macro.

Start recording the macro. Perform the procedures and then stop recording the macro. A window will then pop up as shown in Figure 17.8.

You can select either Visual Script or IDEAScript. Selecting either one will open the appropriate editor window and automatically paste the actions or codes in. When procedures are performed in IDEA, they are logged in the history found under the Properties window. You can copy all the procedures into IDEAScript or selected tasks. In our example in Figure 17.9, we select the "Copy the IDEAScript for the selected task(s)" option since we right-clicked on the record extraction area to bring up the selection. Once the selection is made, the IDEAScript editor opens and the script is automatically created for you.

You can make changes to both the source and output filenames along with the equation from within the IDEAScript editor to suit you. Alternatively, you can add dialog boxes and coding to allow for user input. The dialog box shown in Figure 17.4 was created in the IDEAScript editor's dialogs area, displayed in Figure 17.10.

The companion website makes available a Mod calculation script that allows the user to select the file to apply the script to, select the amount field, and select whether to extract even hundreds, even thousands, or even ten thousands amounts. The script includes a Help button to provide instructions for entering a tax percentage

```
'******************************************************************************
********
'* Script:mod demo.iss
'* Author: Brian Element - brian.element@ideascripting.com
'* Technical Consultant - Sunder Gee
'* Date: April 25, 2014
'* Purpose: Demo script to show basic IDEAScript functionality
'* Disclaimer: This script is provided without any warranty or guarantee.  Anybody using
this script
'* is encouraged to validate the effectiveness and reliability on their own.
'******************************************************************************
********
Dim listbox1$()

Begin Dialog dlgModDemo 51,44,149,101,"Mod Demo (Even Thousands)", .NewDialog
  Text 10,12,87,11, "Select Field to run test on", .Text2
  OKButton 11,51,40,14, "OK", .OKButton1
  CancelButton 71,51,40,13, "Cancel", .CancelButton1
  DropListBox 10,31,109,11, listbox1$(), .DropListBox1
End Dialog
Option Explicit

Dim sFilename As String
Dim sFieldname As String
Dim bExitScript As Boolean

Sub Main
        Call mainMenu
        If Not bExitScript Then
                Call extraction
        End If
End Sub

Function mainMenu()
        Dim iButton As Integer
        Dim dlg As dlgModDemo
        Dim source As database
        Dim table As table
        Dim rst As recrodset
        Dim field As field
        Dim fields, i, j As Integer

        sFilename = getCurrentDatabase()

        If sFilename = "" Then
                MsgBox "Please select an IDEA database"
        Else
                Set source=client.opendatabase(sFilename)
                Set table=source.tabledef
                Set rst =source.recordset
                fields=table.count
```

(continued)

```
                                ReDim listbox1$(fields)
                                j = 1
                                For i = 1 To fields
                                        Set field=table.getfieldat(i)
                                        If field.IsNumeric Then
                                                listbox1$(j) = field.name
                                                j = j + 1
                                        End If
                                Next i
                                If j = 1 Then
                                        MsgBox "This file does not have any numberic fields"
                                Else
                                        iButton = Dialog(dlg)
                                        If iButton = -1 Then
                                                sFieldname = listbox1$(dlg.DropListBox1 + 1)
                                        Else
                                                bExitScript = True
                                        End If
                                End If
                        End If
                End If

        End Function

        Function extraction()
                Dim db As database
                Dim task As task
                Dim dbName As String

                Set db = Client.OpenDatabase(sFilename)
                Set task = db.Extraction
                task.IncludeAllFields
                dbName = client.UniqueFilename("MOD Thousand")
                task.AddExtraction dbName, "", sFieldname & " % 1000 = 0"
                task.PerformTask 1, db.Count
                Set task = Nothing
                Set db = Nothing
                Client.OpenDatabase (dbName)

        End Function

        Function getCurrentDatabase() As String
                Dim db As database
                On Error GoTo errorHandler
                Set db = Client.CurrentDatabase
                getCurrentDatabase = db.Name
                Set db = Nothing
                Exit Function
        errorHandler:
                Set db = Nothing
                getCurrentDatabase = ""
End Function
```

FIGURE 17.5 Even Thousands Extraction IDEAScript

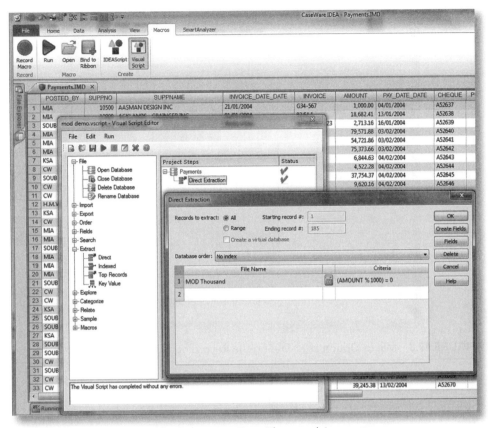

FIGURE 17.6 Visual Script for Extracting Even Thousand Amounts

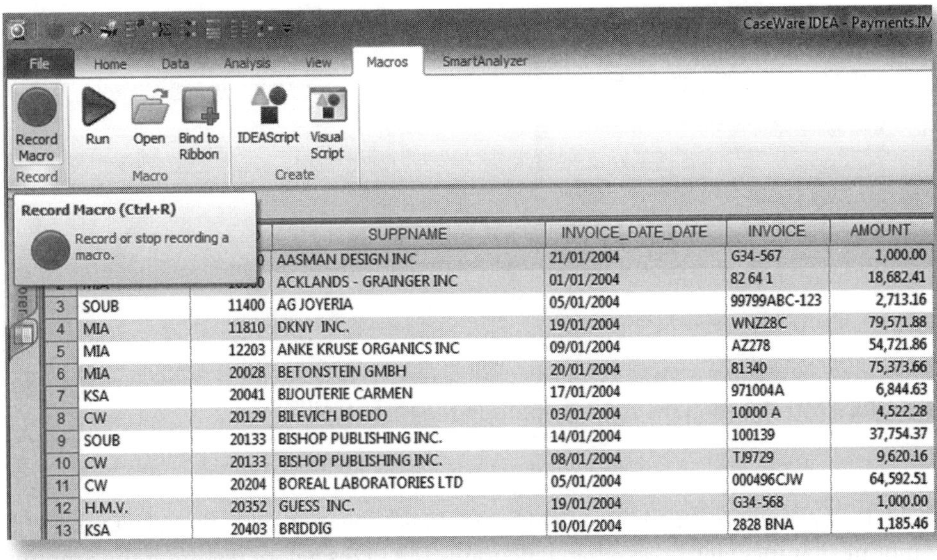

FIGURE 17.7 Recording a Macro

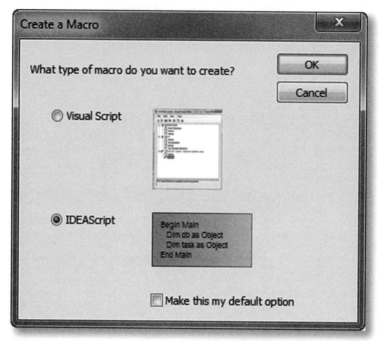

FIGURE 17.8 Macro Option after Ending the Recording of Macros

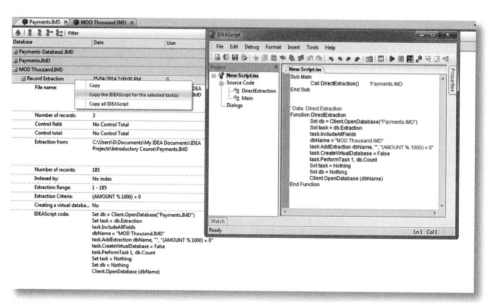

FIGURE 17.9 Creating the IDEAScript from the History File

field. In cases where an amount field before taxes does not exist, the script takes the amount that includes taxes, then calculates the taxes before testing if the amount matches the even amount selection. Refer to Figure 17.11.

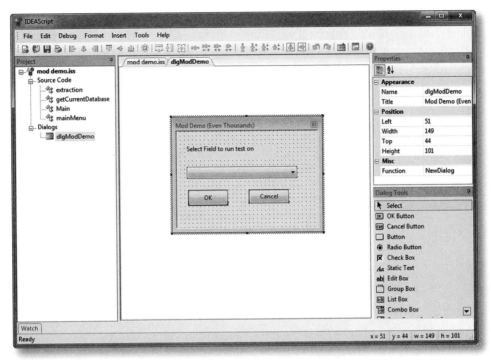

FIGURE 17.10 IDEAScript Dialog Editor

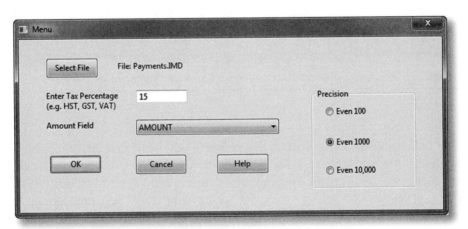

FIGURE 17.11 Mod Calculation Script Dialog Box

To complete the overview, custom functions should also be introduced as they are written using IDEAScript. Custom functions are used just like the included @Functions within IDEA. The custom functions are accessible in the equation editor in the same area as the @Functions. Custom functions are prefixed with the # symbol instead of the @ symbol as in regular functions, and have the file extension .ideafunc. Custom functions should be located under the active IDEA project in the Custom Functions.ILB folder. A sample of a short but very effective custom function is shown in Figure 17.12. The custom function converts a character field containing date information into a date field in IDEA format.

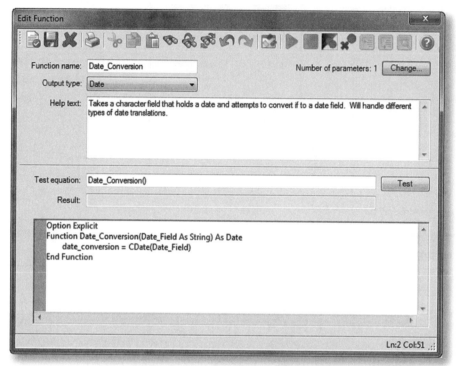

FIGURE 17.12   Custom Function to Convert a Character Field into a Date Field

CDate is a Visual Basic function that converts a character date field into an actual date field that is usable by IDEA. For example, the function can convert April 26, 2014, Apr 26/14, or 4/26/14 characters to an IDEA date field in the default format of DD/MM/YYYY. CDate can also be used to convert a time string into IDEA's time format. This custom function allows access to a specialized Visual Basic function that is not available in the IDEA equation editor.

Companion Website IDEAScripts

IDEAScripts are available for download from the companion website. These scripts were created based on IDEA version 9. Newer versions of IDEA may cause the scripts to be inoperable by producing error messages. Unless there is a complete overhaul of the scripting module by CaseWare IDEA, minor modifications to the scripts may be necessary to operate in newer versions of IDEA.

An understanding of the procedures automated by an IDEAScript provides confidence in the script. The following scripts are described step by step in Chapters 5 and 6 of this book.

- Number duplication
- Z-score
- Relative size factor (RSF)
- Same-same-same (SSS)
- Same-same-different (SSD).
- Mod calculation (even amounts)
- GEL-1
- GEL-2

Other useful IDEAScripts available from the companion website are:

- **Text search:** The script allows for input of up to 10 search terms that includes a wildcard character and Boolean operators to expand the capabilities of the search. The power of this script is that it allows you to load a predefined text file of search terms. The text file does not have the 10 search-term limit and can be used in conjunction with the search-term entry boxes.
- **Top records extraction exclusion:** The script extracts the top records for the user-selected field and then creates a new file with those records that did not form part of the top-record extraction.
- **Payment date versus due date:** The script allows you to select extractions based on two dates where the first date field is prior to the second date field, the first date field is the same as the second date field, or the first date field is after the second date field. The script then can summarize the resulting files by the year and the month.
- **Benford's Law second, third, and fourth digit tests:** The script creates up to three separate files for performing the second digit test, the third digit test and the fourth digit test as selected by the user. The analysis will be performed on each key field, such as a client field.
- **Benford's Law first digit test:** IDEA's Benford's Law first digit test is applied to the entire data set. This script allows the user to select a field where the test will be applied to each unique key in that field. An example would be where by selecting the vendor field, the first digit test of Benford's Law is applied to each vendor within the entire data set.
- **First two digits:** IDEA's Benford's Law first two digits test is applied to the entire data set. This script allows the user to select a field where the test will be applied to each unique key in that field. An example would be where by selecting the vendor field, the first two digits test of Benford's Law will be applied to each vendor within the entire data set.
- **Cross join:** To join files within IDEA, there must be a common key in each of the files. This script takes two files that do not have a common key and joins all records from both files.

- **Compare multiple fields:** IDEA can only compare a single numeric field between two files. The script allows for comparison with numeric, character, and date fields. Up to eight fields can be selected for comparison. One use can be to compare the same file at different points in time.

- **Date extraction:** The script allows the extraction of up to 24 dates entered or the upload of previously defined dates from a text file. In addition, specific days of the week may be selected for extraction. The script has an extract inverse option where all dates not selected are outputted.

- **Identify blank—repeat fields:** The script scans all the fields in an IDEA database and identifies fields that contain two or more different values. Those fields are logged in a text file. Those fields that do not contain different values are either blank or repeated information, such as the same company code that populates the entire field. Blank or repeated fields are earmarked to allow the user to select those fields to be removed from the database.

- **Review status:** The script appends up to five multistate and five comment fields to the database. A multistate field is where you can click on a record in the multistate field to cycle through icons—a checkmark, *X*, question mark, or blank. It allows a user to track the review of transactions and permits notation entries relating to the review.

- **Import multiple files:** This script allows you to select multiple files of the same format and import them into IDEA at the same time. It is capable of importing dBase, MS Access, MS Excel, print report, PDF, EBCDIC, fixed length test, delimited text, and XML files.

- **Export delimited files:** IDEA exports a character field with quotes encapsulating the text when exporting to a delimited file. This script allows you to eliminate the quotes or allows you to select your own encapsulating character. You can also define any field or decimal separator.

- **Luhn algorithm:** This script allows you to validate the checksum based on the Luhn algorithm. Credit card numbers, Canadian social insurance numbers, Canadian business numbers, Canadian GST/HST number, U.S. national provider identifier, along with older U.S. Social Security numbers (issued prior to June 2011) are among those that use the Luhn algorithm.

 ## CONCLUSION

Whether custom functions, Visual Script, or IDEAScript are used, they can all save time in performing procedures and tasks within IDEA. The real power lies with IDEAScript. In using IDEAScript, work is performed faster, the results contain fewer errors, and you can complete tasks that are difficult to do without some of the functionalities of IDEAScript.

Macros can be recorded or can be created from the history log file. The scripts can be edited to make them more usable. By creating message boxes and input boxes, flexibility is greatly increased when interaction with the user is possible. Macros can be attached to the tool bar menu for ease of access.

This chapter introduces the possibilities and potential available in IDEAScript for the automation of procedures. Programming is beyond the scope of this book, but here are some resources to increase your IDEAScript knowledge.

- *Mastering IDEAScript: The Definitive Guide* by John Paul Mueller (Hoboken, NJ: John Wiley & Sons, 2011), www.wiley.com/WileyCDA/WileyTitle/productCd-1118004485,descCd-description.html
- CaseWare IDEA Inc., Resource and Support Website: Available to all license holders of the IDEA software at www.ideasupport.caseware.com.
- IDEAScript for Programmers: Classroom training provided by CaseWare IDEA Inc., www.caseware.com/training/trainingCourseDetail?UID=4f4f5a63a4ed4af38c01 9a0d67b5a052.
- IDEAScripting and More website: A free site providing IDEA-related material including IDEAScripts at www.ideascripting.com.

CHAPTER EIGHTEEN

Conclusion

THIS BOOK TAKES THE READER from the beginning to the end of applying data analytics with practical uses in mind. The first two chapters introduce fraud and fraud detection. The third chapter is a critical one to read before commencing any data analytics, as it details how to obtain good data for use with data analytical software. Chapter 4 provides the reader with a basic understanding of statistics. Statistical theory is the underlying basis of many analytical tests. Chapter 5 and onward details general data analytical tests and specific tests for various fraud scheme areas. Chapter 17 shows the reader how to automate procedures to simplify the data analytical process.

To conclude the book, we will take a look at financial statement fraud and learn why this important area of fraud was omitted from this book. We will also review a listing of features demonstrated with the IDEA software and end this book with a few additional words about data analytics.

 ## FINANCIAL STATEMENT FRAUD

Financial statements are summarized transaction records obtained from detailed accounting records that are used to provide information about the financial position of the business entity. The main users of financial statements include:

- Prospective investors to determine whether to invest.
- Owners, managers, and shareholders who make business decisions.
- Lending institutions when deciding to lend or continue to lend funds.
- Vendors when establishing a business relationship.
- Government entities such as the tax authorities.

Since financial statements are key documents used in making significant decisions, financial statement fraud impacts users of these statements at great costs. Due to the magnitude of losses from financial statement fraud, this is a hot media topic. Many studies have been made on financial statement fraud and are included in most fraud literature. The studies have found that the frauds are committed by those who have the greatest motive and receive the greatest benefits; that is, senior management. The fraud can be committed by using the accounting system to generate the desired results, to provide falsified information into the accounting system, or merely by creating falsified financial statements. Financial statement fraud schemes include:

- Enhancing revenue with fictitious sales.
- Omitting expenses and liabilities.
- Providing incorrect valuations for assets.
- Manipulating results by using timing differences.
- Improper disclosures by addition or exclusion.

At the transactional level, data analytics may detect some of the categories of financial statement schemes by using the tests described in earlier chapters of this book. However, the most significant fraud items impacting financial statements would not likely be in the detailed transactions, but rather in journal entries or outside of the normal business transactions. As such, general tests to detect anomalies within the data may not be the best place to start. Certainly, if there was a specific area targeted for investigation, data analytics can assist with the verification of the details summarized on the financial statements.

A good starting point for testing for financial statement fraud would be from the financial statements themselves. This fundamental analysis can be done by calculating and interpreting both vertical and horizontal ratios. The categories of ratios that can be performed include:

- Profitability
- Debt
- Operating
- Liquidity
- Cash flow
- Investment valuation

Data analysis software is not suitable for these types of calculations and analysis. Spreadsheet software such as Excel would be more appropriate. The formula for the calculations of the ratios within each of the categories can be found in most auditing books and by Internet searches. A website that provides this is www.caclubindia.com/articles/analytical-review-3850.asp.

Before calculating the individual ratios, it would be beneficial to employ the Beneish model test. This test consists of eight financial ratio variables to calculate a score value. The score reflects the degree to which earnings may have been manipulated. If the score is greater than –2.22, there are potential earnings manipulation. The Beneish ratios along with an Excel spreadsheet to perform the calculations for you can be found at http://investexcel.net/beneish-m-score.

IDEA FEATURES DEMONSTRATED

Listings of the IDEA features outlined in this book, along with equations with @Functions, are summarized here. It is the author's hope that if some of the features, equations, and functions are new to the reader, exposing the reader to them opens up additional potential uses for data analytics. IDEA features demonstrated include:

- Summarize: Summing on average in addition to the default total
- Join: Using the options of "Matches only" and "Records with no secondary match"
- Chart: Join two years (periods) of similar files and create a chart for visual comparisons
- Rename fields
- Append fields
- Index fields
- Equations editor
- Multistate field type
- Duplicate key detection
- Duplicate key exclusion: It displays just one exclusion, but use the SSD IDEAScript to overcome this
- Gap detection
- Criteria and criteria view
- History
- Top record extraction
- Stratification
- Key value extractions
- Search
- Boolean operators
- Sampling
- Correlation
- Trend analysis
- Time series analysis
- Benford's Law
- Pivot table
- Exporting field statistics to Excel
- Visual Script
- IDEAScript

Equations and @Functions demonstrated include:

- @Precno( ): Returns the physical record number in the data file.
- @Val(@Left(@Str(ACCOMMODATION, 2, 2), 2)): Converts the ACCOMMODATION field to a character field using the @Str function to output a minimum of two characters with the second "2" as the number of decimal places. The @Left function extracts the first two characters starting from the left position. The @Val function converts everything back to numeric.

- (PAYAMOUNT_SUM – @FieldStatistics("PAYAMOUNT_SUM", 11))/@ FieldStatistics("PAYAMOUNT_SUM", 18): Z-score calculation of the PAYAMOUNT_SUM field amount minus the average amount obtained from the field statistics, and then divide the net by the population standard deviation amount obtained from the field statistics.

- (PAYMENT_AMOUNT % 10000) = 0 .AND. PAYMENT_AMOUNT < > 0: Equation to extract records with even tens of thousands amounts.

- PURCHASE_ORDER_CONTRACT_NUMBER = = " ".AND. PAYMENT_AMOUNT < > 0.00: Extracts payments where the purchase orders are blank (no purchase order numbers).

- @Age(PAYMENT_DATE_2, INVOICE_DATE_2): Calculates the difference in dates between the invoice date and the payment date.

- @Workday: Returns a "1" if the date falls on a weekday and "0" if falls on a weekend day.

- @Dow(PAYMENT_DATE_2): Returns the day of week for the payment date.

- @Strip(@Left(SUPPLIER_ADDR, 10)): The equation takes the first 10 characters of the supplier address and then removes or strips any spaces, control characters, and punctuations from the address.

- @Upper(@Strip(@Left(ADDRESS,10))): The equation takes the first 10 characters of the address and then removes or strips any spaces, control characters, and punctuations from the address. The results are then converted to uppercase.

- @If(@GetNextValue("CHECK") – CHECK = 1, 10, 11): The equation takes the next value in the CHECK field, subtracts the current check value and, if the difference is 1, then the number 10 is returned in the new field. If the difference is not 1, then the number 11 is displayed in the new field. All items with 11 are transactions not in sequence.

- LAST_NAME + " " + FIRST_INITIAL + " " + MIDDLE_INITIAL: Concatenate the last name, first initial, and middle initial fields into one field with blank spaces between the fields.

- LAST_NAME == " " .AND. AMOUNT < > 0.00: Extract for payments amounts made where the last name is blank.

- @If((LAST_DAY_OF_MTH – 3) < DAY, 1, 2): The equation would return the number 1 if the last day of the month field (minus three days to account for the weekend and one holiday) is a smaller number than the day of another field, such as the payment day. If the condition does not match, then the field would display the number 2 to represent not paid on the last day of the month.

- @If(DATE_DIFF > 0, ACCOMMODATION/DATE_DIFF, ACCOMMODATION): In the equation, if the date difference represents days traveled, it provides us with the average accommodation amounts if days traveled are greater than 0, and returns the accommodation amount if traveled on the same day.

- PAY_TYPE = = "VOID" .OR. @GetNextValue("PAY_TYPE") = = "VOID": The equation instructs IDEA to extract any record where the payment type field contains the word VOID and also extract any records where the next record (that is, get the next value that matches) in the payment type field contains the word VOID. The result will determine if there is a matching sale for every void transaction.

- @FinYear(BUSDATE_DATE, "0331"): Returns the financial or fiscal year of the date field where the year-end is specified as March 31.
- @Qtr(BUSDATE_DATE, "0331"): Returns the financial quarter of the date field where the year-end is specified as March 31.
- @Dtoc(BUSDATE_DATE, "YYYY-MM"): Converts the date format to a character field laid out in the new format described within the quotes.

PROJECTS OVERVIEW

One last feature to mention that was not previously demonstrated is the *Project Overview* feature. It displays all the steps taken within IDEA and can be applied from the Home tab. Similar to the *History* feature that retains the steps taken for individual files, the project overview visually displays all steps and procedures applied to the entire project. Figure 18.1 shows the project activities from Chapter 7, which only demonstrated a few procedures.

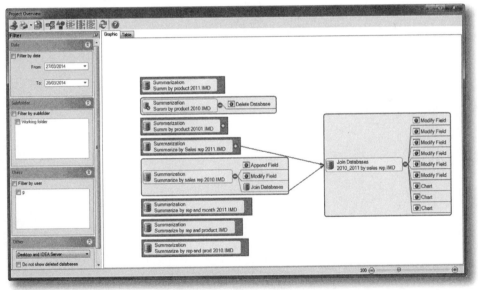

FIGURE 18.1 Project Overview of Chapter 7 Skimming and Cash Larceny Analysis of Files

The project overview graphically brings together all actions, including creating, modifying, and deleting databases. Interactions and relationships between databases are also displayed. All actions at the task level are included and can be seen by clicking on the + sign to expand actions taken within each database. Figure 18.2 is difficult to read but is shown as a typical example that shows a number of databases and their relationships to each other.

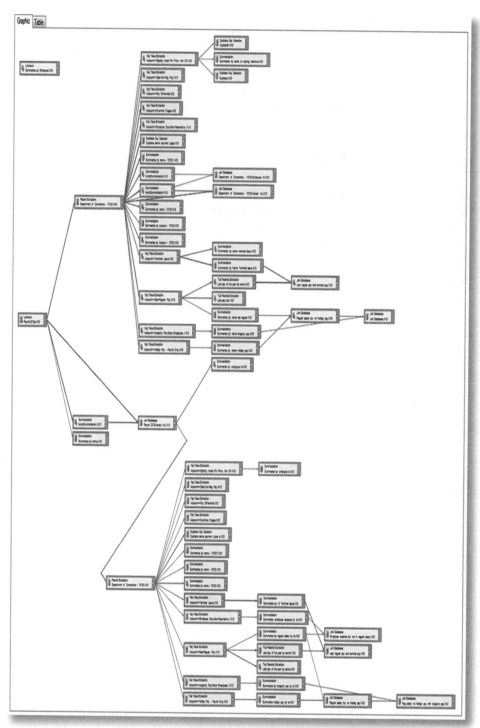

FIGURE 18.2 Project Overview of Chapter 10 Payroll Fraud Analysis of Files

DATA ANALYTICS: FINAL WORDS

In "The Global Economic Crime 2014 Survey"[1] from PricewaterhouseCooper (PwC), data analytics was added as a new category in the methods of how serious fraud was initially detected. The survey reported that data analytics was responsible for initial detection as follows:

- 9 percent globally
- 4 percent in the United States
- 10 percent in Canada

Does this mean that other methods of fraud detection such as from tips, routine internal audits, and so on are much more effective? When we couple this survey with a 2014 Deloitte survey[2] that found less than 26 percent of the organizations use data analytical tools to manage risk in their supply chain, we can postulate that the low detection rate may be due to the low usage of data analytics.

Many risks occur every day. Most are inconsequential but some can be significant and damaging. Risk is not something that can be or should be eliminated. After all, if organizations did not take some risk, they would never grow and may not even survive. Risk brings opportunities and rewards. The key is to manage risk. Data analytics can help mitigate the risks of fraud by analyzing all transactions, whether in the thousands or in the millions, to identify anomalies in those transactions.

Data analytics is not without challenges. One of the biggest challenges is to limit the number of false positives when using data analytical techniques. Large numbers of anomalies result in too many transactions to investigate. However, any significant amount of exceptions indicates weaknesses with internal controls. Rather than shifting through all the exceptions, additional techniques can be used to highlight those transactions with higher risks. It is not difficult to rerun the tests with different or higher thresholds. If many of the anomalies are of similar characteristics, subsets of the transactions can be extracted for review. Since tests are easily applied, especially if they are automated, auditors and investigators are more likely to take these timesaving steps. Due to the ease of use and high speed of data analytical software, it is appropriate to utilize an all-inclusive or comprehensive approach to apply any analytical test that may reveal red flags of fraud. It takes very little effort and the tests can be adjusted after viewing the initial results.

Another challenge is that there will be attempts to conceal fraud. The fraudster may try to hide the fraud by having the fraudulent transactions stay under the radar by aiming to include the transactions to fall within normal data patterns. Most data analytical tests will not flag those types of transactions as anomalies. However, as the fraudster grows more confident with the success of the fraud and gets greedier, accelerated patterns and trends will emerge. There will be spikes that will occur. Comparative analysis by day, by day of month, or by month may detect these patterns. The most productive type of data analytics are those that compare different data sets to look for matches where there should not be any or nonmatches where there should be. These techniques are discussed in the earlier chapters of this book.

As technology changes and organizations grow, so do the opportunities for fraud. Technology provides fraudsters with the means both to conceal traditional fraud schemes and to perpetrate new schemes. There will be a constant need for the organization to combat fraud by assessing and reassessing the effectiveness of controls, prevention tools, and detection tools. Fraud is ever evolving and anti fraud tools, including data analytical software, should strive to maintain and improve its effectiveness. Auditors and investigators need to invest in training and in continuing professional education to be a successful part of this evolution.

 NOTES

1. PricewaterhouseCoopers, "PwC Global Economic Crime 2014 Survey: The Many Varieties of Fraud," accessed April 27, 2014, www.pwc.com/gx/en/economic-crime-survey/economic-crimes/index.jhtml.
2. Deloitte LLP, "Deloitte Survey: Organizations in Need of Data Analytics to Detect Supply Chain Fraud, Waste and Abuse," accessed April 24, 2014, www.deloitte.com/view/en_US/us/press/2919b272ad125410VgnVCM3000003456f70aRCRD.htm.

About the Author

Sunder Gee is a CPA, CMA, and CIDA (certified IDEA data analyst) who retired from the Canada Revenue Agency (CRA) in 2013. Prior to his retirement, he held the position of Electronic Commerce Audit Advisor for the Head Office. In that position, he provided consultation on electronic commerce issues and computer-assisted audit techniques, both within the agency as well as to other tax authorities worldwide. Sunder also has extensive auditing experience, ranging from sole proprietorships to the largest companies in Canada, in the resource and high-technology sectors. Additionally, he has trained many CRA auditors in the use of laptop computers and software applications.

Sunder has developed extensive training material on a wide variety of topics for the CRA, CaseWare IDEA Inc., and local colleges. For example, he has developed presentations and workshops on electronic sales analysis, obtaining electronic data, auditing online vendors, forensic accounting, intelligence gathering, anti–money laundering, and data analytics.

Sunder is a certified CaseWare IDEA instructor and consultant. He also consults for tax lawyers and tax accountants, predominantly in the area of electronic data. His current focus is on data analytics for forensic analysis and he presents on related topics such as:

- "Advanced Statistical Methods for Finding Fraud" at the Association of Certified Fraud Examiner (ACFE) Canadian Conference, October 2012.
- "Bringing Sophistication to Data Analytics" at the ACFE Asia–Pacific Conference, November 2012.
- "Detecting Electronic Suppression of Sales: A Data Analytics Approach" at the Federation of Tax Administrators Technology Conference, July 2013.
- "Busting Barriers—Fighting Fraud" at the North America IDEA User Conference, May 2014.

Sunder is currently developing an online forensic accounting course at a local college.

About the Website

THE COMPANION WEBSITE (www.wiley.com/go/fraud_detection) offers the IDEA data files used in the examples and demonstrations of the step-by-step procedures outlined in this book. Using the data files, IDEA users can follow along to enhance their data analytic skills. The IDEAScripts listed and described in Chapter 17 are also included. IDEA users can run the scripts using the included data files or apply them to their own data sets to immediately test for anomalies of potential fraud.

The password to enter the site is: fraudelement.

The reader can obtain a demonstration version of the most current version of the IDEA software at: www.caseware.com/IDEACDBook1.

Complete the web form and the link to a downloadable demo will be sent to your e-mail address. At the bottom of the page, from the Book pull-down menu, please choose "Fraud and Fraud Detection."

The demonstration version of IDEA is fully functional, but data files are limited to 1,000 records each.

Download the "Fraud and Fraud Detection.zip" file from the companion website and unzip the files under the IDEA Projects folder as shown in the following graphic. The zip file size is 200MB and will unzip to 3GB.

The Custom Functions.ILB folder contains the Date_Conversion.ideafunc custom function. The Macros.ILB folder contains a Visual Script and the IDEAScripts that are displayed in the following screenshot.

In the Source Files.ILB folder, all the IDEA files are also available in CSV delimited format. You can import these delimited files into other data analytical software if you wish. CSV files can also be opened in Excel within its number of records limitation. Two dBase files are also included.

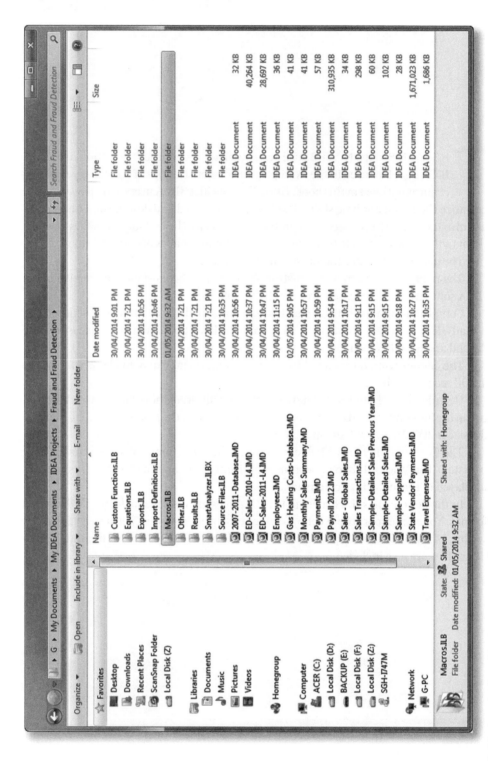

Folders and Files of IDEA Project on the Website

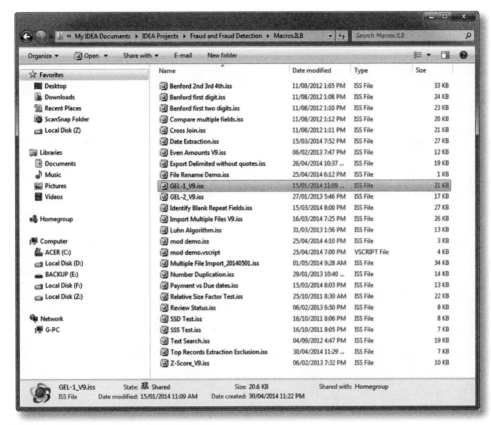

Included Visual Script and IDEAScripts

Index